HEAD-UP DISPLAYS

To the memory of Jim Newman, 1967–1986

Oh, I have slipped the surly bonds of earth
And danced the skies on laughter-silvered wings;
Sunward I've climbed, and joined the tumbling mirth
Of sun-split clouds – and done a hundred things
You have not dreamed of – wheeled and soared and swung
High in the sunlit silence. Hov'ring there
I've chased the shouting wind along, and flung
My eager craft through footless halls of air.
Up, up in the long, delirious, burning blue
I've topped the windswept heights with easy grace
Where never lark, or even eagle, flew,
And, while with silent, lifting mind I've trod
The high untrespassed sanctity of space,
Put out my hand, and touched the face of God.

John Gillespie Magee, Jr.
High Flight

Head-Up Displays

Designing the way ahead

Richard L. Newman

Routledge
Taylor & Francis Group

LONDON AND NEW YORK

First published 1995 by Ashgate Publishing

Published 2016 by Routledge
2 Park Square, Milton Park, Abingdon, Oxon OX14 4RN
711 Third Avenue, New York, NY 10017, USA

Routledge is an imprint of the Taylor & Francis Group, an informa business

A catalogue record for this book is available from the British Library

Library of Congress Catalog Card Number: 95-75645

ISBN 13: 978-0-291-39811-6 (hbk)

Acknowledgements

The many helpful discussions with Robert E. (Hawkeye) Hughes, Loran A. Haworth, and Thomas G. Foxworth caused the genesis of most of the ideas presented here. Their contributions are greatly appreciated.

Tom Foxworth solicited my first human factors paper in 1970. Unfortunately Tom died in September 1994 as this book was going to press. I shall miss his lengthy discussions about aviation and head-up displays.

John Hall of DRA, Bedford provided updated figures of the Fast-Jet HUD symbology. His help is appreciated.

Flight Dynamics, GEC Avionics, Kaiser Electronics, and Sextant Avionique provided photographs of installations which are used to illustrate current HUD state of the art. Their help and permission to use these photographs is acknowledged. They also reviewed the technical data presented and provided corrections to the draft.

Flight Visions and Jet Electronics and Technology also reviewed the technical data and provided corrections to the draft. Their assistance is also acknowledged.

Terry Lutz provided comments on the operation of several HUDS, particularly the F-16. His personal experiences and viewpoints were quite helpful.

Portions of the work which led to this document were sponsored by the Air Force Flight Dynamics Laboratory, Air Force Wright

Aeronautical Laboratory, and by the Joint Cockpit Office, Wright Laboratory, United States Air Force, Wright-Patterson AFB.

The Air Force Project Engineer, William L. Augustine, was instrumental in providing this support. Bill passed on in September 1993. His contributions to HUD research and development will be missed.

Note: pilots have been referred to as 'he/him' throughout the book, though these references should be understood as to include 'she/her', as appropriate.

Contents

List of illustrations

List of tables

List of abbreviations

A/A	Air-to-air combat
A/G	Air-to-ground combat
a.c.	Alternating current
ACM	Air combat maneuvering
ACRL	Aircraft reference line
ADI	Attitude director indicator
AERP	Alert eye reference point
AFB	Air Force Base
AFIFC	Air Force Instrument Flight Center
AIAA	American Institute of Aeronautics and Astronautics
AOA	Angle of attack
ARP	Aerospace recommended practice
ARS	Aircraft reference symbol
AS	Aerospace standard
ASL	Azimuth steering line
BFL	Bomb fall line
CAS	Calibrated airspeed
CCIL	Continuously computed impact line
CCIP	Continuously computed impact point
CDM	Climb–dive marker
CHPR	Cooper–Harper Pilot Rating
CRT	Cathode ray tube
d.c.	Direct current

DCP	Display control panel
DERP	Design eye reference point
DH	Decision height
DME	Distance-measuring equipment
DOD	Department of Defense
EADI	Electronic attitude director indicator
EFA	European Fighter Aircraft
EMI	Electromagnetic interference
ERP	Eye reference point
EU	Electronic unit
EVS	Enhanced vision system
FDI	Flight Dynamics
FAA	Federal Aviation Administration
FISP	Flight Instrumentation Standardization Program
FLIR	Forward-looking infrared
FOR	Field of regard
FOV	Field of view
FPA	Flight path angle
FPM	Flight path marker
FRL	Fuselage reference line
GPIP	Glidepath intercept point
GS	(1) Groundspeed; (2) Glideslope
HDD	Head-down display
HMD	Helmet-mounted display
HOCAC	Hands on collective and cyclic
HOTAS	Hands on throttle and stick
HOTAY	Hands on throttle and yoke
HSI	Horizontal situation indicator
HUD	Head-up display
I^2	Image intensifier
IAS	Indicated airspeed
IFOV	Instantaneous field of view
ILS	Instrument landing system
IMC	Instrument meteorological conditions
INS	Inertial navigation system
IVSI	Instantaneous vertical speed indicator
KIAS	Knots, indicated airspeed
LCD	Liquid crystal display
LCOS	Lead-compensating optical sights
LED	Light-emitting diode
loc	Localizer
LOP	Line of position
LOS	Line of sight

LRU	Line replaceable unit
MMWR	Millimeter wave radar
N/P	Non-precision
NASA	National Aeronautics and Space Administration
NVG	Night vision goggles
PDU	Pilot display unit
PF	Pilot flying
PFP	Potential flight path
PFR	Primary flight reference
PIO	Pilot-induced oscillation
PNF	Pilot not flying
PVSA	Primary visual signal area
RAE	Royal Aircraft Establishment
RAF	Royal Air Force
SDO	Spatial disorientation
SETP	Society of Experimental Test Pilots
SID	Standard instrument departure
STAR	Standard terminal arrival route
STOL	Short takeoff and landing
SVS	Synthetic vision system
TACAN	Tactical air navigation (system)
TAS	True airspeed
TFOV	Total field of view
TLX	Task load index
TOF	Time of flight
TOGA	Takeoff/go-around
UA	Unusual attitude
UK	United Kingdom
US	United States
USA	United States of America
USAF	United States Air Force
V/STOL	Vertical/short takeoff and landing
VAM	Visual Approach Monitor
VFOV	Vertical field of view
VISTA	Variable Stability Inflight Simulator Test Aircraft
VMC	Visual meteorological conditions
VOR	Very high frequency omnirange (navigation system)
VSI	Vertical speed indicator
VTOL	Vertical takeoff and landing
VV	Velocity vector

List of symbols

Symbols

A_G	Approach angle
A_i	Depression angle to point i
D_i	Distance to point i
h	Height above touchdown
H	Altitude
$\dot{H}$	Vertical speed (altitude rate)
LA_i	Lateral angle to point i
L_G	Length: threshold to GPIP
L_R	Runway length beyond GPIP
P_k	Probability of kill
q	Pitch rate in body axis coordinates
Q	Quickener term
Q_1	Washed-out pitch quickener term
Q_2	Pitch rate quickener term
s	Laplace transform variable
V_G	Groundspeed
V_{MO}	Maximum operating airspeed
V_T	True airspeed
V_x	Longitudinal component of inertial velocity
V_Y	Lateral component of inertial velocity

V_z	Vertical component of inertial velocity
W	Runway width
x_i	Lateral position of point i in HUD coordinates
X_i	Lateral position of point i in runway coordinates
y_i	Vertical position of point i in HUD coordinates
Y_i	Longitudinal position of point i in runway coordinates
z	Intensity of CRT image
α	Angle of attack
β	Angle-of-sideslip
γ	Flight path angle
δe	Elevator deflection
σ	Ratio of ambient air density to at sea level standard density
δ_G	Glideslope deviation
δ_L	Localizer deviation
τ	Quickening time constant
Θ	Pitch attitude
ϕ	Bank angle
Φ	Lateral flight path angle
Ω	Heading
Ω_A	Aircraft heading
Ω_R	Runway heading (course)

Subscripts

$(\ )_i$	Inertial
$(\ )_a$	Air-mass
$(\ )_0$	Glidepath intercept point (GPIP) on runway centerline
$(\ )_1$	Approach threshold at left side of runway
$(\ )_2$	Approach threshold at right side of runway
$(\ )_3$	GPIP at left side of runway
$(\ )_4$	GPIP at right side of runway
$(\ )_5$	Departure end at left side of runway
$(\ )_6$	Departure end at right side of runway
$(\ )_7$	Approach threshold on runway centerline
$(\ )_8$	Departure end on runway centerline
$(\ )_A$	Actual pitch or flight path angle
$(\ )_D$	Displayed pitch or flight path angle
$(\ )_R$	HUD reference for roll axis
$(\ )_{PL}$	Pitch ladder

1   Introduction

Head-up displays (HUDs) provide the pilot with a means to view real-world cues simultaneously with on-board flight information. This combination of real-world cues and artificial cues requires displays collimated at infinity.

The major advantages of head-up displays are seemingly obvious:

- *Reduced pilot workload*   Pilot workload is reduced when the overall piloting tasks require head-up, outside-the-cockpit flight references.
- *Increased flight precision*   The expanded scale of the HUD data and its overlay on the external visual scene allows the pilot to fly more precisely.
- *Direct visualization of trajectory*   A conformal display allows the pilot to assess the aircraft performance directly.
- *Increased flight safety*   Essential flight information presented on the HUD reduces eyes-in-the-cockpit during critical flight maneuvers.

Purpose

In spite of these advantages, the use of HUDs as flight instruments has not been totally successful. Since the late 1970s, a number of reports

1

$(1–4)$[1] have been published citing significant deficiencies in HUD symbology and installations. These deficiencies include lack of failure detection, lack of standardization, and increased tendency toward spatial disorientation.

This document reviews historical HUD experience and recommends a set of HUD design criteria. These are based on operational experience and on HUD research where appropriate. The material should help engineers develop new head-up displays. It should also help airlines and other potential HUD operators understand the limitations of existing HUD specifications and avoid repeating mistakes of the past.

Scope

We will restrict the discussion to displays which display flight information in virtual images in the pilot's forward field-of-view. The discussion will not consider helmet-mounted displays worn by the pilot.

HUDs considered include those displays used for routine flying maneuvers, for all-weather instrument landing, for weapons delivery, and for other specialized uses. The recommendations for HUD design are intended for all fixed-wing aircraft, tactical, transport, and specialized mission aircraft. Where appropriate, recommended values will be shown for each type of aircraft.

The recommendations are based on characteristics of HUDs found in the past to have desirable characteristics based on pilot opinion (and on characteristics which have demonstrated problems in operational use).

Display design

Reviews of operational HUDs lead to the conclusion that the HUD design process itself may be deficient. There seems to be a tendency in developing HUDs to include everything that can possibly be useful to the pilot. This results in a very cluttered display.

Traditionally, display designers have sought expert pilot opinion for guidance during the development of new flight displays. While user opinion is helpful, pilots tend to have diverse (and strongly held)

[1]Italic numbers in parentheses, (), indicate references listed at the end of each chapter.

opinions. In addition, pilots with limited background in display evaluation often limit the design of novel systems to those concepts with which they are familiar.

Pilots also have a tendency to 'gold plate' specifications and may not realize the consequences of minor additions.

The design process

The display design must consider why the pilot needs the data and what the pilot is expected to do with the data. According to Singleton (*5*), the following questions should be considered during the development of a display:

- Does the pilot's need justify the display?
- What data does the pilot need that has not been provided?
- Can the average pilot obtain what is required easily?
- Does the display conform
  - to the real world?
  - to other cockpit displays?
  - with previous pilot habits and skills?
  - with required decisions and actions?

Wickens (*6*) proposed a 'proximity compatibility' principle to develop displays. This principle uses proximate displays for tasks that are closely related and vice versa. Others have amplified this approach for cockpit displays (*7*). These display design techniques have been applied to cockpit instrument panels, but not to HUDs.

Previc(*8*) proposed HUD design based on physiological principles. Previc's analysis appears to provide a theoretical basis for the basic instrument 'T', albeit several decades after its development.

Following completion of the display design, its evaluation must be based on objective, performance-based criteria and measures of the display's effect on mission performance. It is up to the evaluation team to determine what the appropriate measures are. These should reflect the intended mission of the aircraft and include all mission segments.

Clutter

When deciding what information to display, the designer must use the Hippocratic approach used by physicians in treating an injury or illness: First, do no harm. Every information element shown on a HUD must serve a purpose and lead to improved performance. Every pixel must be justified. While all displays have a need to minimize display clutter, this is particularly critical with see-through displays. Since HUD symbols are presented in the pilot's view of the real world, obtrusive symbology should be kept to an absolute minimum. Hughes (*9*) expressed this as 'not one "pixel" should be lit unless it "buys" its way onto the screen by providing a demonstrable improvement in performance.'

Global priorities vs. minutia

A final comment: display specifications and, as a result, display designers in the past have over concerned themselves with details of the specific symbols. The general arrangement (location within the field of view) and the algorithms driving the symbols are more important (in our opinion) than the details of the symbols themselves.

The evaluation process

The history of HUDs shows that poorly designed displays were not 'flagged' during the test and evaluation phase, and the deficiencies were not corrected. Because of this, some comments on the testing of displays are in order.

In the past, non-weapon system HUD evaluations were conducted fairly superficially using benign tasks with no particular criteria other than subjective opinion. While subjective opinion should not be ignored, the performance achievable with the display must be specified. The flight tasks must be rigorous, requiring high workload on the part of the evaluation pilot – even to the point of adding secondary tasks to add stress and distractions.

References

(1)   Barnette, J. F. *Role of Head-Up Display in Instrument Flight* (Randolph AFB, Texas: Air Force Instrument Flight Center, 1976), AFIFC LR-76-2

(2)   Newman, R. L. *Operational Problems Associated with Head-Up Displays During Instrument Flight* (Wright-Patterson AFB, Ohio: Air Force Aeromedical Research Laboratory, 1980), AFAMRL TR-80-116

(3)   Lovering, P. B. and Andes, W. S. *Head-Up Display Symbology and Mechanization Study* (Wright-Patterson AFB, Ohio: Aeronautical Systems Division, 1984), ASD TR-84-5023

(4)   Newman, R. L. and Foxworth, T. G. *A Review of Head-Up Display Specifications* (Wright-Patterson AFB, Ohio: Aeronautical Systems Division, 1984), ASD TR-84-5024

(5)   Singleton, W. T., 'Display Design: Principles and Procedures,' *Ergonomics*, **12**,

4

1969, 519–531

(6) Wickens, C. D. *The Proximity Compatibility Principle: Its Psychological Foundation and Its Relevance to Display Design.* (Champaign, Illinois: University of Illinois, 1992), ARL-92-5/NASA–92–3

(7) Andre, A. D., 'Quantitative layout analysis for cockpit display systems,' *Proceedings of the Society for Information Display 1992 International Symposium, Boston,* (New York: Society for Information Display, 1992), Paper 34.2

(8) Previc, F. H. *Towards a Physiologically Based HUD Symbology* (Brooks AFB, Texas: Air Force School of Aerospace Medicine, 1988), AFSAM TR-88-23

(9) Hughes, R. E. *The HUD Coloring Book: Recommendations Concerning Head-Up Displays* (Washington,: Naval Air Systems Command, 1991)

2　Historical review

The first head-up displays (HUDs) were developed during the late 1950s in several countries, based on reflecting gunsight technology. In these gunsights, the aiming symbol is generated from a light source and projected onto a semi-transparent mirror mounted between the pilot and the windshield. The projector is usually located in the top of the instrument panel. The aiming symbol appears to be 'floating' in the pilot's view of the outside world.

Reflecting gunsights were first used in World War II fighters and had, by the late 1950s, progressed to display images generated on cathode ray tubes (CRTs) which were controlled by airborne computers. Reflecting gunsights have several advantages over their precursors, immovable iron sights.

First, the aiming symbol can be moved to compensate for range, bullet drop, acceleration factors, and rate of target closure. With the incorporation of airborne computers, the equations of symbol motion had become quite complex.

Second, the image of the aiming symbol can be focused to form an image which appears to lie in the same plane as the target. This minimizes the pilot's need to accommodate and focus on two distances and eliminates parallax errors.

Third, the brightness of the aiming symbol can be adjusted (manually or automatically) to allow for changes in ambient light levels.

The next step in the development of the HUD was the addition of flight information to the aiming symbol image. In fact, this can be a working definition of a head-up display: a cockpit display presenting flight data in the pilot's view of the real world.

The chief motivation behind the evolution of HUDs was to place flight information where the pilot was looking – out the windshield. Originally this was thought of as a means of improving pilot airmanship during combat. By the early 1960s, HUDs were seen as assisting pilots during landing approaches. In both instances, the HUD provided needed flight information without the need to look 'inside' at the instrument panel.

Another reason for HUD development was the integration of large numbers of separate gauges in the instrument panel into a single coherent display.

HUD development

The British work

Much of the early development of head-up displays took place at the UK's Royal Aircraft Establishment (RAE) in the late 1950s and early 1960s. In particular, Naish (*1-3*) led these developments at the RAE. He continued his HUD developments with Douglas Aircraft in the late 1960s (*4-5*).

The approach followed by the British was to use a HUD equipped with a single horizon line and aircraft reference symbol. The airplane's flight director computer was used to position a steering cue to guide the pilot during instrument flight. In most HUDs of this type, the airspeed and altitude are shown digitally, although some used fast/slow error cues for airspeed. This type of HUD presentation will be referred to as **unreferenced pitch** symbology.

The British school suggested that a HUD need not be conformal to the real world, but rather that only an approximate overlaying of HUD symbols and real world cues was required (*6*). Their results were based on extensive testing both in simulators and in flight. The success criteria for most experiments was for the minimum tracking error – the ability of the pilot to self-monitor and crosscheck was not usually considered.

In one experiment, however, Naish (*7*) purposely misguided some subject pilots to a touchdown to one side of the runway. He found that pilots tended to ignore the HUD and fly according to real-world cues as soon as they became available.

Part of the reason for the conclusion that a conformal HUD was not required may have reflected the current state of the art at the time. The ability to generate accurate contact analog displays of sufficient accuracy for flight guidance was lacking during this period (*8*).

Another conclusion drawn was that a 1:1 scaling in pitch did not necessarily yield the best pilot performance (*9*). This observation carried forward to early fighter HUDs (AV-8) which used 5:1 pitch scaling. More recently, the RAE has developed the Fast-Jet symbology, which uses a pitch scaling which varies from 1:1 at the horizon to 4.4:1 at the zenith or nadir (*10*).

Visual guidance studies

In the mid-1960s, additional work was being carried on in the USA, chiefly by Sperry under US Navy support. This work, led by Gold, emphasized two facets of HUDs: the use of the display in visual landing approaches and the necessary optical qualities of the display. Gold concluded that, for the visual approach, a single directed cue which the pilot could used to fly to the touchdown point was superior to a combination of a flight path marker and target glideslope scale (*11*). This same conclusion was reached in subsequent studies (*12–13*).

The difference between these visual approach techniques and the unreferenced pitch British school lies in the data processing. The British approach provides left/right, up/down guidance cues from a conventional flight director computer, while Gold's visual approach technique provides guidance from the pilot flying the airplane. By placing the aiming symbol on the desired touchdown spot, appropriate feedback computation is used to move the symbol (within the HUD) to guide the airplane to a desired touchdown.[1]

The other studies by Gold and his co-workers dealt with the optical characteristics of the HUD. These included the appropriate field-of-view (FOV) requirements and the maximum allowable visual disparity between each of the pilot's eyes (*14–16*).

Contact analog HUDs

A contact analog HUD was developed by Klopfstein in the mid-1960s (*17*). Klopfstein's HUD, shown in Figure 2.1, displayed a synthetic

---

[1] It is not absolutely necessary to have visual contact with the runway. If an accurate synthetic runway cue can be generated, placing the symbol on this synthetic cue will suffice.

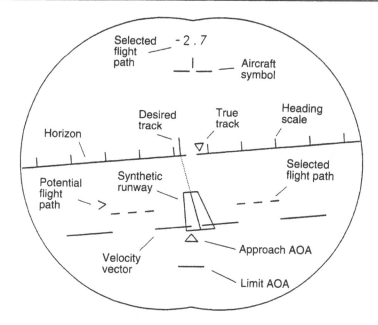

Figure 2.1   Klopstein HUD symbology (*18*)

runway outline which was a contact analog of the real runway.

Klopfstein also incorporated flight path information in the form of the flight path angle through the air. When viewed through the HUD, the angle of attack became obvious to the pilot. This HUD presented guidance information based on a perspective view of the synthetic runway and longitudinal control based on the angular relationship of aircraft pitch and flight path angle.

Other contact analog HUD symbologies were developed by Bergstrom; DeCelles, Burke, and Burroughs; Wilckens; Gallaher, Hunt, and Williges; and Carel (*19-23*). The synthetic runway analog, known as the **Klopfstein runway**, has been adopted in some civil HUDs intended for low visibility landings (*24, 25*).

Military applications

In the early 1970s, the HUD concept had developed to the point that it could be included in the weapon delivery systems for military fighters. The first two significant US aircraft to use head-up displays were the A-7D/E and the AV-8A. Both aircraft were single-seat ground-attack aircraft. In both cases, the driving rationale for using a HUD was to upgrade the gun/bombsights used in previous attack airplanes.

These two HUDs differed from one another in their presentations. The AV-8A HUD is a direct outgrowth of the early British approach to head-up displays (*26*). Aside from its unique vertical takeoff and landing (VTOL) mode, the AV-8A HUD was quite similar to the HUDs shown in reference (*8*), with the primary aircraft symbol displaying pitch attitude.

On the other hand, the A-7D/E HUD is based upon a flight path vector symbol driven by an inertial platform (*27*). This HUD was the first of a series of HUDs in which the primary aircraft symbol is the flight path relative to the ground. While the horizon and pitch references are conformal to the real-world cue, the display is not a contact analog. It has a conformal, symbolic HUD format.

Since the introduction of the head-up display in the A-7D/E and the AV-8A aircraft, HUDs have been used operationally on A-10, AV-8A, F-14, F-15, F-16, F-18, F-111, and F-117 fighters in the US inventory plus a large number of foreign aircraft. HUDs have also been installed on transport aircraft including B-727, B-737, MD-80, C-130, A-320, and Mercure transports. Other HUD installations include the Beech King Air and the Bell 230 helicopter. There are other programs developing HUDs for other airplanes at the time of writing.

Applications to all-weather landing

Head-up displays have been suggested as an aid to alleviate many of the problems faced by pilots during a landing approach under adverse weather conditions. These problems, although known to pilots for some time, were studied by Lane and Cumming in the 1950s (*28, 29*). They studied the visual cues used by pilots during final approach to landing and concluded that a suitable visual aiming device could be used to assist the pilot in judging his approach.

Lane and Cumming were primarily concerned with the problems of the pilot in judging his final approach path in visual meteorological conditions (VMC), although they did discuss the effect of night or weather in obscuring the cues. The cues most widely used by pilots were the relative angle of the touchdown point below the horizon, the shape of the runway or runway light patterns, and the 'center of expansion.' Naturally some of these cues are affected by night or reduced visibility.

Other researchers have studied these cues or rather their absence. Carroll and Swartz *et al.*, described the deterioration in these visual cues during low-visibility landings (*30, 31*). In general, the perception of vertical errors is much more difficult than the perception of lateral errors. This same point was made in the National Transportation Safety Board's study of approach and landing accidents (*32*).

Kraft and Elworth studied the effect of night visual approaches in a simulator study and found that the slope of the terrain and the distribution of lights in front of or behind the airport had a strong effect on the visual glidepath actually flown by pilots (*33*).

At this point we should separate the two specific problem areas: (1) the visual approach and (2) the transition from instrument meteorological conditions (IMC) to a visual landing. During a visual approach, the pilot's problem is to fly a stabilized approach on a safe glidepath – usually of the order of three degrees. Because of varying and often misleading visual cues, such as described by Kraft and Elworth, the pilot can be misled into flying a dangerously low flight path. (While the opposite problem, flying too high, can occur, it is not as critical for obvious reasons.)

The transition from IMC to a visual landing has some of the same problems; however, the problem here is not flying a safe flight path down to the landing flare, it is flying the flare itself. During an instrument approach, the pilot flies head-down using his panel instruments. Upon reaching visual contact, he must come head-up and complete the landing visually. If any illusions are present, the pilot can be led by these illusions into error. The problem is compounded by the very short time interval between ground visual contact and touchdown. This short interval makes it difficult to assess the direction of the flight path. In addition, the reduced visual range can be perceived as a lowering of the horizon caused by an aircraft pitch-up.

Visual landings As a result of these problems, the head-up display was suggested as a viable aid for the visual approach to landing.

During visual landings, the HUD could provide visual guidance, as described by Gold (*11*). Such a HUD was tested in simulated night visual approaches (*34*) and was used operationally by Pacific Western Airlines flying in arctic 'whiteout' conditions (*35*).

Further evidence that a head-up display can be valuable in improving landing safety was demonstrated by a threefold reduction in carrier landing accidents when the US Navy compared the HUD-equipped A-7E with the pre-HUD version, the A-7A (*36*).

Instrument landing system approaches The use of the HUD in the second problem area, transition to a visual flare, was addressed by the British using their 'flight director on the windshield' HUD. During the instrument approach phase, the pilot simply flies the HUD as he would a panel instrument. By placing the flight data in the windshield, the

11

transition to purely visual flight would be aided, giving the pilot more time to assess real-world cues without giving up the instrument ones. This type of HUD was extensively tested, both in Europe and in the USA(*1–4, 37–39*).

The Klopfstein HUD was proposed as an improvement (*17*).[2] By placing a contact analog of the runway where the real runway would appear, the pilot could fly a safe approach path relying on artificial cues. The use of air-mass flight path information was promoted as a safety factor during the approach phase since it provided better aerodynamic information (angle of attack) than the panel instruments (airspeed).

A derivative of the Klopfstein air-mass HUD was used by Air Inter, the French internal airline, as a monitor for very low-visibility landings (*40*). This HUD uses air-mass data but no synthetic runway, and provides a fail-safe option for autopilot malfunctions during the landing flare. The pilot monitors the progress of the automatic landing system using the HUD and uses the HUD as a landing aid if there is improper autoland performance during the flare.

In the early 1980s, the DC-9-80 (later called the MD-80) used a similar concept for monitoring the instrument landing system (ILS) approach. This HUD was operated by Swissair and Austrian Airlines and briefly by Pacific Southwest Airlines (*41*). Both the Mercure and the MD-80 HUDs were not designed as the primary ILS flight aid, but rather as a monitoring system for the automatic landing equipment allowing the redundancy level of the autoland system to be reduced from a triplex system (three channel) to a duplex system.

A triplex system is fail-operational, which means the system can continue to function even with the failure of a single channel. The duplex system, on the other hand, is fail-passive. This means the system will disconnect upon failure of either channel and require the pilot to take over. The HUD provides a take-over capability. This type of systems approach can be cost-effective since a HUD usually is much less expensive than a third autoland channel.

In the late 1980s, Alaska Airlines began to operate using the Flight Dynamics (FDI) HUD in B-727 aircraft. This HUD is not limited to use as an independent monitor, but can be used as a primary instrument approach aid allowing the pilot to manually land in very low visibilities. Using the HUD, Alaska routinely operates to landing visibilities as low as 700 ft and takeoff visibilities as low as 300 ft (*42*).

Synthetic vision/enhanced vision   The addition of sensor image data to

[2]See Figure 2.1.

the HUD has been proposed as a further aid to the all-weather landing (*43*). Both forward-looking infrared (FLIR) and millimeter wave radar (MMWR) have been proposed as sensor sources. Since 1989, the Federal Aviation Administration (FAA) has been conducting an evaluation of such a concept in concert with the United States Air Force (USAF)(*44, 45*). Flight tests in a Gulfstream II were recently completed. Preliminary results indicate the suitability of MMWR radar as an aid. A number of issues remain to be studied, however (*46, 47*).

Northwest Airlines has proposed using a combination of FLIR and MMWR radar to fly to low minima based solely on an image of the runway shown on the HUD (*48–50*). A proof-of-concept system has been flying on a Cessna 402 using FLIR imagery (*51*).

The terms **synthetic vision** and **enhanced vision** have been applied to these types of systems. There is some difference in philosophies between proponents. The term 'enhanced vision' has been advanced by some airlines, such as Northwest, to emphasize that the system would simply augment direct pilot vision much like landing lights or runway lights and allow the pilot to operate by direct visual reference to the image through the HUD. In other words, visual flight augmented by an electronic image.

'Synthetic vision', on the other hand, has come to mean systems in which electronic fusion of sensor images, computer-aided image enhancement, computer-aided runway edge line detection and fixing of stroke symbols to the runway edges occur. This implies that synthetic vision systems (SVS) are navigation/guidance systems requiring more rigorous certification than enhanced vision systems (EVS).

Overview of HUD evolution

As the HUD evolved from the early non-conformal pitch referenced HUDs to conformal inertial-flight path referenced HUDs, there were two evolutions to consider: conformality and the choice of flight reference. Figure 2.2 shows the evolution of head-up displays from the early unreferenced pitch format to the modern symbologies.

No attempt was made in the early HUDs to achieve conformality. This was probably a reflection on the state of the art in aircraft sensors, although Naish makes the case that a compressed pitch scale and lack of conformality promote situational awareness (*52*).

Later HUDs were conformal and scaled 1:1 in both pitch and roll, although most fighter HUDs used compressed heading scales. Still later, the trend is to part-time conformality, with pitch compression being introduced during extreme attitudes (*10*).

Meanwhile, the evolution in the symbol used for airplane control

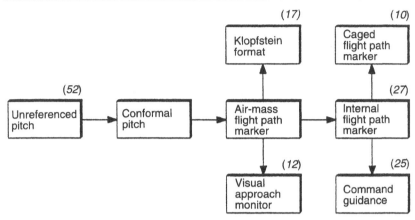

Figure 2.2   Evolution of head-up displays (italic numbers in parentheses indicate references)

began with the pitch symbol used in the early British studies. This may have reflected the state of the art or it may have reflected the use of the traditional head-down control symbol. The symbol progressed to air-mass flight path angle, to inertial flight path angle (17, 27).

Along the way, difficulties with the use of inertial flight path arose. These are caused by strong crosswinds which move the symbol to one side and can make flying by reference to the HUD impossible in very strong winds. Some HUDs provide for a 'cage' mode to force the airplane symbol to the center. Recently, the British standard symbology keeps the airplane reference in the center and displays a separate symbol showing the aircraft trajectory (10).

Operational problems

At the present time, HUDs are operational on most fighter or attack airplanes. While HUDs were first placed on these airplanes to serve as gunsights or bombsights, pilots have found the HUD to be extremely useful in routine flight. USAF pilots flying A-7D and F-15 aircraft reported that they use the HUD as an important part of their instrument scan (53). The Navy treated the HUD as the primary flight reference for both A-7E and F-18 aircraft. In fact, HUD symbology is the only source of attitude information in the F-18 during instrument flight (other than the standby attitude indicator).

In the mid-1970s, the USAF Tactical Air Command requested guidance on the use of HUDs from the Air Force Instrument Flight

14

Center (AFIFC). The AFIFC found that while the HUD did represent a significant aid as a flight reference, the lack of adequate failure detection, an increased tendency to spatial disorientation, and inadequate standardization limited the HUD's usefulness as a primary flight reference (*54*).

A second study attempted to further define some of the problem areas noted above. This study concluded that there appeared to be a dichotomy between HUDs which provided useful flight information to the pilots and those which were not useful as primary flight displays under instrument meteorological conditions (IMC). A number of issues were raised: (1) inadequate symbol dynamic response specifications; (2) lack of standardization in terms of symbology, nomenclature, and operational use; (3) inadequate FOV; (4) inadequate capability to dim the HUD at night; and (5) an increase in reports of spatial disorientation (*53*).

Since the publication of this survey, some of these issues have been addressed. Complaints of inadequate brightness control have diminished. The FOV issue has apparently been satisfactorily addressed with the introduction of diffraction HUDs, although there seem to always be requests from pilots for more FOV. During an interview, one pilot said 'There is no such thing as too much field of view.'

In the early 1980s, another program was undertaken to develop new, standardized HUD criteria. As part of this effort, a design guide was prepared to assist the HUD designers and ensure that the next generation HUD will be suitable for mission tasks (*55*). The design guide also developed guidelines for HUDs intended for use as the primary flight display during IMC. This program also addressed HUD safety issues (*56, 57*).

Recent accident histories of modern tactical aircraft indicate that spatial disorientation (SDO) is a major problem in military airplanes (*58–61*). Quite often the HUD is blamed for causing the pilot to become disoriented. As is usually the case, blaming an accident or series of accidents on a single isolated cause is overly simplistic.

Nevertheless, it is becoming increasingly obvious that there is a problem. Many factors are involved: aircraft-handling qualities, poor head-down instrument layouts, HUDs that are not designed for instrument flight, instrument procedures that do not recognize the effect of the velocity vector, and inadequate instrument training.

Development of specifications

Reviews of electronic display standards and specifications show a limited number of attempts to standardize. Existing specifications and standards for electronic head-up, head-down, or helmet-mounted displays are listed in Table 2.1. Six of these specifications apply to military aircraft; four to civil transport aircraft; and one applies to both civil and military aircraft. Of the civil documents, two are industry recommended standards, one is an Advisory Circular, and one a draft Advisory Circular.

There have been several critical reviews of HUD specifications. In the mid-to-late 1970s, the US Naval Aeromedical Research Laboratory reviewed existing HUD specifications and found a lack of data to substantiate these specifications (*62, 63*).

In the early 1980s, two Air-Force-sponsored studies reviewed HUD specifications (*74, 75*). These reviews found that there was little objective data to substantiate specifications, evaluations, or design choices. In the absence of objective performance data, most were found to be based on subjective opinion. Furthermore, it appeared that utility as a flight reference had not been considered.

This situation developed since electronic displays and associated symbology have traditionally been procured as part of the weapon system, not as part of 'aircraft instruments.' Classed as contractor-furnished rather than government-furnished equipment, adherence to general military standards and specifications was not always required. Symbology drive laws and dynamics have frequently been missing from the specifications.

Since HUDs were not considered 'flight instruments,' no need was seen to establish their suitability for use as flight references.

Table 2.1   Electronic display standards

Specification	Military	Civil	HDD	HUD	HMD	Ref
MIL-D-81641(AS)	X			X		64
MIL-STD-884	X		X	X	*	65
MIL-STD-1295	X			*	X	66
MIL-STD-1787	X		X	X	*	67
TR-87-3055	X	X		X		55
TR-91-01	X			X		68
Fastjet	X			X		69
ARP-4053		X		X		70
AS-8034		X	X			71
AC-25-11		X	X			72
FAA Draft Paper		X		X		73

* Not discussed in specification. However, the display type shown is within the scope of the specification.

Consequently, few flight procedures were developed and limited training provided to pilots on how to use the HUD in routine flight.

Following these studies, the US Air Force sponsored a program to develop HUD criteria. The result was a guide to assist the HUD designer in an attempt to ensure that next-generation HUDs will be adequate for their tasks (*55*).

There have been a number of recurring problems with HUD specifications. The most common are as follows:

- *No dynamic requirements* None of the government display specifications list any dynamic response requirements, other than platitudes such as 'shall be free from unacceptable jitter.' The specifications also fail to specify any sampling interval. As systems capability grows, increased computer workload can force the computation interval to grow from 20–40 ms to 80–100 ms. At some point in the lengthening of this interval, the display quality will degrade dramatically.

  There appears to be a common misconception that 100 ms is a magic computation interval below which there will be no display problems. This seems to be based on the idea of a 0–1 s human reaction time. In fact, sampling intervals of the order of 100 ms can seriously degrade tracking in fighter aircraft (*76*).

- *Standardization* HUD specifications show an almost complete lack of standardization. As an example, in many HUDs the angle of attack (AOA) is shown by an error bracket which moves relative to the velocity vector. Some show a fast error as the AOA bracket above the velocity vector, others show a fast error as the AOA bracket below.

- *Hidden specifications* There are several 'hidden' specifications. One example was the 100 ms computer frame time mentioned before. Another is the precession which occurs as the airplane passes ±90° in pitch. This is a carry-over from electromechanical attitude indicators to prevent gimbal lock. An electronic display has no need to keep this feature. Yet, many HUD designers feel that it is an essential feature – one designer even stated that there was a military specification requiring such a precession!

- *Gold-plated specifications* Finally, many recent standardization attempts have been based on a wish list for HUDs that will do everything. In the civil community, the would-be drafters of requirements assume that all future aircraft will carry wide FOV holographic HUDs with a complete inertial navigation system and precision DME available. The draft specifications appear to preclude non-conformal HUDs for many smaller corporate aircraft. There is a similar tendency in the military community.

When drafting specifications and standards, we should remember that there are places for displays with narrow fields of view driven by gyro platforms presenting air-mass data. These HUDs may not allow us to fly to category III minima, but they may still enhance the mission for which they are intended.

The HUD and spatial disorientation

In early surveys of pilots flying HUD-equipped airplanes, approximately 30% described an increased tendency to spatial disorientation (SDO), attributed to their use of the HUD (53, 54). Later, Newman and Foxworth found that only 14% of pilots flying HUD-equipped F-18s, and no pilot flying HUD-equipped Mercures reported an increased tendency to SDO (75). This was attributed by Newman and Foxworth to better cockpit/HUD integration (F-18 pilots) and to better HUD training (Mercure pilots).

HUD-induced SDO is reported to occur within one of several scenarios, the most common of which is flying in and out of clouds. Other SDO-sensitive situations include such extreme maneuvers as night pull-ups from a target, air combat maneuvering (ACM), and unusual attitude (UA) recoveries. With or without a HUD, these are conditions under which SDO tendencies are most likely to occur.

Causes of HUD-induced disorientation

Tyler and Furr describe the primary cause of SDO as conflicting or reduced visual cues, not abnormal stimulation of the vestibular system (77). In HUD flying, the pilot may have difficulty in interpreting some of the visual cues characteristic of the HUD, such as:

- absence of color and texture cues to identify upright from inverted flight;
- display clutter;
- digital airspeed and altitude presentations, which make rate assessments difficult;
- full-scale angles combined with small fields of view (FOVs), which make aircraft attitude assessment difficult during a UA;
- disorienting precession of the pitch ladder when the airplane passes through the zenith or nadir;
- accommodation traps in the symbology or the combiner

18

structure which cause the pilot's eyes to accommodate to a distance much less than optical infinity;

- framing effects in the symbology or the combiner structure which produce a sense of verticality aligned with the airplane, rather than with the real world; and
- use of the velocity vector as a control parameter rather than as a performance parameter.

Absence of upright versus inverted cues   Conventional attitude director indicators (ADIs) use black (or brown) and blue (or light grey) hemispheres to denote earth and sky. These hemispheres help the pilot distinguish upright from inverted flight. Many ADIs also provide patterns on one or both hemispheres to simulate ground texture or clouds.

The HUD, on the other hand, is limited to monochromatic lines and must avoid textures and patterns which might block external visual cues. It is unlikely that HUDs will be able to incorporate color with sufficient contrast in the foreseeable future. Regardless of technological advances, it would not be practical to use blue and brown to denote sky and ground; blue symbols would not be clearly visible against the actual sky, and brown symbols would not sufficiently contrast with some terrains.

Instead of color-coding the HUD, other cues have been used, such as solid lines above and dashed lines below the horizon. Taylor proposed slight asymmetries in the pitch ladder – displaying the numbers on one side or changing the location of the ticks at the end of the pitch lines (*78*). These appeared promising during static testing, but less so during simulations (*56*).

The F-18 HUD uses slanted pitch lines at large pitch angles to indicate the direction to the horizon (*79*). The Royal Air Force (RAF) Fast-Jet symbology uses pitch lines which appear to taper, becoming shorter as the angle from the horizon increases (*10*). The current USAF HUD standard combines these two approaches and uses articulated/dashed pitch lines below and tapered/solid above the horizon (*68*).

Such coding schemes *by themselves*, however, are unlikely to be entirely successful during the dynamic situation of a UA recovery.

Clutter   A visually cluttered display can prevent the pilot from interpreting the cues needed for prompt recognition and recovery from UAs. Defined in a Federal Aviation Authority (FAA) advisory circular:

A cluttered display is one which has an excessive amount of information in the number and/or variety of symbols, colors, and spatial position relationships. A large fraction of this information may be pertinent to the task at hand, but if an evaluation shows that the secondary information detracts from the interpretation necessary for the primary task, or increases the display interpretation error rate, irrelevant or lower priority information should be removed.(72)

The 2¹/₂° pitch line spacing on early F-16 HUDs has been criticized as distracting clutter, as has the presentation of excessive data on this and other HUDs. In an extreme UA, almost complete declutter may be necessary until the airplane has been stabilized.

Digital data and rate information   The HUD's digital displays have been criticized by some pilots because they make the determination of airspeed and altitude rate information difficult. This should be more of a problem with airspeed than altitude, since the velocity vector provides altitude rate information. However, most pilot complaints have been directed at digital altitude scales.

The RAF Fast-Jet HUD symbology incorporates a circular scale with a pointer and reference marks surrounding the digital airspeed and altitude displays (10). When either the airspeed or altitude change, the circular motion of the pointer provides the pilot with rate information.

Full-scale pitch angles   It can be difficult to assess aircraft pitch attitude with the HUD's full-scale but limited FOV display. The conventional ADI's compressed angular scales make aircraft attitude interpretation easier during dynamic maneuvering. The compressed scales slow down the angular rates on the display and the wider FOV keeps the displayed horizon in view.

Early HUD studies in the United Kingdom found that a slight pitch scale compression resulted in tighter approach tracking performance than did 1:1 scaling (9). Later studies found that pitch scale compression could also be helpful during ACM or acrobatics (80). Pitch scale compression is helpful during UA recognition and recovery as well.

Pitch ladder precession passing zenith or nadir   Most HUDs roll their pitch ladders 180° when the airplane's velocity vector passes through 90° nose-up or nose-down. This was incorporated in their design to emulate the familiar controlled precession made by most ADIs to avoid gimbal lock. At best, this rotation in the HUD's reference frame makes controlled flight difficult during nose-up or nose-down attitudes; at worst, it creates disorientation. Some F-15 squadrons use this effect to induce UAs for training purposes(*53*).

In a recent F-15 UA incident, the negative effect of this HUD feature is apparent (*81*). The pilot stated that he rolled wings-level and pulled, when, in fact, careful viewing of the videotape shows that he actually pulled through from the inverted position in a split-S recovery. Viewed frame by frame, the video recording clearly shows that the apparent roll was actually the display's controlled precession.

Accommodation traps The issue of HUD accommodation traps has been raised by Roscoe and his students, who maintain that the pilot's eyes will accommodate to a relatively close distance, in spite of the HUD symbology being collimated to optical infinity (*82–85*). They assert that when the pilot shifts focus between HUD symbols and real-world objects, these large changes in accommodation produce SDO.

HUD studies have not supported this accommodation concern. An early survey based on interviews with operational pilots flying HUDs found no mention of eye discomfort, focusing problems, or anything resembling accommodation difficulties (*53*). Additionally, while the accommodation argument predicts much shallower HUD landing approaches with greater dispersion than non-HUD approaches (*86*), every HUD study to date has indicated the opposite.[3]

In any event, the accommodation distance of the HUD is at least the distance of conventional instruments, and there have been no suggestions that looking from head-down instruments to the outside scene causes disorientation. Weintraub and Ensing discussed the accommodation issue in some detail (*87*), and this reference is recommended for further reading.

Framing A concern discussed at an AIAA/SETP-sponsored cockpit workshop, is the sense of verticality imposed by the combiner structure or by the symbology (*88*)[4] During the F 15 incident, the airplane was rolled 90° while the pilot thought he was wings-level (*81*). As observed on the videotape, the vertical altitude and airspeed scales, along with

[3]Parenthetically, my observation has been that a clearer view is available through the HUD combiner than around it when flying through rain. With the HUD symbology turned off, the view through the combiner becomes about the same as the previous view around the combiner. My subjective conclusion is that the HUD symbology makes the real world clearer and more in focus. The raindrops and streaks on the windshield seem to act as accommodation traps at windshield distance, whereas the HUD symbology focuses the eyes at a further distance.

[4]This reference has been misinterpreted by many later reviewers as describing accommodation effects rather than framing effects (*82–84, 89*).

the horizontal heading scale, led to this sense of verticality. The edges of the pitch ladder, lining up in horizontal rows, emphasized this effect.

Conventional head-down ADIs are round, thereby avoiding part of this problem. Many ADIs also have pitch lines that lengthen as they extend further below the horizon and thus do not form parallel lines. This does not lead to a false sense of horizontal orientation when the airplane is rolled 90°. This would be an argument in favor of tapered pitch ladder lines.

Velocity vector control   The tendency of pilots to use the HUD velocity vector as a control parameter can result in problems during UAs. Particularly at large angles of attack, this can create situations in which the pilot needs to push on the control stick, but pulls instead because of the extreme negative flight path angle (γ). This confusion results from pilots' standard training experience, which uses aircraft pitch (Θ) as a control parameter.

Surveys of operational fighter pilots revealed that they possess a very superficial understanding of the implications of using γ as a control parameter rather than Θ. Some HUDs do not even display Θ (*53, 54*).

The Klopfstein HUD symbology was the first design to emphasize the angular Θ–α–γ relationship(*17*). This symbology was not widely accepted because of the early symbol generator which could only produce a set of straight lines and displayed no airspeed or altitude data. Its critics admitted, however, that a pilot could use the presentation well enough to allow for precise pitch and airspeed control. This format is shown in Figure 1.1.

HUD disorientation studies

There have been several simulations conducted in the last few years to address spatial disorientation and unusual attitude recovery issues.

A comparison of HUD-based and ADI-based unusual attitude recoveries from unusual attitudes (UAs) was studied by Kinsley and co-workers (*90*). Both a static format and a fixed-base simulation of F-18 airframe dynamics were used for the evaluations. Their results show that use of the ADI ball resulted in faster reaction times and faster overall recovery times than with the HUD format. They found that the visual background did interact with recoveries using the HUD.

In 1986, Guttman compared the F-18 HUD with an electronic ADI (EADI) during UAs in a fixed-base generic simulator (*91*). The results showed that an EADI produces superior recoveries than does a HUD.

Recovery from unusual attitudes was studied by Newman in a study using an F-14 simulator at Patuxent River (*56*). Several variations on a modified F-18 HUD symbology were studied separately. Several modifications were recommended to enhance spatial awareness or to ease of recovery from unusual attitudes: (1) pitch scale compression; (2) automatic change from 1:1 to compressed pitch during unusual attitudes; (3) adding an arrow (Augie arrow) to indicate the recovery direction; and (4) F-18-style slanted pitch lines.

Deaton and co-workers examined the effect of various HUD pitch ladders on unusual attitude recovery and on the ability of the pilot to detect outside visual targets (*92*). They concluded that an enhanced pitch ladder with slanted pitch lines and 'sharks teeth' at extreme nose-low angles would enhance attitude awareness.

Deaton and associates also examined the effect of orientation cues imbedded in the HUD symbology. They found the Augie arrow developed earlier (*56*) to be effective in aiding the pilot during recoveries from unusual attitudes(*93*). Chandra and Weintraub (*94*) found similar results.

In 1989, the Air Force School of Aerospace Medicine (now Armstrong Laboratory) reported the results of static evaluations of various pitch ladder formats on orientation recognition (*95*). Ercoline *et al.* compared articulated (i.e. slanted) pitch ladder lines and combined lines (with articulated lines below the horizon and straight lines above). The combined format was presented in three versions: all lines of equal length; lines becoming shorter (tapering) as the angle from the horizon increases; and lines becoming thicker at extreme negative pitch angles.

The results for pitch recognition favored articulated pitch lines and increasing the thickness as the angle increases from the horizon. For bank orientation, the conclusion was drawn that lateral asymmetry favored bank recognition.

Later studies, however, concluded that articulated pitch ladder lines created problems with bank recognition during unusual attitudes. In 1990, the UK studied alternative pitch ladder formats for the multinational European Fighter Aircraft (EFA). The EFA HUD was to have used F-18-style pitch ladders. The UK Ministry of Defence evaluated this pitch ladder with the tapered pitch lines of the Fast-Jet. The simulation was conducted on the RAE's simulator, which has large amplitude motion cues and a g-seat. The results show a clear subjective and objective preference for tapered pitch ladders over the articulated pitch ladders (*96*). Several pilots made 180° errors in judging bank with the articulated lines and rolled the wrong way during recoveries. This observation was supported by a USAF-sponsored study by Weinstein and Ercoline (*97*), who noted that a large number of

23

evaluation pilots were unable to discern inverted flight and attempted split-S recoveries thus increasing the dive angle.

Ercoline and Gillingham also evaluated airspeed and altitude scales, comparing conventional tapes with various digital and digital plus analog cue formats. The task was maintenance of airspeed and altitude in the presence of disturbances. The results are being evaluated at present. Results indicate that digits plus counter-pointers are preferred. Vertical tapes tended to promote a large number of incorrect responses (*98*).

Current FAA certification practice includes evaluation of unusual attitude recoveries during flight tests. Normally, the most cluttered navigation format is used during UA recoveries. Automatic declutter of navigation data has been incorporated in some civil HUDs to avoid a cluttered format (*99*).

References

(1)   Naish, J. M. *System for Presenting Steering Information During Visual Flight. Part I. The Position of the Presented Information* (Bedford, England: Royal Aeronautical Establishment, 1961), RAE TN-IAP-1132

(2)   Naish, J. M. *System for Presenting Steering Information During Visual Flight. Part II. The Form of the Presented Information* (Bedford, England: Royal Aeronautical Establishment, 1962), RAE TN-IAP-1138

(3)   Naish, J. M. *System for Presenting Steering Information During Visual Flight. Part III. The Influence of Errors and Limitations* (Bedford, England: Royal Aeronautical Establishment, 1964), RAE TN-64026

(4)   Naish, J. M. *Properties and Design of the Head-Up Display* (Long Beach, California: Douglas Aircraft Co., 1970), MDC-J1409

(5)   Stout, C. L. and Naish, J. M. 'Total system concept for category III operations,' in *Proceedings 11th Symposium. Society of Experimental Test Pilots, Beverly Hills* (Lancaster, California: Society of Experimental Test Pilots, 1967), pp. 70–105

(6)   *A Comparison of Electronic World and Flight Director World Head-Up Displays: Their Installation and Philosophy* (Rochester, England: Elliott Brothers, 1968), ADD-229

(7)   Naish, J. M. 'The flight simulator in display research'. *Journal of The Royal Aeronautical Society*, **68**, 1964, 653-659

(8)   Cane, P. 'Head-up display for the airlines', *Shell Aviation News*, no. 363, 1964, 16–19

(9)   Walters, D. J., 'The electronic display of primary flight data', in *Problems of the Cockpit Environment* (Paris: Advisory Group for Aeronautical Research and Development, 1968), AGARD CP-55, Paper 28

(10)   Hall, J. R., Stephens, C. M. and Penwill, J. C. *A Review of the Design and Development of the RAE Fast-Jet Head-Up Display Format* (Bedford, England: Royal Aeronautical Establishment, 1989), RAE FM-WP(89)034

(11)   Gold, T. 'Quickened manual flight control with external visual guidance', *IEEE Transactions on Aerospace and Navigational Electronics*, September 1964, 151–156

(12)   *Engineering Report, Delta Gamma Visual Landing System* (Redmond, Washington:

Sundstrand Data Control, 1971), Report 070-0676-001

(13)   Lowe, J. R., *Improving the Accuracy of HUD Approaches with a New Control Law* (New York: American Institute of Aeronautics and Astronautics, 1978), AIAA Paper 78-1494

(14)   Gold, T. and Potter, E. F. 'Visual suitability – a primary factor in head-up displays', *Sperry Rand Engineering Review*, January 1969, 37–43

(15)   Gold, T. and Hyman, A. *Visual Requirements Study for Head-Up Displays*, (Great Neck, New York: Sperry Rand, 1970), JANAIR 680712

(16)   Gold, T. and Perry, R. F. *Visual Requirements Study for Head-Up Displays* (Great Neck, New York: Sperry Rand, 1972), JANAIR 700407

(17)   Klopfstein, G. *Rational Study of Aircraft Piloting* (Paris: Thomson-CSF, ca. 1966); reprint of 1966 article in *Intrados*

(18)   *All Weather Approach and Landing Monitor, TC-121*, (Paris: Thomson-CSF, no date)

(19)   Bergstrom, B. *Interpretability Studies of Electronic Flight Instruments* (Linköping, Sweden: SAAB, 1967), SAAB TN-61

(20)   DeCelles, J. L., Burke, E. J. and Burroughs, K. 'A real world situation display for all weather landing', in *Crew System Design*, Cross, K. D. and McGrath, J. J. (eds) (Santa Barbara, California: Anacapa Sciences, 1973), pp. 255–263

(21)   Wilckens, V. 'Improvements in pilot/aircraft integration by advanced contact analog displays', in *Proceedings of the 9th Annual Conference on Manual Control, Cambridge* (Cambridge, Massachusetts: Massachusetts Institute of Technology, 1973)

(22)   Gallaher, P. D., Hunt, R. A. and Williges, R. C. *A Regression Analysis to Generate Aircraft Predictor Information* (Washington: National Aeronautics and Space Administration, 1976), NASA TM-X-73170

(23)   Carel, W. L. *Advanced Contact Analog Symbology*, (Culver City, California: Hughes Aircraft Co., 1977), D-7123

(24)   *Head-Up Display for the DC-9 Super 80* (Long Beach, California: McDonnell-Douglas Aircraft, 1979)

(25)   *FDI Model 1000 Head-Up Display System Specification* (Portland, Oregon: Flight Dynamics, 1989), Report 404-0249

(26)   *AV-8A Head Up Display Modification Specification* (St Louis, Missouri: McDonnell-Douglas Aircraft, 1975), MDC-A3589

(27)   *A-7D Navigation/Weapon Delivery System* (Dallas, Texas: Vought Aeronautics, 1974), Report 2-14000/4R-10

(28)   Lane, J. C. and Cumming, R. W. *The Role of Visual Cues in Final Approach to Landing* (Melbourne, Australia: Aeronautical Research Laboratories, 1955), HEN-1

(29)   Lane, J. C. and Cumming, R. W. *Pilot Opinions and Practices on the Approach to Landing: A Questionnaire Survey Among Australian Civil and Military Pilots*, (Melbourne, Australia: Aeronautical Research Laboratories, 1959), HER-1

(30)   Carroll, J. J. 'What the pilot sees during instrument approaches in low-visibility conditions', in *Proceedings 24th International Air Safety Seminar, Mexico City* (Alexandria, Virginia: Flight Safety Foundation, 1971), pp. 63–65

(31)   Swartz, W. F., Condra, D. M. and Madero, R. P. *Pilot Factors Considerations in See-to-Land* (Wright-Patterson AFB, Ohio: Air Force Flight Dynamics Laboratory, 1976), AFFDL TR-76-52

(32)   *Special Study Report on Approach and Landing Accident Prevention* (Washington: National Transportation Safety Board, 1973), NTSB AAS-73-2

(33)   Kraft, C. L. and Elworth, C. L. 'Night visual approaches', *Air Line Pilot*, June

1969, 20–22

(34)   Palmer, E. A. *Night Visual Approaches – Pilot Performance With and Without a Head-Up Display* (Moffett Field, California: National Aeronautics and Space Administration, 1972), NASA TM-X-62188

(35)   Mackie, R., 'The jet turbine aircraft in the Canadian Arctic', paper presented at *Canadian Aeronautics and Space Institute Symposium on Aircraft Operations in the Canadian Arctic, Edmonton* (Edmonton, Alberta: Pacific Western Airlines, 1973)

(36)   Hoerner, F. C. 'HUD military aspects', in *Proceedings of the Flight Operations Symposium, Vancouver* (Redmond, Washington: Sundstrand Data Control, 1979), Vol. II, pp. 53–58, 117–142

(37)   Naish, J. M. *Flight Tests of the Head-Up Display (HUD) in DC-9-20, Ship 382* (Long Beach, California: McDonnell-Douglas Aircraft, 1970), MDC-J0878

(38)   Naish J. M. and Von Wieser, M. F. 'Human factors in the all-weather approach', *Shell Aviation News*, no. 374, 1969, 2–11

(39)   Von Wieser, M. F. 'Operating a head-up display', *Shell Aviation News*, no. 411, 1972, 14–19

(40)   Roland-Billecart, A. and Deschamps, J. G. 'Operational experience with HUD in CAT III', *Proceedings of the Flight Operations Symposium, Vancouver* (Redmond, Washington: Sundstrand Data Control, 1979), Vol. II, pp. 122–157

(41)   *Head-Up Display for the DC-9 Super 80* (Redmond, Washington: Sundstrand Data Control, 1979)

(42)   Johnson, T. *Alaska Airlines Experience with HGS-1000 Head-Up Guidance System* (Warrendale, Pennsylvania: Society of Automotive Engineers, 1990), SAE Paper 901828

(43)   Glines, C. V. 'Synthetic vision will let pilots see through precip', *Professional Pilot*, August 1990, 62–67

(44)   *Synthetic Vision Technology Demonstration Program. Report on the Certification Study Team Meeting* (College Park, Maryland: University of Maryland, 1989), URF-89-1803

(45)   *Proceedings of the 7th Plenary Session of the Synthetic Vision Certification Issues Study Team, Williamsburg* (Hampton, Virginia: Federal Aviation Administration, 1992)

(46)   Foyle, D. C. *et al. Enhanced/Synthetic Vision Systems: Human Factors Research and Implications for Future Systems* (Warrendale, Pennsylvania: Society of Automotive Engineers, 1992), SAE Paper 921968

(47)   Kruk, R. V. *Issues Associated with Enhanced Vision Systems* (Warrendale, Pennsylvania: Society of Automotive Engineers, 1992), SAE Paper 921935

(48)   *Request for Proposal for a Head-Up Display for the Northwest Airlines B-747-100/200 and DC-10 Aircraft* (St Paul, Minnesota: Northwest Airlines, 1991)

(49)   Mages, J. G. 'Northwest Airlines HUD/EVS Program', (St Paul, Minnesota: Northwest Airlines, May 1992), Unpublished briefing materials for SAE G-10 Committee

(50)   Nordwall, B. D., 'Northwest Airlines developing HUD/EVS for more on-time flights', *Aviation Week*, 20 July 1992, 50–51

(51)   Daly, K., 'Looking ahead', *Flight International*, 22 July 1992, 22–23

(52)   Naish, J. M. *Review of Some Head-Up Display Formats* (Moffett Field, California: National Aeronautics and Space Administration, 1979), NASA TP-1499

(53)   Newman, R. L. *Operational Problems Associated with Head-Up Displays During Instrument Flight* (Wright-Patterson AFB, Ohio: Air Force Aeromedical Research Laboratory, 1980), AFAMRL TR-80-116

(54)   Barnette, J. F. *Role of Head-Up Display in Instrument Flight* (Randolph AFB, Texas:

Air Force Instrument Flight Center, 1976), AFIFC LR-76-2

(55) Newman, R. L. *Improvement of Head-Up Display Standards. I. Head-Up Display Design Guide* (Wright-Patterson AFB, Ohio: Air Force Wright Aeronautical Laboratory, 1987), AFWAL TR-87-3055, Vol. I

(56) Newman, R. L. *Improvement of Head-Up Display Standards. II. Evaluation of Head-Up Displays to Enhance Unusual Attitude Recovery* (Wright-Patterson AFB, Ohio: Air Force Wright Aeronautical Laboratory, 1987), AFWAL TR-87-3055. Vol. II

(57) Newman, R. L. *Improvement of Head-Up Display Standards. III. Evaluation of Head-Up Display Safety* (Wright-Patterson AFB, Ohio: Air Force Wright Aeronautical Laboratory, 1987), AFWAL TR-87-3055, Vol. III

(58) *Proceedings of the HUD/Instrument Conference, Langley AFB* (Langley AFB, Virginia: Tactical Air Command Headquarters, 1983)

(59) *Flight Instrumentation Conference*, Pentagon (Washington: US Air Force, 1985)

(60) *Aircraft Attitude Awareness Workshop, Wright-Patterson AFB* (Wright-Patterson AFB, Ohio: Air Force Wright Research and Development Center, 1985), WRDC TR-85-7009; ASD TR-85-5020

(61) Benson, A. J. (ed.) *The Disorientation Incident* (Paris: Advisory Group for Aeronautical Research and Development, 1972), AGARD CP-95

(62) Egan, D. E. and Goodson, J. E. *Human Factors Engineering for Head-Up Displays: A Review of Military Specifications and Recommendations for Research* (Pensacola, Florida: Naval Aeromedical Research Laboratory, 1978), Monograph-23

(63) Frank, L. H. *Comparison of Specifications for Head-Up Displays in the Navy A-4M, A-7E, AV-8A, and F-14A Aircraft* (Pensacola, Florida: Naval Aeromedical Research Laboratory, 1979), NAMRL SR-79-6

(64) *Military Specification, Display, Head-Up, General Specification for* (Philadelphia, Pennsylvania, Naval Publications and Forms Center, 1972), MIL-D-81641(AS)

(65) *Military Standard, Electronically or Optically Generated Displays for Aircraft Control or Combat Cue Information* (Philadelphia, Pennsylvania, Naval Publications and Forms Center, 1975), MIL-STD-884C

(66) *Military Standard, Human Factors Engineering Design Criteria for Helicopter Cockpit Electro-Optic Display Symbology* (Philadelphia, Pennsylvania, Naval Publications and Forms Center, 1984), MIL-STD-1295A

(67) *Military Standard, Aircraft Display Symbology* (Philadelphia, Pennsylvania, Naval Publications and Forms Center, 1989), MIL-STD-1787A

(68) Bitton, D. F. and Evans, R. H. *Report on Head-Up Display Symbology Standardization* (Randolph AFB, Texas: Air Force Instrument Flight Center, 1990), AFIFC TR-91-01

(69) Hall, J. R. *Symbology for the Presentation of Flight Information on Head-Up Displays* (Bedford, England: Royal Aeronautical Establishment, 1993), Draft NATO Standard

(70) *Aerospace Recommended Practice: Flight Deck, Head-Up Displays* (Warrendale, Pennsylvania: Society of Automotive Engineers, 1988), SAE ARP-4102/8

(71) *Aerospace Standard: Minimum Performance Standards for Airborne Multipurpose Electronic Displays* (Warrendale, Pennsylvania: Society of Automotive Engineers, 1982), AS-8034

(72) *Transport Category Airplane Electronic Display Systems* (Washington: Federal Aviation Administration, 1987), FAA AC-25-11

(73) *Criteria for Operations and Airworthiness Approval of Head-Up Displays for Air Carrier Aircraft* (Washington: Federal Aviation Administration, no date), draft advisory circular

(74) Lovering, P. B. and Andes, W. S. *Head-Up Display Symbology and Mechanization*

Study (Wright-Patterson AFB, Ohio: Aeronautical Systems Division, 1984), ASD TR-84-5023

(75) Newman, R. L. and Foxworth, T. G. *A Review of Head-Up Display Specifications* (Wright-Patterson AFB, Ohio: Aeronautical Systems Division, 1984), ASD TR-84-5024

(76) Newman, R. L. and Bailey, R. E. *Improvement of Head-Up Display Standards. IV. Head-Up Display Dynamics Flight Tests* (Wright-Patterson AFB, Ohio: Air Force Wright Aeronautical Laboratory, 1987), AFWAL TR-87-3055, Vol. IV

(77) Tyler, P. R. and Furr, P. A. 'Disorientation: fact and fancy', in *The Disorientation Incident* Benson, A. J. (ed.) (Paris: Advisory Group for Aeronautical Research and Development, 1972), AGARD CP-95, paper A4

(78) Taylor, R. M. 'Some effects of display format variables on the perception of aircraft spatial orientation', *Proceedings AGARD Symposium on Human Factors Considerations in High Performance Aircraft, Williamsburg* (Paris: Advisory Group for Aeronautical Research and Development, 1984), AGARD CP-371

(79) *F-18 Flight Manual* (Washington: Naval Air Systems Command, no date, ca 1984), NAVAIR-A1-F18AC-NFM-000

(80) Monagan, S. J. and Smith R. E., 'Head-up display flight tests', in *Proceedings, 24th Annual Symposium, SETP, Beverly Hills* (Lancaster, California: Society of Experimental Test Pilots, 1980), pp. 75–87

(81) *F-15 Spatial Disorientation*, (Langley AFB, Virginia: First Tactical Fighter Wing, no date, ca 1986), videotape briefing

(82) Roscoe, S. N., 'Designed for disaster', *Human Factors Society Bulletin*, **29**, [6], June 1986, 1–2

(83) Roscoe, S. N. 'Spatial misorientation exacerbated by collimated virtual flight display', *Information Display*, September 1986, 27–28

(84) Roscoe, S. N., 'The trouble with HUDs and HMDs', *Human Factors Society Bulletin*, **30**, July 1987, 1–2

(85) Iavecchia, J. H. *The Potential for Depth Perception Errors in Piloting the F-18 and A-6 Night Attack Aircraft* (Warminster, Pennsylvania: Naval Air Development Center, 1987), NADC 87037-20

(86) Randle, R. J., Roscoe, S. N. and Petit, J. C. *Effects of Magnification and Visual Accommodation on Aimpoint Estimation in a Simulated Landing Task* (Moffett Field, California: National Aeronautics and Space Administration, 1980), NASA TP-1635

(87) Weintraub, D. J. and Ensing, M. *Human Factors Issues in Head-Up Display Design: The Book of HUD* (Wright-Patterson AFB, Ohio: Crew System Ergonomics Information Analysis Center, 1992), CSERIAC SOAR-92-2

(88) Norton, P. A. *et al.* 'Findings and recommendations of the Cockpit Design Subcommittee', in *Proceedings of the 1981 Test Pilot's Aviation Safety Workshop, Monterey*, C. A. Tuomela (ed.) (New York: American Institute of Aeronautics and Astronautics and Lancaster, California: Society of Experimental Test Pilots, 1981), pp. 19–47

(89) Sanford, B. D. 'Head-up displays: effects of information location on the processing of superimposed symbology', Thesis, San Jose State University, 1992

(90) Kinsley, S. A., Warner, N. W. and Gleisner, D. P. *A Comparison of Two Pitch Ladder Formats and an ADI Ball for Recovery from Unusual Attitudes* (Warminster, Pennsylvania: Naval Air Development Center, 1986), NADC 86012-60

(91) Guttman, J. *Evaluation of the F/A-18 Head-Up Display for Recovery from Unusual Attitudes* (Warminster, Pennsylvania: Naval Air Development Center, 1986), NADC 86157-60

(92)   Deaton, J. E. *et al. The Effect of Windscreen Bows and HUD Pitch Ladder Format on Pilot Performance During Simulated Flight* (Warminster, Pennsylvania: Naval Air Development Center, 1989), NADC 89084-60

(93)   Deaton, J. E. *et al.* 'Evaluation of the Augie arrow HUD symbology as an aid to recovery from unusual attitudes', in *Proceedings of the 34th Annual Meeting of the Human Factors Society, Orlando* (Santa Monica, California: Human Factors Society, 1990), pp. 31–35

(94)   Chandra, D. and Weintraub, D. J. 'Design of head-up display symbology for recovery from unusual attitudes', in *Proceedings of the 7th International Symposium on Aviation Psychology* (Columbus, Ohio: Ohio State University, 1993)

(95)   Ercoline, W. R. *et al.* 'Effects of variations in head-up display pitch-ladder representations on orientation recognition', in *Proceedings of the 33rd Human Factors Society Annual Meeting, Denver* (Santa Monica, California: Human Factors Society, 1989), pp. 1401–1405

(96)   Penwill, J. C. and Hall, J. R. *A Comparative Evaluation of Two HUD Formats by All Four Nations to Determine the Preferred Pitch Ladder Design for EFA* (Bedford, England: Royal Aeronautical Establishment, 1990), RAE FM-WP(90)021

(97)   Weinstein, L. F. and Ercoline, W. R. 'HUD climb/dive ladder configuration and unusual attitude recovery', in *Proceedings of the 35th Annual Meeting of the Human Factors Society, San Francisco* (Santa Monica, California: Human Factors Society, 1991), pp. 12–17

(98)   Ercoline, W. R. and Gillingham, K. K. 'Effects of variations in head-up display airspeed and altitude representations on basic flight performance', in *Proceedings of the 34th Annual Meeting of the Human Factors Society* (Santa Monica, California: Human Factors Society, 1990), pp. 1547–1551

(99)   Newman, R. L. *Flight Test Report. Flight Visions FV-2000/KA HUD Installed in a Beechcraft BE-A100* (San Marcos, Texas: Crew Systems, 1993), TR-93-09

3 A review of HUD technology

In order to understand the shortcomings of existing head-up display designs, some understanding of HUD principles is needed. This chapter discusses the three aspects of HUD design: the image source, the optics, and data processing. The chapter also reviews both historical and current HUD designs.

The source of the displayed image in most HUDs is a cathode ray tube (CRT), which is driven by a symbol generator. The symbol generator takes input data from a mission computer or flight management computer and converts the data into meaningful symbology to convey information to the pilot. Some HUDs combine the functions of the symbol generator and mission computer into one black box.

Image sources

Cathode-ray tubes

The source of the displayed image in most modern HUDs is a cathode ray tube (CRT), which is driven by a symbol generator.

CRTs create images by generating an electron ray[1] which strikes the

[1] From the cathode, hence cathode-ray tube.

face of the tube, which is coated with phosphors. The phosphors give off light when the electrons impinge upon the face. The beam is focused by coils near the cathode source in the neck. Deflection plates move the resulting beam of electrons to the desired spot on the tube face by applying varying voltages to the deflection plates.

The intensity of the beam determines how bright the image will be. There is a tradeoff between brightness and tube life. For a given tube, the speed at which the spot moves determines the brightness of the symbol: the faster the motion, the less bright the symbol.

Typically, the symbols or images are redrawn fifty or sixty times a second. If the refresh rate is slower than 50 Hz, then the image may flicker or jump. If the refresh rate is much faster than 60 Hz, the image may not be bright enough.

If too many symbols are incorporated into the symbology, there might not be enough time to generate them all during a single refresh pass. Most displays truncate the symbology and omit symbols down on the list. It may be possible to have some symbols (such as digital data blocks) written during alternate passes, but this adds complexity to the symbol generator and may result in flicker.

Stroke symbology   The symbol generator may produce symbology in the form of stroke symbols using cursive lines and arcs drawn on the face of the CRT. In this case, the symbol generator output converts the symbology to $x(t) - y(t)$ coordinates as functions of time and sends appropriate voltages to the deflection plates in the CRT. It may also send intensity as a function of time, $z(t)$, as well. This is used to turn the line image off (i.e. $z(t)=0$) when the trace would move from one symbol to another.

Varying the intensity could be used to vary the symbol intensity, although this is not usually done. The most common way to enhance a symbol is double-writing.

Raster symbology: The symbol generator may produce an image in video format composed of a raster image, similar to a video picture. A raster image sweeps over the face of the CRT in a standard pattern of parallel lines and then returns to the starting point in a rapid trace called the flyback. In this type of display, the $x(t)$ and $y(t)$ traces are predetermined and the intensity, $z(t)$ is used to generate a pattern showing the image. The image is composed of a series of pixels following the trace of lines.

If symbology is to be incorporated in the raster image, two mechanizations can be used. One is to embed the image into the raster image.

31

This has the disadvantage of changing line drawings into a series of dots. 'Stair-stepping' and other distortions can result. Stair-stepping is an effect when a line is drawn at a very shallow angle to the lines tracing out the image. The result will be a line that follows one line trace for a short distance, then jumps to the next trace and so on.

Raster/stroke symbology Stroke symbology can also be combined with raster by allowing the CRT trace to draw the symbols during the flyback. This allows the original line drawing of arcs and straight lines, but the period during which the symbols can be drawn is very short. Because the flyback time is short, symbol brightness can be limited compared with pure stroke symbols or with symbols embedded within a raster image. Short flyback time can also limit the amount of symbology that can be drawn.

Comparison of symbology Stroke symbology is composed of lines and arcs. This is true of both pure stroke or stroke-during-flyback symbols. The chief limitation is the number of separate lines that can be drawn. This limitation is more critical with flyback symbols. Symbols drawn during flyback will tend to be less bright.

Raster-embedded symbols do not suffer from write-time limitations since the raster trace will cover the entire tube face with or without symbology. Raster symbol generators will be more complicated than pure-stroke symbol generators.

Table 3.1 compares stroke, embedded symbols, and flyback image sources.

Electromechanical systems

Some early HUDs created moving images by using electromechanical meter movements which were lighted or which reflected beams of

Table 3.1   Types of symbols used in HUDs

Type of symbol	Symbols	Numbers of symbols	Brightness of symbols	Symbol generator complexity
Stroke	Sharp	Limited	Bright	Minimal
Embedded symbols	Distorted (pixels)	Generally not limited	Generally acceptable	Complex
Flyback Stroke	Sharp	Severely limited	Limited	Intermediate

light (*1*). Typically, these used moving wires heated to incandescence located in an optical path. Since multiple meter movements interfere with one another, this type of image source was quite limited in the number of symbols that could be displayed. It was also more difficult to modify the symbols being shown than would be true with CRT displays.

There is one advantage to an electromechanical symbol source. Since the symbol is created by physically moving the heated wire, its location can be monitored. This can provide a direct monitor of the output (displayed) data. It is difficult to monitor the output using a CRT.

This type of image source is no longer being manufactured.

Light-emitting diodes

Light-emitting diodes (LEDs) have not been used for HUDs to date because of limited brightness. If the brightness could be made sufficient, the reduced power and size requirements of LEDs would make them attractive.

LEDs cannot display stroke symbols, but map the symbols onto an array of pixels. Thus symbols will be distorted as with raster-embedded symbols (*vide supra*).

Liquid-crystal displays

Likewise, liquid-crystal displays (LCDs) have not been used for HUDs to date because of limited brightness. A see-through LCD HUD was proposed and evaluated, but the lack of collimation made it impossible to view the symbology and the real world simultaneously without double images (*2*). LCDs have been proposed as touch sensitive screens for HUD control panels (*3*). These would allow the control panel to display flight or navigation information when not being used for HUD control.

Similar to LEDs, LCDs cannot display stroke symbols, but must map the symbols onto an array of pixels.

Optical designs

The view of the symbology is a virtual image of the HUD symbols appearing to float in space overlying the real-world view, as is shown in Figure 3.1.

The virtual image is created by a backwards extension of the rays

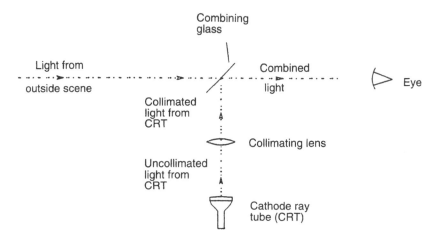

Figure 3.1   Head-up display arrangement

impinging on the pilot's eye. The virtual image doesn't exist in the sense that it can be detected by a photographic plate. It appears only when viewed through another lens (such as the lens in a human eye or a camera lens).

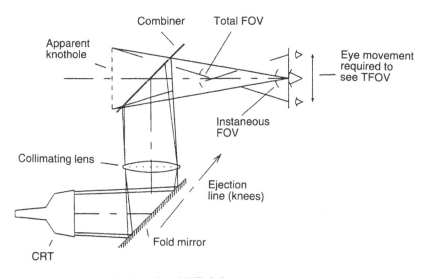

Figure 3.2 Typical refractive HUD (5)

34

Traditional HUDs

The traditional HUD uses a refractive optical design with a combining glass to superimpose the HUD symbols and the real world. Such a system is shown in Figure 3.2.

In a system of this type, the image of the CRT is passed through a collimating lens (or series of lenses) to produce a parallel set of rays. Often the light rays are reflected in a 'folding mirror' to allow for more room in the instrument panel. These parallel rays are reflected by the semi-transparent combining glass back to the pilot's eyes. The view from the external scene passes directly through the combining glass to the pilot's eyes.

In this type of HUD, all of the optical collimation takes place in the collimating lens – the combiner contributes no optical power. Hence, it is called a **refractive HUD**. This is the general arrangement of early HUDs, such as the RAF Buccaneer (the first production HUD, 1964). The Buccaneer HUD display unit is shown in Figure 3.3.

Figure 3.3   Buccaneer HUD display unit (courtesy of GEC Avionics)

35

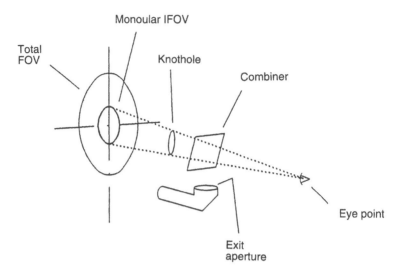

Figure 3.4   Monocular instantaneous field of view

Optical effects

Field of view   The exit aperture of the collimating lens will limit how much of the virtual image is visible at a particular pilot eye location and creates an effect called the porthole or knothole effect (*4*). Only part of the virtual image can be seen at a time. If the viewer's eye is shifted, all of the image can be seen, but only part at a time.

This creates an effect known as the **instantaneous field of view** (IFOV), which is a function of the exit aperture and the exit aperture-eye distance. The **total field of view** (TFOV) is the total image size that can be seen by the viewer by moving his head. Figure 3.4 shows the difference between the IFOV and the TFOV, and the knothole effect.

Figure 3.4 actually shows monocular FOVs. Because the pilot's eyes are located in different locations, each will see a slightly different image. There will be two monocular FOVs, one for each eye as shown in Figure 3.5. The combined FOV is the sum of the two and is sometimes called the **ambinocular FOV**.

The symbology that is seen by both eyes at the same time is the intersecting binocular FOV. If symbology is visible to one eye, but not the other, it is not in the intersecting IFOV. The term binocular FOV should not be used without a qualifying adjective. While most use binocular FOV to mean the combined FOV, others have used it to mean the intersecting FOV (*6*).

36

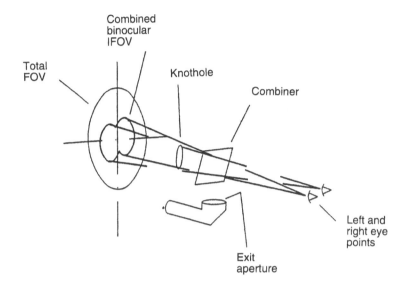

Figure 3.5   Combined binocular instantaneous field of view

The previous discussion of monocular and binocular FOVs referred to instantaneous FOVs. The TFOV is independent of the number of eyes since it is based on the locus of eye positions from which symbology can be seen.

Double combiners can also be used to increase vertical IFOV (VFOV) by creating a double 'knothole.' This is shown in Figure 3.6.

In a HUD where the combiner doesn't contribute to collimation, the combiner can be shifted to move the IFOV (within the total field of view). The A-7D/E HUD shifted the combiner to move the IFOV down during landing approach (7). This allowed the flight path marker to remain in the IFOV.

Transmissivity of combiner   An important property of the combining glass is the transmissivity. The transmissivity is the percentage of light that is transmitted through the glass. The reflectivity or percentage of light reflected, is 100 minus the transmissivity.

The lower the transmissivity, the brighter the HUD symbology will be, but the dimmer the view of the external scene. Diffraction combiners have an advantage since the transmissivity can be quite low for the specific wavelength of the CRT output and still be high for the total visible spectrum.

Most HUD combiners have transmissivities of the order of 70%–90%

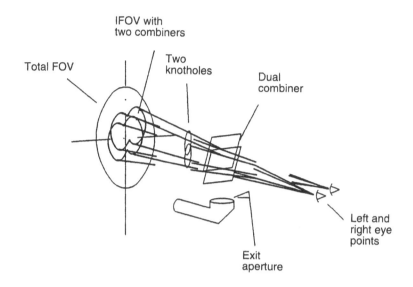

Figure 3.6 Double combiner

with diffractive combiners at the upper end. These values do not appear to present any problem with blocking of external vision (*8*).

Brightness The brightness of the HUD image is influenced by the CRT characteristics, the time spent writing the symbols, and the transmissivity of the combiner. The general requirement for brightness is the need to be visible when viewed against the range of backgrounds. The brightest backgrounds normally encountered in flight are cloud tops illuminated by bright sunlight.

At night, the brightness control must be sufficiently sensitive to allow viewing against a dark background. Early CRT based HUDs were deficient in this respect (*8*).

Stray reflections must also be avoided, from internal reflections and glare during night operations and from external reflections from lights and sunlight. Multiple combiner designs have proven susceptible to stray reflections and should be avoided (*9*).

Distortion The image of the symbology may be displaced from the intended location of the image. A simple displacement error should not affect flight solely by reference to the HUD since all symbols will be moved. If, however, the displacement varies over a short angular distance, the image may appear distorted. Distortion can increase pilot workload by making symbol interpretation difficult.

Similarly, the view of external objects may be displaced or distorted by passage of rays through the combiner.

Disparity The location of the symbology may differ from one eye to the other. This binocular disparity will cause the two eyes to look in slightly different directions. The pilot's eyes will shift to make the retinal images coincide. This response maximizes visual acuity. There is a possible cost in discomfort, which was the basis for early disparity standards (*10*).

Double images can be produced if the effect is strong. Double images have been reported as a problem with the F-16 HUD, but this appears to be a result of the windshield having a significant optical power (*11*).

Eye reference point The field of view available to the pilot will be a function of the diameter of the exit aperture and the distance from the pilot's eye to that point. Obviously, increasing the size of the exit aperture can increase the FOV. Moving the location of the exit aperture closer to the pilot can also increase available FOV.

Military HUDs are limited in how close the installation can be located to the pilot because of the need to clear the path for ejection seat escape. Figure 3.2 shows an ejection clearance line constraint on a typical installation.

Transport HUDs do not have ejection seat constraints. These HUDs frequently have overhead mounts, which can provide shorter eye relief and consequently larger FOVs.

As the pilot's eye is moved from the design eye point, optical performance (distortion, accuracy of symbol location, etc.) can degrade. Since the pilot will move his head during flight, it is better to speak of an eyebox volume rather than a single eye point. The performance specifications should be met at any location within this eyebox, rather than at a single point. Most early HUDs did not specify an eyebox volume, but assumed a fixed eye location.

Other optical designs

Reflective HUDs A second HUD optical arrangement is created where the optical power and the combining functions are combined into a single curved combiner (*1*).

Collimation is accomplished by reflection on the combiner surface as shown in Figure 3.7. It is necessary to shape both surfaces of the combiner to allow the rays from the external scene to pass through

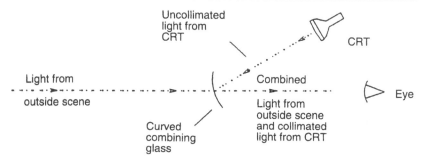

Figure 3.7   Reflective HUD arrangement

without being distorted. This type of HUD is referred to as a **reflective HUD** since the optical collimation is accomplished using the principle of reflection.

Reflective HUDs combine the exit aperture with the total reflecting surface. As a result, the IFOV and TFOV are identical. There is a problem associated with identical IFOV and TFOV: the loss of all symbology when the pilot moves his head out of the eyebox.

In an air-to-air (A/A) engagement, the pilot may move his head to keep his adversary in view. As he returns to the HUD, he may not be in the design eye reference point (DERP). In a conventional, refractive HUD, symbology will usually remain visible as the pilot moves his head and can guide him back to the DERP. A reflective HUD may be 'lost' and require additional effort to regain the symbology.

A second disadvantage of reflective HUDs has been the need to create an off-axis mirror. Fabrication of off-axis optical components usually requires grinding a larger surface than is needed. This is inefficient in terms of material and can be difficult to engineer.

Diffractive HUDs A diffraction grating can also be used as the combiner and final collimating element. A diffraction grating must be tuned for a specific wavelength. Since most CRTs used in HUDs use phosphors with a fairly narrow bandwidth, diffractive optics can be effective.

The major advantage of a diffraction grating combiner is identical with a reflective combiner: the IFOV can be the same as the TFOV. However, the same disadvantage of 'losing the picture' when moving outside of the DERP exists.

The diffraction grating will be tuned for a specific wavelength. Diffractive combiners can provide high reflectivity for the phosphor, thus enhancing symbol brightness. At the same time, the diffraction grating can have a high transmissivity for all other wavelengths, minimizing light attenuation with the external visual scene.

Diffraction gratings for HUD combiners are usually created by forming a hologram of the interference pattern on a photosensitive film. This film is sandwiched between two optical plates for physical ruggedness. Because of the fabrication using holograms, they are often referred to as **holographic HUDs**.

Many modern HUDs are diffraction HUDs; however, there are still refractive HUDs being manufactured, particularly where cost is a major concern.

Multiple combiners Some diffractive HUDs have been designed with multiple combiners to allow the use of on-axis optical designs for collimation. Multiple combiner designs often have problems with extraneous reflections and should be used with care. The complexity of light paths and reflections is shown in Figure 3.8.

Solid optical path The MD-80 uses a solid optical path HUD. In this HUD, the optics are contained in a solid block, with the combining surface being an interface between two blocks of acrylic (*12*).

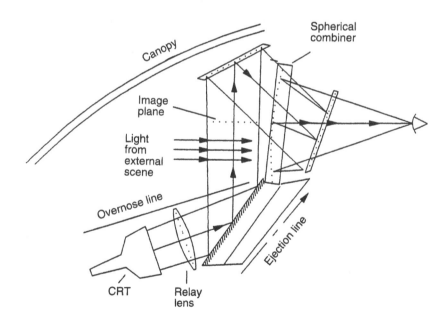

Figure 3.8 Light paths with multiple combiner (5)

41

Data processing

Most HUDs require considerable data processing as they take data from a variety of sensors and integrate the information into a computer graphics output. The system architecture determines how this data will be manipulated and how the HUD will perform error checks and system validation. The following section outlines system architectures for civil and military systems.

Following the discussion of system architecture, we will outline flight path computations and the generation of synthetic runways.

System architecture

The processing of data to be displayed on the HUD takes place in two functional areas: the mission computer and the symbol generator. The **mission computer** takes available sensors and calculates airplane performance data, such as flight path vector information. The mission computer also performs navigation and weapons delivery computations.

Some sensor data is simply passed through the mission computer, such as barometric altitude. Other data is highly processed, such as ILS deviation data, absolute altitude, and aircraft radar attitude, when used to generate the lines of sight for a synthetic runway.

The various items of data to be displayed (flight path angle, aircraft attitude, navigation deviation data, etc.) are sent to the symbol generator. The **symbol generator** takes this calculated data and converts it into symbols (a series of lines, arcs, and characters) which are sent as x–y positions to the display unit. Figure 3.9 shows a typical architecture for a military HUD.

One of the reported shortcomings in using military HUDs for instrument flight has been a lack of failure tolerance (*8, 13*). In spite of considerable recent effort in qualifying HUDs for instrument flight, little has been accomplished in this regard.

Civil HUDs usually combine the mission computer and symbol generator functions in one electronic unit (EU). Most military HUDs simply pass flight director steering cues thorough to the symbol generator. Civil HUDs usually compute steering cues in the HUD computer.

Most civil HUDs are fail-passive and have considerable internal checking including parallel sensor and computation paths up to the symbol generator. Any computed discrepancy is designed to prevent the display of false data. Figure 3.10 shows a typical system architecture for a civil HUD.

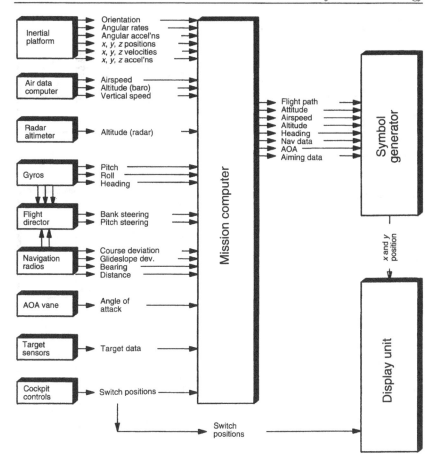

Figure 3.9   Typical military HUD data architecture

Flight path calculations

There are two frames of reference for flight path calculations: air-mass and inertial flight paths.

Inertial flight path   Inertial flight path angles are calculated from Equations (1) and (2):

$$\gamma_i = \tan^{-1}(\frac{V_z}{V_x}) \tag{1}$$

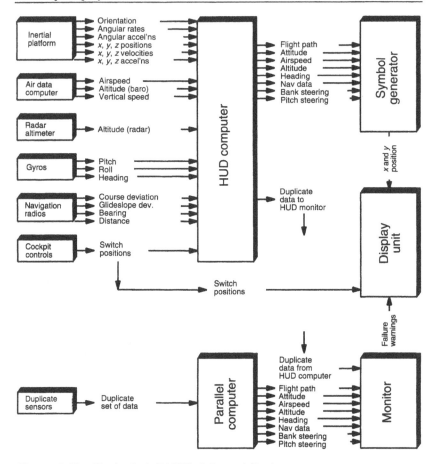

Figure 3.10   Typical civil HUD data architecture

$$\Phi_i = \tan^{-1}\left(\frac{V_Y}{V_X}\right) \tag{2}$$

where γ is the flight path angle and Φ is the lateral flight path (i.e. the drift angle). The subscript 'i' refers to an inertial frame of reference. The remaining terms are the body axis velocities: the longitudinal component (V_X), the lateral component (V_Y), and the vertical component (V_Z). The vertical should be derived from the inertial platform, although barometric data can be used.

In the event of a system failure, V_G from other sources (such as a Doppler radar) has been used for a backup source of data.

If a climb–dive marker is to be drawn, it must be translated to the center of the HUD FOV along a line parallel to the horizon line. The horizontal location of the CDM will be zero, the vertical component will be lowered by $\Phi\tan\phi$. This can create problems at bank angles of 90°. Some military HUDs limit the value of $\tan\phi$ to avoid this problem. Others use modified CDM geometry allowing for some lateral motion.

Air-mass flight path If we substitute true airspeed for V_X and use barometric vertical speed data, we obtain air-mass data:

$$\gamma_i = \tan^{-1}(\frac{\dot{H}}{V_T}) \qquad (3)$$

Normally the lateral component of air-mass flight path will be determined directly from the angle of sideslip (β).

$$\Phi_a = \beta \qquad (4)$$

An alternate source of air-mass flight path data is the angle of attack signal:

$$\gamma_a = \Theta - \alpha \qquad (5)$$

Generally, angle of attack (and sideslip) vanes are noisy and do not provide a satisfactory source for HUD data.

Pitch ladder calculations

The pitch ladder is normally created as a global symbol (see Figure 3.11). In a typical HUD, the [pitch] line spacing is a series of five degree ladders (plus the horizon line).

In most pitch ladders, only the numbers change from line to line. If articulation or tapering is included, the line inclination or length will also change from line to line.

In most HUDs, the pitch lines continue beyond the ±90° points. Future HUDs may replace the ±90° lines with zenith/nadir symbols.

Compression If pitch scale compression is incorporated, the ladder is drawn with the compression in place. Most HUDs change compression in discrete steps of 2:1, 3:1 etc. The physical line spacing will remain five degrees making the indicated line spacing 10°, 15°, etc.

Having lines at multiples of 5° (as viewed by the pilot) also requires that changeover points be restricted to angles that are multiples of the

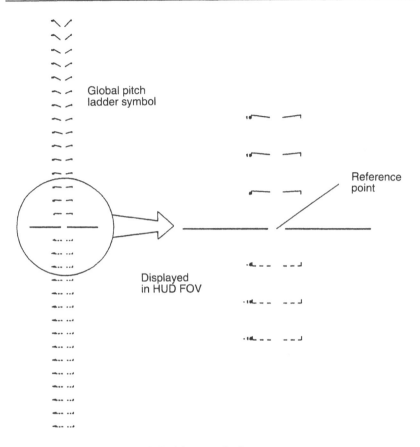

Figure 3.11   Global pitch ladder symbol

line spacing on both sides of the change: that is, a change from 1:1 to 3:1 can only occur at 15°, 30°, etc.

Using fixed line spacing makes programming the symbol easier compared with continuously variable compression. Fixed line spacing restricts the choices in compression.

We must distinguish between the actual pitch angle and the displayed angle. The **actual pitch angle** is the actual angle of depression or elevation as the pilot looks through the HUD. The **displayed angle** is the angle he reads from the pitch ladder scale. For pitch ladders with 1:1 scaling, the two are obviously the same. For HUDs with compression, the two angles will vary in their relationship. Figure 3.12 shows the relationship between displayed angle and pitch

46

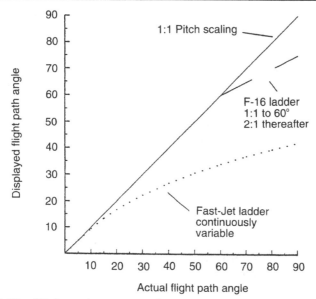

Figure 3.12   Pitch-scale compression

angle for three representative pitch ladders.

Ladder reference All symbols need a reference point, a point which defines their location. The global pitch ladder symbol's reference point is the center of the horizon line (the point midway between the two horizon lines).

Dynamic location of CDM During flight, the HUD symbol generator first locates the climb–dive marker (CDM). This is positioned in the HUD FOV to overlie the airplane's flight trajectory using Equations (1)–(3).

The primary aircraft symbol is drawn on the HUD FOV relative to the aircraft boresight (which is Θ degrees above the horizontal angle: that is, if a flight path marker (FPM) is used, the symbol will be $\Theta-\gamma$ degrees below and Φ degrees left of the boresight. If a CDM is used as the reference, the symbol will be $\Phi-\gamma$ degrees below the boresight and centered in the FOV.

Location of pitch ladder reference The pitch ladder reference point will be located γ_D below the aircraft symbol where the γ to γ_D transformation is defined by Figure 3.12. This is indicated in Figure 3.13a. Next, the ladder is rotated around the aircraft symbol by ϕ, the bank angle, as

47

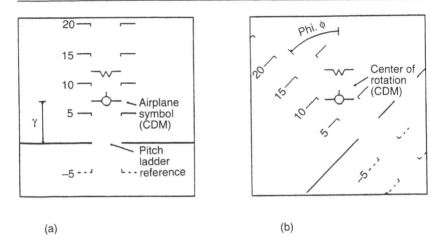

(a)   (b)

Figure 3.13   (a) Pitch ladder placement and (b) pitch ladder rotation (CDM reference)

shown in figure 3.13b.

This is equivalent to saying the location of the pitch ladder reference point will be

$$x_{PL} = -\gamma_D \cos \phi \qquad (6)$$

$$y_{PL} = \gamma - \gamma_D \sin \phi \qquad (7)$$

Use of FPM versus CDM   If the flight path marker (FPM) is used as the location of the primary aircraft symbol (as in the F-16 with drift cutout disabled), the pitch ladder will move laterally with the motion of the FPM, as shown in Figure 3.14:

$$x_{PL} = \Phi - \gamma_D \cos \phi \qquad (8)$$

Pitch symbol   The most common means of displaying the aircraft pitch symbol (waterline or gun cross) leaves it fixed in the HUD FOV. In essence it is 'painted on the glass.' As a result, if the pitch scale is compressed, the pitch symbol will not read correctly when read against the CDL. This has created difficulties in the past with the F-16 when the pitch scale is compressed.[2]

To show the aircraft pitch properly, the waterline symbol should be

[2]T. Lutz (Buffalo, New York), personal communication, 1992.

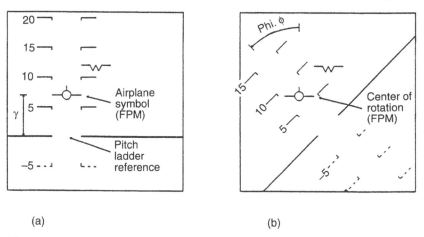

(a)   (b)

Figure 3.14 (a) Pitch ladder placement and (b) pitch ladder rotation (FPM reference)

relocated by an amount $\Theta_D - \gamma_D$.

Invalid FPM/CDM   When the flight path calculations are not valid, the pitch ladder must be referenced to the waterline. In this case, the pitch ladder reference point will be located Θ_D below the gun cross, where the Θ to Θ_D transformation is defined by Figure 3.12. Next, the ladder

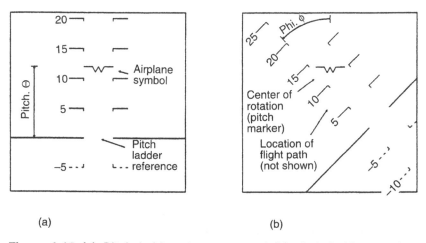

(a)   (b)

Figure 3.15 (a) Pitch ladder placement and (b) pitch ladder rotation (pitch reference)

is rotated around the gun cross by ϕ, the bank angle. This is indicated in Figure 3.15, which shows the same flight conditions as Figure 3.13. The location of the CDL reference point is

$$x_{PL} = -\Theta_D \cos \phi \qquad\qquad (9)$$

$$y_{PL} = \Theta - \Theta_D \sin \phi \qquad\qquad (10)$$

Quickening

One problem with the use of flight path angle as a control variable is the inherent lag of the variable. Pilots are accustomed to flying by reference to pitch attitude. With a longitudinal control input, the aircraft pitch attitude and angle of attack will change rapidly. The flight path will lag behind because of the aircraft inertia and will change to its final value relatively slowly (as shown in Figure 3.16a).

If the pilot is using flight path angle as the control variable, no immediate response will be apparent until the aircraft begins to change its vertical velocity component. With most aircraft, the aircraft pitch will change fairly rapidly, but the angle of attack (and as a result, the flight path) will lag behind the change in pitch. This has the effect of making changes in flight path difficult to make predictably. The

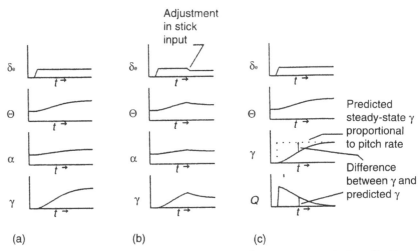

Figure 3.16   Quickening to improve transient response to longitudinal stick input: (a) response to step input in pitch; (b) need to adjust input caused by poor γ response; (c) incorporation of pitch rate term in γ to predict steady-state.

pilot must either make the change based on a change in pitch and wait for the flight path to catch up or make the change in flight path in several steps (Figure 3.16b).

Symbol quickening may be required to yield a 'flyable' flight path marker symbol. Quickening is signal augmentation used to improve predictability during changes in a control output (*14*). It is designed to provide a predictive signal of the final output variable, in our case the flight path.

Quickening is not a new technique; the instantaneous vertical speed indicator (IVSI) incorporates mechanical quickening based on load factor. The turn coordinator used in most light airplanes uses roll rate to quicken the rate-of-turn indicator (*15*).

Quickening adds a term to the flight path which corrects the initial flight path by adding a temporary term to the flight-path signal. The magnitude of this temporary term is adjusted to make the initial response approximate the final steady-state flight path. This is shown in Figure 3.16c. Either a washed-out pitch term or a pitch rate term is appropriate to quicken flight path.

Pitch rate quickening Some HUDs apply a pitch rate term to the vertical component of velocity, V_z or $\dot{H}$.

$$\gamma_1 = \tan^{-1}(\frac{V_z + K\dot{\Theta}}{V_G})$$ (11)

Freiburg used the flight path of a location 8 ft forward of the aircraft center of gravity, effectively making $K = 8$ (*16*).

Washed-out pitch quickening The implementation of the RAE Fast-Jet symbology for the Harrier adds the aircraft pitch change and then washes it out with a time constant approximating the heave time constant of the airplane (*17*). Equation (12) shows the vertical position for the CDM:

$$\gamma_A = \cos\phi \cdot \tan^{-1}\left(\frac{V_z}{V_G}\right) - \alpha_F \cdot \sin\phi + Q$$ (12)

$$\Phi_A = 0$$ (13)

The aircraft reference is driven by the flight path angle for wings-level flight and by angle of attack in 90° banked flight. The quickening term, Q, is equal to Q_1 for pitch attitudes within ±10° of the horizon

51

blending linearly and Q_2 for pitch angles beyond $\pm 30°$:

$$Q_1 = G \cdot \cos \phi \cdot \left(\frac{\tau s}{1 + \tau s} \right) \cdot \Theta \qquad (14)$$

$$Q_2 = G \cdot \left(\frac{\tau s}{1 + \tau s} \right) \cdot q \qquad (15)$$

where $G = 0.7$ and τ varies as $1/\sigma V_T$. For the Harrier at sea level, $\tau = 1.65\,s$ at 200 KIAS and $0.97\,s$ at 400 KIAS. G and τ were determined experimentally and will be aircraft-dependent.

Thus, the Fast-Jet quickening is a washed-out pitch term (with a time constant of the order of 1–2 s) at small pitch angles and becomes a pitch rate term at large pitch attitudes.

It is important to note that the pitch rate term q is in body axis coordinates from a rate gyro. If q is derived from another source, care must be taken to ensure that the result Q_2 is continuous and varies smoothly through the $\pm 90°$ points.

It is also important that the quickener term goes to zero in steady level flight to prevent false indications. This can be a problem with noisy data from the sensors. A suitable filter for incoming sensor data may be required. Further, the quickener calculation may drive the computer frame time to short intervals.

Q_1 is also discontinuous through the $\pm 90°$ points since the pitch rate will change signs. Q_1 can take a long time to recover. The Fast-Jet algorithm reduced the time constant to a small value ($\tau = 0.3\,s$) with $|\Theta| > 60°$.

Caveats   The accuracy of the quickening algorithm will depend on the exact control inputs applied by the pilot. As a result, there is no 'right' quickening term. In practice, the test pilot will have to evaluate the goodness of the particular algorithm, adjusting the constants to produce the 'best' quickening.

Some HUDs in the past have provided a level of augmentation to the point where the flight path symbol was not representative of the aircraft flight path. The designer must be careful to keep the quickening to the minimum level which creates a flyable symbol. The error should be on the side of too little rather than too much quickening.

In particular, care must be exercised to ensure that quickening of flight path symbols does not show non-conservative trajectories when maneuvering near obstacles or terrain. This will be most critical in the landing configuration, particularly for 'backside' aircraft.

Symbol quickening should not change automatically (within a given mode). It should also be kept to the minimum necessary to provide a flyable symbol.

Perspective runway calculations

Geometry The basic runway coordinates are shown in Figure 3.17. The origin for the coordinates is the runway centerline at the glidepath intercept point (GPIP). The coordinate system is aligned with the line of sight (LOS) from the pilot's eye to the GPIP. Points 1 and 2 define the threshold; points 5 and 6 the departure end. Points 3 and 4 are on the runway edges abeam the GPIP. Points 7 and 8 define the centerline of the runway.

The localizer deviation angle, δ_L, is the aspect angle the runway makes with respect to the LOS.

The runway coordinates are given in Equations (16a)–(16h) and (17a)–(17h).

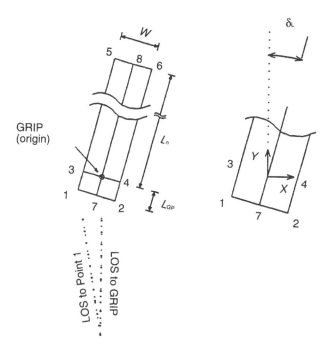

Figure 3.17   Runway coordinates

$$X_1 = -L_G\sin(\delta_L) + \tfrac{1}{2}W\cos\delta_L \tag{16a}$$

$$X_2 = -L_G\sin\delta_L - \tfrac{1}{2}W\cos\delta_L \tag{16b}$$

$$X_3 = \tfrac{1}{2}W\cos\delta_L \tag{16c}$$

$$X_4 = -\tfrac{1}{2}W\cos\delta_L \tag{16d}$$

$$X_5 = L_R\sin\delta_L + \tfrac{1}{2}W\cos\delta_L \tag{16e}$$

$$X_6 = L_R\sin\delta_L - \tfrac{1}{2}W\cos\delta_L \tag{16f}$$

$$X_7 = -L_G\sin\delta_L \tag{16g}$$

$$X_8 = L_R\sin\delta_L \tag{16h}$$

$$Y_1 = -L_G\cos\delta_L + \tfrac{1}{2}W\sin\delta_L \tag{17a}$$

$$Y_2 = -L_G\cos\delta L - \tfrac{1}{2}W\sin\delta_L \tag{17b}$$

$$Y_3 = \tfrac{1}{2}W\sin\delta_L \tag{17c}$$

$$Y_4 = -\tfrac{1}{2}W\sin\delta_L \tag{17d}$$

$$Y_5 = L_R\cos\delta_L + \tfrac{1}{2}W\sin\delta_L \tag{17e}$$

$$Y_6 = L_R\cos\delta_L - \tfrac{1}{2}W\sin\delta_L \tag{17f}$$

$$Y_7 = -L_G\cos\delta_L \tag{17g}$$

$$Y_8 = L_R\cos\delta_L \tag{17h}$$

We can now calculate the distance from the airplane to each point, as shown in Equations (18a)–(18h).

$$D_1 = \sqrt{[(D_0-L_G\cos\delta_L+\tfrac{1}{2}W\sin\delta_L)^2+(L_G\sin\delta_L-\tfrac{1}{2}W\cos\delta_L)^2]} \tag{18a}$$

$$D_2 = \sqrt{[(D_0-L_G\cos\delta_L-\tfrac{1}{2}W\sin\delta_L)^2+(L_G\sin\delta_L+\tfrac{1}{2}W\cos\delta_L)^2]} \tag{18b}$$

$$D_3 = \sqrt{[(D_0+\tfrac{1}{2}W\sin\delta_L)+(\tfrac{1}{2}W\cos\delta_L)^2]} \tag{18c}$$

$$D_4 = \sqrt{[(D_0-\tfrac{1}{2}W\sin\delta_L)+(\tfrac{1}{2}W\cos\delta_L)^2]} \tag{18d}$$

$$D_5 = \sqrt{\{(D_0 + L_R\cos\delta_L + {}^1\!/_2 W\sin\delta_L)^2 + (L_R\sin\delta_L + {}^1\!/_2 W\cos\delta_L)^2\}} \qquad (18e)$$

$$D_6 = \sqrt{[(D_0 + L_R\cos\delta_L - {}^1\!/_2 W\sin\delta_L)^2 + (L_R\sin\delta_L - {}^1\!/_2 W\cos\delta_L)^2]} \qquad (18f)$$

$$D_7 = \sqrt{[(D_0 - L_G\cos\delta_L)^2 + (L_G\sin\delta_L)^2]} \qquad (18g)$$

$$D_8 = \sqrt{[(D_0 + L_R\cos\delta_L)^2 + (L_R\sin\delta_L)^2]} \qquad (18h)$$

The LOS depressions from the pilot's eye are based on these coordinates and are shown in Equations (19a)–(19h).

$$A_1 = \tan^{-1}\left(\frac{h}{D_1}\right) \qquad 19a$$

$$A_2 = \tan^{-1}\left(\frac{h}{D_2}\right) \qquad 19b$$

$$A_3 = \tan^{-1}\left(\frac{h}{D_3}\right) \qquad 19c$$

$$A_4 = \tan^{-1}\left(\frac{h}{D_4}\right) \qquad 19d$$

$$A_5 = \tan^{-1}\left(\frac{h}{D_5}\right) \qquad 19e$$

$$A_6 = \tan^{-1}\left(\frac{h}{D_6}\right) \qquad 19f$$

$$A_7 = \tan^{-1}\left(\frac{h}{D_7}\right) \qquad 19g$$

$$A_8 = \tan^{-1}\left(\frac{h}{D_8}\right) \qquad 19h$$

The lateral LOS angles from the line of sight to the GPIP point are shown in Equations (20a)–(20h).

$$LA_1 = \tan^{-1}\left(\frac{-L_G\sin\delta_L + {}^1\!/_2 W\cos s\delta_L}{D_1}\right) \qquad 20a$$

$$LA_2 = \tan^{-1}\left(-\frac{-L_G \sin\delta_L - \frac{1}{2} W \cos\delta_L}{D_2}\right) \qquad \text{20b}$$

$$LA_3 = \tan^{-1}\left(\frac{\frac{1}{2} W \cos\delta_L}{D_3}\right) \qquad \text{20c}$$

$$LA_4 = \tan^{-1}\left(\frac{-\frac{1}{2} W \cos\delta_L}{D_4}\right) \qquad \text{20d}$$

$$LA_5 = \tan^{-1}\left(\frac{L_R \sin\delta_L + \frac{1}{2} W \cos\delta_L}{D_5}\right) \qquad \text{20e}$$

$$LA_6 = \tan^{-1}\left(\frac{L_R \sin\delta_L - \frac{1}{2} W \cos\delta_L}{D_6}\right) \qquad \text{20f}$$

$$LA_7 = \tan^{-1}\left(\frac{-L_G \sin\delta_L}{D_7}\right) \qquad \text{20g}$$

$$LA_8 = \tan^{-1}\left(\frac{L_R \sin\delta_L}{D_8}\right) \qquad \text{20h}$$

These angles, A_i and LA_i, show the location of each of the runway points relative to the horizontal plane and the line of sight from the pilot to the GPIP.

Correction for pitch, bank, and heading We must now shift these angles to account for the heading of the airplane relative to the LOS to the GPIP. This means we must change each LA, by the angle $\delta_L - (\Omega_R - \Omega_A)$. In other words,

$$x_i = LA_i - \delta_L + \Omega_R - \Omega_A \qquad (21)$$

These angles must be shifted to account for the airplane's pitch attitude relative to the horizon. We must change each A_i by the aircraft pitch attitude, Θ, as described in Equation (22):

$$y_i = A_i - \Theta \qquad (22)$$

The aircraft bank angle will make the points, as displayed on the HUD, rotate about the aircraft roll axis. The projection of the aircraft roll

axis, normally the pitch marker, is x_R, y_R.[3]
The correction for bank angle is

$$x_i(\phi) = (x_R-x_i)\cos\phi + (y_R-y_i)\sin\phi + x_R \tag{23a}$$

$$y_i(\phi) = (y_R-y_i)\cos\phi + (x_R-x_i)\sin\phi + y_R \tag{23b}$$

Additional symbology is usually added to the display to make the pilot's tracking task easier. Two glideslope reference lines are added just outboard of points 3 and 4, but depressed from the horizon by the glideslope angle (normally 3°). A runway course reference tick is usually placed on the horizon at the heading angle corresponding to the runway alignment (runway course). These have been added to the HUD depiction in the figures. A triangle has been added as an additional runway course reference near the heading lubber. This serves the same function as the horizon tick, except this scale is compressed 4:1 as is typical of HUD heading scales.

Figures 3.18 and 3.19 show the view. The airplane is on course and glideslope in Figure 3.18, high and to the left in Figure 3.19. In both figures, the airplane is on a 1.5 mile final. An inset of the head-down

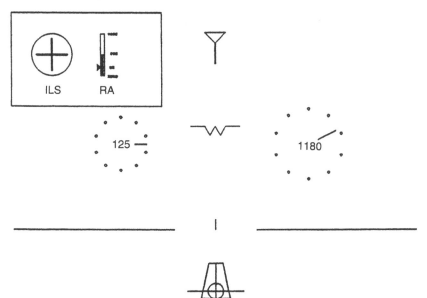

Figure 3.18   HUD perspective runway (on localizer and glideslope)

[3]But not always.

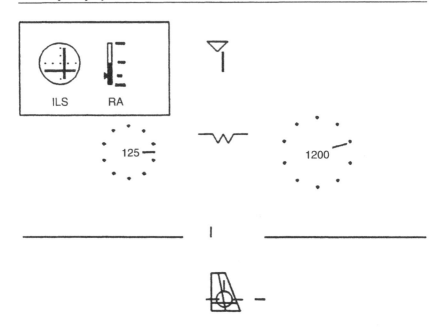

Figure 3.19   HUD perspective runway (high and left)

deviation indicator and radar altitude is shown for further clarification on each figure.

Examples of HUD designs

Optical characteristics

Table 3.2 lists some optical characteristics of representative HUDs.

Symbologies

Figure 3.20 shows the current US military specification for HUD symbology (*18*). Two additional HUD standards have been proposed: the RAE Fast-Jet symbology (*19*), shown in Figures 3.21a and 3.21b, and the USAF proposed standard (*20*), shown in Figures 3.22a and 3.22b. Figure 3.23 shows a typical transport HUD symbology.

Figure 2.1, 4.4, and the figures in the appendix show the symbologies available in head-up displays. Figures 3.23, 13.2, 13.3, 13.5–13.11, 13.13–13.16, and 13.18 show operational HUD

Table 3.2 Optical properties of HUDs

Head-up display	Field of view (deg)		Accuracy (mrad)		Vergence[a] (mrad)	Brightness (FL)	References
	IFOV	TFOV	Centr	Edge			
A-4M		20	1.9	–		10000	21
A-7D/E	11x17	20	2.0	5.0		10000	22, 23
A-10	13x13	20	1.5		1.0D/2.3C	10000	24, 25
	14x14	20					26
A-320	11x15	15x24	1.0	–		10000[b]	Note (b)
A-330	24x30	24x30				10000	Note (b)
AV-8A	18x20	25	1.5	–			22, 27
B-737,–747	26x40	26x40			7	10000	Note (b)
C-17	22x25	24x30					28
F-5E/F	16x17	25	1.5	4.5		10000	Note (c)
F-14A	11x17	20	1.0	1.0			22, 29–31
	11x14						26
F-14D	17x21	17x21					26
F-15	12x17	20					22, 32–34
	19x18	20					26
F-15E	18x28	24x30					26
F-16A/B	9x13	20	1.7	4.5	0.0D/2.0C	10000	35–36
F-16C/D	14x21	25					26
LANTRIN	19x30	19x30					Note (c)
F-18	16x16	20					26
F-111	15x16	20	0.3	2.5	2.0	10000	13, 22
MD-80	26x30		2.4	2.4		10000	12, 41
Mercure	12x18		1.0	1.3	0.3D/6.7C		42, 43
MiG 21	12x18	20	1.7	4.5		10000	Note (c)
Mirage	18x18[b]	24	1.0	–		10000[b]	37
Rafale	18x18	24	1.0	–		10000	Note (b)
T-38	14x20	25				10000	Note (c)
FDI 1000	24x30	24x30	2.0	7.0	1.0D/2.0C		38
FVI 2000	9x9						39
JET 9000	22x11[d]	30x15	1.7	–	1.5D/4.0C[d]	10000	40
TC-121		20	1.1	–			44
VAM	12x22	12x22	1.1	–			1

Notes: [a] Key: D = divergence; C = convergence.
[b] A. Leger (Sextant), personal communication, 1993.
[c] P. Wiseley (GEC Avionics), personal communication, 1994.
[d] D. Christensen (Jet), personal communication, 1994.

symbologies. Figures 13.1, 13.4, 13.12, 13.17, and 13.20 show HUD symbologies that are no longer operational. Figures 2.1, 4.4, and 13.19 show significant experimental or developmental HUD symbologies.

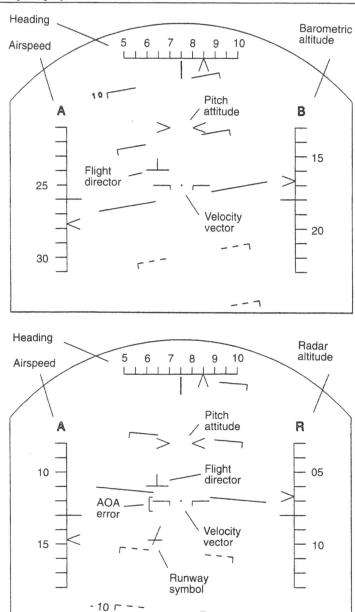

Figure 3.20   MIL-D-81641(AS) HUD symbology (*18*)

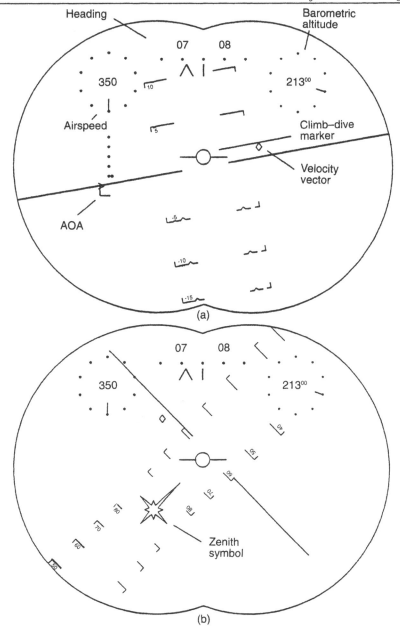

Figure 3.21   RAE Fast-Jet HUD symbology (*19*) (a) basic; (b) during unusual attitude

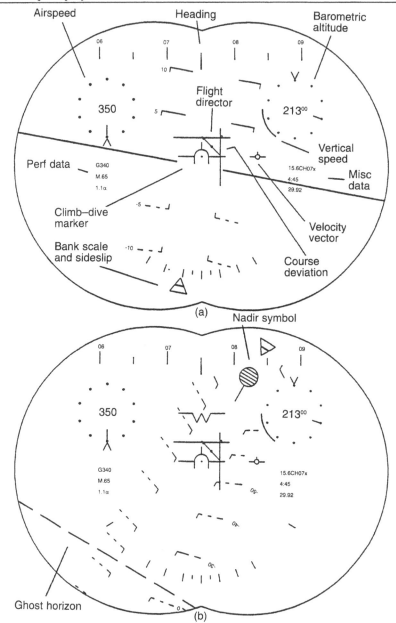

Figure 3.22   Proposed USAF HUD symbology (a) basic (*20*); (b) during unusual attitude (*20*)

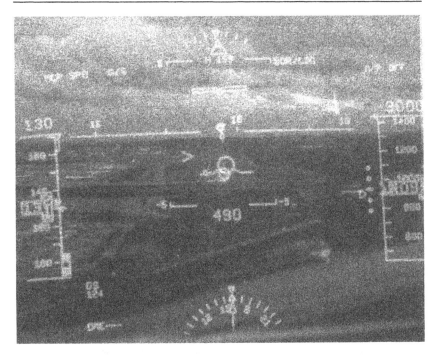

Figure 3.23   Typical transport HUD symbology (courtesy of Flight Dynamics

Installations

Table 3.3 lists some data and computational characteristics of representative HUDs.

Figures 3.24 and 3.25 show typical fighter installations in early airplanes. A late model 'glass airplane' is shown in Figure 3.26.

Figures 3.27 and 3.28 show transport airplane installations.

References

(1)   *System Specification: Visual Approach Monitor for the B-737 Aircraft System No. 960-2008* (Redmond, Washington: Sundstrand Data Control, 1977), Report 060-1624

(2)   Newman, R. L. *LCD Head-Up Display Evaluation* (San Marcos, Texas: Crew Systems, 1992), Memorandum C202-17

(3)   'Liquid crystal up-front control panel', (Rochester, England: GEC Avionics, Ltd., 1991), presentation to Air Force Wright Laboratory

Table 3.3   Computational properties of HUDs

Head-up display	Update rates Att. (ms)	Hdg. (ms)	Air (ms)	Refresh rate (Hz)	Flight path reference	References
A-4M	N/A[a]	N/A[a]	N/A[a]	50[b]		21
A-7D/E	20	20	N/A[a]	50	Inertial	23, 45
A-10	N/A[a]	N/A[a]	N/A[a]		None	25
F-16A/B				60	Inertial	36
FDI 1000	50	50	50	60	Inertial	38
JET 9000	75	100	150	60	Air-mass	40
MD-80	50	N/A[a]	N/A[a]	50	Air[c]	41, 12
Mercure	N/A[a]	N/A[a]	N/A[a]	N/A[d]	Air-mass	42
VAM	N/A[a]	N/A[a]	N/A[a]	N/A[d]	Air-mass	1

Notes: [a] Analog input.
 [b] 33 Hz during computation-intensive periods.
 [c] Highly augmented and filtered.
 [d] Continuous image.

(4) Sleight, G. R. and Lewis, C. J. G. *Practical Experience with Electronic Head-Up Displays in Transport Aircraft* (Rochester, England: Elliott, 1969), Report 29/11/2/BO5

(5) Hussey, D. W. 'Wide angle head-up display design and application to future single seat fighters', *Impact of Advanced Avionics Technology on Ground Attack Weapon Systems, Aghios-Andreas, Greece* (Paris: Advisory Group for Aeronautical Research and Development, 1981)

(6) *Flight Deck, Head-Up Displays* (Warrendale, Pennsylvania: Society of Automotive Engineers, 1988), SAE ARP-4102/8

(7) *A-7D Flight Manual* (Washington: US Air Force, ca. 1984), TO-1A-7D-1

(8) Newman, R. L. *Operational Problems Associated with Head-Up Displays During Instrument Flight* (Wright-Patterson AFB, Ohio: Air Force Aeromedical Research Laboratory, 1980), AFAMRL TR-80-116

(9) Gard, J. H. 'Holographic HUDs de-mystified', in *Proceedings National Aerospace Electronics Conference (NAECON '82)* (New York: Institute of Electrical and Electronics Engineers, 1982), pp. 752–759

(10) Gold, T. and Hyman, A. *Visual Requirements Study for Head-Up Displays,* (Great Neck, New York: Sperry Rand, 1970), JANAIR 680712

(11) Genco, L. V. 'Visual effects of F-16 canopy/HUD (head up display) integration', in *Proceedings Conference on Aerospace Transparent Materials and Enclosures, Dayton* (Dayton, Ohio: University of Dayton, 1983), pp. 793–807

(12) *Head-Up Display for the DC-9 Super 80* (Redmond, Washington: Sundstrand Data Control, 1979)

(13) Barnette, J. F. *Role of Head-Up Display in Instrument Flight* (Randolph AFB, Texas: Air Force Instrument Flight Center, 1976), AFIFC LR-76-2

(14) Birmingham, H. P. and Taylor, F. V. 'A design philosophy for man–machine control systems' in *Proceedings of the IRE,* **42**, December 1954, 1748–1758; reprinted in Sinaiko, H. W. (ed.), *Selected Papers on Human Factors and Use of Control Systems* (New York: Dover, 1961), pp. 67–87

Figure 3.24   Fighter installation (F-5E) (courtesy of GEC Avionics)

(15)   Stinnett, G. W. *The Turn Rate Indicator – Its Interpretation as Affected by Installation and True Airspeed* (Warrendale, Pennsylvania: Society of Automotive Engineers, 1971), SAE Paper 710380

(16)   Frieberg, U. 'Basic about scale one-to-one head-up display', in *Proceedings 15th Symposium, Society of Experimental Test Pilots, Beverly Hills* (Lancaster, California: Society of Experimental Test Pilots, 1971), pp. 77–85

(17)   Hall, J. R., Stephens, C. M. and Penwill, J. C. *A Review of the Design and Development of the RAE Fast-Jet Head-Up Display Format* (Bedford, England: Royal Aeronautical Establishment, 1989), RAE FM-WP(89)034

(18)   *Military Specification, Display, Head-Up, General Specification for* (Philadelphia, Pennsylvania, Naval Publications and Forms Center, 1972), MIL-D-81641(AS)

(19)   Hall, J. R. 'The design and development of the new RAF standard HUD format', in *Symposium on Combat Automation for Airborne Weapon Systems* (Paris:

Figure 3.25   Fighter installation (MiG 21) (courtesy of GEC Avionics)

Advisory Group for Aeronautical Research and Development, 1992); AGARD CP-520, Paper 11

(20)   Bitton, D. F. and Evans, R. H. *Report on Head-Up Display Symbology Standardization* (Randolph AFB, Texas: Air Force Instrument Flight Center, 1990), AFIFC TR-91-01

(21)   *Specification for Head-Up Display Set AN/AVQ-24B* (Rochester, England: GEC Avionics Ltd, 1986), EA-017-0042-C05, Revision E

(22)   Augustine, W. L. *Head-Up Display Area Survey* (Wright-Patterson AFB, Ohio: Air Force Flight Dynamics Laboratory, 1972), AFFDL TM-72-11-FGR

(23)   *Procurement Specification for Display Set, Pilot Head-Up for A-7D/E Airplane* (Dallas, Texas: Vought Aeronautics, 1967), Specification 204-16-19

(24)   *A-10A Flight Manual* (Washington: US Air Force, ca. 1984), TO-1A-10A-1

(25)   *Critical Item Development Specification for Head-Up Display* (Hagerstown, Maryland:

Figure 3.26   Fighter installation (F-18A/B) (courtesy of Kaiser Electronics)

Fairchild Aircraft, 1976), Specification 16OS417001B

(26)   Gard, J. H. *HUDs in Tactical Cockpits. A Basic Guidebook* (San Jose, California: Kaiser Electronics, 1989)

(27)   *AV-8A Flight Manual* (Washington: Naval Air Systems Command, ca. 1984), NAVAIR-01-AV8A-1

(29)   *F-14A Flight Manual* (Washington: Naval Air Systems Command, ca. 1984), NAVAIR-01-F14AAA-1

(30)   Benjamin, M. E. 'F-14 uses digital display method', *Aviation Week*, 1 July 1970, 45–46

(31)   Doucette, A. R. 'Design decisions for a head-up display', IEEE Spectrum, **13**, August 1976, 28–32

(32)   *F-15A Flight Manual* (Washington: US Air Force, ca. 1984), TO-1A-15A-1

(33)   Plummer, C., 'HUD ... basic symbology, hardware, and navigation modes', *McDonnell-Douglas Product Support Digest*, **21**, 1974, 8–10

(34)   Behm, D. 'HUD: radar and air-to-air modes', *McDonnell-Douglas Product Support Digest*, **21**, 1974, 11–12

(35)   *F-16A Flight Manual* (Washington: US Air Force, ca. 1984), TO-1A-16A-1

(36)   *Prime Item Development Specification for the F-16 Head-Up Display Set, CDRL-ELIN-A008* (Fort Worth: General Dynamics, 1978), Specification 16ZE017C

(37)   *HUD/HLD Combined Head-Up/Head-Level Display, VEM-130/TMM-1410* (Paris, Sextant Avionique, no date)

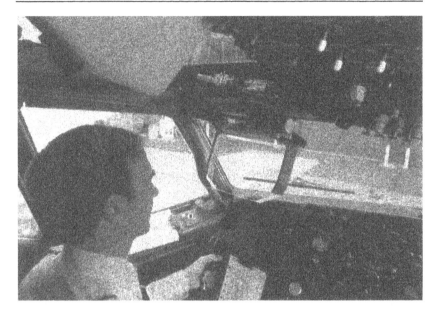

Figure 3.27 Transport overhead installation (courtesy of Flight Dynamics)

(38)   *System Description: FDI Model 1000 Head-Up Display* (Portland: Flight Dynamics, 1983), Report 404-0097

(39)   Newman, R. L. *Symbology for the FV-2000/KA Head-Up Display* (San Marcos, Texas: Crew Systems, 1991), TR-91-11

(40)   *Product Description: Head Up Display System, Model 9000A* (Grand Rapids, Michigan: Jet Electronics and Technology, 1985)

(28)   *Head-Up Display for McDonnell Douglas C-17* (Rochester, England: GEC Avionics, 1987)

(41)   *Head-Up Display for the DC-9 Super 80* (Long Beach, California: McDonnell-Douglas Aircraft, 1979)

(42)   *Cahier des Charges du Collimateur TH-CSF Type 193M* (Paris: Thomson-CSF, 1973), AVG/OP-73/169C

(43)   Roland-Billecart, A. and Deschamps, J. G., 'Operational Experience with HUD in CAT III', in *Proceedings of the Flight Operations Symposium, Vancouver* (Redmond, Washington: Sundstrand Data Control, 1979) Vol. I, pp. 122–153

(44)   *All Weather Approach and Landing Monitor, TC-121* (Paris: Thomson-CSF, no date)

(45)   Crews, L. L. and Hall, C. H. *A7D/E Aircraft Navigation Equations* (China Lake, California: Naval Weapons Center, 1975), NWC TN-404-176

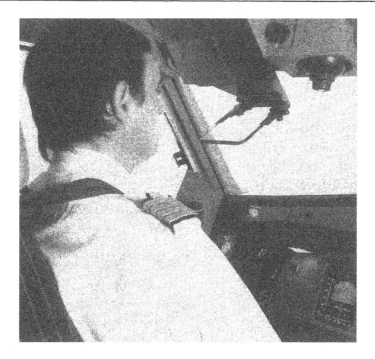

Figure 3.28   Transport overhead installation (courtesy of Sextant Avionique)

4 Symbology lessons learned

This chapter describes head-up display (HUD) symbologies which have been tried in the past – some successfully and some not. The symbology designer can use these historical results to choose a best set of symbology for a given application.

Standardization

Standardization of HUD symbology across aircraft is important to maximize positive and minimize negative transfer of learned habits. In spite of this, standardization, while desirable, must play a secondary role to the effectiveness of the display for the particular aircraft and mission. While some aspects of standardization should not be changed arbitrarily,[1] variations in mission, aircraft performance and agility, sensors available, and HUD field of view (FOV) should allow flexibility in symbology standards.

In addition, it is much more important for modes within a given HUD to be similar than for standardization across aircraft types. This concern is based on the pilot of a given aircraft being exposed to multiple formats in the same aircraft on a daily basis while only infrequently being

[1]Such as airspeed on the left/altitude on the right or the shape of some primary symbols.

exposed to new aircraft.

For example, use of a variable-compression pitch scale and a climb–dive marker could have significant advantages during HUD instrument modes, but could present difficulties during air-to-ground (A/G) weapon-delivery operations. In this case, an A/G airplane may need to avoid the use of variable compression pitch scales in all modes, even if the HUD standard prescribes variable-compression for instrument modes.

We must not become slaves to standardization for its own sake. Historical symbology standards often reflect the limitations of symbol generators at the time they were developed and should not be allowed to restrict development of advanced display formats. The primary goal should be enhanced pilot/aircraft performance *with HUDs designed and tested with mission performance in mind.*

General format description

Symbol definition

HUD symbology definition is often thought of as symbol definition, but in reality three areas must be considered: shape, size, and meaning of individual symbols; symbol placement within the FOV; and motion of the symbol relative to other symbols.

As an example, the climb–dive marker (CDM) is constructed of a winged circle with a 10 mrad circle and an overall wingspan of 30 mrad. An optional 5 mrad tail may be added. This defines the symbol size and shape.

The CDM is positioned in the center of the FOV and serves as the point of reference for aircraft control. The symbol moves vertically and provides an indication of the current flight path angle of the aircraft. The vertical motion will be driven by current inertial or air-mass flight path and may or may not have a quickening term added to enhance its flyability. The CDM differs from the flight path marker (FPM) by being constrained laterally to the center of the FOV while the FPM is free to move laterally.

The CDM also serves as the reference for angle-of-attack error, for potential flight path, and for flight guidance cues. All of these items must be described in order to complete the element description. In the past, HUD symbology descriptions have overemphasized the details of symbol size and shape and tended to ignore the other elements of the description.

As HUDs became widespread, certain *de facto* standards have

71

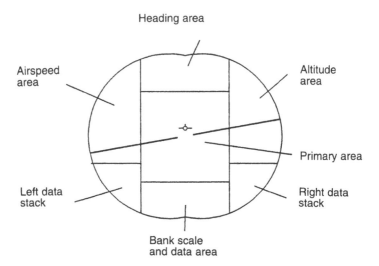

Heading area

Airspeed area

Altitude area

Primary area

Left data stack

Right data stack

Bank scale and data area

Figure 4.1 Functional field assignments

emerged. Some represent the positive results of trial and error, but others are merely expressions of 'it's always been done that way.' HUD design must be based on the mission needs of the aircraft and pilot, and will evolve as technology and missions change. It is important to ensure that any changes from historical HUDs should not be dangerously incompatible with existing pilot techniques and learned habits.

General format description

Figure 4.1 labels the generally accepted locations of the data displayed in a HUD, in the same fashion that the Basic-T describes the placement of head-down display elements.

Effect of FOV size

Figure 4.2 represents a roughly-to-scale layout of the basic symbology on a 25° horizontal/20° vertical display surface. The dimensional units most often used to describe symbol size and position are milliradians (mrad) of angular arc, and thus a specified viewing distance is required to convert to equivalent linear dimensions for the CRT tube face.

If a HUD with significantly different FOV is being developed, the designer is cautioned against merely scaling the symbols up or down. In particular, the primary flight information scales (airspeed, altitude, and

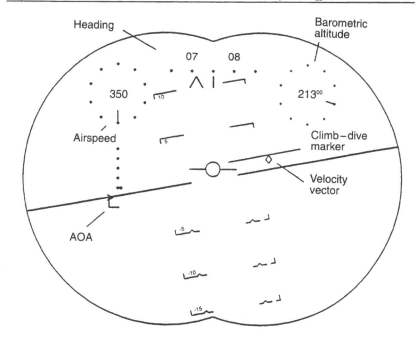

Figure 4.2   Basic symbology (25° x 20° FOV)

heading) should not be moved further away from the center of regard for HUDs with larger FOVs. Moving them further than about 4° requires that a scanning eye movement be performed in order to reference the altitude and airspeed information. It is, however, generally preferable to move secondary fields (such as navigation digital data blocks) away from the center of regard.

As the FOV is reduced from the typical 25°x20° degree size, the designer is faced with a serious problem. It will not be possible to shrink the data scales and maintain legibility. The airspeed and altitude scales may have to be compromised and vertical tapes or pure digits used in place of counter-pointers to physically fit the scales in the IFOV. Secondary scales might be relocated outside of the IFOV and displayed elsewhere in the TFOV (requiring some head-motion to view). Figure 4.3 shows the effect of applying the basic symbology in a 12x15 FOV combiner. In an extreme case, a compressed, non-conformal presentation might be necessary in small FOVs (of the order of 9°x9°).

If the FOV is increased from the typical 25°x20° size, the designer is faced with a different problem. He should not feel compelled to expand the scales to the periphery of the FOV nor should he expand the size of

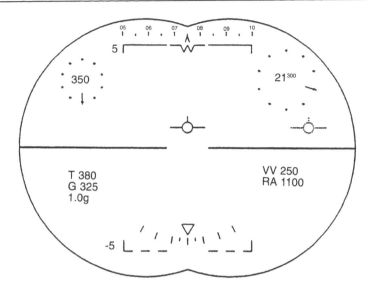

Figure 4.3   Basic symbology (narrow FOV)

the scales to make the HUD difficult to read.

Positioning of primary fields

Experience with HUDs, both during simulations and in flight, suggests that the goodness of a display is largely determined by the placement of the functional elements relative to the airplane reference symbol. In most HUDs, this symbol is the flight path marker or climb–dive marker. As the airplane is flown throughout its operational envelope, the location of this flight path symbol varies. At low speeds, it will appear near the bottom of the HUD FOV; at high speeds, it will move up. As the pilot increases the load factor (pulls gs), it will move down.

The altitude, airspeed and heading scales should be centered around the expected location of the flight path in the FOV. Past experience indicates that having a single changeover point is best. Some systems have done this manually (by changing the combiner glass position in the A-7) or automatically (with gear down in the F-16).

An approach recommended by Hughes (*1*) is to map the expected position of the aircraft flight path for various flight conditions in the HUD instantaneous FOV. He recommends creating two groupings of scales, one based on normal high-speed flight and one for landing. The changeover should be automatic and based on angle of attack (α) or airspeed rather than on configuration change (landing gear) or HUD mode. He recommends such a change at about 230–250 KIAS or 5° below approach α .

When flight path quickening was first implemented, the cluster of altitude, airspeed, and heading symbols tracked with the smooth motion of the CDM. However, simulation results suggest that this has some annoying characteristics, and a fixed location with a single changeover point seems to be a more acceptable baseline (2).

Clutter

Clutter is the major problem with the design of HUD symbologies. There is a tendency for designers to display everything possible in the HUD FOV. This is often based on asking pilots what data they need to fly a mission segment and then displaying everything full-time in the HUD (such as the altimeter setting, which only needs to be checked and set at intervals). This can lead to a cluttered display.

Clutter will adversely affect the ability of the pilot to see through the HUD. This can prevent visual acquisition of other airplanes or targets. See-through is most critical in the center of the FOV and on the horizon. Hughes recommends: '*Keep everything off the horizon as much of the time as possible*' (1).

Clutter is not simply related to density of symbols. A display with only two symbols will be interpreted as cluttered if they touch or clash in such a way as to render them confusing.

The amount of symbology (in terms of numbers of elements, line density, closed figures, etc.) must be limited. Not one pixel should be lit unless it buys its way onto the screen by providing a demonstrable improvement in performance (1). Some of the underlying principles concerning clutter are discussed in some detail elsewhere. The need to see through a HUD is of such overwhelming importance that the underlying principle should be, 'When in doubt, leave it out.'

Dryden states the principle as

> We should quit trying to make HUDs more complicated than they have to be. We should figure out what its truly needed, provide that – and nothing more. (3)

Display refresh

There is a second compelling reason to minimize HUD symbology. Many HUDs with large amounts of symbology can exceed the writing time available for the CRT display at 50–60 Hz. If this happens, the CRT refresh rate must be decreased or the symbol set truncated. The first alternative can cause flicker, while the second can delete needed symbols. This problem can be most severe in combined raster/stroke systems because the time available during flyback for writing the stroke symbols may be quite limited.

It is imperative not only to limit the number of individual symbols, but also to ensure that the symbols chosen comprise the fewest number of lines. Excessive use of text symbols can create problems because of the large numbers of lines needed. In addition, the more important symbols (such as the pitch ladder and airplane symbol) should be written first.

Airplane reference symbol

Choice of reference

Most HUDs today use inertial flight path reference. This has not always been so. As HUDs evolved from the firsts attempts to display flight information, they started out displaying only aircraft pitch with a non-conformal pitch ladder. HUDs progressed through conformal pitch-referenced displays to flight path vector displays. Early flight path displays showed air-mass data (i.e. the flight path was referenced to the air-mass). Figure 2.2 shows the general evolution.

While conventional wisdom suggests that inertial flight path

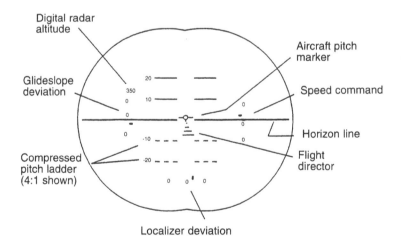

Figure 4.4   Non-referenced pitch symbology

76

referenced HUDs should be the logical choice, there are minority opinions to the contrary. Naish makes a strong case for the unreferenced pitch-based HUD with a flight director (*4*). An example of such a HUD is shown in Figure 4.4. Naish claims that such a display has superior performance in terms of transition to visual flight, of discrepancy detection, and in terms of resistance to symbol fixation.

Klopfstein developed an air-mass-based flight path symbology which made use of the unique relationship between flight path angle, pitch attitude, and angle of attack (*5*) (see Figure 2.1). While no formal tracking performance studies were reported, anecdotal evidence indicates that very precise airspeed control was possible with Klopfstein's symbology even in the absence of airspeed or angle-of-attack symbols (*6–8*).

Klopfstein emphasized the use of air-mass vector data to show α as the difference between two vectors. Air-mass reference should have advantages during up-and-away missions where ground reference is not important and aerodynamic performance is (such as A/A combat).

The point is: there are good and valid reasons to deviate from the conventional inertial flight path reference to either an air-mass flight path reference or to a pitch attitude reference. Reasons might include emphasis on up-and-away mission tasks, supporting equipment (i.e., lack of inertial reference), or FOV constraints forcing a compressed pitch ladder. While much of the remaining discussions will consider symbology in terms of inertial flight path, the designer should not forget other frames of reference.

Some HUDs include other inputs into the flight path symbol, such as vertical and horizontal deviation. This has been done to ease the tracking task, making it a compensatory task versus a pursuit task. While this has resulted in improved tracking accuracy, *there is invariably a cost in situational awareness*. We strongly urge that the flight path symbol be driven by inertial (or air-mass) flight path only, with a minimum level of quickening or filtering (if needed).

Aircraft reference symbol

The aircraft reference symbol (ARS) is the symbol which the pilot uses to control the airplane. Most HUDs use the flight path marker for this purpose. Other HUDs use the caged velocity vector (climb–dive marker) or aircraft pitch marker as the aircraft reference.

One school suggests that the same symbol should be used as the ARS. The ARS could, for example, represent flight path during an instrument approach and show aircraft pitch during the missed approach. This allows the pilot to fly with only one symbol. It also allows the use of the most effective symbol (normally the winged/tailed circle).

The other approach is to use separate symbols. While this requires the pilot to switch symbols, it does enhance his situational awareness.

The symbol of choice for the ARS is the 10 mrad circle with 10 mrad wings (and optionally a 5 mrad tail). This symbol has the highest degree of saliency (i.e. is most clearly perceived as the airplane). If aircraft pitch is used, a separate symbol should be used to make it clear that pitch, not flight path, is being used for aircraft control. The use of a single symbol for both caged and uncaged flight path does not appear to present problems.

The tail is not required, but does appear to enhance the perception of 'airplaneness' to some pilots. While most current implementations include the tail, the US Navy (*1*) and the British(*9*) have deleted it. Their rationale is that the tail clutters the most critical area of the display, and the guidance cues do not require stand-off indexing such as is needed for an α bracket or airspeed error tape. While we continue to recommend the tail, its omission is likely of little consequence.

The tail could be deleted when the flight path marker is caged to indicate this fact. Some HUDs display or remove the tail to indicate data degradation, but the effectiveness of this has not been demonstrated (*9*).

There is no need for a central dot, since the pilot can easily center the circle with guidance cues if required.

Pitch marker (waterline)

The pitch marker symbol is a '-W-' symbol with 10 mrad wings. The -W- serves as a mnemonic for the aircraft waterline. Some civil HUDs use a winged -V- symbol. The -W- is preferred because of the ability to use the central apex as a reference if the pitch is used as the aircraft reference symbol. The symbol is also known as the **waterline symbol**. Henceforth, we will use waterline in place of pitch marker.

When the waterline is referenced to the pitch ladder, the result is a value in degrees representing the aircraft pitch attitude. The pitch attitude is the angle between a selected fuselage longitudinal reference line (waterline) and the local-level plane. This angle is usually represented by Θ. The waterline refers to where the aircraft is pointed, not where it is going in terms of its flight path. This key distinction will be further discussed under flight path symbology below.

Different airframe manufacturers use different conventions for the definition of waterline. From a pilot's perspective, the most useful location would be the zero lift line to more clearly indicate angle of attack. In weapon aiming, the boresight would be preferred. As a result, in high speed flight, the flight path symbol will come to rest slightly below the waterline.

The waterline is a fixed reference in the display if the pitch scaling is 1:1. If the pitch ladder is compressed, the waterline must be displaced to the appropriate position in reference to the pitch scale to show the correct angular information. Failure to make this correction can lead to incorrect pilot responses. This has been reported in the F-16 which uses pitch compression above ±60°.[2]

The waterline is used as the aircraft reference symbol whenever flight path information is not available or is unsuitable for the task. An example is an aircraft during takeoff roll. As the aircraft accelerates on the ground, the flight path will continue to show level flight. Rotation for takeoff must be set by using the waterline. Another example occurs during vertical or short takeoff and landing (V/STOL) applications whenever sufficient forward motion for flight path generation is not available.

To minimize clutter, the waterline can be removed during *en route* flight if a valid flight path reference is available. There is little to be gained by displaying the waterline in up-and-away flight particularly if the flight path reference has pitch quickening included.[3]

Caged vs uncaged flight path

Most early HUD applications were developed for attack aircraft as super gunsights, and were heavily biased in favor of air-to-ground implementation schemes. The A-7D/E, for example, used a full-time ground-referenced flight path marker as the sole flight path representation, and in high crosswind conditions the symbol was displaced so far to the side that it interfered with the various scales for airspeed and altitude. This interference may have been aggravated because there was no occlusion protocol and the symbols were simply drawn over each other.

Pilots have reported that maneuvering an aircraft with a markedly displaced flight path marker feels funny because the aircraft does not seem to roll about its aerodynamic axes (*1*). Current commercial transport applications still favor the single uncaged ground conformal flight path marker, possibly because maneuvering is limited.

In addition, some HUDs included a sideslip (β) term in the lateral equations for the inertial flight path symbol. In some cases, the β signals

---

[2]T. Lutz (Buffalo, New York), personal communication, 1992.
[3]Showing the waterline full-time may enhance situational awareness recognition of UAs.

were quite noisy, producing a flight path symbol with excessive lateral motion.

Because of the maneuvering difficulties with the laterally free flight path symbols, various manual caging schemes were introduced to constrain the flight path marker to the vertical centerline. Because pilots wanted to know where the airplane was going, the F-18 HUD introduced a ghost velocity vector. This scheme allows both the ease of use of the caged symbol and the ground reference of the uncaged. It is used during low-level flight, A/G weapon delivery, and landing approach.

In the F-18, the pilot has the option of caging or uncaging the flight path symbol. The RAE developed a similar scheme using full-time caging (9). In the Fast-Jet, the caged symbol is called the **climb–dive marker** and is always constrained to the center of the FOV.[4] A separate velocity vector symbol (a small diamond) is shown whenever the lateral drift exceeds 2°.

The Fast-Jet symbology does not give the pilot a cage/uncage option – the aircraft reference symbol is always uncaged. This can present difficulties during air-to-ground weapon delivery since the bomb-fall-line must be referenced to the laterally free symbol. The RAE did not report testing their format during steep dive-bombing maneuvers.

Caged flight path

The recommended scheme is to give the pilot the option of caging or uncaging. With caging, a diamond velocity vector will be shown at the correct lateral position of the flight path. The constrained symbol (called the climb–dive marker, CDM) will be the reference for flight symbology (α error, energy cues, etc.). The ghost VV will be the origin of the bomb-fall-line. This provides the best of both worlds concerning maneuvering and ground prediction information and is recommended as the normal mechanism. It is shown in Figure 4.5.

Neither the dashed ghost symbol nor the diamond VV is preferred. The dashed ghost symbol might be confused with the CDM, although there are no reports of this. The diamond VV might be mistaken for some targeting symbols. If either is used, sufficient testing should be undertaken to ensure that the symbol chosen will not be confused with any other symbol used in the HUD. Another option is to use the wings and tail only (i.e., delete the circle) of the flight path marker.

---

[4]The term **pseudo-air-mass** has been used for such caged symbols. However, this term is misleading.

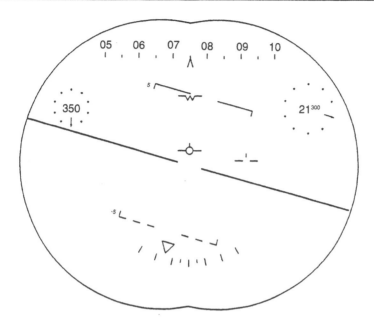

Figure 4.5   Caged flight path symbology

Uncaged flight path

The pilot should have the option of a free or uncaged flight-path marker (FPM). In the uncaged mode, all references will be in relation to the laterally free flight path marker (as shown in Figure 4.6). Other than ground referenced weapon delivery, uncaging is generally only needed, if at all, during high crosswind visual approaches when the α error might be annoyingly far from the ground-referenced touchdown point.

Climb–dive marker/flight path marker symbols

A brief review of the suggested terminology is in order. The aircraft reference symbol (ARS) is the symbol used by the pilot to fly the airplane. Flight and guidance symbols use the ARS as their reference. The ARS also serves as the center of rotation for the horizon and pitch ladder.

In caged mode, the pilot will use the climb–dive marker as the ARS. In the uncaged mode, the flight path marker will serve as the aircraft reference. If reliable flight path data is not available, the waterline will serve as the ARS. Table 4.1 shows the various choices.

81

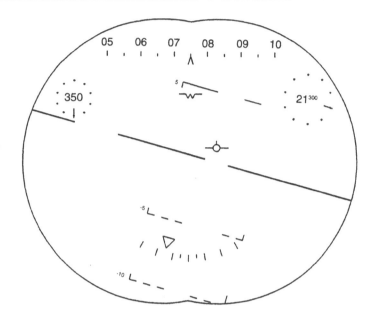

Figure 4.6   Uncaged flight path symbology: note occlusion around airspeed and altitude

For the balance of this document, we will use the abbreviation CDM/FPM to mean the aircraft reference.

Alternative symbols Some civil HUDs have modified the flight path symbol from a straight winged circle to an inverted gull-wing circle (sometimes referred to as the flat-footed duck) (*10*). This was done to ensure that the wings would be visible regardless of the location of the horizontal deviation signal (a horizontal line). It was also supposed to ease the pilot's task in maintaining 30° banked turns. This symbol is not recommended because of the presence of two vertical references: the wingtip and the center of the circle.

The proposed USAF standard uses an open half-circle for the CDM with two legs presumably representing landing gear (*11*). This was chosen to avoid the use of the winged/tailed circle which had been traditionally used for the velocity vector. A central dot is added to enhance the pilot's perception of the location. A small version of the winged/tailed circle is used to display the velocity vector. Advantages of this symbology have not been validated. A similar symbol was proposed earlier to differentiate between inertial and air-mass and inertial flight

82

Table 4.1 Aircraft reference symbols

Condition	Aircraft reference symbol	Symbol(s)	Data displayed
Caged	CDM	Winged circle Wings/tail (no circle)	Flight path angle Velocity vector
Uncaged	FPM	Winged/tailed circle	Velocity vector
Pitch only	Waterline	Winged 'W'	Aircraft pitch; flight path data not available

path data.

The ghost velocity vector (VV) has been used in the F-18 as the ground-referenced flight path symbol and is drawn as a winged circle drawn with dashed lines. There is still discussion on what the configuration of the VV should be. Some pilots find the dashed circle too big and distracting and prefer the British implementation, which uses a small diamond.

Symbol drive laws

The details of the flight path symbol drive laws will not be described here, but it is extremely important that the vehicle characteristics and control sensitivities are matched to the display motion. Many current HUDs suffer in this regard, particularly with respect to the incorporation of an unsmoothed β (sideslip) term into the symbol behavior.

One significant advance in the field of HUD implementation has been the incorporation of methods to lead-compensate (or quicken) the flight-path symbols. The improvement in controllability provided by a suitable quickening scheme can be dramatic, and is particularly evident during hard maneuvering. The quickening implementation scheme is discussed in Chapter 3.

A word of caution: there is sometimes a fine line between enhancing the pilot's tracking task and removing situational awareness cues. There is a potential, if too much compensation is applied, to dramatically improve tracking performance and simultaneously dramatically reduce situational awareness. There is no question that the addition of pitch rate terms or a washed-out pitch signal to the flight path signal can improve the pilot's workload during aggressive tracking tasks, particularly during aggressive maneuvering to capture a tracking parameter. The designer must ensure, however, that misleading flight path information is never allowed to be shown. For example, STOL aircraft, low thrust-to-weight transports, and/or delta-wing fighters in backside or near-backside regions of the drag curve might well show dangerously misleading quickened flight path information in response to pitch inputs. Any quickening algorithm must be validated over the entire flight envelope.

The effect of the quickening algorithm during the high body-axis rates of an unusual attitude has not been investigated and might hinder recovery.

The advantages of quickening are great, and quickening of the CDM symbol should certainly be considered. Incorporation of quickening will probably eliminate the need to display the waterline for takeoff/go-around initiation. Quickening of the velocity vector symbol should also be considered, but with caution because of the concerns expressed in the previous paragraphs.

Horizon line

The horizon line establishes the position of a horizontal plane passing through the aircraft at approximate eye level. Some HUDs have used horizon lines which were heavier or thicker to differentiate them from the other pitch lines. These are not recommended because of obscuration involving the most valuable area of real estate in terms of outside view. The length of the horizon line (to the edge of the FOV) should provide enough differentiation from the balance of the ladder lines.

Various attempts have been made to show the ground side of the horizon line (the side toward the earth) using ticks on the lateral limits of the line (pointing toward the ground) or little trees pointing to the sky side. The effectiveness of such implementations have never been demonstrated. Ticks are not well accepted when they are placed at the center gap, since they become clutter in the most critical part of the FOV (*1*).

The horizon line is drawn relative to the CDM/FPM. It is displaced from the reference by the flight path angle and then rotated about the CDM/FPM to show aircraft bank angle.

The horizon line should have a center gap slightly wider than the wings of the aircraft symbol; 33–36 mrad are suggested. The center gap should remain as part of the horizon line and pitch reference lines even when the reference lines are well displaced from the aircraft reference symbol.

It is extremely important that a wide horizon line does not clash with or run through other symbols on the display, but rather runs behind and is occluded by them with good margins. For details on the philosophy and mechanization of occlusion and priority refer to the section 'Symbol priority' in Chapter 7. Clashing of the line with any other symbol element can be seen as unacceptable clutter, regardless of the overall density of the symbols.

Pitch ladder

The pitch ladder (alternately called pitch lines, pitch scale, or climb–dive ladder) is shown with the horizon line in Figure 4.7. The use of the term **pitch** may be misleading, since the scale is most often used as a climb/dive or flight path angle scale, but this nomenclature enjoys such wide acceptance it would be difficult to change.

Like the horizon line, the pitch ladder is centered on and rotates about the current CDM/FPM. The central gap remains at all times in all the pitch lines, matching the width of the horizon line gap. Perpendicular ticks are usually located at the ends of the pitch lines and provide a cue to the horizon line. Snapping gaps closed is an attention-

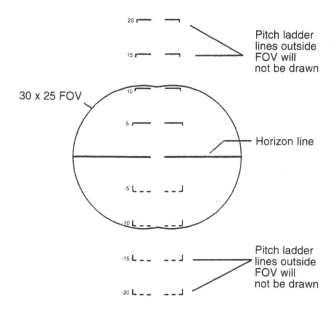

Figure 4.7   Pitch ladder

85

getter, and scrolling them closed can be perceived as a motion cue.

Transport HUDs intended for precision approaches often rotate the pitch ladder about the waterline marker. There have been no reported adverse comments on this. This is likely because maneuvering is limited during instrument approaches. Also, the center gap on these transport HUDs has also been considerably wider than the wings of the airplane reference symbol.

The pitch ladder should rotate around the pitch marker when the CDM/FPM is invalid or not available. Some have suggested that the CDM/FPM be deleted during unusual attitudes or at high angle of attack (*12*).

Composition

Most US HUDs use the convention of solid lines for positive angles and dashed lines for negative angles, although the reverse has been employed. Dashing the sky lines would provide more intuitive recognition properties of attitude, but the current installed base of HUD systems using the other convention makes the change from this *de facto* standard inadvisable.

The pitch lines above the horizon should be solid and the lines below the horizon dashed (approximately of the dimensions shown in Figure 4.7). Three to five dashes per line appears to be optimum. The space-to-solid ratio of the line is somewhat critical. If the spaces are too short, the line may appear solid when rapidly moving on the display surface; conversely if the individual solid segments are too long and the spaces too large, the pilot may fixate on one segment and misinterpret its meaning.

Perpendicular ticks of 5 mrad length are located at the outboard ends of the pitch lines and are oriented as a cue to point toward the horizon line. Some HUDs display the ticks on the inboard end of the ladder lines below the horizon to further differentiate between climb angles and dive angles. Ticks in the inboard edges add clutter to the central portion of the FOV, and this additional clutter must be weighed against any possible advantage.

Scaling and compression

Most US HUDs have used pitch scaling (also called **gearing** or **compression**) that is 1:1 to the real world, i.e. in direct correspondence with the real world. Experience with tactical applications indicates that the pitch scaling should be 1:1 when the flight path is in the region of the horizon line or when the aircraft is being flown against real-world objects (such as landing approaches or air-to-ground attacks). Failure to do this results in annoying relative motion between the real horizon and the HUD horizon line or between ground objects and the pitch ladder lines. This, however, has never been validated, and early British studies indicate that 1:1 pitch scaling may not be necessary (*13*).

Several unusual attitude studies indicate a strong benefit to compressed pitch scaling to enhance the pilot's ability to recognize and recover from unusual attitudes. Both full-time compression and 1:1 HUDs that switch automatically at extreme pitch attitudes have been recommended (*12*). Compression has been implemented using three approaches: full-time compression, switched compression and variable compression.

Many British HUDs use full-time compression, particularly in air-to-air modes where spatial orientation may be most critical. The F-16 HUD switches automatically from 1:1 to 2:1 at extreme pitch attitudes. The British Fast-Jet format uses a progressive compression scheme from 1:1 at the horizon line to 4.4:1 at the zenith and nadir (*9*).[5]

Both variable gearing and switched gearing do cause apparent variations in pitch rate, which can possibly lead to over-stressing the airplane until the pilot becomes used to the apparent slowness of recovery when the nose is near the 90° nose-down point. It does appear, based on the F-16 experience, that pilots are not bothered by discrete changes in gearing (provided not more than a factor of 2 is attempted) and may not even notice the change.[2] Until the effect of compression on displays conformal with the real world is complete, the designer is cautioned against anything but 1:1 in the range of pitch attitudes where A/G tracking is used. (Using switched gearing can permit delaying the changeover point to well beyond the weapon-delivery dive angle.)

If switched gearing is incorporated, the switching logic should provide hysteresis to avoid annoying repeated changes back and forth. Newman (*12*) suggested that a return to 1:1 be delayed for several seconds after the unusual attitude or maneuver was finished.

Articulation

The pitch scale lines in many current applications are articulated or

---

[5]The choice of 4.4:1 at the zenith and nadir was not based upon evaluations. As the concept evolved, a decision was made to have pitch lines spaced every 5° up to 30° above and below the horizon and every 10° thereafter. A second, independent decision was made to have the lines spaced no further apart then 5° in real angles. To accomplish this, the compression at ±30° was arbitrarily set at 2:1. Since the compression is 1:1 from –5° to +5°, the compression at ±90° is 4.4:1 (J. C. Penwill (Royal Aircraft Establishment, Bedford England), personal communication, March 1992).

bent toward the horizon. The angular pitch value of the line under these circumstances is calibrated at the juncture of the fixed center break. The disadvantages of the 'bendy bars' pitch lines are considerable. First, the numeric value representing the angle is displaced vertically from the CDM/FPM, and it is somewhat confusing, even to experienced pilots, as to what is the actual angle.

Additionally, it is easy to misinterpret one limb of the articulated lines as a roll reference for wings level. This phenomenon is frequently seen when individuals are asked to recover from an unusual attitude to a certain pitch attitude, wings level, and instead stop when they have aligned one limb of the bent pitch line to a level orientation. Finally, the entire goal of the articulation, namely to provide a pointer toward the horizon, is not very well satisfied. Indeed, occasional roll errors of 180° have been seen in simulator studies (*14, 15*).

Tapering

The pitch scale lines in many current applications become shorter as the angle from the horizon increases, in an attempt to provide an extra cue to pitch attitude and direction to the horizon. This approach is generally only significant for compressed pitch scaling, otherwise the tapering will be too small for the pilot to notice. (While the effect has been effective, it does provide a cue pointing away from the horizon.) Tapering also reduces the roll orientation at large pitch attitudes because of the very short lines.

One proposed HUD format tapered the above-horizon lines to point to the horizon in the takeoff/go-around (TOGA) mode (*16*).

Numbering

The current trend in military HUDs displays pitch angle numerics only on the left side when the aircraft is upright (and thus is written upside-down on the right when the aircraft is fully inverted). The number is written on the horizon side of the line (to amplify the horizon-pointing function of the adjacent tick). Minus signs are used with negative pitch values. No symbol for degrees is used. Some implementations suggest placing the numbers and ticks on the inboard side of the negative pitch lines, but this has often met with criticism because of the sensitivity to any clutter in the central area of the display.

Zenith and nadir

Figure 4.8 shows the display configuration as the zenith (90°) is approached from a wings-level pull up. A star is recommended as an intuitive symbol representing the sky. The pitch ladder should be drawn on the far side of the zenith and nadir symbols and not stop at the ±90° point even in transport HUDs.

Alternative zenith symbols include a complete eight-pointed star with a line pointing to the horizon (*9, 11*). A simple five-pointed star has also been recommended (*1*). All of these require more lines than the asterisk which is proposed. The eight-pointed star requires 16 lines and the conventional star five. The asterisk is created with four lines and should be as noticeable as either star format.

Figure 4.8 also demonstrates the approach to the nadir (90° straight down) at approximately 75° of bank. A bulls-eye or target is used as the intuitive straight-down symbol.

Some nadir symbols use multiple concentric circles or circles with multiple lines. In the absence of data supporting the need for these extra lines, these have been passed over in favor of the conventional open circle.

Most formats include a line pointing to the horizon, but this seems redundant since all lines from the zenith or nadir will point to the horizon.

The terms 'CLIMB' and 'DIVE' should never be used as the nadir/zenith cues, since they are subject to misinterpretation as to whether they state ('You are climbing...') or command ('Climb now...').[6]

Pitch ladder asymmetry

Experimental and empirical evidence supports the fact that asymmetrical elements in the pitch ladder add to a pilot's ability to rapidly assess spatial orientation (*17*). In an effort to provide as much asymmetry both in left/right and positive/negative pitch angle references, the following elements are incorporated:

- solid lines for positive angles, broken for negative;
- different line styles above and below the horizon (such as short lines for positive angles, long lines for negative);
- numbers on left side only;
- horizon-pointing ticks;
- numbers on the horizon side of the lines.

A form of extreme asymmetry, pitch lines on one side only, was found to

---

[6]One major airline goes so far as to use the word 'PUSH' at the zenith of their fleet's attitude indicators and the word 'PULL' at the nadir.

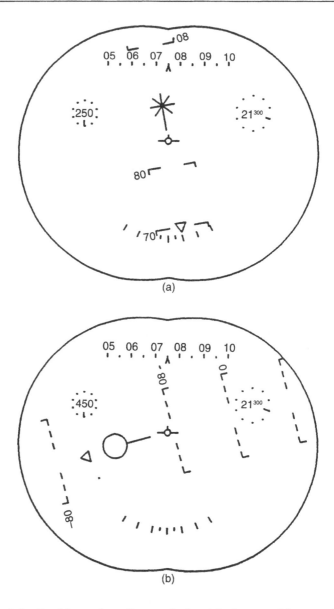

Figure 4.8 **Zenith and nadir symbols. (a) Approaching zenith: 84° climb and 10° right bank (note tapered ladder). (b) Near nadir: 81° dive and 75° left bank**

create difficulties with judging roll attitude during simulator evaluations (*12*).

The use of articulated lines for positive angles/tapered bars for negative angles has been proposed. This, however, introduces the same problems as were discussed above. The HUD designer must decide if the additional vertical symmetry cues outweigh the difficulties introduced by the articulated or tapered lines.

Civil HUDs have not used such asymmetry because few have considered unusual attitude recognition and recovery.

Pitch ladder reference

The center of rotation for the pitch ladder should normally be the airplane reference symbol (ARS). This will ensure that the ARS stays within the center gap.

Some civil HUDs intended for ILS approaches pivot the pitch ladder around the pitch symbol. This can cause the pitch ladder lines to obstruct the ARS. This has not been reported to be a problem because of the limited maneuvering during ILS approaches. Most such HUDs also employ pitch ladders with wide center gaps.

If a CDM is used with a velocity vector, rotating the pitch ladder around the waterline can make the velocity vector appear to be placed on the wrong side of the CDM.

During unusual attitudes or during high angle of attack, the CDM/FPM may not be usable. In these cases, recoveries should be made by reference to the pitch symbol. This will require that the pitch ladder reference be changed to the pitch symbol. This should be accomplished automatically (probably in conjunction with deleting the CDM/FPM). The pitch ladder may jump, particularly at large bank angles. Hysteresis should be incorporated to prevent the pitch ladder from jumping back and forth.

Other pitch ladder cues

One civil HUD modifies the pitch ladder during the takeoff/go-around (TOGA) mode to show an inverted tapering above the horizon line (*16*). The pitch ladder points to the horizon. It is also referenced to the aircraft heading, not to the CDM/FPM. If the airplane heading is the same as the desired heading, the pitch ladder is centered in the HUD; as the airplane turns the ladder shifts, indicating deviation from the desired heading. This approach is suitable only for specific mission tasks, not for general use.

Airspeed

Indicated airspeed

Airspeed is shown in the left portion of the instantaneous FOV. It is placed slightly above the expected level of the CDM (see Figure 4.2). This scale is reserved for indicated airspeed (IAS) only.[7]

The groundspeed or true airspeed values can be selected for display in the subsidiary data block (unboxed and labeled), well removed from the indicated (lift-related) airspeed term. This minimizes the potentially disastrous possibility of misinterpreting a groundspeed readout as a wing lift performance value.

The airspeed scale is placed symmetrically across the display surface from the barometric altitude scale. The counter-pointers should lie slightly above the expected position of the CDM/FPM to minimize the opportunity for interference with the lateral movement of the FPM or VV.

Existing HUD airspeed displays have been either analog or digital. Digital airspeed had the advantage of precise display, but lacked useful rate information.

Analog displays, on the other hand, presented rate information, but of limited precision. Most analog airspeed scales were vertical tapes. These often lead to airspeed reversal errors or false horizon cues (*18, 19*). Vertical airspeed tapes also require that the tape move in the opposite direction to the altitude tape (possibly leading to a false roll cue) or that they be numbered with the large values at the bottom.

The counter-pointer format, however, appears to be the best of both worlds, digital and analog (*9, 12*). In addition to precise digital readouts, it displays analog information that has the following characteristics:

- minimal clutter with high pilot acceptance;
- marked improvement in the ability to smoothly and rapidly change to a new steady-state value;
- marked improvement in the ability to stay at a preselected value for airspeed or altitude without having to constantly read the digital value;
- no need to rescale the size of a tape window to allow for different

---

[7]Strictly speaking, the scale should show calibrated airspeed (CAS). Since pilots use the the terms IAS and CAS interchangeably, the term **indicated airspeed** will be used throughout, and carries the clearest connotation of a dynamic pressure-related term. It is more clearly distinguished from true airspeed or groundspeed than the term **calibrated airspeed**.

rates or phases of flight.

The counter-pointers are shown in Figure 4.9. Ten dots surround the digits and form a circle approximately 45 mrad in diameter. The dots should be barely perceptible (approximately 0.5–1 mrad in diameter), and in fact the dots may not be required at all. The pointer is a line segment with its extended center of origin at the center of the circle. Most implementations have terminated the outer end of the line at a radius corresponding to the circumference of the dot circle; however, extending the lines slightly beyond the dots (1–2 mrad) could enhance visibility.

The airspeed digits obscure that portion of the pointer line that run behind the numbers. The obscuration mask must extend approximately 3 mrad past the edge of any of the airspeed digits to prevent the counter-

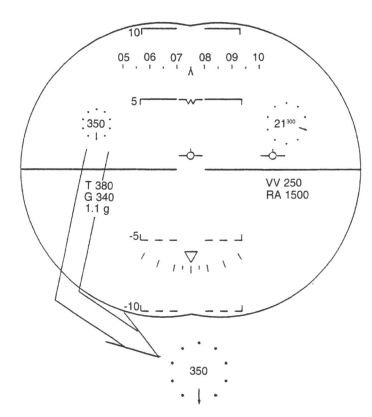

Figure 4.9 Airspeed counter-pointer

93

pointer needle from fusing with the numeral and deforming its apparent shape.

The IAS pointer is set for 100 knots per revolution of the counter-pointer. The performance gains associated with the simple circular analogs have been consistent across a wide range of experimental and operational trials, and they are recommended without reservation. Even so, the ability to declutter the analogs should be provided to the pilot.

The airspeed digits should be expressed to the whole knot with no leading zeros. Scrolling of the moving digits, like a car's odometer, has been suggested to reduce the distraction of the digital value snapping back and forth, but the advantage of this method has not generally been borne out in comparative trials (1).

Some installations use a scrolling digit for the terminal digit. The advantage of this has not been documented. If scrolling digits are rejected because of drawing complications, the units digit should be set to zero at high rates to minimize blurring during rapid changes.

For those airplanes not requiring airspeed trend information, digits only should suffice. There is no need for the airspeed scale to use the same format as the altitude scale. The MB-339C HUD displays digital airspeed and counter-pointer altitude (20).

If an error in the airspeed data is detected, the entire airspeed symbol should be deleted. It is not necessary to specifically enunciate the failure.

Airspeed reference

A reference caret to indicate a selected airspeed, such as a landing approach airspeed should be displayed on the circle of dots at a location corresponding to the tens and units value of the selected airspeed. If the selected airspeed is more than 40 knots from the currently displayed airspeed, this caret should be deleted.

When the airspeed carets are deleted because of being more than 40 knots from the current airspeed, some recommend displaying the value above the counter-pointer circle. The value of displaying the digits must be weighed against the extra clutter.

For the takeoff roll in a transport HUD, the two or three takeoff reference speeds should be indicated: V_1, V_R, and V_2. V_1 and V_R should be deleted after lift-off. For airspeeds more than 40 knots below the takeoff reference speeds, the carets will be deleted and the values should be shown above the counter-pointer circle. The values should be labeled, such as V1 105 etc.

Flight performance data block

Various categories of aerodynamic performance data are displayed in digital format in a data block in the lower left instantaneous FOV below the airspeed scale. The data are available within easy scan range, but not in a position to clutter the display during A/A or A/G activity. The data consist of text written approximately 6 mrad high, each with a numeric value and a short descriptive label. The content includes (but is not limited to) the data types listed below, and the hierarchy from top to bottom represents a consensus of some existing applications. In general, the display of data that goes into the data block should be easily selected or deleted by the pilot.

The digital values should not be boxed. Closed figure symbols (like the box) act to obscure distant objects within the rectangle when viewed through the human perceptual system. The only reason that boxing was utilized in previous applications was to positively separate the value from other surrounding numbers, and this goal can be achieved by reserving the primary scales for indicated airspeed and barometric altitude values only, and making sure that size or position cues will preclude confusion with any other numeric values.

True airspeed True airspeed should be shown digitally, preceded by the letter 'T'. The resolution should be 1 knot (e.g. T 462).

Groundspeed Groundspeed should be shown digitally, preceded by the letter 'G'. The resolution should be one knot (e.g. G 455).

Groundspeed could be displayed here or in the navigation data block. The performance data block was chosen because of the value of having groundspeed during landing approaches for wind shear awareness.

Mach number Indicated Mach number should be shown digitally, preceded by the letter 'M'. The resolution should be 0.01 (e.g. M 0.83). Mach number must be displayed if required for airworthiness considerations.

Load factor (gs) The normal load factor should be shown digitally, followed by the letter 'g'. The resolution should be 0.1 (e.g. 2.5 g). Load factor will normally be displayed only on tactical aircraft.

Angle of attack If needed, α should be shown digitally, preceded by the letter 'α'. The resolution should be 0.1 units or degrees (e.g. α 0.1).

One experimental implementation has mechanized the α and G digits in such a way that they increase in size and move closer to the center of the field as the values increase through certain key points (*1*). The utility of this additional capability for α in the presence of an error bracket cue is questionable, however, and it needs further investigation. Some variations of these methods may prove to be very useful, however, in augmenting other cues (auditory, tactile, or visual) that alert the pilot to the fact that a critical value is being approached.

Airspeed error

The α-error bracket or speedworm (see 'angle-of-attack error' below) could be driven by airspeed error in place of angle-of-attack error.

Altitude

Barometric altitude

For the same reasons discussed above, barometric altitude is shown in a location opposite the indicate airspeed. A counter-pointer arrangement, similar to airspeed, should be used as shown in Figure 4.10. The pointer should make one revolution every 1000 feet. Because more digits must be enclosed in the display, the radius of the circle of dots should be about 55 mrad, slightly larger than the airspeed scale.[8]

The thousands and tens-of-thousands digits should be written larger than the hundreds, tens, and single digits. The tens-of-thousands and thousands digits are the same size as the airspeed digits and the remaining digits about 60%. Below 1000 ft, all the digits are full-size.

Some applications recommend keeping the ones and tens column smaller than the hundreds, thousands, and ten-thousands digits. This is apparently an attempt to be compatible with the 'Flight Level 350' nomenclature, but it is confusing to pilots used to seeing the number of thousands in either larger or reverse colored numerals. This alternative convention should be avoided to prevent twelve thousand/twelve hundred type errors.

The digits should snap, not scroll to avoid reading errors (*22*).

The singles-unit column remains zero (thus display accuracy is to the nearest 10 or 20 ft) to avoid blurring the last digit. This might need to be modified during ILS approaches.

---

[8]Both the Fast-Jet and the USAF standards specify different-size circles intentionally (*21*). While there is no *a priori* need for identical-size symbols, neither is there a demonstrated need for intentionally having different sizes.

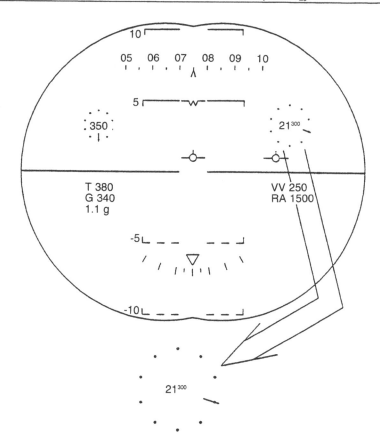

Figure 4.10   Altitude counter-pointer

Altitude reference

A reference caret to indicate selected altitude should be displayed on the circle of dots at a location corresponding to the hundreds, tens, and units value of the selected altitude. If the selected altitude is more than 400 ft from the currently displayed altitude, this caret should be deleted.

When the altitude carets are deleted because of being more than 400 ft from the current altitude, some recommend displaying the value above the counter-pointer circle. The value of displaying the digits must be weighed against the extra clutter.

The altitude caret should indicate the same altitude as is set in the altitude alerter.

97

Absolute altitude

Both analog and digital scales for radar (or absolute) altitude have been used. In most HUDs, radar altitude will be automatically displayed whenever the absolute altitude is below a threshold value (normally 1500 ft). The optimal position of this composite display in the HUD FOV must be carefully determined both in high speed low-level flight and during landing approaches so that maximal awareness is matched to minimal clutter.

Normally, radar altitude will display values to the nearest 10 ft down to 500 ft (or some similar altitude) and display values to the nearest foot below.

Digital absolute altitude   Two positions for radar altitude digits have been used, both with success: below the aircraft reference symbol or in a digital data block below the barometric altitude. This location usually requires an 'R' prefix to distinguish it from the other digits in the data block.

Some HUDs intended for ILS Category III approaches have used a center-bottom location for the absolute altitude. This location doesn't appear to require a label.

Analog absolute altitude   The most successful analog cue is a vertical tape with an associated reference caret which can be set by the pilot. Usually, these scales are nonlinear (as are most panel radar altimeters), and small dots or ticks are used as scale references. The total height should be about 50 mrad to minimize clutter and framing effects.

Other analog cues that have been used include a rising runway type of cue for the landing approach. These have generally been successful. Such a display should generally not be enabled until late in the ILS approach.

Vertical speed

In aircraft using attitude reference instrument systems, the vertical speed indicator (VSI) is an important altitude lead instrument, and instrument pilots use it extensively to maintain altitude.[9] A second use of the VSI lies in the use as a control parameter to establish glide slope by integrating the aircraft speed and wind data. In flight path reference systems both of these functions are provided by the CDM/FPM, which

[9]We use the term **vertical speed** rather than the military term **vertical velocity** for two reasons. Vertical velocity sounds too similar to velocity vector. In addition, vertical speed is a scalar, not a vector quantity.

gives a direct reading of the variable of interest, flight path angle.

Given some experience and training with flight path systems, many pilots elect to declutter vertical speed and this capability should be provided. Civil airworthiness requirements may require vertical speed.

This does however give up a cross-check in case of failure of the flight path reference ('the CDM is below the horizon line, but the vertical speed is positive...'). While this type of failure check is best left to automatic devices, pilots should have the option to display VSI. Since VSI will be required in the event of a loss of flight path reference, an argument could be made to display it full-time to minimize the effect of a transition from a flight path reference to a pitch/VSI reference.

Both digital and analog vertical speed displays have been used.

Digital vertical speed   Digital vertical speed is generally located immediately below (above in some HUDs) the barometric altitude display. The digits would be preceded by a 'V' to prevent confusion with radar altitude. The value represents feet per minute rate of climb or descent. Many pilots have complained that digital vertical speed scales are unusable.

Analog vertical speed   Analog vertical speed displays have expanding-tape scales or moving carets. When used with vertical tape altimeter displays, these have tended to improve performance during level-off from climbs or descents (*23*).

A novel modification to the expanding tape bends it around the counter-pointer circle of dots (*11*). Expanding-tape scales have been successful, but do add considerable clutter.

Altimeter setting

Some HUDs display the current altimeter setting digitally in the navigation data block. It could also be shown near the barometric altitude scale. However, the pilot's need for this information is insufficient to justify displaying it in the HUD FOV. If it must be displayed in the HUD, consideration should be given to displaying it only during data entry, and removing it shortly after a change has been completed.

Heading

The most common heading suite used in head-up displays is a horizontal scale in the upper portion of the display. The scale, shown in Figure 4.11, should be optimized to reduce clutter, minimize the framing effect of long linear scales, and yet give plenty of lead information for hard maneuvering to a new heading.

The scale provides coverage of 40° at approximately 4:1 to 6:1 horizontal compression. There is little to be gained for most airplanes by making the scaling conformal. To do so may result in degraded control of the heading because of the rapid motion of the numbers during rapid changes.

No digital readout of the heading is included. The added benefit of a digital value in the presence of a well-designed scale is minimal, although some pilots would rather have a centered unboxed digit as the sole heading symbol, and forgo the scale entirely.

There may rarely be a need to display it in an alternative position at the bottom of the field but this should be avoided if possible. While this would preserve the 'T' concept, it would force the bank scale to the top of the FOV which is not desirable. It would also make the heading less easy to see against a ground-clutter background.

Using the recommended scale, at least three numbers will be displayed at any time if 10° interval labels are used. Longer scales may lead to a false horizon sense. Two digit numbers are used as labels (the same convention as runway numbering except leading zeros are used, so that 01 means 010°). A fixed centered lubber line is used as the index. If a heading reference symbol is utilized, it should be represented by a caret, but this may meet with some resistance since the heading scales in some current aircraft (notably the F-18) use the caret symbol as the lubber index.

The numbers should scroll horizontally into the central display area instead of snapping the complete numerals onto the ends in a distracting fashion.

Some civil HUDs have placed the heading numbers on the horizon line. These HUDs invariably use a 1:1 relationship between displayed numbers and the real world. Since these HUDs are typically used during ILS approaches, compression may not be necessary since the airplane will not be maneuvering aggressively. Difficulties related to obscuration of the scale behind the CDM during any level flight segment and apparent rolling of the scale out of the readable plane when the aircraft rolls argue against this mechanization.

Heading references

Heading references, such as selected heading and course information, can be a useful addition to a heading scale. It is important that these be identical to those shown on any head-down instrument. They should be

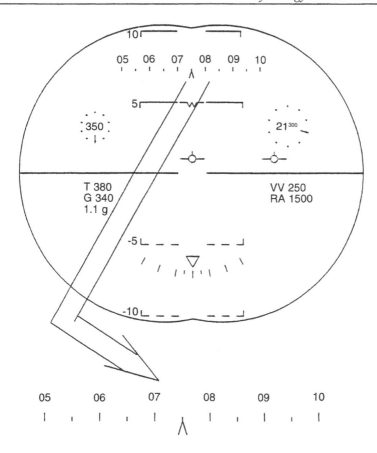

Figure 4.11   Heading scale

marked with symbols similar to those shown on the head-down instruments. A caret is normally used for a selected heading and a single or double bar is used for navigation course.

The value of the selected markers (or bugs) should be obvious to the pilot. If the marker would be off scale, it should be located just off the side of the heading window and turned on its side. A digital indication of the set value could be shown for pilot reference.

Ground track

Some HUDs display ground track, often as an inverted 'T'.

101

Orientation cues

Horizon-pointing cues

The addition of a horizon pointer attached to the CDM/FPM dramatically improves a pilot's ability to recover from an unusual attitude. It improves the HUD's generally dismal performance in this area, and may even exceed the capabilities of a full head-down attitude gyro for the unusual attitude (UA) recovery wings level task. It must be stressed that the arrow-type recovery cues only affect the ability to recover from unusual attitudes and do not markedly improve UA prevention.

Three implementations have been suggested. The **Augie arrow** is a horizon-pointing arrow centered on the ARS, the **pacman** is a 45° cutout of the velocity vector circle, and the **ghost horizon** is a thick dashed horizon surrogate near the periphery of the FOV. These are shown in Figure 4.12.

Attitude awareness cues

Two global attitude awareness cues have also been proposed. The **orange peel** is an attitude cue surrounding the ARS. The orange peel is a thick circle which rotates to show roll angle, and expands and contracts to show pitch. The French have proposed a small attitude ball (called **le boule**) in the lower-left corner of the FOV as a global attitude awareness cue.[10] These are shown in Figure 4.13. These attitude awareness cues should have the advantage of enhancing attitude awareness on the part of the pilot – preventing UAs, not merely helping in their recovery.

Mechanization

Orientation cues are generally mechanized to appear when the horizon disappears from the FOV. They should be oriented to point to the horizon so that the pilot can simply roll to the cue and pull, regardless of attitude. Because of this, a horizon pointer is preferred to a pointer mechanized to point to the sky.

Because UAs may be associated with unreliable flight path information, reversion to a pitch reference will be likely. For this reason, the orientation cue should work well with the waterline.

The orange peel or le boule symbols have usually been presented full-

---

[10]The choice of the lower-left corner was presumably based on directing input into the right brain hemisphere.

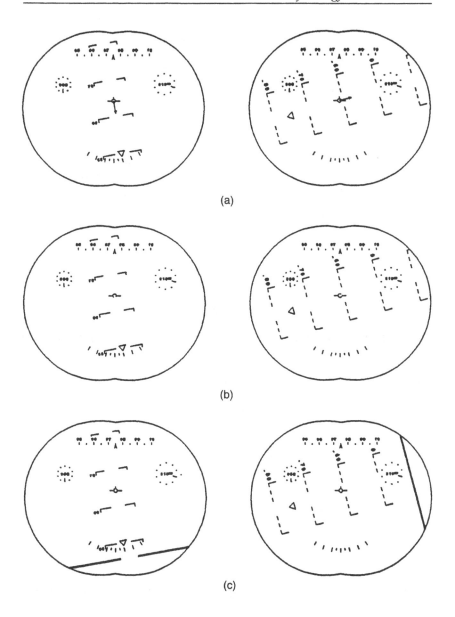

(a)

(b)

(c)

Figure 4.12   Orientation cues: (a) Augie arrow; (b) finless pacman; (c) ghost horizon

103

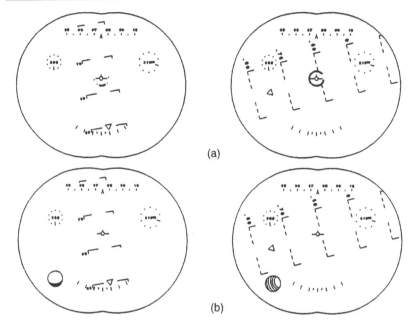

**Figure 4.13   Attitude awareness cues: (a) orange peel; (b) French ADI
ball (*le boule*)**

time. The orange peel has also been proposed as a substitute for the
pitch ladder.[11]

The Augie arrow has been evaluated and found to be a very useful aid
to UA recognition and recovery (*12, 24*). Tests on the ghost horizon
were included in the tests of the proposed USAF standard with mixed
opinions (*25, 26*). Results of tests on the others have not been published
nor have any been compared with one another.[12] Table 4.2 compares the
features of the five cues.

Angle-of-attack cues

Angle of attack, α

If needed, angle of attack, α, is displayed as an unboxed digital value in

---

[11]P. Weger (MBB, Munich, Germany), personal communication, January 1992.
[12]Simulator tests using both the pacman and orange peel have been completed, but
the results have not been reported.

Table 4.2   Horizon-pointing cues

Horizon-pointing cue	Symbol	Clutter	Effectiveness
Augie arrow	Horizon pointing arrow	Slight increase	Demonstrated in several simulation experiments; results favorable
Pacman	45° gap	None	Has not been implemented; will not work with waterline or with open circle
Ghost horizon	Dashed horizon at edge of FOV	Increased at edge of FOV	Mixed results; difficult to place – too near edge of FOV and not apparent, too far from edge clutters
Orange peel	'Hollow' attitude indicator around ARS	Considerable able in center of FOV	Anecdotal reports indicate considerable effectiveness
Attitude ball 'le boule'	Small AD1 in lower left of FOV	minor	Anecdotal reports indicate considerable effectiveness

the lower-left data block (see 'Flight performance data block' above). An 'α' symbol is used as a label preceding the value. The units are expressed in tenths of units, with 0.1 being the minimum interval. Deletion of the α digits in the cruise ranges reduces clutter, but a method of allowing the pilot to easily obtain the α value at any time should be provided.

Angle-of-attack error

The α-error bracket, shown in Figure 4.14, consists of a C-shaped bracket which is referenced to the horizontal centerline (left wing) of the CDM/FPM symbol. If no flight path information is available, the bracket is referenced to the left wing of the waterline. In general the total length of the bracket represents a nominal 4α units, although this value may depend on the specific scaling factor of the aircraft α units scheme.

In the past these brackets have been mechanized in two diametrically opposite schemes: the bracket moves up if the airplane is fast (α less than reference) or the bracket moves down in the same situation. The first mechanization is the conventional pilot display of 'fly the little airplane to the symbol' – fly to.

The second mechanization scheme stems from the original Klopfstein

HUD format which made use of the unique relationship between angle of attack, flight path angle, and aircraft pitch. By depressing the pitch scale by an amount corresponding to the reference, the pilot could easily maintain a target (and airspeed). This was adopted in the Mercure HUD. These French HUDs were air-mass based and the emphasis was placed on maximizing aerodynamic information transfer.

When the A-7D/E HUD was introduced, the same scheme was taken (contrary to the specification) even though the HUD displayed an inertial flight path. The α-error bracket was now a fly-from display. Later HUDs had the option of either matching the A-7D/E or using the more natural fly-to sense. The potential for confusion with mixed fleets is obvious.

The bracket should be mechanized to move upward in relation to the CDM/FPM to indicate the fast situation (α less than optimal). This is the so-called fly-to mechanization. Using an example of an α system with a range of about 18°, the α-error bracket will ordinarily be enabled when α is less than reference minus 5°. A 0.5° hysteresis should be incorporated to prevent flickering. The bracket should be enabled by α value and not by HUD mode or aircraft configuration.

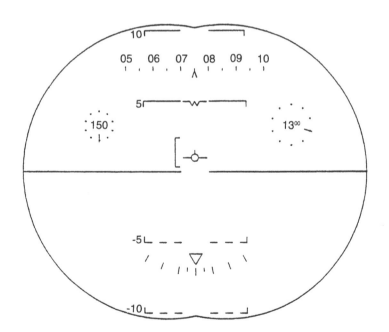

Figure 4.14   Angle-of-attack error bracket (showing slightly fast)

106

Speed worm Civil transports have tended to use a slightly different cue, the so-called speed worm. This is a tape scale growing out of the left wing of the ARS, above the wing for airspeeds faster than reference/α less than reference. While most transports have used airspeed error to drive this cue, α mechanization is an alternative.

Anecdotally, the speed worm was introduced to avoid instances where pilots lost the α-error bracket when the IAS was much greater than the reference approach speed during an initial approach.

Analog angle-of-attack

In some HUDs, an α thermometer has been used in the lower left hand FOV (*9*).

Energy cues

Recently, a number of flight performance cues have emerged displaying energy management or potential flight path. The input data is normally based on longitudinal acceleration. We will discuss the most common implementation, **potential flight path** (PFP). PFP has been developed for the landing approach and for the initial climb. This is not meant to preclude other energy cues designed for other phases of flight.

PFP represents the flight path angle which will maintain the existing airspeed based on current thrust and drag. The vertical displacement between the CDM/FPM wings and the PFP indicates the magnitude of the acceleration (positive or negative) along the flight path. The PFP symbol is shown in Figure 4.15 and consists of a caret which runs in a vertical path parallel to and displaced just to the left of the α bracket.

Generally, the PFP caret is enabled any time the bracket is displayed. Some HUDs have an additional mirror-image caret to the right of the CDM/FPM. The zero index for the caret is horizontal alignment with the CDM/FPM wings (and not the α bracket) for airspeed maintenance. If the caret is level with the horizon, the total aircraft energy is constant, although the pilot may be trading airspeed for altitude.

Bank scale

A bank scale is located in the lower part of the instantaneous FOV as shown in several of the figures. The index points down (in earth coordinates), so that a right bank is shown as a deflection of the index to the right. Some HUDs show the bank scale at the top. This should be

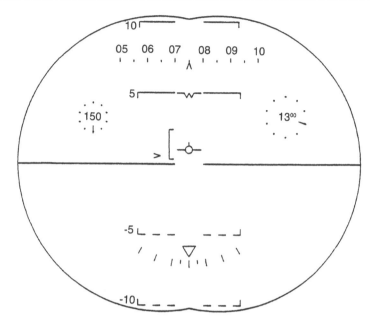

Figure 4.15   Potential flight path (showing slightly fast with airspeed decreasing)[13]

avoided since the pointer cannot remain perpendicular to the horizon unless it is reverse-sensed.[14]

The bank angle scale is an arc segment fixed and centered on the apparent center of the IFOV in most current HUDs, but there is no reason not to tie the position of the scale to the center of regard in the airspeed–heading–altitude constellation of symbols (see 'Positioning of primary fields' above). Some HUDs tie the scale to the CDM/FPM, but this can result in unwanted motion. Some HUDs tie the scale to the waterline but this may add clutter to the center of the FOV.

If the center of the arc is not the same as the center of rotation of the pitch ladder, there may be unwanted motion of the bank pointer relative

---

[13]The airplane is trading airspeed for altutide. The total energy is increasing since the caret is above the horizon, but airspeed is descreasing since it is below the CDM/FPM wing.

[14]A secondary reason for placing the heading at the top and the bank scale at the bottom is their use during maneuvers at low altitude in visual conditions. Under these conditions, the scale at the bottom of the FOV will tend to become lost in ground clutter. Heading is the more important of the two information fields and should thus be placed at the top of the FOV.

to the pitch ladder.

The scale has radial ticks at 0°, 10°, 20°, and 30° on either side. Some add ticks at 45°. The proposed USAF standard includes ticks at 45° and 60° that are shown only when the bank angle exceeds 20° (*11*). Generally, the ticks should be 3 mrad, with the zero and 30° ticks being slightly longer (5 mrad).

The pointer is a small triangle (about 3 mrad on a side), although some may have avoided this closed symbol in favor of a caret because of perceived denseness. In some current symbologies, the bank indicator is allowed to run all the way around the outer rim of the IFOV, so that the roll index is in effect a ground pointer Thus inverted flight results in the arrowhead residing above the heading scale at the top of the display regardless of nose-up or nose-down orientation. Despite some apparent use in certain weapon-delivery modes, this implementation is a poor unusual attitude cue since it is difficult to find under most conditions, and it points down rather than to the horizon (*12*).

One recent HUD proposal uses a bottom bank arc but with an upward pointing sky pointer (*11*). This mixing of cues can lead to confusion and should be avoided.

Certain missions may require accurate roll orientation, and sensor gimbal limits may be required as additional markings on the scale. Some transport HUDs use roll whiskers to show maximum bank at touchdown.

However, many pilots will be satisfied to estimate roll angle from the pitch line angles, and choose to declutter the entire bank scale.

Sideslip (β) cue

Sideslip has not been a major issue with HUDs because most HUDs have been installed in military fighter aircraft. As HUDs become common in transport and VTOL aircraft, the display of sideslip will be quite critical during engine-out flight or in VTOL operations. A sideslip cue is essential for transport HUDs.

Four formats have been recommended. The first uses a ball-bank analog similar to the traditional slip–skid indicator. This is not normally displayed and only appears when a sideslip threshold is reached. The scale remains visible until after all sideslip has been removed. The sense of the indicator is 'step on the ball' to remove any sideslip. Figure 4.16 shows the various sideslip formats.

The second format places a flagpole on the waterline, which displays a flag. The length of the flag shows the amount of sideslip. Again, the symbol is not visible until the sideslip reaches a threshold value.

The third format splits the triangle used for the bank index. This is not

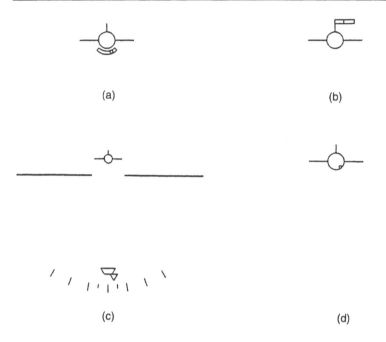

(a)

(b)

(c)

(d)

Figure 4.16   Sideslip scales: (a) ball scale; (b) flag; (c) bank scale; (d) mini-ball

recommended for several reasons. First, the cue is removed from the aircraft reference and will require the pilot to look away from his primary flight cue. Second, the sense will not be apparent ('step on the point of the triangle' or 'step on the base'). The proposed USAF standard HUD inverts the bank triangle from the accepted civil arrangement. This clearly compounds the opportunity for confusion. If the USAF standard is adopted, as appears likely, there will be two 'standards' for displaying sideslip on the bank pointer.

For fighters or tactical applications, the sense will become even more confused at high bank angles or in inverted flight.

The use of the bank pointer for sideslip is not recommended.

A fourth format uses a small ball-scale inside the CDM/FPM circle. The symbol is compatible with prior training with needle/ball applications, and can be displayed in all modes without inducing clutter. The enhancing feature of this mechanization is that although tiny in terms of area, the symbol is useful because of the unambiguous location as part of the CDM/FPM symbol.

Guidance cues

Situational vs steering data

The symbols used for lateral and vertical guidance must first be categorized as either raw (situational) data or flight director data. Confusion and potentially lethal errors can occur when a clear differentiation is not maintained. Comments such as 'I thought I was on centerline because the [flight director] cue was centered...' are typical of the potential misinterpretations.

Flight directors function on the basis that if a pilot keeps the symbol centered, the aircraft will be directed along a calculated track to intercept and hold an intended course such as a final approach course and glide path. The weakness of a flight director is that it gives the pilot no information about where the aircraft is in relation to that course or glide path. Hence a rule of flight director implementation is: always provide a source of raw (situational) steering data along with the flight director (1).

Concepts to ease the pilot's task in making changes to the aircraft trajectory, such as symbol quickening or the use of flight director cues, tend to weaken his situational awareness. A word of warning: be very careful to provide clear situational cues when using these task enhancement tools.

There is a tradeoff between situation awareness and the tracking performance achieved by the pilot. One can design a display emphasizing one over the other. While there is a tendency to emphasize task performance (e.g. ILS localizer or glideslope-tracking error) as a figure of merit, the designer must also ensure satisfactory situation awareness. Imposing a situation awareness criterion may well result in a slight degradation in task performance. The trick is to ensure a level of task performance *satisfactory* to the certification authority and the operator and a *satisfactory* level of situation awareness, not just attempt to maximize tracking performance.

Guidance cues

Unfortunately, there is no standardization on the symbology to show guidance data. In addition, there is limited data comparing one symbol over another. Table 4.3 lists various HUDs with their choice of symbols, while Figure 4.17 shows several sets of symbols.

Side scales One of the first navigation presentations for HUDs was a surrogate of the course deviation scale as shown in Figure 4.4. Both lateral (localizer) and vertical (glideslope) scales have been used. Location has

Table 4.3 Landing guidance cues

Head-up display	Raw data cue	Flight director cue	Reference
Operational			
A-7D/E	Perspective cue	Tadpole	27
A-14	Needles	Tadpole	28
F-15	None[a]	Cross	29
F-16	Needles	Tadpole	30
F-18	Needles	Tadpole	31
B-727	{ Course line (loc) { Synthetic runway	Circle/tadpole	10
MD-80	Deviation box	Circle/tadpole	32
Experimental			
PERSEPOLIS	{ Deviation box { Synthetic runway	None[b]	33
Klopfstein	Synthetic runway	None[b]	5
Naish	Side scales	Perspective cue	4
King Air	Side scales	Wings	23
Proposed			
MIL-D-81641	Course line	Inverted T	34
USAF std	{ Needle (loc) { Side scale (GS)	Needles	11
USN std	{ Large box[c] { Tadpole[c]	Rotating box	1

Notes: [a] This HUD does not display raw data.
[b] This HUD has no flight director.
[c] This HUD has two sources of raw data.

varied from the top of the FOV to the bottom of the FOV for lateral deviation and either left or right side for vertical deviation. Naish recommends using side scales in conjunction with a center flight director (*4*). Another HUD (not yet operational) placed lateral deviation scales between the aircraft reference symbol and the heading (*23*).

Arguments in favor of side scales are generally based on similarity to head-down instruments or reducing clutter near the center of the FOV.

Arguments against using side scales for deviation include interference with other required data or on the need to divert attention from the center of the HUD.

An additional consideration for the use of lateral deviation side scales is the need to provide selected VOR or TACAN course information elsewhere in the HUD to maintain pilot orientation during an approach.

Cross-pointers/needles   For ILS tracking, the use of cues analogous to the ILS cross-pointers has been used. These needles can be referenced to the

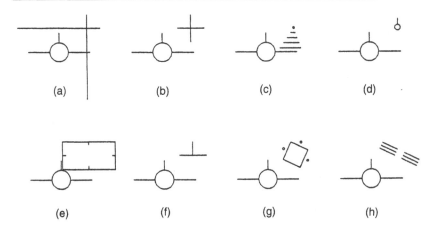

Figure 4.17   Guidance cues (all showing fly up and right): (a) cross-pointers; (b) cross; (c) perspective cue; (d) tadpole; (e) box; (f) invented tee; (g) rotating box; (h) wings

CDM/FPM or to some fixed point in the HUD FOV. The use of the CDM/FPM as the zero point has been the most common (resulting in a compensatory tracking task). The F-16 displays roll-stabilized ILS cross-pointers (*30*).

Some HUDs have used a reference point that appears to overlie the actual touchdown target – a point in the FOV corresponding to the azimuth to the runway and depressed by the glideslope depression angle. This results in the ILS tracking task being performed as a pursuit tracking task.

In addition, the cross-pointers/needles have been drawn in both roll-stabilized and non-roll-stabilized formats.

Non-roll-stabilized cross-pointers/needles have also been used to provide flight director steering cues. All known implementations of such steering cues have been referenced to the CDM/FPM. This has been proposed as an Air Force standard (*11*).

Depending on the format of the head-down ILS raw data and flight director, the use of cross-pointers in the HUD will mimic the panel or conflict with it. Using cross-pointers for raw data frequently results in complaints by pilots used to split-cue head-down flight directors.

A major advantage of the split-cue cross-pointers is the ability to convey glideslope failure to the pilot by removing the vertical deviation pointer or pitch steering bar.

Cross   Rather than use split needles/cross-pointers, some HUDs use a moving cross for flight director steering information. Similar to the cross-pointers, the cross is be referenced to the CDM/FPM or ARS (*23*).

The cross could also be used to provide raw deviation data. No known operational HUDs have used this symbol.

An advantage of the cross is the ability to convey glideslope failure to the pilot by replacing the cross with a vertical line.

Perspective cue A perspective cue has been used as both a raw data deviation cue (*27*) and as a flight director cue (*4*).

Circle/tadpole A small circle has been used in many HUDs as a steering cue (*10, 27, 30, 33*). The aircraft is flown so as to place the CDM/FPM circle around the smaller circle. Quite precise tracking performance can result. Frequently a vertical tail is added to the steering circle (tadpole).

This symbol has been the flight director with the best-documented performance. It has also been the most widely used flight director symbol. No conflict with head-down flight-director symbols (either split-cue or single-cue) has been reported.

This symbol has also been proposed for raw data(*1, 35*).

Box A deviation box has been used in a manner similar to the ILS cross to show raw deviation data (*32, 33*). The center of the box is the on-course location. The dimensions of the box present a cue for the maximum acceptable deviation. Often the box dimensions change and represent maximum windows for category I and II decision heights.

Rotating box A small box has been proposed for a flight-director cue. The size is scaled such that the CDM/FPM circle will just fit inside the box. This allows precise tracking performance.

The box rotates as well as translating laterally indicating the approximate bank angle being commanded. When the flight-director cue is satisfied, the box will be oriented parallel to the wings of the CDM/FPM and the circle will just fit inside the box.

Small dots which translate and rotate with the box are often added. These dots are to be superimposed over the wing-tips (and tail) of the CDM/FPM to further enhance the cue.

Inverted T An inverted T has been used. It is similar to the cross except that the bottom leg is omitted (*34*). It has only been proposed for flight-director data, not for raw data.

Wings This is a single-cue flight-director symbol in which the wings of the CDM/FPM are flown to match a set of stylized wings (*23*). When the two pairs of wings are superimposed, the flight-director cues have been satisfied.

Rotating HSI cue   For lateral tracking (VOR/TACAN/ILS), the use of a cue analogous to the horizontal situation indicator (HSI) rotating deviation cue has been used. The symbol is a direct analog of the lateral deviation cue which rotates to show the relative angle between the desired course and the aircraft heading. These needles can be referenced to the CDM/FPM or to some fixed point in the HUD FOV. If used for ILS tracking, normally a side-scale deviation indicator showing glideslope deviation is employed. An example is shown in Figure 4.18.

Such a cue has been most successful in presenting situational information during course intercepts. The HSI-style format has generally been used in locations away from the CDM/FPM, both above and below the center of the FOV.

When used near the center of the HUD FOV, the deviation dots can create unwanted clutter. Logic must be developed to removed the dots when the airplane is tracking the desired course within some predetermined tolerances.

When the CDM/FPM has been employed as the reference, frequent complaints about disorientation have followed. Locations away from the CDM/FPM seem to produce fewer such complaints. In addition, the rotating HSI reference may produce a false roll cue if the CDM/FPM is the reference. For this reason, if used, it should be relegated to a navigation field in the FOV.

Synthetic runway   This is a perspective cue of a runway outline which is drawn to overlie the real-world runway and is shown in Figure 4.19. The perspective cue allows the pilot to fly quite precise approaches using visual techniques. This is often called the **Klopfstein runway** (5).

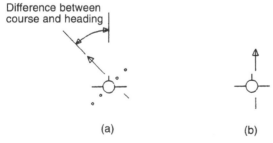

(a)   (b)

Figure 4.18   Rotating HSI deviation cue: (a) indication during course intercept; (b) indication during tracking (display logic removes dots)

115

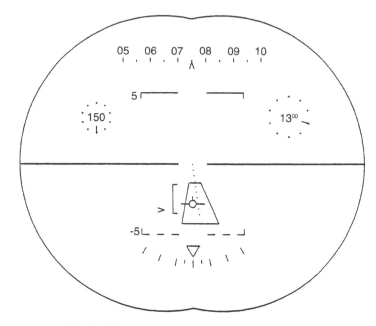

Figure 4.19   Synthetic runway cue

The lateral deviation is shown by the angle made by the runway centerline, with vertical representing on-course. The pilot can usually determine this accurately.

The vertical deviation is shown by the depression angle of the runway threshold. This usually requires reference tick marks at the glideslope approach angle to aid the pilot.

The Klopfstein synthetic runway has been reported to produce excellent tracking performance even without the use of a flight director and, at the same time, to permit a high degree of spatial orientation.

Course line   A course line similar to the centerline of the synthetic runway has been used as a lateral deviation cue for ILS approaches (*10*).

General comments

Generally, most of these symbology concepts work as far as tracking performance during an ILS approach. Virtually any HUD allows the pilot to track an ILS far tighter than with head-down instruments. In fact, tracking performance is generally such that it is difficult to conduct an experiment to distinguish between HUD symbologies without imposing external workload on the evaluation pilot. What is not clear is how well the pilot can maintain situational awareness (including checking for consistency of raw data) when using these symbologies.

It is necessary to ensure that the symbols chosen for flight-director and raw data complement each other. The operational airplanes in Table 4.3 indicate symbol combinations which have been tried. While the issue of the best ILS tracking symbology remains to be settled, the following combinations appear to work well together:

- Raw data: Deviation box
  Flight director: Circle/tadpole (*32*)
- Raw data: Cross-pointers/needles
  Flight director: Circle/tadpole (*30*)
- Raw data: Synthetic runway
  Flight director: Circle/tadpole (*16*)
- Raw data: Deviation box
  Flight director: Rotating box (*35*)
- Raw data: Synthetic runway
  Flight director: None (*5*)

Combinations of symbols with large numbers of horizontal or vertical lines tend to be confusing.

Bearing symbols

Two bearing symbols which have been tested are shown in Figure 4.20. The compass rose symbol (Figure 4.20a) allowed good overall situational awareness, but resulted in extremely high workload during ADF approaches. The compass rose was too small to allow accurate tracking. The digital bearing did help with using the ADF as a cross-bearing aid.

The quadrant symbol (Figure 4.20b) was created in an attempt to allow tracking. Tracking experiments indicated an improvement in tracking workload with minimal effect on overall situational awareness. Based on these tests, this symbol is recommended. The symbol shows one quadrant of a conventional RMI. The quadrant is centered on the bearing pointer.

The simplified symbol (Figure 4.20c) has been proposed for a military standard, but has not yet been tested (*11*). Based on data from compass rose testing, it is not recommended (*23*).

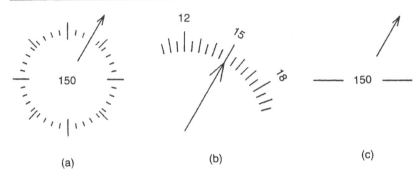

(a)   (b)   (c)

Figure 4.20   Bearing cues: (a) compass rose; (b) RMI quadrant; (c) simplified

Digital data

A data block reserved for information concerning weapon status (upper portion) and text navigational data (lower portion) is located in the lower-right FOV. Only imperative data should be shown. Some indication of Master Arm On should be displayed. Navigation parameters (time-to-go, waypoint status, latitude and longitude, time, etc.) should be easily selectable by the pilot. A stopwatch function should be available.

Text size slightly smaller than 6 mrad may be acceptable in the NAV section.

Advocates of left-brain/right-brain specialization suggest that orientation cues be placed in the left visual field and numeric data and text be placed in the right. The positioning of the global attitude ball in the lower-left corner follows this train of thought.

The HUD should not be used to display information unless it is critical to the mission and is required to be displayed in the pilot's forward FOV. One pilot suggested that a particular display item should be removed to make room for something more important – nothing.

Consideration should be given to displaying information in this data block on request, with a readily available declutter option.

Warnings and cautions

Master warning or caution

The basic requirement for a HUD master warning or caution symbol is that it cannot be missed if you are looking through or near the HUD. However, the warning symbol must not compromise the ability to

118

continue to fly the aircraft in reference to the basic HUD flight symbology.

A barber-pole (a set of oblique parallel lines) with an area of about 15° x 15° in the center of the field with loose spacing (approx 30 mrad) between lines, flashing at 3–4 Hz, has been used in the past to satisfy these requirements. The symbol density of these lines will generally not cause over-illumination effects at night.

Some HUDs use text warnings for critical failures written in a specific location. Examples include specific warning messages for failure of ILS guidance during approaches or loss of attitude data. Use of a dedicated warning window in the bottom of the FOV has been successful. Locations away from the HUD center of regard may not be successful.[15]

Pull-up cues (typically replacing the HUD data with a large 'X') have been effective in obtaining the pilot's attention. However, replacing the HUD data effectively prevents the pilot from using the HUD data to continue to fly the airplane. This would not be acceptable for a primary flight display.

HUD data integrity

The integrity of the data presented on the HUD must be assured. Normally, simply removing the data is thought to be sufficient, although some argue that specific warnings (such as X-ing out the bad data) are required.

Critical data (loss of attitude data or loss of guidance during low instrument approaches) will require specific warnings if tests show that the pilot will not react rapidly to simply removing the data. In particular, loss of a glideslope signal or flare guidance must be clearly annunciated.

A promising cue to warn of attitude gyro failure has been to remove the pitch ladder and horizon line and replace them with a double-written ghost horizon line at the last valid horizon position (*23*).

All evaluations of potential HUD symbologies should conduct tests to determine the ability of the pilot to detect discrepancies and to switch to another source (such as the head-down panel).

Weapon displays

This section will discuss several weapon-aiming symbols. These should be considered basic formats. For obvious reasons, discussion of weapon symbology must be limited.

---

[15]Generally, the text warnings near the periphery of the FOV have not incorporated flashing to attract the pilot's attention (*36*).

Air-to-air

Gun aiming Air-to-air targeting was the origin of the head-up display. The simplest lead-compensating optical sight (LCOS) shows an aiming reticle to show the bullet path at some range ahead of the airplane. The reticle moves as the airplane maneuvers because of changes in airspeed, loads, etc. If the range is available from radar or other means, the range can be found directly.

The earliest gunsights used stadiametric ranging. The aiming reticle incorporates a circular ring. If the pilot knows the wingspan of the adversary, he can adjust the size of the ring with a controller until the wingspan just fills the aiming ring. This size determines the range and the aiming reticle is positioned accordingly.[16]

Modern gunsights show a continuously computed impact line (CCIL). This shows the bullet flight path as a wavy line emanating from a fixed point on the HUD, usually called the gun cross. This represents the boresight of the weapon. Cross ticks are shown for several time-of-flight (TOF) points (0.5, 1.0, 1.5s, etc.). The aiming reticle moves along this line and is driven by the range to the target. Figure 4.21 shows a CCIL format.

Target range is usually shown by a circumferential scale on the aiming reticle. A typical format has two reference ticks, at 9 o'clock (maximum usable range) and 3 o'clock (minimum range). A movable tick shows the actual range.

Missile aiming Since most air-to-air missiles will track an adversary, a CCIL or LCOS symbology is inappropriate. Most missile aiming symbologies show a pattern showing the missile sensor field of regard (FOR). The pilot must maneuver the airplane so that the missile FOR overlays the target position. Once the missile acquires the target, the symbol changes to show that the missile sensor is tracking the target. This may include a range indication to assist the pilot in firing at the maximum in the P_K (probability of kill) curve.

Normally, different-shaped FOR and tracking symbols are used for different missiles to emphasize to the pilot which missile system is being used.

Air to ground

A typical air-to-ground (A/G) symbology displays a continuously computed impact point (CCIP) marker. The CCIP marker is a moving

---

[16]The earliest use of these sights computed the bullet trajectory at a single, predetermined range. The pilot set the ring to match the adversary's wingspan at this range. He then closed until the wingspan filled the sight.

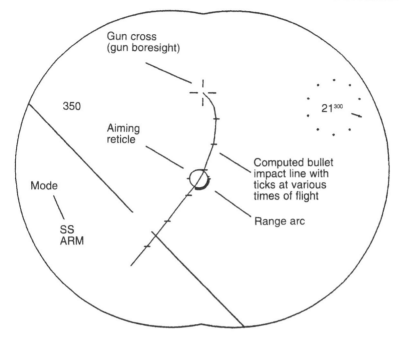

Figure 4.21 Typical CCIL format (20)

symbol showing the ground impact location if the munition were to be released at that instant. The CCIP marker and the aircraft velocity vector/flight path marker are connected by a bomb fall line (BFL) which represents the locus of points the munition will strike on a horizontal plane at the target altitude. The BFL is perpendicular to the horizon line. Normally a free flight path marker is used during A/G operations rather than the CDM with a separate velocity vector.[17] A typical CCIP format is shown in Figure 4.22a.

If target coordinates are available to the mission/weapon computer, the target location can be displayed on the HUD. The target can be designated visually by placing a cursor shown in the HUD FOV over the target and pressing a designate button. The HUD LOS to the target will allow the mission computer to determine the target coordinates and position a target symbol on the HUD. Boxes, diamonds, etc. have been used for this purpose.

Alternative designations methods, such as reflecting laser beams from the target, can be used as well.

[17]The RAF Fast-Jet symbology (9) is an exception, retaining the CDM and drawing the BFL from the VV diamond.

121

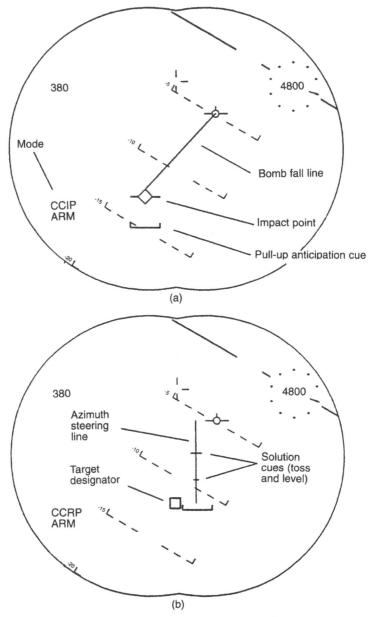

Figure 4.22 **Typical air-to-ground formats (*20*): (a) CCIP symbology;
(b) CCRP symbology**

122

Once the target has been designated, a steering cue, the azimuth steering line (ASL) can be drawn – a vertical line with an azimuth location midway between the target symbol and the FPM. This gives the pilot a direction to maneuver to align the munition trajectory with the target. Target designation is required before an ASL can be drawn.

Solution cues appear on the ASL to indicate the point for release. These are horizontal bars on the ASL. The spacing from the FPM is proportional to the time to release. Solution cues for both dive-bombing and toss-bombing are possible. The solution cues move up the ASL. When they reach the FPM, the bomb should strike the target provided the ASL steering has been satisfied. Figure 4.22b shows a typical ASL symbology.

Other

Weapon status Somewhere in the HUD field of view, some indication of system status, weapon selected, and an armed/safe annunciation is required. This is normally provided by data in one of the digital data blocks. If different symbols are used for different weapons (e.g. radar missiles use one format, IR seekers use another), text requirements will be minimized.

Target symbols The choice of target symbols varies from system to system. The RAF Fast-Jet (*9*) was criticized by US pilots because the diamond velocity vector symbol was identical to some US target symbols.

Standby reticle Early HUDs had a standby reticle available in the HUD FOV. The standby reticle was a fixed aiming symbol with manually adjustable depression. It had a separate power supply. It is not clear if these were incorporated because of a real or a perceived lack of reliability. In any event, standby reticules are probably no longer necessary.

Breakaway It is essential to warn the pilot during air-to-ground or low-level flight if ground impact is imminent. This is usually accomplished by deleting all aiming or steering data and writing a large 'X' in the center of the FOV. This tells the pilot that he must pull up with at least some specified (usually 4*g*) load factor.

References

(1) Hughes, R. E. *The HUD Coloring Book: Recommendations Concerning Head-Up Displays* (Washington,: Naval Air Systems Command, 1991)

(2) Eksuzian, D. J. *et al. TRISTAR I: Tri-Service Symbology Test and Research* (Moffett Field,

California: Tri-Service Flight Symbology Working Group, in final stages of publication), FSWG TR-91-01

(3)   Dryden, J. B., 'Flying through the glass', *Code One*, April 1992, 12–15

(4)   Naish, J. M. *Review of Some Head-Up Display Formats* (Moffett Field, California: National Aeronautics and Space Administration, 1979), NASA TP-1499

(5)   Klopfstein, G. *Rational Study of Aircraft Piloting* (Paris: Thomson-CSF, ca. 1966); reprint of 1966 article in Intrados

(6)   Foxworth, T. G. *A New Concept of Flying: Flying the TC-121 All-Weather Head-Up Display* (Egham, England: International Federation of Air Line Pilots Associations, 1973)

(7)   McCloskey, St J. *Flying the TC-121: A Visit to Bretigny to Fly the Thomson-CSF Head-Up Display* (Egham, England: International Federation of Air Line Pilots Associations, 1973), Report 74C95

(8)   Ertzgaard, J. H. *IFALPA Flight Test Report: Thomson-CSF TC-121* (Egham, England: International Federation of Air Line Pilots Associations, 1976), L76C228

(9)   Hall, J. R., Stephens, C. M., and Penwill, J. C. *A Review of the Design and Development of the RAE Fast-Jet Head-Up Display Format* (Bedford, England: Royal Aeronautical Establishment, 1989), RAE FM-WP(89)034

(10)   *FDI Model 1000 Head-Up Display System Specification* (Portland, Oregon: Flight Dynamics, February 1989), Report 404-0249

(11)   Bitton, D. F. and Evans, R. H. *Report on Head-Up Display Symbology Standardization* (Randolph AFB, Texas: Air Force Instrument Flight Center, 1990), AFIFC TR-91-01

(12)   Newman, R. L. *Improvement of Head-Up Display Standards. II. Evaluation of Head-Up Displays to Enhance Unusual Attitude Recovery* (Wright-Patterson AFB, Ohio: Air Force Wright Aeronautical Laboratory, 1987), AFWAL TR-87-3055, Vol. II

(13)   Naish, J. M. 'Control gains in head-up presentation', in *Proceedings of 6th Annual Conference on Manual Control, Wright-Patterson AFB* (Wright-Patterson AFB, Ohio: Air Force Flight Dynamics Laboratory, 1970), pp. 19–46

(14)   Penwill, J. C. and Hall, J. R. *A Comparative Evaluation of Two HUD Formats by All Four Nations to Determine the Preferred Pitch Ladder Design for EFA* (Bedford, England: Royal Aeronautical Establishment, 1990), RAE FM-WP(90)021

(15)   Weinstein, L. F. and Ercoline, W. R. 'HUD climb/dive ladder configuration and unusual attitude recovery', in *Proceedings 35th Annual Meeting of the Human Factors Society, San Francisco* (Santa Monica, California: Human Factors Society, 1991), pp. 12–17

(16)   Steenblik, J. W. 'The diamond, the shark, and the inverted Christmas tree', *Air Line Pilot*, December 1991, 28–31

(17)   Taylor, R. M. 'Some effects of display format variables on the perception of aircraft spatial orientation', in *Proceedings AGARD Symposium on Human Factors Considerations in High Performance Aircraft, Williamsburg* (Paris: Advisory Group for Aeronautical Research and Development, 1984), AGARD CP-371

(18)   Norton, P. A. *et al.* 'Findings and recommendations of the Cockpit Design Subcommittee', in *Proceedings of the 1981 Test Pilot's Aviation Safety Workshop, Monterey*, C. A. Tuomela (ed.) (New York: American Institute of Aeronautics and Astronautics and Lancaster, California: Society of Experimental Test Pilots, 1981), pp. 19–47

(19)   Ercoline, W. R. and Gillingham, K. K., 'Effects of variations in head-up display airspeed and altitude representations on basic flight performance', in *Proceedings of the 34th Annual Meeting of the Human Factors Society, (Santa Monica, California: Human Factors Society 1990)*, pp. 1547–1551

(20)   *MB-339C Aircraft Pilot's Guide* (Varese, Italy, Aermacchi, ca. 1993), PIPG01-9CB

(21)   Kinsley S. A., Warner, N. W. and Gleisner, D. P. *A Comparison of Two Pitch Ladder Formats and an ADI Ball for Recovery from Unusual Attitudes* (Warminster, Pennsylvania: Naval Air Development Center, 1986), NADC 86012-60

(22)   Marthinsen, H. F. 'The killer instrument – the drum pointer altimeter', *IFALPA Quarterly Review*, December 1990, 14–21

(23)   Newman, R. L. *Symbology for the FV-2000/KA Head-Up Display*, (San Marcos, Texas: Crew Systems, 1991), TR-91-11

(24)   Deaton, J. E. *et al.* 'Evaluation of the Augie arrow HUD symbology as an aid to recovery from unusual attitudes', in *Proceedings of the 34th Annual Meeting of the Human Factors Society* (Santa Monica, California: Human Factors Society, 1990), pp. 31–35

(25)   Bailey, R. E. and Knotts, L. *Flight and Ground Simulation of the Proposed USAF Head-Up Display Standard* (New York: American Institute of Aeronautics and Astronautics, 1993), AIAA Paper 93-3605

(26)   Turner, A. D. and Hattendorf, P. E. *Standardized Head-Up Dis-play Symbology Evaluation* (Edwards AFB, California: Air Force Flight Test Center, 1993), AFFTC TR-92-15

(27)   *A-7D Flight Manual* (Washington: US Air Force, ca. 1984), TO-1A-7D-1

(28)   *F-14A Flight Manual* (Washington: Naval Air Systems Command, ca. 1984), NAVAIR-01-F14AAA-1

(29)   *F-15A Flight Manual* (Washington: US Air Force, ca. 1984), TO-1A-15A-1

(30)   *F-16A Flight Manual* (Washington: US Air Force, ca. 1984), TO-1A-16A-1

(31)   *F-18 Flight Manual* (Washington: Naval Air Systems Command, ca. 1984), NAVAIR-A1-F18AC-NFM-000

(32)   *Head-Up Display for the DC-9 Super 80* (Long Beach, California: McDonnell-Douglas Aircraft, 1979)

(33)   Suisse, H. *Head-Up Display System: PERSEPOLIS Symbology* (Vaucresson, France: Avions Marcel Dassault-Breguet Aviation, 1979), DGT-16433

(34)   *Military Specification, Display, Head-Up, General Specification for* (Philadelphia, Pennsylvania, Naval Publications and Forms Center, 1972), MIL-D-81641(AS)

(35)   Huff, R. W. and Kessler, G. K. 'Enhanced displays, flight controls, and guidance systems for approach and landing', in *Aircraft Ship Operations* (Paris: Advisory Group for Aeronautical Research and Development, 1991), AGARD CP-509, pp. 8.1–8.22

(36)   Cox, W. J. *Evaluation of Situation Versus Command Guidance Symbology in Hybrid Landing System Applications* (Washington: Federal Aviation Administration, in preparation)

125

5 Primary flight reference criteria

Primary flight references (PFRs) are displays which provide sufficient information for the pilot to fly the airplane during a particular mission segment.[1] 'Sufficient information' means that contained in the traditional head-down 'basic T,' such as airspeed, altitude, and attitude. Appropriate substitutions can be made, depending on the phase of flight: α for airspeed, radar altitude for barometric altitude, etc.

PFRs provide data for the pilot to control the airplane – climb or descend, turn left or right. Navigation or systems data is not normally included unless critical to the mission segment. An example of critical to the mission segment is the need for guidance cues during an instrument approach.

Normally, a HUD should be treated as a PFR since the pilot will likely use it as such as if it were the primary flight reference regardless of disclaimers in the flight manual.

Data requirements

The development of any display must start with the basic principle of analyzing the mission requirements. The information required by the

[1]Instrument meterological conditions (IMC) are assumed.

pilot and crew must be cataloged. Only then can the display symbology be designed. Head-down instruments did not change greatly for many years. As a result, designers forgot this basic principle and concentrated on matching the format of the 'basic T.'

Ketchel and Jenney (*1*) reviewed the informational requirements of electronic displays in 1968. They outlined the general need for an informational requirements study and reviewed 16 such studies. They charted the information requirements for each study and summarized them for selected phases of flight (takeoff, *en route*, and landing). In their review, the needs of the pilot were assumed to be proportional to the number of times each data item was mentioned – a vote basis. They do mention that such a summation is no substitute for a detailed analysis, but only as an approximation of the needs.

As an example, Ketchel and Jenney mention a pull-up warning to avoid terrain. This was only listed twice (out of 16 reports), but is obviously an important information item. This points out a major limitation of pilot surveys or summaries in determining informational requirements and the need for careful consideration of all relevant issues.[2]

Singleton (*2*) described a generic approach to display design. He recommends: (1) justifying the display need; (*2*) determining what data is required; (*3*) ensuring that an average pilot can use the display; and (*4*) ensuring compatibility of the display with the environment and pilot.

The need for course deviation, navigation, or systems data during a specific mission segment is a matter requiring some attention. Many engineers and pilots will add data after data to the list if there is a slight need. This approach should not be taken. Data should only be displayed on a HUD if there is a clear and unambiguous need.

The designer must determine if a specific parameter (e.g. course deviation) is to be required. The choice depends on how critical constant reference to a specific data parameter is and whether or not the pilot can refer to inside instruments safely. Table 5.1 lists typical data requirements for a PFR in terms of traditional data likely to be on a HUD. The table shows these requirements for various mission segments.

This data may be replaced by other data which will allow the pilot to accomplish the mission segment. For example, α might be an acceptable substitute for airspeed on final approach, but not during an

---

[2]Ketchel and Jenney mentioned sideslip information and concluded that it was of limited importance to fixed-wing aircraft. This may reflect a large proportion of fighter aircraft in their survey sample. It may also reflect no thought for engine-out control

Table 5.1 Primary flight reference HUD data requirements

Parameter	To roll	Clmb	Crse	Desc	ILS appr	N/P appr	TOGA	A/A	A/G
				Mission segment[a]					
Pitch ladder	–	X	X	X	X	X	X	–	X
Waterline	?	X	–	–	–	–	X	X[b]	–
CDM/FPM	–	X	X	X	X	X	X	X	X
Altitude	U	X	X	X	X	X	X	X	X
Vertical speed	–	X	X	X	X	X	X	–	–
Radar altitude	–	–	–	U	U	U	U	–	X
Baro setting	–	–	–	–	U	U	U	–	–
Vert deviation	–	–	U	–	–	–	–	–	–
Selected alt	U	U	U	U	U	U	U	–	–
Airspeed	X	X	X	X	X	X	X	X	X
TAS digits	–	–	?	–	–	–	–	–	?
GS digits	U	–	U	–	U	U	U	–	U
Mach digits	–	–	X[c]	X[c]	–	–	–	X	–
Selected a/s	U	U	–	U	U	U	U	–	U
Speed/AOA error	–	U	–	–	U	U	U	–	U
Heading	X	X	X	X	X	X	X	–	–
Selected course	U	N	N	N	U	U	N	–	–
Selected headg	U	U	U	U	U	U	U	–	–
Ground track	–	–	–	–	U	U	–	–	–
Bank scale	–	–	–	U	U	U	U	–	?
Sideslip	–	X[d]	U	–	–	–	X[d]	?	X
Energy	U	U	U	U	U	U	U	U	U
Flight director	N	N	N	N	U	U	N	–	–
Lateral deviation	N	N	N	N	X	X	N	–	–
Glideslope	–	–	–	–	X	–	–	–	–
Stopwatch digits	U	–	–	–	U	U	–	–	–
Time of day	–	N	N	N	–	–	–	–	–
ETA	–	N	N	N	–	–	–	–	–
Distance (DME)	–	N	N	N	N	N	N	–	–
Navaid tuned	N	N	N	N	X	X	N	–	–
Wlnd information	?	–	–	–	U	U	U	–	?

Notes: [a] Code: X = required; U = useful information; N = depends on navigation requirements.
[b] Weapon boresight (gun cross).
[c] If required for operational limits.
[d] Required for multi-engine aircraft.

air-to-ground weapon delivery. The HUD designer must develop a table similar to Table 5.1 based on an analysis of the particular HUD, aircraft, and mission.

Declutter of non-required data (any data not marked with an X) should be permitted. Declutter of required data (marked with an X) could be allowed provided the pilot can regain the decluttered data without removing his hands from the aircraft controls (the hands on throttle and stick, HOTAS, concept). This will permit declutter of data during VMC traffic patterns to improve visibility of traffic, etc.

Correspondence with head-down displays

If the HUD is to be a primary flight reference, it must be possible to view substantially the same data on the head-down panel. This is required for several reasons: as a backup to the HUD symbol generator, to allow the pilot to view the display without the view of the external real-world cues, and to allow the pilot to have a close focus when cross-checking instrument panel data. The inability to use the HUD when flying directly into the sun absolutely requires that PFR data be available head-down.

'Substantially the same data' means the head-down data must be compatible with the HUD – differing scale compressions and declutter options may be used. It is not necessary that the presentations be identical. In particular, the use of vertical tapes on the head-down display does not preclude the use of counter-pointers on the HUD. Strict commonality between head-up and head-down displays should not be required.

Some designers have felt that if the HUD is oriented relative to the FPM or CDM, the head-down PFR should be also. This is a case of 'it seemed like a good idea at the time'. Switching from a flight path based HUD to an attitude-based HDD has not been reported to be a significant problem in terms of attitude awareness in previously fielded HUD equipped airplanes. If a head-down flight path display is used, care must be taken to ensure that the display doesn't present a misleading presentation when compared with both the HUD and a standby attitude indicator.

Many HUDs have not complied with the strict interpretation of the basic T, which requires the heading below the attitude. For civil HUDs, this deviation from the standard (*3*) requires justification on the basis of equivalent level of safety (*4*). There is sufficient experience with HUDs having heading at the top of the FOV to satisfy deviation from the basic T. The HUD designer should be aware of the equivalent safety rule and not be afraid to deviate from the basic T arrangement.

If the heading is located at the bottom of the FOV, other changes will be required. In particular, the bank scale must be relocated to avoid interference.

Additional data, not present on the HUD, may be present on the head-down display if there is no interference with the use of the display to fly the airplane. The head-down display might be a color display while the HUD is monochromatic. The two displays, HUD and head-down, should use the same mode switch and data sources to ensure that they are operating coherently.

It is desirable that the head-down display be visible in the primary visual signal area (PVSA) at all times. If panel space is limited, this requirement can be relaxed if the primary flight display can be recalled to the panel with one button push (following the HOTAS or HOTAY[3] principle). This would allow, for example, the replacement of the head-down primary flight display by an expanded map or radar display.

HUD symbology

Unusual attitude recovery

A primary concern for PFRs, not just for HUDs, is the need to prevent occurrence of and to aid in the recovery from unusual attitudes (UAs). To this end, HUDs must be designed and tested with UA recovery and spatial disorientation in mind in all modes, even ILS approaches.

Aircraft pitch attitude, not velocity vector, is of primary importance during UA recovery. At large angle of attack, the velocity vector may not be responsive to control inputs. In particular, a large α indicated by a large negative flight path angle (FPA) and a nose-high Θ must not cause the pilot to attempt recovery by raising the velocity vector by pulling on the control column.

With present HUD formats and existing pilot backgrounds, two symbology features are essential: (1) the pitch ladder must clearly indicate aircraft pitch during extreme pitch excursions, and (2) the velocity vector information (CDM/FPM) must not mislead the pilot by indicating a pull during high angle of attack conditions.

The HUD must clearly distinguish nose-high angles from nose-low. This can be accomplished with different-style pitch ladder lines above and below the horizon. Additional distinctions include dashed lines below the horizon. The dashing of the lines should be at three to five dashes per 'rung'. Positive angles should use solid horizontal lines with tick marks at the outside edge.

The pitch reference for a HUD intended for a PFR should use a complete pitch ladder, not just a horizon line or a horizon line and a pitch mark. While the use of a horizon line alone has been suggested

---

[3]HOTAY means 'hands on throttle and yoke,' the transport equivalent of HOTAS.

in the past for transports, the possibility of an UA in a transport must not be ignored. A horizon line only (or a horizon line plus a pitch mark) would be acceptable only if a clear improvement in performance can be shown and if reversion to a conventional pitch ladder is automatic during UAs before the horizon leaves the IFOV.

Global attitude cues, such as a small attitude ball or 'orange peel' in the HUD IFOV may allow for a horizon-line-only symbology. These have not been evaluated.

Some designers who insist on having both head-up and head-down indicators use the same location for the bankscale. Using different bank scales was studied during simulator experiments (5) and not found to be a problem.

De-emphasizing the velocity vector at large α's has been accomplished by deleting the CDM/FPM when α becomes excessive. Simulator (5) and flight experiments (6) indicate that deletion of the velocity vector symbol at high α is satisfactory.

Other data

Other data shown on the HUD will depend on the specific requirements of the mission segment. The aircraft master warning and master caution annunciation should be repeated on the HUD unless they are visible near the HUD. Many recent proposals for HUDs intended for PFRs have included a great deal of digital data: altimeter setting, radio navaids tuned, etc. This information is needed, but care should be taken in displaying it on the HUD. In the unlikely event that this data cannot be displayed head-down, display on the HUD may be required. The pilot should have the ability to declutter such status data.

The annunciation of status information should vary from task to task. During instrument approaches, the display of navigation information (such as the facility identification) on the HUD may be warranted.

Use by the non-flying pilot

As HUDs become more common in transport airplanes, a major consideration is the ability of the non-flying pilot (PNF) to monitor the information being displayed to the pilot flying the airplane (PF). It is not possible for one pilot to view the HUD being used by the other pilot. Therefore, some consideration must be devoted to ensuring that the PNF can readily determine the sources of data, HUD modes, and selected references (such as selected course) being used by the PF.

Transport HUDs to date have only considered the single flight task of the low-visibility approach. These normally begin with pre-approach briefings and use identical data for both the PF and PNF. While ILS approach monitoring has been carefully thought out for Category II and III approaches, the problem has not been addressed for other flight phases.

During routine terminal area maneuvering, the wrong choice of selected course can lead the crew to excessive errors. It is not enough to say that the PNF should detect deviations as they occur. He should be able to detect incorrect settings before deviations occur.

This may require additional head-down data in the cockpit, such as digital indicators showing selected course, and heading bugs in use on the other pilot's HUD.

HUD mode switching

A problem area in recent HUD flight testing is the location of many of the HUD and navigation controls. Many HUDs have not been well integrated into the cockpit, requiring multiple data entries, often with diverse locations for the selections – the glareshield, the center console, and the overhead panel. This is exacerbated with HUDs by the need to maintain a head position within the eyebox. The added workload may not be evident during low workload operations, such as during simulator evaluations or during flight testing in low-traffic areas. The problem may only be apparent well into flight testing.

There are two schools of thought on HUD modes. One recommends a large number of modes with no options within a given mode. The second favors limited numbers of modes with a number of declutter options within each mode. This is discussed later (see 'Clutter' in Chapter 7).

Automatic HUD mode switching is not desirable for a display intended as a primary flight reference. An exception is the reversion to a basic instrument mode when an unusual attitude is detected.

Unusual attitude mode

The HUD designer should establish bank and pitch limits beyond which it is assumed that there is an unusual attitude. If the primary flight display is not shown head-down, it must be returned to the pilot's view.

Any HUD intended as a PFR should incorporate a basic instrument mode which can always be selected by the pilot regardless of the other

132

modes being used. This might be accomplished automatically when pitch and bank limits are exceeded. When these limits are exceeded, the HUD should delete all information beyond a minimum set necessary to recover from an unusual attitude. In particular, some navigation data can rotate to show false roll cues. These should be deleted during the 'unusual attitude' mode.

The limits for 'unusual attitude' switching depend on the aircraft type and mission. The limits for a fighter would obviously be different from a passenger carrying transport. For example, a corporate turboprop airplane might recall the head-down primary flight display when the bank exceeds 35° and delete the non-essential HUD information when the bank exceeds 45°, the nose is more than 15° nose low, or when the airspeed exceeds V_{MO}. There should be some hysteresis incorporated to prevent the displays from flickering if the airplane is flown at these limits.

The pilot should be able to select the head-down PFR without removing his hands from the flight controls. This could be accomplished by a dedicated switch on the stick or throttle. This is necessary because the pilot might not wish to look at the HUD because of the background (such as when the sun is in view through the HUD FOV).

Other automatic modes

The HUD could employ automatic switching based on weight-on-wheels to switch from takeoff roll symbology to takeoff/go-around (TOGA) symbology. The touchdown following an approach could also trigger an automatic switch to a rollout mode.

Reliability

The reliability of a HUD primary flight display, in general, should match or exceed that of the head-down instruments it is replacing.

When incoming data or processing that affects primary symbology is identified as invalid, the affected symbology should automatically be deleted or should revert to a backup mode.[4] The processor should check the incoming data needed to generate the primary symbology for reasonableness with respect to physical aircraft parameters. It should also cross-check related data for predetermined differences if more than one source of data is available.

[4]Such as reversion to air-mass data when inertial calculations are no longer valid.

133

The pilot must be able to rapidly and reliably detect the deletion of data or the reversion to backup modes. If the change is too subtle, specific annunciations must be provided. The ability of the pilot to detect changes and revert to alternative displays or alternative procedures must be evaluated during HUD acceptance.

Redundancy

At a minimum, there should be two symbol generators available to provide symbology to the HUD (one of which can drive the symbology for the head-down display discussed previously).

Standby attitude indicator

The standby attitude indicator must be clearly visible at all times without pilot selection. A general rule is that the standby indicator must be more reliable than the primary indicator. Given sufficient reliability, there is no reason why the standby indicator cannot be an electronic display.

The use of a touch-sensitive LCD screen for the HUD up-front control panel has been proposed (7) for a standby attitude indicator. This display would display attitude information except when touched. At this time, it would display a menu allowing for pilot input to the HUD.

Inertial vs air-mass data

Historically, the choice of whether to use inertial or air-mass velocity vector data has depended on whether or not an inertial navigation system (INS) was installed in the airplane. This is not a valid reason for this decision. The needs of the pilot may dictate a need for air-mass data.

There are valid reasons to choose either air-mass or inertial velocity vector data. The use of air-mass data allows direct integration of aerodynamic information. Where this information is critical (such as high α or engine-out situations), the use of air-mass data may be preferred. Air-mass data is also recommended for air-to-air combat.

Summary

The main point of this chapter is the need to perform a careful, methodical information and task analysis and not simply rely on pilot opinion.

The designer must also recognize that design is a series of tradeoffs and that display design is no exception. In addition to the tradeoff between information and clutter, the location of the display icons is also a tradeoff. For example, placing a scale in a different location (such as heading at the bottom) requires relocating several other display elements. These may be obvious (bank scale) or subtle (navigation data, sideslip, or warning messages).

References

(1) Ketchel, J. M. and Jenney, L. L. *Electronic and Optically Generated Aircraft Displays: A Study of Standardization Requirements* (Washington, Office of Naval Research, 1968), JANAIR 680505

(2) Singleton, W. T. 'Display design: principles and procedures', *Ergonomics*, **12**, 1969, 519–531

(3) 'Instruments: arrangement and visibility', *Airworthiness Standards: Transport Category Airplanes* (Washington, DC: Federal Aviation Administration, no date), Federal Aviation Regulations paragraph 25.1321(b); see similar paragraphs for other categories of aircraft: 23.1321(d) for light airplanes and 29.1321(b) for transport rotorcraft

(4) 'Issue of type certificate: normal, utility, acrobatic, commuter, and transport category aircraft; manned free balloons, special classes of aircraft; aircraft engines; propellers', *Certification Procedures for Products and Parts* (Washington, DC: Federal Aviation Administration, no date), Federal Aviation Regulations paragraph 21.21(b)(1)

(5) Newman, R. L. *Improvement of Head-Up Display Standards. II. Evaluation of Head-Up Displays to Enhance Unusual Attitude Recovery* (Wright-Patterson AFB, Ohio: Air Force Wright Aeronautical Laboratory, 1987), AFWAL TR-87-3055. Vol. II

(6) Bailey, R. and Knotts, L. *Flight and Ground Simulation Evaluation of the Proposed USAF Head-Up Display Standard* (New York: American Institute of Aeronautics and Astronautics, 1993), AIAA Paper 93-3605

(7) 'Liquid crystal up-front control panel,' (Rochester, England: GEC Avionics, 1991), GEC Avionics presentation to Air Force Wright Laboratory

135

6 Equipment considerations

Field of view

The HUD should be designed and installed to meet the operational requirements for the specific application. In particular, the system should be designed to permit the pilot to look in normally expected directions with minimal loss of symbology because of the knothole effect. The FOV should be centered on the centerline of the pilot.

The pilot should not have to move his head to view the primary symbology. In other words, the IFOV should include the major flight-data symbols in the HUD under normal viewing conditions. Head motion has a tendency to cause or exacerbate spatial disorientation or vertigo and the HUD should be designed to minimize this. Further, it is desirable that primary flight data be contained within the intersecting binocular FOV.

Secondary symbology, such as radio frequencies or altimeter setting data, if required, can be shown outside the IFOV.

If the displayed flight information includes conformal ground reference symbols, such as a runway or target symbol, the lateral FOV should be sufficient to permit conformal viewing of the symbols during all anticipated crosswinds. Runway symbols should be conformal during crosswind approaches at the maximum approved landing crosswind. A lack of adequate lateral FOV has been identified as a major limitation during crosswind landings (1).

136

Vertical FOV requirements are more important in fighter aircraft where the weapon cues may have a large vertical motion, particularly in airplanes that are used in both the A/A and A/G modes. Generally, A/A weapon symbols are high in the FOV and A/G symbols low.

The FOV should be specified for each installation. Suggested minimum values of combined binocular IFOV are shown below:

Tactical aircraft: 20° vertical
                      20° lateral
Transport aircraft: 12° vertical
                      25° lateral

Some have suggested mandating that the IFOV should be equal to the TFOV. The rationale has been that symbology can be 'lost' when it leaves the IFOV. Such a requirement would eliminate refractive HUDs for all practical purposes. Since the previous discussion restricts the primary flight symbology to the IFOV, there is no need to insist that the IFOV and TFOV be equal.

In the past, minimum TFOVs have been specified. Again, restricting the primary flight symbology to the IFOV makes a TFOV requirement redundant. Nevertheless, a minimum TFOV is specified for transport and fighter aircraft to allow for pilot head motion, particularly when IFOV is restricted by cockpit geometry.

Suggested minimum total field-of-view values are

Tactical aircraft: 25° total
Transport aircraft: 25° total

The use of non-conformal HUDs with compressed pitch scaling may allow relaxation of these FOV limits.

No minimum FOV is recommended for trainer or business aircraft. FOV requirements for these aircraft should be evaluated on a case-by-case basis.

Some sensors have limited FOV when compared with the HUD FOV. The effect of flying a raster HUD with a small 'inset' image has not been determined.

Optical quality

Brightness

The brightness control should provide a suitable contrast between symbols and external visual cues over the range of ambient lighting conditions expected in service. In the past, problems have been encountered during night operations where the HUD intensity could not be set low enough to provide a comfortable display against a dark background. At the same time, HUDs intended to be used to track aerial targets (such as A/A weapons targeting) should ensure that the symbols can be easily seen against bright clouds.

Unless specially enhanced, all symbols should be equally bright. This does not preclude allowing different symbols' brightness to be controlled independently. Aircraft master warning or other critical warning messages should appear fully bright when they are first shown in the HUD FOV, if practical, regardless of the brightness setting. Canceling warning or alert messages in the HUD FOV should require some pilot action.

When set for manual operation, the HUD brightness should be adjustable from zero to full intensity. In automatic, the HUD brightness should track the ambient light level to maintain a constant (pilot selectable) contrast ratio. Automatic HUD brightness, if available, should track the background brightness with sufficient speed to avoid large variations in contrast ratio. The pilot should have the capability to select manual brightness (i.e. a manual brightness control is required; an automatic brightness control is optional).

Daytime brightness   A recommended daytime background brightness is 10000 FL (sunlit snow).

Night-time brightness   The minimum controllable brightness should provide smooth control of HUD intensity at very low ambient light levels (less than 15 FL). Some HUDs have used a two position manual brightness control with both a day and a night range of settings. This was identified as a problem area in early CRT HUDs (*1*).

Brightness variations   The brightness of a uniform display should not vary significantly over the FOV.

Raster brightness   The brightness of a raster image may adversely affect the ability of the pilot to look through the HUD. The effect has not been determined.

It is currently difficult to achieve very bright stroke images because the stroke symbols must be written during the 'fly-back' portion of the display frame. This may create difficulties in viewing stroke symbols when operating in a stroke/raster mode.

Visual disparity

Binocular disparity has been shown to be a limiting factor in the pilot's adaptation to a HUD (*2–4*). Any disparity should be minimized. If a choice must be made for slight horizontal disparity, a slight convergent disparity (i.e. the symbols appear closer than optical infinity) is preferred over a divergent disparity. The binocular disparity of the displayed symbols should be specified over the TFOV. Normally the binocular disparity is measured over a number of viewing angles from several locations within the eyebox. The convention is that 95% (2 sigma) of the measured values should be less than the specification.

The original *Design Guide* (*5*) recommended no tolerance for divergent disparity (0.0 mrad) and a larger one for convergent (2.5 mrad). This was primarily based on Gold's work (*2–4*), which used visual discomfort as the criterion. Recent accommodation arguments (see 'Accommodation traps' in Chapter 2) suggest that pilots may accommodate at distances fairly close to the combiner glass (*6–8*). Having convergent disparity may exacerbate this effect. We do not agree with this argument; nevertheless, there is no need to have a design guide which may make the problem worse. For this reason, the present recommendation for convergent disparity is set at 1.0 mrad. This value is also within the current state of the art.

The divergent limit has relaxed to 1.0 mrad. A slight divergence, i.e. the HUD imagery should appear to be beyond optical infinity, may reduce the tendency to near accommodation. In any event, 1 mrad is well within the comfort range found by Gold and Potter (*2*).

Recommended maximum values for visual disparity within the central portion of the FOV are:

Horizontal:	divergence:	1.0 mrad
	convergence:	1.0 mrad
Vertical:	dipvergence:	0.5 mrad

If the real-world cues appear to be closer than optical infinity, because of windshield distortion or because the HUD is intended to be used while viewing nearby cues (such as during refueling operations), the convergence and divergence limits may be adjusted so the virtual image does not appear to be further away than the external cues.

Color

Colors used in monochromatic HUDs should be specified for each installation. Any color used should be assessed for acceptable contrast against all likely background conditions. The use of a P-43 phosphor has been found in the past to provide acceptable contrast.

If night-vision goggles (NVGs) are likely to be worn in conjunction with HUD use, then the colors used should also be compatible with the NVGs. Normally, a P-43 phosphor and a narrow-bandpass green filter will ensure compliance with this paragraph.

Night filters have been used to provide adequate control or acceptable contrast during night operations. Such a filter should only be incorporated if an improvement over an unfiltered display can be demonstrated. Any night-filter color specification should be matched with the color specification for the HUD itself.

Combiner

Transmittance   The average transmittance of the combiner to external light should be as high as practical. Minimum values of combiner transmittance should be specified for each installation. A suggested minimum value for combiner transmittance is:

Combiner transmittance: 70% (based on ambient sunlight, averaged over all wavelengths)

No credit for part-time use of the HUD should be allowed in specifying combiner transmittance.

The combiner should not color the ambient light to produce misleading color cues of real world objects.

Workmanship and construction   The combiner shall be free from defects which will affect the appearance of the glass or which may affect its serviceability.

The entire periphery of the edges and the surface should be gray-ground to reduce objectionable highlights (*9*). The combiner edges and mounting can produce 'accommodation traps', which may defeat the purpose of collimating the HUD image. For this reason, the combiner mounting should be as unobtrusive as practicable.

Displacement error

When objects are viewed through the combiner, the combining glass should not cause real-world objects to appear to be displaced significantly. Recommended maximum displacement errors are:

Within central 12° of FOV: 0.6 mrad

Within 12°–24° annular FOV: 1.2 mrad
Beyond 24 deg annular FOV: 2.0 mrad

Distortion

The combiner should not discernibly distort real-world objects when they are viewed through it.

If the windshield or canopy is a major source of distortion, the symbol placement may be modified to allow conformal symbols to overlie their real-world equivalents when viewed through the canopy.

Eyebox

The eyebox should contain the HUD design eye reference point (DERP). Within the eyebox, the optical specifications should be met. The minimum size of the eyebox should be such to allow for reasonable pilot head motion. Recommended minimum dimensions are:

Tactical aircraft:
    Longitudinal: 4 in
    Lateral: 4 in
    Vertical: from 1 in below DERP
        to highest practical
        seating height
Transport aircraft:
    Longitudinal: 4 in
    Lateral: 4 in
    Vertical: 2 in

If an alert eye reference point (AERP) is specified, the eyebox should contain the AERP.

There should be a means provided to indicate the proper DERP to the pilot while sitting in his seat. This may be accomplished on the ground prior to flight (i.e. it is not necessary to provide this indication in flight, although such capability is desired for transport aircraft).

Specific consideration should be paid to the typical practice of sitting as high as possible in tactical aircraft to maximize the external view. In tactical aircraft, the HUD DERP need not be the aircraft DERP used to design the flight instruments (*10*). The HUD DERP will be specified by the operator.

The HUD DERP for transport aircraft should be identical to the DERP used in the design of the flight instruments (*10–11*).

141

Consideration should be paid to the likelihood of transport pilots moving out of the eyebox during long cruise segments.

Fatigue

The HUD should be designed to minimize personnel fatigue caused by viewing. In particular, the visual disparity required may be more stringent if the HUD is to be used for extended periods compared with HUDs used briefly during specific mission tasks.

The pilot should be able to view the HUD while sitting comfortably in his normal sitting position.

Glare

Glare and other unwanted visual signals should be minimized. Stray reflections from cockpit lights, from the sun, moon, or external lights should not interfere with the use of the HUD, with the view of real-world objects, or interfere with other crewmembers.

For a HUD intended for use as a primary flight reference (PFR), glare and other unwanted visual signals should be minimized. Stray reflections from cockpit lights, from the sun, moon, or external lights should not interfere with the use of the HUD, with the view of real-world objects, or interfere with other crewmembers not using the HUD.

Multiple reflection combiners should only be installed if necessary, since they can be a source of stray reflections. There should be no secondary real-world images visible over the entire FOV when viewed from within the eyebox. Solar images should be held to a maximum intensity of 2.5% with 0.5% as a design goal.

Multiple images

For HUDs intended for use as PFRs, there should be no secondary symbology images visible over the entire FOV when viewed from within the eyebox.

Care must be taken to avoid unwanted images from the aircraft windshield if the windshield and combiner are in close proximity. An anti-reflective coating should be used on all optical surfaces to minimize unwanted reflections.

Sensor requirements

Accuracy

The accuracy of the gyroscopic reference has been a problem with the retrofit of HUDs in the past. Generally, conventional aircraft gyros have not had the required accuracy and have presented problems with mismatch with the HUD symbols and the real world.

The following gyro platform accuracies are recommended:

All aircraft (non-contact analog):
Heading:	1.0°
Pitch:	1.0°
Roll:	1.0°
Pitch zero:	0.5°
Roll zero:	0.5°

All aircraft (contact analog)
Heading:	0.2°
Pitch:	0.5°
Roll:	0.5°
Pitch zero:	0.2°
Roll zero:	0.5°

The final judge of gyro platform accuracies is the lack of interference with non-contact analog symbols or the absence of a discernible mismatch with external visual cues for contact analog symbols. The preceding gyro accuracies are presented as a guide.

If the available gyro platform accuracy does not meet these standards (as may be the case with retrofit installations), compressed pitch-scale formats may allow relaxation of these accuracies.

Sensor response

The response of sensors input to the HUD can have a significant impact on the HUD characteristics. In general, the two sensors that can cause the most difficulty are the response of the gyro platform and the response of the angle of attack (AOA) and sideslip sensors.

Gyro platform   In general, the gyro platform should provide accurate data at a rate approximately four times the response rate of the aircraft. Recommended minimum platform response rates (providing acceptable accuracies) are:

143

Tactical aircraft:
    Pitch: 180°/s
    Roll: 400°/s
    Heading: 90°/s
Transport aircraft:
    Pitch: 90°/s
    Roll: 120°/s
    Heading: 30°/s

Angle of attack (AOA)   The AOA sensor should provide a signal without excessive oscillations or noise, but with sufficient response for the HUD symbols on which it is based. No specific recommendations can be made at this time. It is quite likely that angle of attack data requirements will be more stringent for a HUD using AOA to generate an air-mass velocity vector than for one displaying only α or α error.

Reliability

The HUD system should be designed to achieve the highest practical level of reliability. Design reliability should be determined using the standard methods (*12*).

Primary flight reference

The system reliability for HUDs intended to be used as primary flight references during flight in instrument meteorological conditions (IMC) should be at least that of the head-down instruments. The system should be designed such that the displaying of incorrect attitude information is extremely improbable.

Instrument landing

The system reliability for HUDs intended to be used as primary flight references during instrument approaches and landing will generally be much higher than for other HUDs. The overall system reliability will be specified by the operator or the certification authority. Considerations should be given to incorporating fail-passive or fail-operational designs. The system should be designed so that the displaying of incorrect attitude or guidance data is extremely improbable.

Non-primary flight reference

The system mean time between failures for HUDs not intended to be used as primary flight references in IMC should be specified by the operator.

HUD controls

Specific controls

Power   The HUD should incorporate an on/off switch to completely remove power from the unit (except power to the standby reticle, if installed). This switch can be included with the brightness control provided a suitable detent is used. If a stowable combiner is used, the on/off switch may be incorporated with the stowing or unstowing of the combiner.

Brightness   The HUD should have a manual brightness control, an automatic brightness control (if specified by the user), and a manual standby reticle brightness control (if a standby reticle is installed).

- *Manual*   The manual brightness control should continuously vary the intensity of all symbols from zero to full intensity.
- *Automatic*   With automatic brightness on, the brightness control should track the ambient light level to maintain a constant contrast ratio. For an increase in ambient brightness as detected by the light sensor, there will be an associated increase in display intensity to maintain a constant contrast ratio.
- *Standby reticle*   If a standby reticle is installed, its brightness control should continuously vary its intensity from zero to full intensity. It should incorporate a detent to remove power from the standby reticle. A separate power supply should be used for the standby reticle.

Declutter   A means of selectively removing symbols from the display should be provided. See 'Clutter' in Chapter 7.

Mode   If automatic mode switching is incorporated, it is highly recommended that a manual mode selection switch be available to allow the pilot to override the automatic selection.

Test   A test switch should be provided to allow the pilot to initiate self-testing of the HUD. This may be omitted if an automatic test function is applied with initial power-up.

Relation to head-down instruments

Controls related to display modes and pilot inputs (such as altimeter settings or heading selection) should be combined with those of the head-down instruments. This has been identified as a major issue in civil HUD programs.

Software design

The HUD system software should be developed in accordance with appropriate software criteria (*13, 14*).

Primary flight reference

The software for HUDs intended to be used as primary flight references during flight in instrument meteorological conditions (IMC) should be developed and verified to level I of DO-178 (*14*).

If the HUD is designed as a supplementary display, level II verification can be allowed provided failures are 'fail obvious.' The pilot must be able to recognize failures and switch his reference to the head-down display.

If the level II option in the previous paragraph is taken, the amount of time taken to detect a failure and switch to the primary display should be determined. This time will determine any operational limitations such as minimum altitude for use of the HUD in IMC.

For those HUDs intended as PFRs, changes to software (including changes to the symbol generator) will normally require extensive analysis before approval for use in IMC.

Non-primary flight reference

A HUD not intended to be used as a primary flight reference in IMC need only have its software designed and verified to level II.

Design and construction

This section contains standard requirements for all airborne avionics equipment. It is included for completeness.

The materials and processes used in the construction of the HUD system should conform to accepted aeronautical practices. Limited life parts, except for CRTs, should be avoided.

Weight

The weight of HUD components should be kept to the minimum commensurate with design objectives. Handles or grasp surfaces should be provided on all line replaceable units (LRUs) that are heavy or that are difficult to grasp, remove, or carry.

Cabling and connections

The wiring connections of the HUD system should conform to appropriate military or civil cabling standards *(15)*. Connectors should be provided with a positive index to prevent misconnection.

All HUD systems should be provided with a wiring interface diagram defining the system inputs, outputs, and power supply requirements.

Interchangeability

All HUD parts having the same part number should be interchangeable with each other with respect to installation and performance.

Electromagnetic interference (EMI)

The HUD system is essentially no different with respect to EMI than any other electronic system. The HUD should not be susceptible to interference from other aircraft systems, considering both interference of signal sources to the HUD and disturbances to the aircraft power system. The HUD in turn should not be a source of EMI to other critical aircraft systems.

Since HUDs interface with many other aircraft systems as signal sources, it should be demonstrated that these interfaces have no deleterious effects on those systems or their outputs to other instruments.

Maintainability

The HUD system should be designed for maintainability. The design of the equipment should provide for easy access to internal parts, terminals, and wiring. All modules, connectors, adjustment or

147

alignment controls, and test points should be marked or identified. The design should be such that it is impossible to incorrectly install a module in the unit. All alignment or adjustment controls should be accessible with a minimum of need to remove the system or assembly from the aircraft. Scheduled maintenance should be limited to periodic cleaning of exposed optical surfaces, replacement of a CRT, or servicing of optical desiccant material.

Identification

Nomenclature, serial number assignment, and identification marking should conform to appropriate military or civil standards (*16–18*).

Environmental conditions

The HUD system should be designed to the environmental conditions specified in military HUDs or for civil HUDs (*19, 20*). Relaxation of performance standards is often allowed during initial warm-up at very cold temperatures or during the firing of aircraft guns.

Human engineering

The HUD system should be designed and developed with the objectives of enhancing the man–machine interface. MIL-STD-1472 (*21*) provides criteria for the application of human engineering principles and procedures.

Cooling requirements

The HUD cooling requirements should be specified for each aircraft installation. Cooling failure should not cause HUD loss. Overheating of the HUD system should be annunciated to the crew.

Warm-up time

The HUD equipment should be functionally operational and conform to all accuracy and performance requirements within 2 min of being switched on at any condition within the environmental envelope specified. Power transients of up to 10 s should not require re-warm-up for periods longer than the power loss.

Installation criteria

This section contains standard requirements for all airborne avionics equipment: however, head-up displays have some unique requirements.

Pilot display unit (PDU) mounting

Mounting of the PDU or PDU components should be such that the display accuracy and readability are not degraded by the environmental conditions normally expected in flight.

Mounting The mounting of the PDU or PDU components should be designed to withstand the vibration, turbulence, maneuvering, and pressurization loads expected in service. The PDU mounting should provide for both lateral optical and vertical optical adjustments.

The PDU should make the least practicable interference with mounting the primary head-down flight instrument in the primary visual signal area (PVSA). As a design goal, the PDU should not interfere with mounting the primary head-down flight instrument in the PVSA.

Replacement Replacement of the PDU should not require optical adjustment.

Stowable combiner If a stowable combiner is used, it should be easily stowed by the pilot with his restraint system fastened (shoulder harness locked). There should be a positive means to ensure that the combiner is fully deployed before symbols are displayed.

Egress The PDU should not interfere with crew escape, including bailout or ejection seat use, if appropriate. Minor infringement on the ejection plane may be tolerated if this infringement is confined to the central portion of the panel and does not create an unacceptable risk to pilots during ejection (*22*).

Crashworthiness Protruding parts of the PDU should incorporate impact protection for the crew, such as the use of foldaway or breakaway structures or padded structures.

External light HUDs designed for use in combat aircraft (including transports) should not be visible from outside the aircraft during night operations.

Combiner windloads   For aircraft in which the front part of the canopy is removed prior to ejection, the combining glass and its mounting structure should withstand without breakage the wind loading and temperature differential associated with the sudden removal of the canopy in flight. This requirement is imposed to avoid injuries to the pilot from combiner debris during an ejection.

Bird strike   The design of the combiner should consider canopy or windshield deflection during a birdstrike. If the canopy or windshield could contact the combiner during a birdstrike, the combiner and its mounting should be designed to prevent large, sharp, or high-velocity fragments from injuring the pilot when the combiner is struck along its upper edge.

Recording capability   The PDU should be designed with the ability to install a camera to record the HUD symbology and the visual scene through the combiner.

Display control panel (DCP) mounting

Mounting of the HUD control unit should allow the pilot to easily make mode changes and enter necessary data during normal flight operations. The effect of turbulence and normal clothing (including gloves) should be considered.

Electronic unit (EU) mounting

The mounting of the HUD EU or EU components should be designed to withstand the vibration, turbulence, maneuvering, and pressurization loads expected in service. The EU mounting should also allow for ease of removal and replacement during maintenance.

Power requirements

Again, this section contains standard requirements for all airborne avionics equipment.

Electrical power

HUD systems should normally operate on a combination of 400Hz, 115Va.c. and 28Vd.c. power as specified by the operator. The power requirements should not exceed the load specified by the user

150

organization/customer. If a standby reticle is installed, it should have a power supply independent from the primary HUD power supply.

Trainer or business aircraft may not have a.c. electrical power available. HUDs designed for such aircraft should be designed to operate on d.c. power only.

Electrical transients

Electrical overload The HUD system should contain overload protection devices for all internal power supplies. These devices should automatically reset when the overload condition no longer exists.

Power interruptions The HUD should be designed to provide for monitoring of and proper response to interruptions of the primary electrical power. For isolated short-term power interrupts, the HUD should go blank for the duration of the interrupt and restore the display following reapplication of power.

Undervoltage protection The HUD system should not be damaged by voltages below those specified above, and should automatically resume normal operation when the undervoltage condition no longer exists.

Documentation

The HUD system design should be documented by:
1. design drawings, schematics, wiring diagrams including interfaces, and parts lists;
2. detail specifications;
3. test procedures defining methods of verifying and evaluating characteristics and performance;
4. environmental test reports documenting design performance over the full range of applicable environments;
5. analyses verifying reliability, maintainability, and safety (the HUD software design should be documented as described in DOD-STD-2167 (*13*) or in DO-178 (*14*);
6. flight manual material or supplements; and
7. maintenance manual material or supplements

References

(1) Newman, R. L. *Operational Problems Associated with Head-Up Displays During Instrument Flight* (Wright-Patterson AFB, Ohio: Air Force Aeromedical Research Laboratory, 1980), AFAMRL TR-80-116

(2) Gold, T. and Potter, E. F. 'Visual suitability – a primary factor in head-up displays', *Sperry Rand Engineering Review*, January 1969, 37–43

(3) Gold, T. and Hyman, A. *Visual Requirements Study for Head-Up Displays* (Great Neck, New York: Sperry Rand, 1970), JANAIR 680712

(4) Gold, T. and Perry, R. F. *Visual Requirements Study for Head-Up Displays* (Great Neck, New York: Sperry Rand, 1972), JANAIR 700407

(5) Newman, R. L. *Improvement of Head-Up Display Standards. I. Head-Up Display Design Guide* (Wright-Patterson AFB, Ohio: Air Force Wright Aeronautical Laboratory, 1987), AFWAL TR-87-3055, Vol. I

(6) Roscoe, S. N. 'Designed for disaster', *Human Factors Society Bulletin*, **29**, (6), June 1986, 1–2

(7) Roscoe, S. N. 'Spatial misorientation exacerbated by collimated virtual flight display', *Information Display*, September 1986, 27–28

(8) Roscoe, S. N. 'The trouble with HUDs and HMDs', *Human Factors Society Bulletin*, **30**, July 1987, 1–2

(9) *Military Specification: Reflector, Gunsight Glass* (Philadelphia, Pennsylvania, Naval Publications and Forms Center, no date), MIL-R-6771B

(10) *Military Standard: Aircrew Station Geometry for Military Aircraft* (Philadelphia, Pennsylvania, Naval Publications and Forms Center, no date), MIL-STD-1333A

(11) *Aerospace Recommended Practice: Location and Actuation of Flight Deck Controls for Commercial Transport Type Aircraft* (Warrendale, Pennsylvania: Society of Automotive Engineers, 1984), SAE ARP-268F

(12) *Military Handbook: Reliability Stress and Failure Rate Data for Electronic Equipment* (Philadelphia, Pennsylvania, Naval Publications and Forms Center, no date), MIL-HDBK-217D

(13) *Defense System Software Development* (Philadelphia, Pennsylvania, Naval Publications and Forms Center, no date), DOD-STD-2167

(14) *Software Considerations in Airborne Systems and Equipment Certification* (Washington: Radio Technical Commission for Aeronautics, no date), DO-178A

(15) *Military Specification: Wiring Aerospace* (Philadelphia, Pennsylvania, Naval Publications and Forms Center, no date), MIL-W-5088H

(16) *Military Specification: Nomenclature Assignment, Contractors Method for Obtaining* (Philadelphia, Pennsylvania, Naval Publications and Forms Center, no date), MIL-N-7513

(17) *Military Specification: Plate, Identification* (Philadelphia, Pennsylvania, Naval Publications and Forms Center, no date), MIL-P-15024

(18) *Certification Procedures for Products and Parts* (Washington: Federal Aviation Administration, 1972), AC-21.303-1A

(19) *Military Specification: Electronic Equipment, General Specification for* (Philadelphia, Pennsylvania, Naval Publications and Forms Center, no date), MIL-E-5400

(20) *Environmental and Test Procedures for Airborne Equipment* (Washington: Radio Technical Commission for Aeronautics, no date), DO-160C

(21) *Military Standard: Human Engineering Design Criteria for Military Systems, Equipment, and Facilities* (Philadelphia, Pennsylvania, Naval Publications and Forms Center, no date), MIL-STD-1472

(22) *Military Standard: Aircrew Station Geometry for Military Aircraft* (Philadelphia, Pennsylvania, Naval Publications and Forms Center, no date), MIL-STD-1333A

7 Display criteria

The HUD may repeat, augment, or replace head-down displays and information for any and all phases of flight. HUD systems that are designed to replace head-down displays should contain the information required by the pilot for manual control during the selected flight phase. It is understood that this information need not be identical in content or format to the head-down information.

Compatibility with head-down displays

The HUD should display data which is compatible with the head-down instruments. It is important that the control strategies used head-up by the pilot be compatible with those used head-down. This does not mean that the HUD must be constrained to show only that data that is shown head-down. It might not be feasible to display all HUD parameters on a head-down electromechanical instrument and would not be wise to limit an electronic HUD to only those parameters available head-down.

It does mean that the same pilot will fly the airplane both head-up and head-down. If only pitch information is available head-down, then pitch information should be displayed on the HUD so that in critical flight situations the pilot can use the same information and control strategies. A large interaction with pilot training is implied by these

154

arguments.

The HUD must be integrated into the cockpit. This means that the procedures used to fly by reference to the head-up display and those used to fly by reference to the head-down panel must not lead to problems when the pilot switches from one display to the other. For example, the use of longitudinal controls by reference to flight path angle (FPA) on the HUD should not lead to problems if the pilot mistakenly uses the techniques for flying by reference to pitch (Θ) on the head-down panel.

It is not necessary for the HUD to use exactly the same format as the head-down panel. Specifically, if the head-down display uses tapes, this should not require the HUD to use tapes. Many successful HUD installations have mixed round displays with tapes and round dials with pure digits.

Clutter

A cluttered display is one with an excessive amount of information contained in the number or variety of symbols. The designer must guard against the urge to add more and more data to the display. Not one pixel should be lit unless it 'buys' its way onto the screen by providing a demonstrable improvement in performance (*1*).

The pilot should also have a means to reduce the amount of extra, low-priority information if it is not desired. There are two primary means to accomplish this: using few HUD modes with declutter options or using many HUD modes with fewer declutter options.

We favor installations using a limited number of modes with declutter logic over a large number of modes.

Declutter logic

One design philosophy allows the pilot to manually select from one or more declutter options. In the extreme, this approach would allow the pilot to select whatever symbols are wanted from a menu.

The simplest form of declutter is a 'scales' switch. This removes secondary information so the pilot can concentrate on the symbols of greater importance. Early HUDs used this approach to delete airspeed, altitude, vertical velocity, and heading from the HUD. Because this 'all or nothing' approach leaves something to be desired, some modern HUDs have two or more declutter options, removing part of the secondary displays at one position and the rest at another.

It is highly recommended that HUDs have a minimum of two levels of declutter. This is easily accomplished with a sequential push button on the stick or yoke. The first push could remove non-essential data, the second could remove navigation data, and the third could restore everything.

It is also recommended that, while a basic selection of symbols to be displayed be programmed into the HUD controls, the pilot be given the option to modify the programming and select which symbols are included with each level of declutter.[1]

It is also recommended that the pilot be given some ability to change the scales format. For example, the pilot could select counter-pointers or digits for airspeed or altitude.

Mode logic

The second declutter philosophy uses a large number of modes with symbols chosen for each mode. When this option is used, there is less need for multiple declutter choices. Nevertheless, some declutter choice is desirable.

It is recommended that HUDs have some format of declutter logic available even if there are large numbers of modes available.

It is also recommended that, while a basic selection of symbols to be displayed for each mode be programmed into the HUD controls, the pilot be given the option to modify the programming and select which symbols are included with each level of declutter.

Automatic declutter

Under some limited circumstances, it may be desirable to automatically declutter the HUD without pilot intervention. This option must be used sparingly. Instances where this might be desirable include large pitch or roll excursions typical of unusual attitudes, windshear encounters in transport aircraft, or excessively low altitude during A/G weapons delivery where a mandatory breakaway is commanded. During such cases, all non-essential data should be eliminated.

Extreme care should be used when incorporating these automatic declutter modes. For example, during air combat maneuvers (ACM) in tactical aircraft, pitch or roll attitudes might trigger such declutter. Such automatic action should not detract from the use of the HUD or from the mission.

---

[1] This option could be accomplished on the ground prior to flight.

Raster clutter

The raster image itself may adversely affect the ability of the pilot to look through the HUD. The effect has not been determined. It is very likely that raster clutter criteria will be more stringent than for stroke-only HUDs.

Accuracy

The accuracies of symbol placement should be commensurate with the intended use of the symbol and the operational requirements. All accuracies, except boresight accuracy, should be considered system accuracies, not just HUD accuracies.

Boresight

The recommended boresighting accuracy specifications are:

Tactical aircraft:	1 mrad
Transport aircraft:	3 mrad
Trainer aircraft:	3 mrad
Business aircraft:	3 mrad

Contact analog symbols

Positioning of contact analog symbols should produce no discernible mismatch with the real-world cues. If a mismatch is unavoidable, symbolic rather than realistic symbols should be used (such as a runway centerline versus a complete runway, for example).

Other symbols

Recommended positioning tolerances of other symbols are:

Conformal symbols:	1 mrad
Non-conformal symbols:	3 mrad

Raster images

In a raster HUD, the raster image should conform to the real world cues and to stroke symbols. Recommended image tolerance is:

157

Raster image to real world: 1 mrad
Raster image to stroke symbol: 1 mrad
One raster image to another: 1 mrad

Some sensors have limited range. These can present misleading images. The effects have not been determined.

Standby reticle

If installed, the positioning accuracy of the standby reticle should be commensurate with the intended use of the HUD.

Dynamic response

The motion of all analog symbols on the HUD should be smooth, with no objectionable overshoot, and should generally track the short period of the airplane. Symbols should be stable with no discernible flicker or jitter.

Flicker

Symbols should show no discernible flicker. A minimum symbol refresh rate of 50 Hz is recommended. The use of 60 Hz may enhance recordability with video recording equipment.

The HUD should be synchronized with other CRT displays visible to the pilot. This is particularly important when basic refresh rates less than 60 Hz are used.

Jitter

Symbols should be stable with no discernible jitter, i.e. less than the minimum linewidth. Motion at frequencies above 0.25 Hz is considered jitter.

Noise

Display noise should not cause symbol forms or accuracies to exceed recommended or specified limits. Display noise should not interfere with the intended use of the HUD.

Frame times

Recommended minimum sampling rates for aircraft attitude, inertial velocities, and accelerations are:

Tactical aircraft: 25 Hz (up-and-away)
12.5 Hz (landing configuration)

Trainers: 25 Hz (up-and-away)
12.5 Hz (landing configuration)

Transport aircraft: 10 Hz

Business aircraft: 10 Hz

These rates correspond to frame times of 40 ms for tactical air trainer aircraft (up and away) and 80 ms for in the landing configuration. They are equivalent to 100 ms for transports. Slower sampling rates (3–4 Hz) may be used for some slowly changing quantities, such as altitude.

Airspeed data for air-mass velocity vector calculations should be sampled at the rates shown for aircraft attitude unless no degradation in performance can be shown for slower rates.

In any event, the ultimate criterion is the ability of the pilot to use the display. These recommended sampling rates should be validated in flight in the particular installation.

Raster update rate

A raster image may be updated fairly slowly when compared with other HUD data. This will be particularly true with radar images. In addition, signal processing may add to the image latency. These effects may adversely affect the ability of the pilot to fly using the HUD and to make decisions concerning continuing the approach. The effect has not been determined.

Some sensors have limited range. These can present misleading images if incorporated into raster images. Although no criteria have been established, sensor images will require evaluation to ensure that dangerously misleading images do not occur and that the pilot can use the images to perform mission tasks.

Quickening

Symbol quickening may be required to yield a 'flyable' flight path marker symbol (See 'Quickening' in Chapter 3). Symbol quickening should not change automatically (within a given mode) in a non-failure state. Symbol quickening must be kept to the minimum necessary to provide a flyable symbol.

Some HUDs in the past have provided a level of augmentation to the point where the flight path symbol was not representative of the aircraft flight path. The designer should be careful to keep the quickening to the minimum level which creates a flyable symbol. The error should be on the side of too little rather than too much quickening.

In particular, care should be exercised to ensure that quickening of flight path symbols does not show non-conservative trajectories when maneuvering near obstacles or terrain. This will normally be most critical in the landing configuration, particularly for 'backside' aircraft.

Damping

Symbol damping may be required to yield a 'flyable' symbol. Symbol damping should not change automatically (within a given mode) in a non-failure state.

Electronic displays do not have the mechanical damping present in many mechanical indicators. Some HUDs in the past have not allowed for noisy sensors (particularly in sideslip). Again, any error should be on the side of too little rather than too much electronic damping.

Digital displays

Digital displays, such as airspeed, altitude, etc., should not be refreshed on the display faster than 3–4 Hz. The data should be updated at a faster rate if required in the flight control computations, but the data displayed on the HUD should change no faster than indicated.

Fault alerts

HUD data

The HUD should not display false or misleading information. If invalid data is received from HUD input sources, then the HUD should indicate the loss in validity by deleting the symbol(s) in question.

Symbols that are calculated using backup or reversionary sources (such as calculating velocity vector based on air data instead of inertial data) should clearly indicate this to the pilot.

Symbols that are incorrectly positioned because of FOV limitations should clearly indicate this to the pilot. In the past, this has been successfully accomplished by placing an 'X' over the symbol, by truncating the symbol at the FOV limit, or by adding an arrow to the symbol. *Flashing a symbol alone is not acceptable.*

Particular care should be taken so that two symbols which are positioned relative to each other do not change this relationship when placed at or near the limit of the FOV. An example would be the flight director and the velocity vector (if the flight director is shown relative to the velocity vector, as is common practice). When the velocity vector, is limited by the FOV limit, this should not affect the relative location of the director steering symbol relative to the velocity vector. This might be accomplished by limiting the velocity vector slightly inside the FOV limit so the director steering symbol can still move around it.

The use of flashing symbols to indicate degraded or FOV limited data is not acceptable by itself.

Symbols that can be deleted by declutter should have a secondary warning when they are deleted because of faulty data. An example might be the annunciation 'INVALID' in place of radar altitude digits if the data were deleted because of invalid data. In this case, if radar altitude data was invalid, but had been deleted by a declutter option, the 'INVALID' message would not be shown.

Aircraft master warning/master caution

The HUD should repeat the aircraft master warning and master caution annunciation. Specific annunciations should be included only if necessary for safe flight. If specific indications are used, they should conform to MIL-STD-411 (*2*) for military HUDs or AS-425 (*3*) for civil HUDs.

Pitch-scaling considerations

Generally one-to-one pitch scaling of HUD data has been preferred, although other scalings have been shown to be advantageous under some circumstances. A slight compression (of the order of 1.5:1 or 2:1) has been shown to improve ILS tracking performance and may be useful if a conformal display is not needed (*4*).

This pitch compression or more can be of assistance to the pilot during large-amplitude maneuvers (such as ACM, acrobatics, or unusual attitude (UA) recoveries). An unusual attitude mode has been suggested (5) with an automatic step change in pitch compression data to assist the pilot during spatial disorientation. This step change was well received by the evaluation pilots. Such a mode is recommended for all aircraft, transport as well as tactical. The RAF Fast-Jet format (6) provides for continuously variable pitch compression.

One-to-one scaling is indicated during ground reference maneuvers with conformal displays (such as air-to-ground tracking).

Recent HUDs (7) intended for retrofit in airplanes with conventional gyros have used compression to mask the platform inaccuracies of these gyros (see 'Sensor requirements' in Chapter 6).

Reference for error displays

Reference

Traditionally, the location of the reference for error displays (course deviation information, airspeed error, angle of attack error, etc.) has been the aircraft reference symbol. Normally this location would be recommended; however, some recent successful HUDs have used the intersection of the horizon line and the selected course as the reference for ILS deviation error. Further, recent studies indicate that increased use of the pitch symbol as a reference may enhance resistance to spatial disorientation.

It is premature to insist that navigational deviations and error symbols be referenced to the primary flight symbol. In some cases, it may be disadvantageous to do so.

Flight director information should have its zero reference located at the primary airplane symbol unless enhanced performance can be demonstrated using another reference.

Fly-to vs fly-from considerations

All error symbols should be 'fly-to' symbols. The only exception has historically been the angle of attack error which, in some airplanes, has had a 'fly-from' sense.

The choice for the angle of attack sense is based on two conflicting criteria. The conventional criterion of always 'flying-to' an error, and the geometrical criterion of attempting to show, the relationship between α, γ, and Θ, which leads to a 'fly-from' sense. Selection on one choice would be premature at this time.

Compressed pitch-scaling consideration

If compressed pitch-scaling is used to assist in unusual attitude recognition or for use in acrobatic flight, it will not be possible for the various HUD symbols to all be conformal. The common choices in compressed pitch-scale use are to have the aircraft pitch symbol (waterline) remain fixed in the HUD FOV, to have the horizon symbol remain conformal with the real-world horizon (zero pitch angle), or have the displayed velocity vector symbol remain conformal with the true velocity vector. For most applications, it is recommended that the HUD horizon remain conformal with the real-world horizon. Other than weapons delivery, no operational advantage can be seen for the practice of keeping the waterline fixed.

For ground-referenced maneuvers (A/G weapons delivery, landing approach, or terrain following) with inertial velocity vectors, then the displayed HUD velocity vector should remain conformal with the true velocity vector.

In either case, the angular relationships between α, γ, and Θ should be retained (although compressed): that is, the HUD pitch symbol with pitch compression would be moved so that it matches the appropriate angle on the pitch ladder.

Target (or traffic) symbols should overlie the actual target rather than at the indicated angles on the pitch-scale.

Directed decision cues

The use of a directed decision cue must be held to an absolute minimum and confined to those situations where loss of the aircraft is imminent if the trajectory is continued (e.g. a breakaway commanded because of impending ground impact). For example, landing minima, if annunciated, should use 'DECISION HEIGHT' not 'GO-AROUND.'

The use of directed decision cues during combat, such as 'SHOOT' should be avoided since this requires the pilot to follow specific tactics which may not be desired in all situations. An 'IN RANGE' annunciation is preferred to 'SHOOT.'

Symbol priority

A table of symbol priority must be established for those symbols that can move within the FOV. If any symbols can overwrite one another, the symbol generator should use this symbol priority table to blank the symbol of lower priority to prevent interference with the legibility of the higher-priority symbol.

A table of symbol priority must be established for those symbols that can move within the FOV. If two symbols can overwrite each other, the symbol generator should use this symbol priority table to blank the symbol of lower priority. This will minimize symbol interference.

Recommended symbol priorities are shown in Chapter 8.

Coding

Each symbol should be unique by virtue of at least two coding characteristics. Color coding is acceptable; however, colors should be consistent with head-down displays. Flashing of symbols should be minimized. Flashing may be used to attract attention to a symbol, but should not be used by itself to denote data error, FOV limits, decision height, etc.

Color

Colors should only be used where an improvement over monochrome can be shown. Colors used should be consistent with head-down instruments. Each color used should be assessed for acceptable contrast against all likely background conditions. (These requirements may provide conflict, such as the need to use blue to show pitch up and a color other than blue to contrast with the sky background.) Color should not be the only distinction. In a degraded or monochromatic mode, a color display must remain legible and unambiguous. Color displays should have a means for the pilot to select a monochromatic display.

Size and shape of symbols and characters

Symbols should appear clean-shaped, clear, and explicit. Lines should be narrow, sharp-edged, and without halo.

The meaning and behavior of symbols should be consistent for all modes of a given display. Generally, the symbols in MIL-STD-1787 (*8*) are recommended. Where other symbols are recommended, these are shown in Chapter 8.

Symbol characteristics (such as shape and size) which are suitable for stroke symbols may have to be revised if the symbology is embedded in the raster image.

Line width

The recommended line width is 1.0 mrad. Enhanced lines are not recommended.

Size of characters

The size of alphanumeric characters will depend on the degree of importance attached to the particular character. Recommended size guidelines are:

Basic size: 4 x 7 mrad
Enhanced: 7 x 12 mrad

Shape of characters

The shape of alphanumeric characters has not been specified in the past. Two recommended fonts are the Mitre font and the Leroy fonts (*9, 10*).

Raster issues

A number of issues arise when raster images are incorporated into a HUD. Some of these have been discussed above (image brightness, image registration, and clutter). Others require additional research. A limited number of criteria have been published (*11*), while other issues are as yet unresolved.

Kruk (*12*) and Foyle *et al.* (*13*) have discussed outstanding issues.

References

(1)   Hughes, R. E. *The HUD Coloring Book: Recommendations Concerning Head-Up Displays* (Washington,: Naval Air Systems Command, 1991)
(2)   *Military Standard: Aircrew Station Signals* (Philadelphia, Pennsylvania, Naval Publications and Forms Center, no date), MIL-STD-411D
(3)   *Aerospace Standard: Nomenclature and Abbreviations for Use on the Flight Deck* (Warrendale, Pennsylvania: Society of Automotive Engineers, 1985), SAE AS-425C
(4)   Naish, J. M. 'Control gains in head-up presentation', in *Proceedings of 6th Annual Conference on Manual Control, Wright-Patterson AFB*, (Wright-Patterson AFB, Ohio: Air Force Flight Dynamics Laboratory, 1970), pp. 19–46
(5)   Newman, R. L. *Improvement of Head-Up Display Standards. II. Evaluation of Head-Up Displays to Enhance Unusual Attitude Recovery* (Wright-Patterson AFB, Ohio:

Air Force Wright Aeronautical Laboratory, 1987), AFWAL TR-87-3055. Vol. II

(6) Hall, J. R., Stephens, C. M., and Penwill, J. C. *A Review of the Design and Development of the RAE Fast-Jet Head-Up Display Format* (Bedford, England: Royal Aeronautical Establishment, 1989), RAE FM-WP(89)034

(7) Newman, R. L. *Flight Test Report. Flight Visions FV-2000/KA HUD Installed in a Beechcraft BE-A100* (San Marcos, Texas: Crew Systems, 1993), TR-93-09

(8) *Military Standard, Aircraft Display Symbology* (Philadelphia, Pennsylvania, Naval Publications and Forms Center, 1989), MIL-STD-1787A

(9) Weintraub, D. J. and Ensing, M. *Human Factors Issues in Head-Up Display Design: The Book of HUD* (Wright-Patterson AFB, Ohio: Crew System Ergonomics Information Analysis Center, 1992), CSERIAC SOAR-92-2

(10) Shurtleff, D. A. *How to Make Displays Legible* (La Mirada, California: Human Interface Design, 1980)

(11) *Military Specification: Displays, Airborne, Electronically/Optically Generated* (Philadelphia, Pennsylvania, Naval Publications and Forms Center, 1987), MIL-D-87213A

(12) Kruk, R. V., *Issues Associated with Enhanced Vision Systems* (Warrendale, Pennsylvania: Society of Automotive Engineers, 1992), SAE Paper 921935

(13) Foyle D. C. *et al.* 'Enhanced/synthetic vision systems: human factors research and implications for future systems', in *Enhanced Situation Awareness Technology for Retrofit and Advanced Cockpit Design* (Warrendale, Pennsylvania: Society of Automotive Engineers, 1992), SAE SP-933, pp. 59–66

8 Recommended standard symbology

The following symbol sets can be recommended at this point in time based on previous experience and the results of tests. This is not to say that other combinations are not acceptable; they can be acceptable if they can be shown to improve pilot performance.

Recommended symbols

Airplane reference symbol

The primary ARS should be the climb–dive marker with a ghost velocity vector or a flight path marker. The pilot should have the option to uncage to the FPM or cage to the CDM. The CDM/FPM should use the winged circle with the tail optional.

The backup reference is the winged W, pitch marker. No recommendation is made concerning full-time display of the waterline. The added situational awareness of full-time pitch information must be balanced against added clutter on a case-by-case basis.

Horizon line/pitch ladder

The horizon line should extend to the periphery of the FOV. The

167

pitch ladder should not employ 'bendy bars'. The use of different pitch ladder lengths, tapering, tick marks, etc. should be employed to distinguish above from below the horizon. Tick marks should be located on the outboard ends of the ladder rungs. Omitting tick marks above the horizon should be considered.

Insufficient testing of variable pitch scale compression has been conducted to recommend it without reservation. In the interim, progressive automatic switching from 1:1 to 2:1 at ±30° of pitch and from 2:1 to 4:1 at ±60° is recommended. The F-16 automatic switching from 1:1 to 2:1 at ±60° could also be used. In either case, care must be taken to ensure that the pitch symbol is rewritten to show the correct pitch angle when read against the pitch ladder. The switch back to the lower pitch compressions should employ a delay of 3–5 s to prevent rapid switching back and forth.

The simple zenith and nadir symbols should be used to minimize the write time. While the horizon-pointing line may be unnecessary, it will certainly do no harm.

Airspeed and altitude scales

Counter-pointers should be used for the primary airspeed and altitude display. Subsidiary scales, true airspeed, groundspeed, load factor for airspeed and vertical speed, radar altitude, etc. for altitude, should be displayed digitally below the primary scale. These should be displayed only if needed and the pilot should be able to declutter them quickly and easily. He should also have the option to quickly recall them if needed.

The pilot should also have the option to declutter the counter-pointer and circle of dots for airspeed, altitude, or both.

Heading scale

Generally the traditional compressed heading scale at the top of the FOV should be used.

HUDs intended for precision landing approaches could make use of 1:1 heading marks on the horizon, but this is discouraged for other flight phases.

Orientation cue

At this time, the Augie arrow is recommended, although testing of other options is incomplete. Based on anecdotal evidence, the French attitude ball (*le boule*) in the lower left could be used in place of the

Augie arrow.

Guidance cues

No particular recommendations can be made at this time except for negative ones. Much testing is still required to compare one symbology with another. Additionally, the ability of the pilot to detect discrepancies must be evaluated.

The rotating HSI cue should not be used with the aircraft reference symbol as its center. The potential for false roll cues is too great to allow this.

The use of ILS-style cross-pointers seems to create difficulties because of the large numbers of vertical and horizontal lines and because of confusion between raw deviation data and computed steering commands.

The following sections list the data considered appropriate for specific HUD modes. Data not listed as belonging to the minimum set can be decluttered if desired.

Symbol priority

Each symbol must have a symbol priority. Lower-priority symbols will be occluded by symbols of higher priority. The top priority should be assigned to the aircraft reference symbol – the CDM/FPM. The second highest priority should be assigned to the waterline, the heading, and the airspeed/altitude scales. The lowest priority should be assigned to the pitch ladder and horizon.

Otherwise, moving symbols should occlude fixed symbols.

Basic mode

The data requirements for the basic HUD mode are shown in Table 8.1. The key in the basic mode is to reduce the symbols to the minimum necessary to control the airplane.

Basic display

Figure 8.1 shows the basic symbology.

Unusual attitude recovery display

The unusual attitude symbology should be displayed whenever the

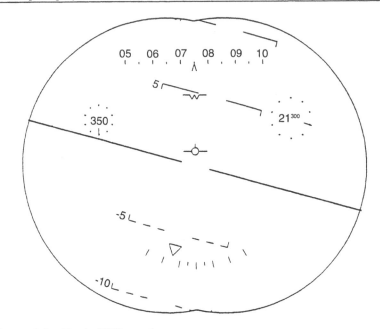

Figure 8.1   Basic HUD mode

pitch and bank exceed predefined limits. These limits will vary from aircraft type to aircraft type. The trigger point should be set just beyond those bank and pitch angles encountered during routine flying. Figure 8.2 shows the unusual attitude symbology.

The orientation cue should be displayed whenever the horizon is out of view or when exceeding normal bank and pitch limits. The climb–dive marker should be deleted at high angle of attack.

An Augie arrow or other orientation cue is recommended to enhance recovery.

The pitch ladder may be compressed to enhance UA recognition and recovery. A 2:1 compression is recommended. These recommendations may be modified if an orange peel or *le boule* symbol is used.

During an unusual attitude, all symbology not necessary to recover the airplane should be deleted.

Takeoff/go-around

The data requirements for the TOGA HUD mode are shown in Table

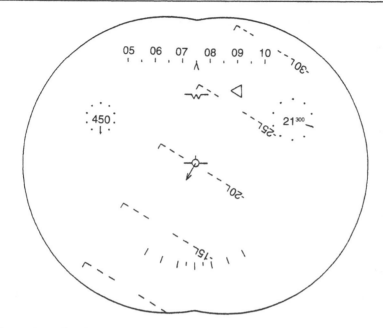

Figure 8.2   Basic mode – unusual attitude recovery

8.2. Angle of sideslip is required for multi-engine or VTOL aircraft.

An energy cue (potential flight path) is recommended for the climb mode. A runway acceleration cue is desired for the takeoff roll.

The use of air-mass data could enhance aerodynamic performance.

En-route

The data requirements for the *en-route* HUD mode are shown in Table 8.1. The symbology is shown in Figure 8.3

The *en-route* mode is predicated on normal cruise, not terminal area maneuvering.

Airspeed should delete the pointer and circle of dots and show digits only. The pointer should be retained for altitude to enhance the ability to detect subtle changes from the assigned altitude.

The limits to trigger switching to the unusual attitude mode should be less in the *en-route* mode.

Table 8.1 Basic mode HUD data requirements[a]

Parameter	Minimum set	Typical set	Unusual attitude	*En-route* mode
Pitch ladder	X	X	X	X
Waterline	X	X	X	–
CDM/FPM	–	X	X	X
Altitude	X	X	X	X
Vertical speed	X	X	X	–
Radar altitude	–	U	–	–
Baro setting	–	–	–	–
Vert deviation	–	–	–	U
Selected alt	–	U	–	X
Airspeed	X	X	X	X[b]
TAS digits	–	–	–	–
GS digits	–	–	–	–
Mach digits	–[c]	X[c]	–	X[c]
Selected a/s	–	–	–	–
Speed/AOA error	–	–	–	–
Heading	X	X	X	X
Selected course	–	–	–	N
Selected headg	–	–	–	U
Ground track	–	–	–	–
Orientation cue	–	–	X	–
Bank scale	–	–	X	–
Sideslip	–	–	–	–
Energy	–	U	–	–
Flight director	–	N	–	N
Lateral deviation	–	N	–	N
Glidescope	–	–	–	–
Stopwatch digits	–	U	–	–
Digital nav data	–	–	–	–
Distance (DME)	–	–	–	N

Notes: [a] Code: X = required; U = useful information; N = depends on navigation requirements.
[b] Digits only.
[c] If required for operational limits.

Non-precision approach/landing

The data requirements for the approach and landing task are listed in Table 8.3.

Precision approach/landing

The data requirements are listed in Table 8.3. The choice of a final

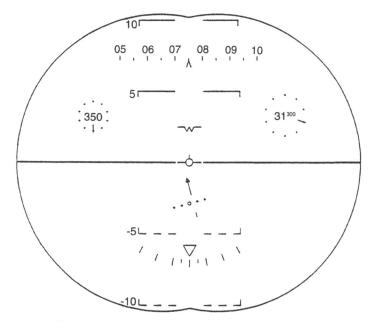

Figure 8.3 *En-route* **mode**

approach symbology requires additional research. The three most likely choices are shown in Figures 8.4–8.6.

Geographic orientation has been difficult with most symbologies employed to date. Intercept symbology also requires additional development.

Tactical modes

The data requirements for typical tactical tasks are shown in Table 8.4.

In the air-to-air mode, the orange peel or *le boule* symbology may allow the use of horizon line only.

Training

The training modes should concentrate on the basic flight mode. The flight path display should be based on air-mass data.

The instructor should have the option to select and remove specific

173

Table 8.2 Takeoff/go-around mode HUD data requirements[a]

Parameter	Minimum set	Typical set	Takeoff run
Pitch ladder	X	X	–
Waterline	X	X	–
CDM/FPM	–	X	–
Altitude	X	X	X
Vertical speed	X	X	–
Radar altitude	–	X	–
Baro setting	–	–	–
Vert deviation	–	–	–
Selected alt	–	U	–
Airspeed	X	X	X
TAS digits	–	–	–
GS digits	–	–	–
Mach digits	–	–	–
Selected a/s	–	–	–
Speed/AOA error	–	U	–
Heading	X	X	X
Selected course	–	–	–
Selected headg	–	–	–
Ground track	–	–	–
Orientation cue	–	–	–
Bank scale	–	–	–
Sideslip	X[b]	X[b]	–
Energy	–	U	U
Flight director	–	N	N
Lateral deviation	–	N	N
Glidescope	–	–	–
Stopwatch digits	–	–	U
Digital nav data	–	–	–
Distance (DME)	–	–	–

Notes: [a] Code: X = required; U = useful information; N = depends on navigation requirements.
[b] Required for multi-engine aircraft.

symbols to enhance the training mission.

Narrow-FOV air-to-air fighter

An example of a specific HUD application is presented to illustrate the design principles for head-up displays. This example is an air-to-air fighter intended for all-weather interceptor duties. This is a hypothetical example of how aircraft and mission constraints dictate HUD symbology.

Table 8.3 Approach mode HUD data requirements[a]

Parameter	Minimum set	Non-precision approach	Precision approach
Pitch ladder	X	X	X
Waterline	X	X	X
CDM/FPM	X	X	X
Altitude	X	X	X
Vertical speed	X	X	X
Radar altitude	–	X	X[b]
Baro setting	–	–	–
Vert deviation	–	–	–
Selected alt	–	U	U
Airspeed	X	X	X
TAS digits	–	–	–
GS digits	–	U	U
Mach digits	–	–	–
Selected a/s	–	U	U
Speed/AOA error	–	X	X
Heading	X	X	X
Selected course	–	X	X
Selected headg	–	U	U
Ground track	–	–	–
Orientation cue	–	–	–
Bank scale	–	?	?
Sideslip	–	–	–
Energy	–	U	U
Flight director	N	N	N
Lateral deviation	X	X	X
Glidescope	–[c]	–	X
Stopwatch digits	–	U	–
Digital nav data	–	–	–
Distance (DME)	–	N	N

Notes: [a] Code: X = required; U = useful information; N = depends on navigation requirements.
[b] The landing flare in a Category II or III approach may require special symbology.
[c] Required for precision approach.

Aircraft/mission constraints

The basic mission is all-weather interceptor duties. A secondary mission is day air-to-air combat.

The aircraft in constrained by cockpit geometry to a narrow FOV, of the order of 10° TFOV.

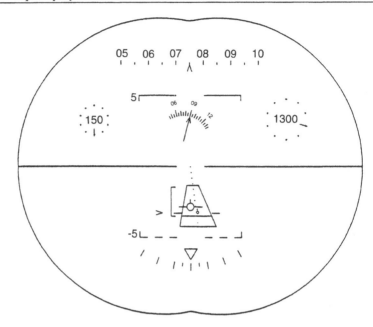

Figure 8.4   Approach/landing mode (synthetic runway)

Data requirements

Aerodynamic performance Performance information must be emphasized. Both angle-of-attack and angle-of-sideslip information are required. Total energy and energy relative to an adversary are also pertinent.

Air-reference Information relative to the ground is less important: that is, there is no overwhelming need for conformality or for ground-referenced flight path information.

Spatial disorientation The combination of narrow FOV and a mission requiring dynamic maneuvering suggests that conventional pitch ladder spacing would not provide for adequate situational awareness. The symbology will have to minimize any tendency to spatial disorientation.

Need for direct view Particularly in the day ACM role, the paramount need is to reduce clutter to an absolute minimum.

176

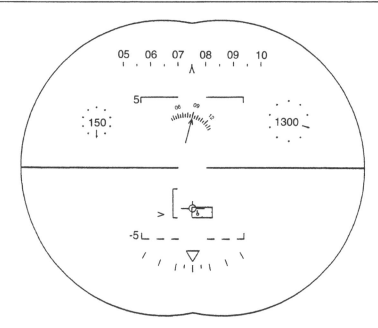

Figure 8.5 Approach/landing mode (deviation box/tadpole)

Symbology choices

Air-mass flight path information   The flight path information should be air-mass-based, not inertially based. This is based on the emphasis on aerodynamic performance and is supported by the absence of a requirement for ground-referenced flight path information.

   If full-time pitch information is presented, the angular relationship between the waterline/gun cross and the air-mass CDM will show angle of attack directly. The lateral motion of the FPM relative to the CDM will show sideslip.

Pitch information   The pitch symbol (waterline or gun cross) should be fixed in the FOV. This will allow it to perform double duty of serving as a weapon boresight and as a reference for judging the AOA by gauging the angle between it and the CDM.

   If adequate pitch information can be obtained with the use of the ADI ball in the lower-left FOV, this is the preferred symbology. The pitch ladder should then be confined to a horizon line only. During other phases of flight, lines at ±5° and ±10° should be added (but not

177

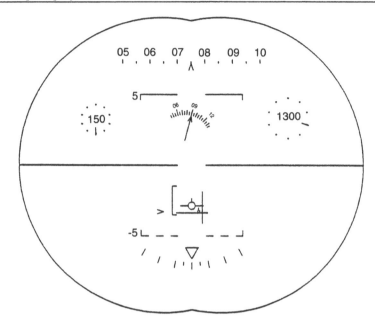

Figure 8.6   Approach/landing mode (cross-pointers/tadpole)

during A/A).

The orange peel could be used to maintain pitch information, but this is not recommended because of added clutter in the center of the FOV.

If the ADI ball does not provide adequate orientation cues, then a conventional pitch ladder should be used.

Pitch-scale compression   If the ADI ball and a horizon line is used, the compression should be 1:1.

Otherwise, full-time pitch-scale compression should be incorporated. This will allow the pilot to view more lines of the pitch ladder and maintain spatial awareness while maneuvering. Since the angle-of-attack information will be shown by the angle between the waterline/gun cross and the CDM, a fixed compression is preferred over a stepped or variable compression.

The preliminary choice is 4:1 compression; however, this must be validated in flight.

The symbols need not be conformal, so it is recommended that the pitch symbol be fixed (as is often the case in present-day HUDs). This symbol might perform double duty as a weapon boresight or gun cross.

178

Table 8.4 Tactical HUD data requirements[a]

Parameter	Terrain-following	Air to air	Air to ground
Aiming symbol	–	X	X
Pitch ladder	X	?	X
Waterline	X	X[b]	X
CDM/FPM	X	X	X[c]
Altitude	X	X	X
Vertical speed	X	X	X
Radar altitude	X	–	X
Baro setting	–	–	–
Vert deviation	U	–	–
Selected alt	–	–	–
Airspeed	X	X	X
TAS digits	–	–	X
GS digits	U	–	–
Mach digits	–	X	–
Load factor	U	X	U
Speed/AOA error	–	–	–
Heading	X	–	–
Selected course	–	–	–
Selected headg	–	–	–
Ground track	U	–	–
Orientation cue	–	–	–
Bank scale	–	–	X
Sideslip	–	–	–
Energy	–	X	–
Flight director	–	–	–
Lateral deviation	N	–	–
Stopwatch digits	U	–	–
Digital nav data	–	–	–
Distance/range	N	X	–
Breakaway	X	–	X

Notes: [a] Code: X = required; U = useful information; N = depends on navigation requirements.
    [b] Gun cross.
    [c] FPM preferred.

Scales Airspeed and altitude are not normally required. If desired, either could be selected by the pilot. If needed, digital airspeed/altitude would minimize clutter with counter-pointers available as needed.

Heading is not required, but could be available as needed.

These scale choices could be set as desired by the pilot before flight with two levels of declutter on and declutter off available. The choice should be independent, i.e. the pilot could select digital airspeed but

179

no altitude or heading as default choice and counter-pointer airspeed and altitude as the alternate choice.

Basic HUD mode The basic instrument mode showing airspeed, altitude, and heading must be available with the push of a single button without the need to remove the pilot's hand from the stick or throttle (HOTAS).

Energy cue The rate of change of aircraft energy should be indicated by a moving cue relative to the CDM. If possible, this should be referenced to the adversary, showing the rate of energy change relative to the target aircraft.

Reliability

This HUD will be the primary flight display. Its reliability must be equivalent to that required for head-down gyro information. The likelihood of displaying dangerously misleading attitude information must be extremely improbable.

Summary

The final choice for symbology will require flight trials to verify the adequacy of the cues. The two choices are:

1. Version 1 (shown in Figure 8.7):
   - No pitch ladder: horizon line only
     ADI ball in lower left FOV 1:1 compression
   - Air-mass CDM with velocity vector
   - Gun cross pitch symbol
   - Declutterable scales: airspeed/altitude, no heading
   - Energy cue
   - Weapon cues as needed
2. Version 2:
   - Conventional pitch ladder: 4:1 compression
     ADI ball in lower-left FOV
   - Air-mass CDM with velocity vector
   - Gun cross pitch symbol
   - Declutterable scales: airspeed/altitude, no heading
   - Energy cue
   - Weapon cues as needed

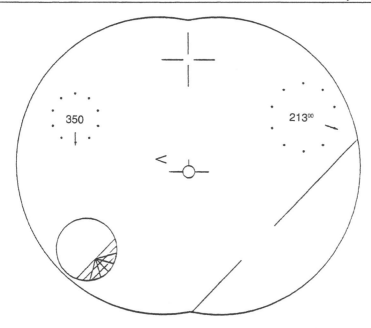

Figure 8.7   Proposed narrow-FOV air-to-air symbology

Narrow-FOV turboprop business aircraft

A second example is a turboprop business aircraft intended to fly to secondary airports. Category III ILS approaches are not required; however, non-precision approaches, including ADF approaches, are to be considered.

Aircraft/mission constraints

The basic HUD goal is to provide a supplementary display and not replace the head-down instruments. The aircraft is constrained by cockpit geometry to a narrow FOV, of the order of 10° TFOV. The aircraft has no inertial navigation system. The HUD should use conventional aircraft gyros, if possible.

Data requirements

Need for conformality Information relative to the ground is less important. Most instrument approaches will be non-precision or ILS

181

Category I approaches. Category II approach capability is desired, but not essential.

There is no overwhelming need for conformality or for ground-referenced flight path information.

Attitude sensors The performance of conventional aircraft gyros is probably insufficient for full-scale 1:1 HUDs.

Spatial disorientation The narrow FOV suggests that conventional pitch ladder spacing would not provide for adequate situational awareness. The symbology will have to minimize any tendency to spatial disorientation.

Flight director A flight director is available on the head-down instruments. The ILS symbology should be equally able to display flight-directed data and raw data.

Symbology choices

Pitch-scale compression Full-time pitch-scale compression should be incorporated. This will allow the pilot to view more lines of the pitch ladder and maintain spatial awareness while maneuvering or during unusual attitude recoveries. The accuracy inherent in conventional aircraft gyros would also prove bothersome if 1:1 scaling were used. A fixed compression is preferred over a stepped or variable compression.

The minimum compression necessary to allow recovery from UAs and avoid unwanted gyro noise to affect flight performance should be used. The preliminary choice is 6:1 compression; however, this must be validated in flight.

Air-mass flight path information The flight path information should be air-mass based, because of the absence of a suitable sensor.

The angular relationship between the waterline and the air-mass CDM will show angle of attack directly. The lateral motion of the FPM relative to the CDM will show sideslip.

Scales Counter-pointers are preferred for airspeed and altitude. A conventional heading scale (4:1 or 6:1) at the top of the FOV is recommended.

If counter-pointers are used, the narrow FOV width may create clutter. Digital airspeed/altitude would minimize clutter. This should be available as a declutter option. Because of the airspeed range of a turboprop, it may not be necessary to show airspeed trends. In this case, a digital-only airspeed would minimize clutter.

ADF bearing Bearing information is required for flying ADF approaches. The quadrant cue should be used.

ILS presentation While it is premature to select an ILS symbology, the need to show both raw data only and raw data plus steering suggests that using cross-pointers for raw data and a tadpole for steering data would be the initial choice.

All switching, setting of course/heading bugs, etc. must use one setting for both the HUD and instrument panel.

Reliability

This HUD will not be the primary flight display but will repeat data shown head-down. HUD failure must be improbable. The likelihood of displaying dangerously misleading attitude information must be extremely improbable.

Operational limits must be set which take into account the time necessary for the pilot to detect a failure, determine if he/she must switch to the head-down instruments, and accomplish the switch to these instruments.

Summary

The final choice for symbology will require flight trials to verify the adequacy of the cues. The recommended symbology is:

- Conventional pitch ladder: 6:1 compression
- Air-mass CDM with velocity vector
- Scales:
    counter-pointer airspeed (declutterable to digits)
    counter-pointer altitude (declutterable to digits)
    conventional heading
- Navigation cues:
    ADF: quadrant bearing cue
    VOR: HSI deviation cue
- Tadpole flight director cue
- ILS cues:
    intercept: HSI cue/side GS scale
    final: cross-pointers

This symbology is very similar to that shown in Figure 8.6.

9 HUD evaluations

History of vote/performance evaluations

The following comments apply to evaluation methods, not to the particular displays or display concepts involved.

Performance-based studies

HUD studies in the 1960s in the United Kingdom were performance-based. Naish measured approach-tracking performance, lateral and glideslope errors (1–3). Among the conclusions was that director symbols and slight pitch-scale compression improved tracking performance. A shortcoming of the objective data was the absence of any measurement of the pilots' ability to maintain situational awareness in flight.

In the 1970s, Klopfstein developed a landing symbology as an aid to flying ILS approaches. This display featured a synthetic runway and used a unique angular presentation of angle of attack (4) (see Figure 2.1). Anecdotal evidence by pilots who evaluated this display reported that precise airspeed control and tracking performance resulted even though no airspeed information was shown on the HUD (5).

In the mid-1980s, the US Air Force studied the effect of HUD symbology on unusual attitude recovery and measured a variety of recovery parameters (6). The conclusions supported the early studies and recommended the use of compressed pitch-scale and a recovery cue. This study also indicated that air-mass data might be beneficial. The conclusions lend weight to the need for an overall objective performance-based test methodology.

In spite of these results, there has been reluctance to use the compressed pitch-scale, the synthetic runway outline, or air-mass data in operational HUDs. This reluctance has not been based on these performance-based evaluations, but, rather, is based on individual pilot opinions.

Opinion-based decisions

The AOA bracket and the orientation of airspeed and altitude scales are two issues where conflicting opinion has created dissimilar formats to display the same information. The use of color coding for head-down displays (HDDs) is another.

At one point, there were two quasi-standards for color HDDs. These were developed by two competing transport airplane manufacturers. They differed in choices of colors for scales, navigation symbols, etc. On review, it appeared that once the decision to have the sky color be blue, the warning color red, and so forth, had been made, only a limited number of choices remained. For example, if the sky is colored blue, the pitch scales can't be blue also. It appeared that each company made a slightly different choice for one or another minor scale and all of the remaining color choices resulted.

At a standardization meeting several years ago it was seriously proposed that the committee take an equal number of choices from each company's list and arrive at an 'acceptable compromise'. The alternative was a vote between the two companies. A performance-based evaluation was not discussed.

Subjective data

It is clear that subjective pilot ratings play a key role in any display evaluation. Historically, pilot ratings have been patterned after one of two forms: the traditional Likert difficulty scale (7) or the Cooper–Harper Pilot Rating (8).

Likert rating scales

Traditional rating scales ask the pilot to rate the difficulty making choices such as 'Very Easy,' 'Easy,' 'Medium,' 'Hard,' or 'Very Hard.' A derivative of this type of scale is the TLX workload rating scale developed by NASA (*9*). Similar ratings have been used in previous HUD simulations (*6*). The chief advantage of a Likert scale is the ease with which a subject can learn it. They can also be useful for 'troubleshooting' an unacceptable display.

One disadvantage of such scales is the reluctance of subjects in general to use extreme values and the reluctance of pilot subjects to use 'difficult' ratings unless the display is quite difficult to fly. As a result, a seven-point scale frequently becomes a three-point scale.

Cooper–Harper pilot ratings

The Cooper–Harper Pilot Rating (CHPR) scale uses a decision tree to allow the pilot to 'walk through' a series of dichotomous alternatives, by answering questions, such as 'Is it [the airplane] controllable?'; 'Is adequate performance attainable with a tolerable workload?'; and 'Is it satisfactory without improvement?' Following these dichotomies, the pilot then makes a choice of three sub-alternatives.

The main advantage of this approach is that the logic tree involved produces consistent results, particularly with trained evaluators. This is evident in the area of aircraft handling qualities ratings.

A second advantage of the logic tree approach is apparent when evaluations are conducted without a control display or control symbology. In this case, we don't compare preferences, but determine if the performance objectives are met and what degree of pilot workload is required to meet them.

The major difficulty is the time that a novice evaluator must spend learning the logic tree. When using CHPRs with untrained evaluators, quite often a copy of the logic diagram is provided as an in-flight aid. Scales based on Cooper–Harper-type logic trees have been used during LANTIRN evaluations (*10*). A similar scale, the Bedford workload scale was used in the UK for HUD evaluations.[1] Another similar scale was developed by Haworth and Newman (*11*).

It is imperative that a rating be taken in the context of a specific flight task flown by a typical operational pilot. Cooper and Harper emphasized this requirement, but it applies to all aircraft control–display evaluations as well. When using a task-oriented evaluation, the evaluator must use consistent performance standards. These should be related to operational standards, but must be clearly stated as shown in Table 9.1.

[1] J. Hall (Royal Aircraft Establishment, Bedford, England), personal communication, February 1990

Table 9.1   Evaluation task performance standards

Desired performance standards	Adequate performance standards
Dynamic maneuvers	
2 s to acquire new attitude.	4 s to acquire new attitude.
5° heading and roll error at key points during maneuver.	10° heading and roll error at key points.
3° heading error on recovery.	5° heading error.
100 ft altitude loss.	200 ft altitude loss. No PIO.
Unusual attitude recoveries	
1.4 s to initial correct control input. Initial control input in accordance with published instrument standards (*12*). No control reversals. No overshoots on recovery to wings-level.	1.8 s to initial correct control input. Initial control input in accordance with published instrument standards (*12*). One control reversal. Single overshoot on recovery to wings-level.
Instrument approach	
Loc/GS error ½ dot,	Loc/GS error 1 dot,
airspeed error 2 knots	airspeed error 5 knots.
for 50% of task.	for entire task.
No overshoots on intercept.	Single overshoot on intercept.
Go around at DH +20/–0 ft.	Go around at DH +40/–0 ft.

Display evaluation

There are two aspects of flight displays that must be considered: can the pilot determine the value of a specific parameter, such as airspeed? and can the display be used to control that variable? These two questions must be answered in the context of a specific task scenario. Because of the widespread acceptance of the CHPR scale in the flight test community, two logic trees were constructed to rate the readability and the controllability of displays, as shown in Figures 9.1 and 9.2. These scales were adapted from reference (*11*).

The readability rating can also be applied to the ease of overall maintenance of situational awareness or attitude awareness.

These display ratings follow the original Cooper–Harper decision tree closely. The difference between the display flyability rating and a handling-qualities CHPR is the requirement that the evaluation pilot consider aircraft control *using the display for information*. This is essentially a CHPR of the airplane-handling qualities in series with the display control laws. This rating for a given symbology will be expected to vary from aircraft to aircraft.

Additional questionnaires

In addition to the basic rating cards, questions should be asked

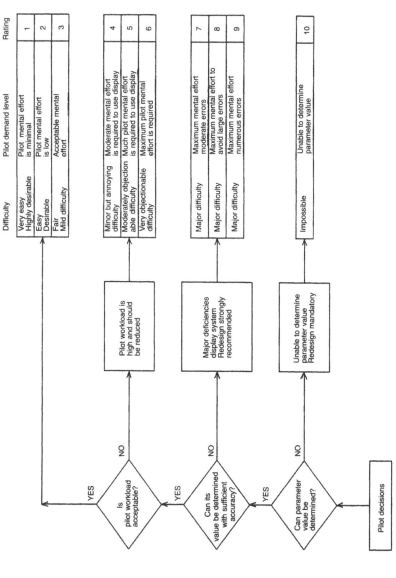

Figure 9.1   Display rating decision tree, I: ease of reading data (*11*)

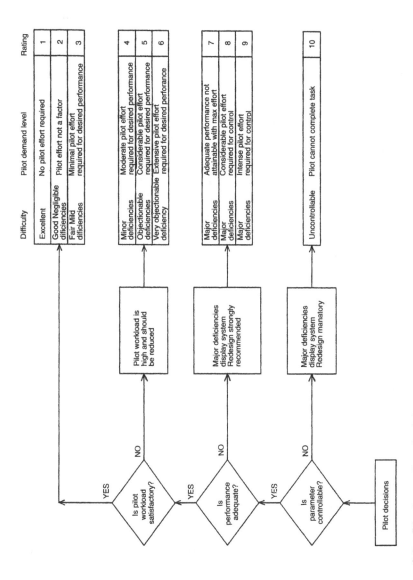

Figure 9.2 Display rating decision tree, II: ease of control (11)

189

addressed to specific test issues, such as perceived problems with a particular display. These can be asked at the same time the rating card is completed (following each data run) or during a debriefing session. The final debriefing questionnaire should also ask for comparisons between displays.

Evaluation flight tasks

Aircraft have many common mission segments: takeoff, climb, cruise, descent, terminal area maneuvering, approach to land, hover, and landing. For the most part, the problems that affect a particular type of aircraft during these common mission segments are the same problems that affect other aircraft. Hoerner (*13*) said that we have most of our problems in the last 15 miles of the flight.

All mission tasks should be further divided to separate visual flight from instrument flight. From a display point of view, each has its particular set of problems.

When evaluating digital flight controls, the control system may be found to be acceptable during routine mission tasks, but highly unacceptable during aggressive tracking tasks. This is sometimes described as a handling qualities 'cliff.' As the pilot tracks more and more aggressively, the handling qualities deteriorate quite suddenly and sharply, i.e. falls off a cliff (*14*). This is often pronounced during such demanding tasks as the landing flare or aerial refueling.

In similar fashion, digital display dynamics can result in similar cliffs when evaluated during aggressive tracking tasks. For example, a velocity vector symbol may be well behaved until the pilot increases his gain to place it on a particular spot on the runway. For this reason, at least some of the experimental tasks should require aggressive tracking on the part of the subject pilots.

Evaluation task requirements

The tasks must be appropriate to the aircraft missions. Regardless of the mission, basic instrument and visual tasks must be flown, even if the display is intended for mission-specific tasks only. One task that is normally required for all aircraft types is an unusual-attitude recovery task.

The tasks must include aggressive pilot tracking to test the so-called cliff. Low-level terrain-following, A/G tracking, landing flare, and unusual-attitude recovery are examples of tasks requiring aggressive pilot inputs. Both instrument and visual tasks should be flown.

190

It is also essential that dynamic maneuvering against real-world backgrounds be flown, particularly when evaluating non-conformal pitch-scaling or the effect of clutter. These flights against real-world background should be flown both day and night.

It is also important to have some performance basis with which to compare different displays. Tracking accuracy is often used as a measure. Unusual attitude recovery uses reaction time to the first correct control input and the number of control reversals during the recovery.

Evaluation tasks

The following tasks have been used in a variety of studies and are recommended as candidate evaluation tasks.

It is also important to develop tasks that are representative of the mission lengths. Short evaluation sorties or simulator sessions may not uncover problems with eye fatigue or high workload.

Unusual attitude recovery   The task involves a recovery from an unusual attitude using HUD symbology only. The airplane should be placed in an unusual attitude and the subject pilot directed to recover to a predetermined heading and altitude.

The head-down instruments should be covered during this task and view of the real-world cues blocked by the blue/amber system or other vision-restriction device. During the entry into the unusual attitude, the HUD should be blanked.

Additional unusual attitudes should be introduced during other tasks. For example, during a simulated air-to-air tracking task, all external visual cues can be removed as if the target airplane flew into a cloud. The pilot would have to recognize the situation and recover.

It is important that the UAs be evaluated with all symbology options and in all HUD modes, not just in a 'basic mode.' The maximum possible level of clutter should be evaluated during UA recovery.

Dynamic maneuvering   The task involves aggressive instrument flight using HUD symbology only. The pilot will be asked to fly a series of maneuvers appropriate to the airplane. Vertical S maneuvers modified to include abrupt changes of pitch and bank are suitable for this task. Instrument acrobatics (steep turns, barrel rolls, cloverleafs, etc.) have also been used. At intervals, the subject pilot can be distracted with a task requiring head-down viewing, such as reading an authentication table arranged by rows and columns.[1]

Aimpoint tracking   Air-to-ground weapons delivery is a highly suitable experimental task for HUDs. It should require aggressive tracking on the part of the subject pilot. For transports, a related task would be a visual approach to landing requiring the pilot to maintain a specific aimpoint with the flight path marker.

This task should help identify any problems associated with a non-conformal display.

Instrument approach   The task involves an approach to a landing or to a missed approach. Approximately half of the approaches will be to a landing and half to a missed approach. Both precision and non-precision approaches should be flown.

This task should include representative terminal maneuvering, not just the final approach phase. Penetration approaches (where indicated) and complex terminal (SID/STAR) profiles should also be flown. Difficulties with altitude maintenance with vertical tapes did not appear until terminal maneuvering was added to the instrument approach tasks in one evaluation (*15*).

Visual approach   The task involves a visual approach to a landing. Some approaches should be flown at night. Both straight-in and circling approaches should be flown.

System failures   During any of the tasks, it is important to consider the effect of system or sensor failures. ILS approach should induce single-axis failures (such as glideslope failure) and determine if the pilot can recognize this event and maintain suitable performance following the failure.

Choice of pilots

One fundamental question is: should test pilots or operational pilots be used as evaluators?

Arguments favoring operational pilots include having pilots with recent mission experience. It is also possible to obtain a range of experience levels from recent pilot-training graduates to experienced pilots.

One problem with using operational pilots is that each pilot is often overtrained on a particular display and may be predisposed to that display – F-16 pilots prefer F-16 symbology, F-18 pilots prefer F-18 symbology, etc. Ideally, one should use operational pilots with no symbology background. Unfortunately, this is not possible. To avoid this problem, the experimenter must ensure that no particular symbology is over-represented and that the subjective data is used with care.

Another problem is the need to train operational pilots, both in how to fly with non-standard displays or techniques and in how to use rating scales. It is imperative that adequate familiarization and instructions be provided. This is most apparent with scales similar to the CHPR. This training can amount to two or three practice sorties per pilot compared with one for a trained evaluator. This problem area cannot be overstated and is one of the most severe restrictions on using line pilots.

Arguments favoring test pilots include having trained evaluators. Properly trained test pilots are used to rating airplane handling and should be familiar with the rating scales, such as the Cooper–Harper type of walk-through ratings. Test pilots are also skilled at communicating with engineers and can provide insight into display or control law problems.

Test pilots are experienced pilots, perhaps not with recent mission experience. They usually have a broad range of experience in different airplanes and with different displays. This allows them to be able to adapt their individual control strategies to the display, such as using the pitch symbol versus velocity vector symbol for aircraft control.

The test pilot must, of course, remain objective. One must be particularly careful if a test pilot has had a major role in designing the symbology. In this case, it would be well for the test pilot to disqualify himself from the final approval portion of the tests.

The need to conduct practice sorties for untrained evaluators can quickly use up the available sorties in a program. For example, if 24 sorties are available, using two test pilots will allow for 22 data sorties. If six operational pilots are used instead, 12–18 practice sorties may be required allowing only 6–12 data flights.

If the display is novel or controversial, it may be necessary to use a group of pilots of varying experience as a final check, although this will not normally be necessary.

Summary

Display evaluation techniques have not kept pace with the rapid evolution of aircraft displays. Display evaluation in the past has been, to a large extent, based on subjective opinion and not on the actual aircraft/pilot performance. Pilot opinion, while valuable, must be tempered with performance measurement.

Modern digital displays interact strongly with aircraft dynamics and cannot be easily separated from the aircraft-handling qualities. Many of the issues in testing fly-by-wire flight control systems are similar to flight display evaluation issues.

Display evaluation is not a simple task. It requires as much attention as any other flight critical system. Some of the problems high-performance aircraft have exhibited in terms of lack of situational awareness or spatial disorientation have had their origins in poor display design and in the following poor display testing.

References

(1)   Naish, J. M. *System for Presenting Steering Information During Visual Flight. Part I. The Position of the Presented Information* (Bedford, England: Royal Aeronautical Establishment, 1961), RAE TN-IAP-1132

(2)   Naish, J. M. *System for Presenting Steering Information During Visual Flight. Part II. The Form of the Presented Information* (Bedford, England: Royal Aeronautical Establishment, 1962), RAE TN-IAP-1138

(3)   Naish, J. M. *System for Presenting Steering Information During Visual Flight. Part III. The Influence of Errors and Limitations* (Bedford, England: Royal Aeronautical Establishment, 1964), RAE TN-64026

(4)   Klopfstein, G. *Rational Study of Aircraft Piloting* (Paris: Thomson-CSF, ca. 1966); reprint of 1966 article in *Intrados*

(5)   Foxworth, T. G. *A New Concept of Flying; Flying the TC-121 All-Weather Head-Up Display* (Egham, England: International Federation of Air Line Pilots Associations, 1973)

(6)   Newman, R. L. *Improvement of Head-Up Display Standards. II. Evaluation of Head-Up Displays to Enhance Unusual Attitude Recovery* (Wright-Patterson AFB, Ohio: Air Force Wright Aeronautical Laboratory, 1987), AFWAL TR-87-3055. Vol. II

(7)   Murphy, G. and Likert, R. *Public Opinion and the Individual* (New York: Harper, 1938)

(8)   Cooper, G. E. and Harper, R. P. *The Use of Pilot Rating in the Evaluation of Aircraft Handling Qualities* (Moffett Field, California: National Aeronautics and Space Administration, 1969), NASA TN-D-5153

(9)   *NASA Task Load Index (TLX), Version 1.0* (Moffett Field, California: National Aeronautics and Space Administration, ca. 1988)

(10)   Papa, R. M. and Stoliker, J. R. 'Pilot workload assessment – a flight test approach', in *The Man–Machine Interface in Tactical Aircraft Design and Combat Automation* (Paris: Advisory Group for Aeronautical Research and Development, 1987), AGARD CP-425, paper 8

(11)   Haworth, L. A. and Newman, R. L. *Test Techniques for Evaluating Flight Displays* (Moffett Field, California: Army Aeroflightdynamics Directorate, 1992), USAAVSCOM TR-92-A-006; NASA TM-103947

(12)   *Instrument Flying* (Randolph AFB, Texas: Air Force Instrument Flight Center, ca. 1986), AFM-51-37

(13)   Hoerner, F. C., 'HUD military aspects', in *Proceedings of the Flight Operations Symposium, Vancouver* (Redmond, Washington: Sundstrand Data Control, 1979), Vol. II, pp. 53–58, 117–142

(14)   Berthe, C. *et al.* 'Fly-by-wire design considerations', paper presented at *20th Annual European Symposium SETP, Linköping* (Linköping, Sweden, Society of Experimental Test Pilots, 1988)

(15)   Newman, R. L. *Symbology Flight Test Report FVI Model FV-2000 Head-Up Display* (San Marcos, Texas: Crew Systems, 1991), TR-91-10A

10　HUD training

Historical HUD training

HUD training has historically been left to the pilot to learn on his own (*1*). Since HUDs were not considered 'flight instruments', no need was seen to develop training syllabi or procedures, other than for mission-specific tasks (such as weapons delivery). As civil operators began to operate HUD-equipped airplanes, more attention was paid to developing HUD-specific training. However, as with military operators, this training was very task specific (such as monitoring a Category III instrument approach).

With this background in mind, we will consider two areas of HUD-involved training: training pilots to fly with a HUD and using HUDs to teach pilots to fly.

Training pilots to fly with a HUD

Instrument pilot training

Early surveys of military HUD pilots (*1*) reported a lack of training in HUD-specific instrument procedures. Pilots did not seem to be completely aware of what the relationship was between the flight path angle and the traditional airspeed, pitch, and vertical speed.

Suggestions that pilots be taught HUD techniques are generally rejected on the grounds that HUD techniques are self-evident and that pilots should learn to fly 'real instruments' first. These arguments are not true, since the techniques of HUD instrument flight (vector instrument flight) are different from conventional instrument flight (attitude instrument flight).

Under some conditions, attitude instrument flight techniques which appear to work under most circumstances for vector instrument flight can backfire. Descent with a high angle of attack is an example of such a condition. During normal flight, pulling on the stick will 'raise' the velocity vector. During a high angle of attack descent, however, this same control input can increase the descent rate and lead to a loss of control.

The increase in spatial disorientation accidents during the 1980s (2) may be a result of a lack of HUD-specific instrument training.

Confusion between vector instruments and attitude instruments apparently caused the pilot of an RAF Jaguar to become confused about the performance of his airplane during a low level flight (3). This apparently led to a loss of awareness of the aircraft trajectory. The resulting accident should not be classed as a 'loss of situational awareness,' since the pilot was quite aware of his proximity to the ground – he simply mistook where the airplane was pointing (attitude flight) from where it was going (vector flight).

These arguments are also refuted by early reviews of HUD training (1) which indicated that over 100 hours were required for the pilots to teach themselves HUD techniques. During trials with the MARS HUD in a C-130 (4), while initial performance with the HUD was better than without, pilot performance was still improving at the 75 h point, indicating that the pilot was still learning how to use the HUD.

The use of HUD-specific instrument flight training would seem to be a natural place to save flight hours which could be better spent in other areas of training.

The argument that pilots should learn to fly 'real instruments' first brings to mind the arguments made when attitude gyros replaced rate gyros (and attitude instrument techniques replaced rate instrument techniques). The author's initial instrument training was clouded by this issue as the turn-and-bank was emphasized over the attitude indicator (i.e. learn to fly 'real instruments' first). This initial instrument training had a negative transfer when the transition to jet aircraft was made.

Based on a review of HUD problems, spatial disorientation incidents, current military training syllabi, HUD research, and personal HUD experience, a sample course syllabus outline (5) was prepared for pilots about to be assigned to HUD-equipped aircraft. In general, the topics include the following items:

- Outline of HUD information
  - Differences between attitude and vector flight
  - Relationship between AOA, aircraft pitch, and flight path angle
  - Difference between air mass and inertial data
- Spatial disorientation
  - Physiology review
  - Head motion
  - Visual accommodation (accommodation 'traps')
  - View of external cues through HUD
- Recognition of aircraft attitude
  - From head-down instruments
  - From head-up display
  - AOA, aircraft pitch, and flight path angle
- Recovery from unusual attitudes
  - Recognition
  - Control strategies
- Channelization of attention
  - Integration of head-up and head-down data

Mission-specific training

Early reviews of HUD training (*1*) indicated that over 100h of experience were required for the pilots to teach themselves. Generally, mission tasks (weapons delivery, Category III instrument approaches, etc.) are taught in the same fashion as pre-HUD tasks by demonstration and repeated practice.

In 1980, a review of French airline HUD training (*6*) was conducted. At the time, Air Inter used an air-mass HUD. Their training included demonstration scenarios designed to convey the concept of air-mass velocity vector to the trainee. For example, the initial demonstration was a visual approach with no wind; the second was an approach with a 90 knot headwind. This clearly demonstrates the effect of wind in a fashion the pilot under instruction will not soon forget. This imaginative use of simulator capability hasn't been used elsewhere.

The HUD itself could be used for training. It is possible to generate a synthetic ground analog with a target located at a safe altitude. Such a simulated target range would allow pilots to practice weapons delivery at a safe altitude and at a safe geographical location. A synthetic aerial adversary could also be projected onto the HUD and used for training.

This type of embedded tasking has been used during recent HUD evaluations; the HUD computer was used to simulate an airborne target (7) or an ILS-in-the-sky (8). Such techniques could be used for mission training.

Training is not solely a military issue; the proposed use of synthetic vision/enhanced vision HUDs will certainly require additional training over and beyond 'conventional HUD' training. With the levels of training activity in both military and airline operations, even a small reduction in training hours can produce major savings.

When to introduce HUD

When should the HUD be introduced to the pilot – early in his basic pilot training or later as part of the aircraft checkout? Current practice is to introduce the HUD during or subsequent to aircraft checkout.

Originally, civil operators felt that simultaneous introduction of a new airplane and a new concept of flying (the HUD) was too much at once. Use of the HUD on the Mercure was delayed for several months after the pilot became qualified on the airplane (6). This approach means that pilots who are already HUD-qualified on another airplane will not be able to use this background from the start or will require a different checkout syllabus. Present day training (9), on the other hand, integrates the HUD into the initial aircraft checkout.

The second approach would introduce the HUD earlier. A dedicated HUD course would outline the special techniques of HUD instrument flying. This could be accomplished in a trainer or in a simulator and be incorporated into fighter lead-in training.

A strong case can be made to introduce military student pilots to the HUD as soon as possible – in primary or basic training, since most will only be flying HUD- and electronic-display-equipped airplanes throughout their careers. As will be discussed below, there are other advantages to this approach.

Using a HUD to train pilots to fly

Recent events indicate that the use of HUDs could enhance training in several areas. As commercial airlines begin to incorporate head-up displays, several hitherto unsuspected benefits have emerged. One of these benefits is a reduced level of training required to checkout in a new aircraft type.

During aircraft checkout

Alaska Airlines is the only US air carrier operating head-up displays. They report a fairly significant saving in hours required during initial aircraft checkout (9). Pilots new to the aircraft are encouraged to use the HUD from the beginning, although proficiency checks are conducted with the HUD off (except for HUD-specific procedures). Alaska pilots have been approved to fly to lowest minima sooner with HUD-equipped aircraft than with non-HUD-equipped aircraft.

There are two reasons for this improvement in training. The biggest task for a pilot making a transition to a new airplane is the need to develop his sight picture (i.e. what does the view from the cockpit look like during approach, flare, and landing) and how does the airplane respond to control inputs.

The HUD certainly aids in developing the sight picture. A properly implemented flight path vector assists the pilot in determining how the airplane responds to his control inputs. It is not surprising that the HUD would help in this transition; what may be surprising to some is that the experience is valid even after the HUD is removed.

What is not known is exactly how much the saving is; whether or not it can be improved by modifying the checkout syllabus; or how long the HUD helps. It does appear that HUD learning continues for a considerable period, even though pilot proficiency is high (4).

During primary pilot training

If the observations concerning checkout benefits incurred by using a HUD are valid, they should also apply to primary pilot training. This would use the HUD as a training tool to teach pilots how to fly. As mentioned earlier, the HUD can help a student pilot learn the sight picture needed to fly an airplane visually. This applies to primary flight training as well as airplane model checkout.

The HUD can also provide immediate feedback to the fledgling pilot on the responses of the airplane to his control inputs. A traditional HUD is a valuable training aid for no other reasons than these. Based on the Alaska Airlines experience (9), we should expect primary training with a HUD to produce better pilots faster.

The argument against the use of HUDs in primary training is that it will create 'HUD cripples' – pilots who are helpless without a functioning HUD. This is rebutted by an informal Navy study (10), which attempted to document the HUD cripple argument. In this study, A-7 pilots were divided into HUD experienced A-7E pilots and those with no HUD-experience (A-7A and B). Their performance was measured in a simulated night carrier landing task with no HUD. The pilots with HUD experience performed better with no HUD.

In addition, the HUD can be used as a training aid to demonstrate concepts that are difficult to present. Angle of attack (AOA) is such a concept. An air-mass HUD can give a student pilot a clear picture of AOA by showing him the angular difference between where the airplane is pointing and the vector through the air. Klopfstein (*11*) first pointed this out. Most pilots are vaguely aware of the term angle of attack, but fail to appreciate it fully until it is shown on the HUD.

The initial lesson should teach the relationship between aircraft pitch, AOA, and flight path. The initial symbology should consist only of a horizon line, a pitch marker, and the air-mass flight path marker. The student should be taught how to maneuver the aircraft with only these cues (and an occasional check of altitude).

Next, airspeed should be presented and its relation to AOA demonstrated. Finally, the effect of power/thrust should be introduced.

At the conclusion of this lesson, the student pilot should have a clear, *workable* understanding of the relationship between pitch, AOA, flight path, airspeed, and power. This understanding will be much clearer than today's initial 'pitch and power' approach. The student can *see* what's happening.

Finally, the HUD symbology should be removed – one at a time – to teach the student how to infer data not presented, such as estimating AOA from airspeed and flight path from pitch and airspeed.

The initial portions of the syllabus should emphasize air-mass flight data. In addition to pitch, AOA, etc., the air-mass symbology can show the effect of sideslip. This could be particularly important during initial multi-engine training.

Later lessons can introduce inertial flight path to teach the student to visualize and predict where the airplane is going. This would be useful during landing practice.

While the benefit seems clear in terms of cost and time savings, there have been no formal studies to quantify the benefit, nor have any HUD-specific curricula been developed.

Use by operators of non-HUD-equipped aircraft

If the observations concerning checkout benefits incurred by using a HUD are valid, there may be benefits to operators of non-HUD-equipped aircraft. If, for example, one out of eight scheduled sorties could be dropped from a checkout syllabus by the use of a properly designed HUD, an operator of a non-HUD aircraft might wish to install a HUD in one aircraft to be used solely for checkout. The savings of 12% could offset the cost of the single installation.

The savings might be even greater if simulators are used for a large portion of the training. In this case, a certified HUD is not needed. In fact, no HUD need be installed – only the HUD symbology included in the computer-generated visual scene.

Training vehicle

Should HUD training be based on classroom training, should it use simulators, or should it be conducted in flight? In general, operators would like to accomplish all of the training in a classroom with no other assets required. In reality, some of the training must be accomplished in a training device, a simulator, or in flight. An assessment must be made of the optimum allocation of resources.

Certainly, a portion of the training in the differences between attitude instrument flight and HUD (or vector) instrument flight requires 'hands on' practice by the pilots. The question is simply how much time and how much can be accomplished in a simulator or other training device. Based on French airline experience (6), the simulator can be very helpful in explaining the differences between air mass and inertial velocity vectors.

Initial HUD exposure should be confined to air-mass data (velocity vector). This is based on several considerations. First, the airplane's performance is a function of airspeed and motion through the air. Using air mass data during training would allow this to be demonstrated directly to the student. Second, many inertial platforms have characteristics that are undesirable for student air work – sluggish responses or restrictions on aircraft attitudes or attitude rates. If an exposure to inertial data is required as part of the training, it should be deferred and be presented after the student is well versed in basic air-mass HUD flying.

A HUD surrogate has several advantages for training instrument procedures. This would normally be a trainer equipped with a HUD that has the navigation/approach modes identical to the operational airplane and has been recommended in a previous HUD study (2).

The HUD trainer should be equipped with a full suite of head-up and head-down CRT displays and should be able to emulate the various symbologies in the fleet. The mission of this airplane should be to

* provide basic introduction to HUD instrument flying;

- provide recurrent HUD instrument checks; and
- develop adequate HUD instrument procedures.

It should also include some form of computer navigation system to acquaint the student pilot with the data entry and monitoring requirements of modern inertial navigational systems and their computers.

A great deal of the problem inherent in modern military airplanes is the high workload of the weapon systems themselves. Often these require considerable effort in inputting data to the on-board computer and in monitoring the systems data. The skills needed to accomplish these tasks are not the same skills emphasized in flying training.

Many of the tasks required are weapon-system-specific. Nevertheless, there is a common thread of the problems. There is a need to learn how to prioritize attention and workload capacity to accomplish the mission.

This training could be accomplished using a generic weapon system computer – to teach the fledgling pilot how to allocate his cognitive resources to his tasks and maintain his awareness. This would be similar in scope to fighter lead-in training, in which student pilots fly generic mission profiles and use generic tactics in T-38s.

The HUD system needs to be optimized for the training mission and should not be just another HUD installation. It would be a mistake to simply adopt a service standard HUD for a trainer.

The HUD controls must be accessible to the instructor pilot, who must also have a means to view the HUD symbology and the real-world cues (perhaps on a television monitor). The symbol generator for the HUD trainer should have a library of all HUD symbologies for the entire fleet of the operator. This will allow the emulation of all HUDs in the service inventory and is essential for recurrent instrument training. A HUD videocamera and video-recording is essential for post-flight debriefing.

It must be emphasized that simply repeating the various HUD symbologies does not make a HUD suitable for training. It is essential that the HUD be able to show each individual symbol to the student one at a time or as desired by the training syllabus. For example, the initial training lesson may well be to show the horizon line and the pitch symbol alone. This and similar modes must be available to support the instructional syllabus.

The primary data source should be air-mass data. The flight path can be derived from accurate AOA and pitch sensors. It is not necessary (and may not be desirable) for this type of airplane to have an inertial navigational platform. The gyro platform will have to be superior to typical trainer aircraft gyros. If advanced navigational systems training is required (simulating an inertial system), then an area navigation system such as Global Positioning System could be used. This would allow training in navigation system data entry and in the associated workload management, similar to the cockpit resource management training of the airlines.

The use of embedded training (see 'Mission-specific training' above) is also strongly recommended for a HUD trainer. At the least, the ability to generate synthetic ILS approaches, synthetic ground targets, or aerial adversaries should be considered.

Unresolved HUD training issues

There are a number of HUD flight training issues remaining for investigation. Some of these issues merely require flight validation of previous simulation results while others involve more complete research efforts.

HUD training

Of most pressing concern is the requirement for training pilots during the initial exposure to head-up displays. This was originally cited as a problem area in the late 1970s (*1*). The training level has improved, primarily as commercial airlines begin to incorporate HUDs in their fleets. There are those who feel that the current airline training amounts to overkill. The current training is almost entirely aimed at the Category III ILS approach procedures.

However, the planned introduction of enhanced vision/synthetic vision systems will present new training needs. In addition, the development of HUDs for smaller airplanes will create additional training requirements:

- Initial HUD training
    - Should basic HUD training be conducted separately from aircraft checkout?
    - If separate, should HUD training precede or follow aircraft checkout?
    - Should basic HUD training be integrated with aircraft checkout?
    - If integrated, what is the best means to conduct integrated HUD/aircraft training?

- Recurrent HUD training
  - What is the best means to conduct integrated HUD/aircraft training?
- Separate HUD training
  - How is basic HUD training best accomplished?
  - As a basic HUD instrument course?
  - Integrated with primary instrument training?
  - Accomplished following initial operating experience?

The results of these questions may differ depending on the operator. Airlines may decide on a different approach than a military organization.

HUD training benefit

Recent data suggests that the HUD can be beneficial as a training tool. The incorporation of a non-optimized HUD may have cost/time savings of up to 30% when compared with training without a HUD. Development of a HUD optimized for the training role may result in even greater savings.

The potential benefit should be documented based on studies of present HUD training being conducted and later with a strawman curriculum.

Training tools

If a HUD curriculum is to be developed (regardless of when), should the HUD be a 'standard' HUD or should it have features which would enhance its use in the training syllabus? The present T-38 Flight Instrumentation Standardization Program HUD (*12*) has several options for the instructor, including the possibility of training-specific HUD modes and symbologies.

Should the instructor have his own combiner, or will a repeater be sufficient? It is worth observing that NASA's Shuttle Training Aircraft uses a different model HUD for the instructor (*13*).

Summary

The HUD appears to shorten training time for aircraft checkout. This is based on anecdotal evidence, but appears to be a valid statement. The amount of savings has been estimated between 10 and 30%.

The benefit of HUD experience lasts after the HUD is no longer available.

The HUD has potential benefit during primary pilot training – even if the pilot will not fly HUD-equipped aircraft in operational use. The benefit of a HUD during primary training for pilots who will use the HUD during their careers is greater.

HUD training to date has not been optimized. There are considerable savings possible for mission-related training.

References

(1)   Newman, R. L. *Operational Problems Associated with Head-Up Displays During Instrument Flight* (Wright-Patterson AFB, Ohio: Air Force Aeromedical Research Laboratory, 1980), AFAMRL TR-80-116

(2)   Newman, R. L. *Improvement of Head-Up Display Standards. III. Evaluation of Head-Up Display Safety* (Wright-Patterson AFB, Ohio: Air Force Wright Aeronautical Laboratory, 1987), AFWAL TR-87-3055, Vol. III

(3)   'Jaguar hit trees', *Flight International*, 19 July 1986

(4)   *Head-Up Display Evaluation* (Hickam AFB, Hawaii: 6594th Test Group, 1976), LTR-76-8

(5)   Newman, R. L. *Head-Up Display Training Syllabus Outline* (Yellow Springs, Ohio: Crew Systems, 1987), TR-87-21

(6)   *Programme Simulateur – Approche Automatique Mode Land* (Paris: Air Inter, 1979)

(7)   Newman, R. L. and Bailey, R. E. *Improvement of Head-Up Display Standards. IV. Head-Up Display Dynamics Flight Tests* (Wright-Patterson AFB, Ohio: Air Force Wright Aeronautical Laboratory, 1987), AFWAL TR-87-3055, Vol. IV

(8)   Gawron, V. J. *et al.* 'Comparison of a head-up display evaluation in ground and flight simulation', Presentation at *36th Annual Meeting of the Human Factors Society, Atlanta* (Santa Monica, California: Human Factors Society, 1992)

(9)   Johnson, T. and Schwab, D. *Alaska Airlines HUD Experience*, (Seattle, Washington: Alaska Airlines, 1992), unpublished briefing to AIAA Aircraft Operations Technical Committee

(10)   *ALPA Head-Up Display Newsletter,* January 1979, 4–5

(11)   Klopfstein, G. *Rational Study of Aircraft Piloting* (Paris: Thomson-CSF, ca. 1966); reprint of 1966 article in *Intrados*

(12)   *T-38 Head-Up Display (HUD) Avionics System Manual* (Wright-Patterson AFB, Ohio: 4950 Test Wing, 1991)

(13)   Ivins, M. 'Space Shuttle applications', in *Proceedings of the Flight Operations Symposium, Vancouver* (Redmond, Washington: Sundstrand Data Control, 1979), Vol. II, pp. 104–117; Vol. IIA, section 6

11 Summary

There are a number of HUD issues remaining for investigation. Some of these issues merely require flight validation of previous simulation results while others involve more complete research efforts.

Table 11.1 summarizes outstanding issues with an estimate of both the priority (i.e. the need for solution) and the complexity of the issue. Table 11.1 also indicates whether the issue requires ground simulation or flight studies for its resolution, or is appropriate for analysis.

It is worth noting that many of these issues are the same issues raised in previous HUD studies for both civil and military HUDs (*1, 2*). This points up the need to take these issues and develop programs to address them in a logical and systematic fashion. Otherwise, ten years hence, we will still be citing the same issues as unresolved.

Some issues apply to all HUDs while others are germane to specific aircraft types (fighters or transports) only.

Flight symbology

There are a number of flight symbology issues which require further study. These include the following prioritized issues.

Table 11.1   HUD issues

Area	Issue	Priority F[a]	T[b]	Complexity	Method[c]		
Flight	Pitch-scale compression	H	L	Medium		IF	
symbology	Primary flight symbol	H	H	High	GS	IF	
issues	Control law issues	H	M	High	GS	IF	AN
	Pitch ladder reference	M	H	Medium	GS	IF	
	Pitch ladder precession	L	–	High		IF	
	Other data	L	L	Low	GS		
Navigation	Flight director symbols	H	H	Medium	GS	IF	
issues	ILS approach symbols	H	H	Medium	GS	IF	
	Course interception	M	H	Low	GS	IF	
	En-route navigation	M	M	Medium	GS	IF	
	Bearing data	M	M	Medium	GS	IF	
	Monitoring vs flying	–	H	Medium	GS	IF	
	Ground roll guidance	L	M	High	GS	IF	
Raster issues	Raster brightness	H	H	Low	GS	IF	
	Raster registration	H	H	Medium	GS	IF	
	Limited sensor range	H	H	Medium	GS		
	Raster update rate	H	H	Medium	GS	IF	
	Registration of multiple images	L	H	High	GS	IF	
	Raster clutter	H	H	High	GS	IF	
	Sensor/raster FOV	M	H	High	GS	IF	
Data integrity	Warning criteria	H	H	High	GS	IF	
issues	Warning methods	H	H	Low	GS		
	Integration with HDD	H	H	High	GS		AN
	Dual display consequences	–	L	Low	GS		AN
Training issues	Training benefit	H	H	Medium	GS	IF	
	Training tools	H	H	Medium	GS	IF	
Operations	Visual accommodation	M	M	High		IF	
issues	HUD-specific procedures	H	H	High	GS	IF	
	Role of non-flying pilot	–	M	Low	GS		
Research	Flight research vehicle	H	H	High		IF	
issues	Desktop prototyping	M	M	High	GS		AN
	Configuration control	H	H	High	GS	IF	AN

Notes: [a] F – fighters   } Priority: L/M/H – Low/Medium/High
[b] T – transports
[c] IF – flight validation, GS – ground simulation, AN – analysis

Pitch scale compression

A major problem with HUDs during aggressive maneuvering or UAs is the full-scale motion combined with the small FOV. This makes the symbols rush across the FOV and makes interpretation and use of the symbology quite difficult.

The obvious solution is to compress the pitch scaling to make more of the pitch ladder visible in the FOV and slow down the movement. A side-effect of this change is the inability to display conformal symbology.

Lack of conformality   The major question concerning compressed pitch scales is 'Does the lack of conformality with the real world interfere with flight or mission tasks other than during full IMC?' Any such problem will be more pronounced during ground referenced maneuvers, such as landing approaches, low level navigation, and A/G weapons delivery.

Amount of compression   The amount of compression suitable for various tasks should be determined. Early work in the UK (*3*) recommended pitch scale compressions between $1^1/_2$:1 and 4:1. More recent simulations found that UA recovery was enhanced with a 6:1 compression, although the pilots voiced strong negative opinions over this much compression (*4*). A 2:1 compression provided almost as much benefit and the pilots' opinion was favorable.

It appears that the best pitch scale compression for spatial awareness is somewhere between 2:1 and 4:1.

Changes in compression   Does a change in compression help or hinder the pilot?

A step compression change may alert the pilot to an otherwise unnoticed UA. The subject pilots' comments were favorable to the concept of switched compressions (*4*). The F-16 HUD uses such a step change, with no adverse pilot comments reported.[1]

In studies using variable pitch compression (*5*), the subjects seem to have not been aware that the compression was changing.

The triggering conditions for switched compression or the control laws for variable compression will need to be evaluated, although any such study should be deferred until the suitability of changing compression is established.

---

[1]In fact, most pilots are not aware of the change (T. Lutz, personal communication, 1991).

209

Previous ground-simulation studies have taken these issues as far as is possible; final resolution requires in-flight validation. The priority studies should deal with the 1:1 versus full-time 2:1 compression and with the effect of switched versus variable gains. Any study of variable gains must have switched gains and full-time compression available as controls.

Subsequent studies should evaluate the effect of other pitch compressions (such as 3:1 or 4:1). If variable or switch compression appears favorable, then a third study might be necessary to examine the gain scheduling or switching points.

The tasks should include ground reference tasks, such as landing approach and A/G tracking, in addition to up-and-away tasks such as unusual attitude recoveries.

While these issues are of paramount importance to fighter aircraft, they will be a factor in any aircraft during an unusual attitude incident. Since transports can enter UAs for a variety of reasons, these issues should be addressed for transport aircraft as well as fighters. In fact, an argument can be made that the relative rarity of UA encounters in transports makes these issues of greater, not lesser importance. Certainly, the B-747 UA incident over the Pacific Ocean (6) points up the hazard of UAs in transport aircraft.

Primary flight symbol

There are several possible options in use for the primary flight symbol, the symbol the pilot uses as his reference when flying the airplane. In most US HUDs the primary flight symbol is based on the aircraft inertial velocity vector. Generally, the velocity vector is free to move laterally unless a cage mode is provided and selected by the pilot. In the caged mode, the symbol is constrained to the center of the HUD. No drift information is available to the pilot when the symbol is caged.

Lateral motion of the CDM/FPM   One issue is how to display the primary aircraft symbol when drift is present. Should a caged mode be incorporated and, if so, do we need to display drift to the pilot?

Should this caged symbol require pilot input to implement, such as a drift-cut-out switch?

Should an uncaged flight path marker symbol be displaced laterally by inputs other than drift? Examples of such inputs are sideslip or lateral deviation inputs in the MD-80 HUD. Sideslip inputs to the flight path marker may explain some of the 'noise' in the lateral motion of the F-16 HUD.

This question has implications for ground-attack missions as well as for low-visibility instrument approaches.

These issues require both simulator study and in-flight evaluation. The flight tasks studied should encompass all mission tasks including unusual attitude recovery. It is particularly important to consider A/G tasks when examining the issue of lateral motion of the primary aircraft symbol.

This issue must be studied in conjunction with the symbol control laws and in conjunction with whichever pitch scale compressions are chosen from the previous section.

Use of air-mass versus inertial data Another question is the use of inertial or air-mass data for the CDM/FPM computations. The use of air-mass data may be appropriate for level cruising flight, for A/A combat, and possibly for initial climb. The use of air-mass data in these flight regimes may ensure maximum aerodynamic performance.

Control law issues

Very little attention has been paid in the past to specifying the drive laws (or equations) for the display symbols (7). The military standard for electronic displays (8) simply states that the velocity vector is normally damped to make it usable but the amount of damping is dependent on the system. The same document also states that the velocity vector should show the motion of the aircraft's center of gravity. A strict interpretation of this last requirement precludes any signal augmentation, such as quickening.

Augmentation is highly aircraft-dependent. Any formula developed for a particular airplane will not be applicable to other aircraft except by coincidence.

Eliminating misleading information Any HUD design must ensure that misleading information is not presented to the pilot. When the CDM/FPM is quickened, it does not show the instantaneous flight path, but rather approximately where the flight path will be when steady state is reached. During flight close to the ground, it must be demonstrated that the displayed flight path symbol will not mislead the pilot into thinking he will clear an obstacle when, in fact, he will not. This can be significant during go-arounds from landing approaches.

This will be more critical with low thrust/weight aircraft (transports or during single-engine landings) or with delta-wing aircraft. 'Backside' or V/STOL aircraft will also be critical.

Effect during unusual attitudes The use of a pitch rate or washed-out

211

pitch term in the motion of the flight path symbol must be investigated during unusual attitudes or during high-rate maneuvering to ensure that the algorithm used does not create difficulties.

Effect of wind-shear encounters The use of a pitch rate or washed-out pitch term in the motion of the flight path symbol must be investigated during wind-shear situations to ensure that the algorithm used does not create difficulties.

The issue is not whether or not quickening or other augmentation will be used. That depends on the dynamics of the airplane. The issue is whether or not the specific implementation is satisfactory and will require validation whenever the quickening algorithm is developed, modified, or applied to a different aircraft. This evaluation is part of the basic certification of the HUD and will encompass analysis, simulation, and flight evaluation.

Pitch ladder reference

In military HUDs, the pitch ladder rotates about the CDM/FPM. In civil HUDs to date, most pitch ladders have rotated about the pitch marker (waterline). The use of a roll reference other than the aircraft reference symbol (ARS) creates relative motion between the pitch ladder and the ARS. At large bank angles, the pitch ladder can interfere with the CDM/FPM. The problem is exacerbated by pitch compression.

It has not been a problem in civil HUDs to date since most civil HUDs have been intended for ILS approaches with limited maneuvering.

The only civil HUD (*9*) intended for all flight phases at this writing was an unreferenced pitch reference HUD in which the pitch ladder rotates about the center of the FOV.

Pitch ladder precession

Should the pitch ladder emulate the same precession similar to conventional mechanical gyros when the aircraft's nose (or flight path) passes through the zenith or nadir? This apparent precession is caused by the singularity when the pitch equals 90°. Passing 90° pitch in an inclined loop, this effect creates an illusion of rolling 180° as the pilot passes over the top. This produces a disorienting effect. The videotape of a recent F-15 spatial disorientation incident (*10*) shows this rapid roll clearly.

There are several approaches to eliminating this problem. One is to use quaternions to redefine the attitude (flight path) of the airplane (*11*). A second approach could redraw the pitch ladder symbology near the 90° points with less emphasis on the roll attitude.

Other data displays

Power/thrust Is there a benefit for presenting power/thrust information on a HUD? Many VTOL aircraft have power/thrust displayed. If the answer is in the affirmative, how best should engine output be displayed?

This issue may be significant for aircraft using a HUD to monitor automatic systems, particularly where auto-throttles do not physically move cockpit thrust levers.

Takeoff monitors NASA has proposed a takeoff monitor system for display on a HUD (*12*). How should this information best be integrated into the takeoff guidance information?

Energy management What is the best means for displaying energy information, particularly in the A/A arena?

Navigation symbology

The navigation issue evaluation must reflect several competing criteria: fine-tracking performance, tracking acquisition, and situational awareness. Often, symbologies that enhance one will detract from the others. As an example, the difficulties with ILS final symbology and course intercept symbology have been cited (see 'Guidance cues', Chapter 4).

The final choice for a symbol set must reflect the needs of the task. A symbology designed for a Category III approach may not look like the symbology designed equally for Category I and non-precision approaches.

The issues listed below should be addressed in simulator studies, although final validation in flight is required.

ILS symbology

There is no agreement on the best means of presenting ILS deviation (raw data) on the HUD. There are a number of formats available ranging from cross-pointers or deviation boxes to synthetic runways (see Figure 4.17). Each of these has its own advantages and disadvantages.

To date, there has been limited comparison of one type of symbology with others to determine the limitations and performance benefits of each. Most studies to date have expressed their results in terms of subjective likes/dislikes of the pilots. Seldom has objective performance criteria been reported.

Any evaluation of ILS symbology must be made in conjunction with flight director symbology. The two symbol sets must be compatible. In addition, the ILS deviation symbology must be useful to fly as raw data only.

Both ILS raw data and flight director symbology must be designed to allow the pilot to quickly detect system failures, particularly loss of glideslope signals or failure of the flight director computer.

Recent preliminary studies (*13*) indicate that it is not always advantageous to locate symbology in the center of the FOV and that a slight scan may not extract a performance penalty. If this is validated, it will ease the design of guidance/flight director symbology by allowing raw data to be removed from the center of the HUD FOV.

Flight director symbology

The best flight director symbology must be selected in conjunction with ILS raw-data symbology as discussed in the previous section.

Course interception symbology

Symbology optimized for minimizing tracking errors near decision height is often less useful during the interception phase of the approach. Some HUDs (*14*) have added an 'HSI-like' indicator near the CDM. Mixing heading and roll angles near the aircraft reference symbol can be confusing, however.

Other HUDs have proposed adding an HSI compass rose near the bottom of the HUD. This leads to clutter. What has happened is that an attempt to correct deficiency in one symbol by adding other symbols has resulted in an overall non-optimum symbology suite. Development and validation of suitable symbology for course interception is needed.

En-route navigation symbology

In similar fashion, *en-route* navigation symbols have often been based on ILS-final symbology. A comparison of appropriate *en-route* symbology choices is needed to aid the symbology designer make choices.

Bearing data

There is a need to determine the best set of bearing information for a HUD. Based on a symbology evaluation in a limited-FOV HUD, one of two format choices was needed depending on the use of the bearing information. Simple orientation tasks (fly to the outer compass locator) could make do with a small pointer and digital bearing data. Flying ADF approaches, however, requires more precision in the analog data.

Monitoring vs flying

The choice of guidance symbology may vary depending on whether the HUD is intended to maximize performance (minimize tracking error), maximize situational awareness, or simply monitor the progress of an instrument approach. To date, no study of how best to design HUDs intended to monitor ILS approaches has been published. The French airline, Air Inter, has used HUDs as ILS monitors. These HUDs are certainly not optimized for use as pilot guidance tools, but are simple monitor devices with minimal guidance capability.

While the Air Inter HUD works, it would be surprising if this design were the optimal HUD for monitoring.

Guidance during ground roll

During ground roll (takeoff roll or landing roll-out), the center of the HUD can become very cluttered with the CDM/FPM lying on the horizon. During low-visibility conditions, the natural runway cues lie at the bottom of the FOV. The combination of clutter at horizon and the removal of the airplane reference from the natural cues could be improved upon.

An appropriate cue to guide takeoff rotation is needed. The use of a FPM or CDM has inherent limitations during this transition. In addition, an optimum cue to guide de-rotation after landing is needed.

Raster issues

There are a number of raster-specific issues which require further study. The following issues have been identified as significant.

Generally, these issues will require in-flight evaluation.

Raster brightness

The brightness of a raster image may adversely affect the ability of the pilot to look through the HUD. The effect has not been determined. This will require in-flight testing during all ambient lighting conditions.

Raster image registration

The registration requirements for the raster image when compared with the stroke symbology or with the real world have not been determined.

A preliminary tolerance of 1 mrad has been recommended based on stroke HUD requirements. This figures requires validation.

Effect of sensor range

Some sensors have limited range. These can present misleading images (*15*). The effects of this on the use of the HUD have not been determined.

Raster update rate

The raster image may be updated fairly slowly when compared with the balance of the HUD data. This will be particularly true with radar images. In addition, signal processing may add to the image latency. These effects may adversely affect the ability of the pilot to fly using the HUD and to make decisions concerning continuing the approach. The effect has not been determined. This will require in-flight testing, although simulation testing may be used for initial studies.

Registration of multiple raster images

When multiple sensors are used (such as simultaneous radar and FLIR images), misregistration of the two images may create difficulties for the pilot. There are presently no criteria to determine how much misregistration is acceptable.

A preliminary tolerance of 1 mrad has been recommended based on HUD experience.

Raster clutter

The raster image itself may adversely affect the ability of the pilot to look through the HUD. The effect has not been determined. This will require in-flight testing during all ambient lighting conditions.

Reduced raster field of view

Some sensors have limited FOV when compared with the HUD FOV. The effect of flying with a small 'inset' image has not been determined.

Image enhancement

If computer-aided feature recognition is incorporated into the synthetic vision/enhanced vision image generator, then the embedding of symbology which is tied to these features must be verified. For example, if runway edge recognition is incorporated and edge lines drawn based on the sensor image, the software then becomes a navigation system. The software integrity must be sufficient to allow operations based on this feature recognition.

HUD data integrity

There are a number of data integrity issues requiring further study. These will generally require ground-based simulation or analytical studies to resolve.

Warning criteria

The common means of handling incorrect or invalid data for a HUD is to simply remove it. There is disagreement over what data failures can be handled this way and which require specific annunciation. Certification authorities have not been consistent in their treatment of invalid data.

A basic criterion has been proposed which determines how long it takes a group of representative subject pilots to detect the failure and take appropriate action. This latency will determine the operating limits for the HUD. This is similar in nature to tests to determine the minimum altitudes for autopilot use.

This will entail simulation followed by flight validation.

Warning methods

A variety of warning methods suitable for head-up displays (removal of data, warning annunciation, etc.) have been used. Because of the immediacy of the display, some of these are less effective than others.

Of particular importance is how to display the degradation, but not the unavailability, of flight data. Examples include reversion to air-mass data, alternate airspeed/altitude data, loss of glideslope, etc.

These warning methods should be studied using the same general criteria as in the previous subsection.

Integration with head-down displays

To facilitate cross-checking, the HUD data should be displayed in a format compatible with the head-down instruments. This does not mean that the formats need be identical (or even should be identical). It does mean that the flight procedures and control strategies should be compatible. The instrument cross-check should be considered as well.

Dual displays

What are the effects of dual HUD displays? Can such an arrangement benefit the overall system reliability?

Is it possible for the pilot not flying (PNF) to monitor the progress of a low instrument approach which is being conducted by reference to a raster image? Can he accomplish this with a head-down display? With a HUD?

HUD training issues

There are a number of flight-training issues which require further study.

HUD training benefit

Recent data suggests that the HUD can be beneficial as a training tool. The incorporation of a non-optimized HUD may have cost/time savings of up to 30% when compared with training without a HUD. Development of a HUD optimized for the training role may result in even greater savings.

The potential benefit should be documented based on studies of

HUD training being conducted and later with a strawman curriculum.

Training tools

If a HUD curriculum is to be developed (regardless of when), should the HUD be a 'standard' HUD or should it have features which would enhance its use in the training syllabus? The present T-38 Flight Instrumentation Standardization Program (FISP) HUD installed in a T-38 (*16*) has several options for the instructor including the possibility of training-specific HUD modes and symbologies.

Need the instructor have his own combiner, or will a repeater be sufficient? NASA's Shuttle Training Aircraft (*17*) uses a different model HUD for the instructor.

Operations issues

There are a number of operational issues which require further study.

Accommodation issues

The issue of HUD accommodation has been raised by Roscoe and his students (*18–21*). They maintain that the pilot's eyes will tend to accommodate to a relatively close distance, in spite of the symbology being collimated to optical infinity. They assert that when the pilot shifts focus between HUD symbols and real-world objects, these large changes in accommodation can cause spatial disorientation. Additionally, the effect should make it more difficult for a pilot to visually acquire other aircraft.

HUD research studies have not supported this accommodation argument. An early survey (*7*), based on interviews with operational pilots flying HUDs, evoked no mention of eye discomfort, focusing problems, or anything resembling accommodation difficulties. Additionally, the accommodation argument predicts HUD landing approaches which would be much more shallow and result in larger touchdown dispersion than non-HUD approaches. Every HUD study to date, however, has indicated the opposite.

In spite of this, these arguments have persisted for some time and have clouded the widespread use of HUDs in non-mission-related tasks. The issue is serious enough to warrant a flight experiment to confirm or reject the hypothesis advanced by Roscoe and colleagues. This cannot be accomplished on the ground.

219

Specific HUD procedures

At present, there is a need to develop HUD-specific flight procedures making use of the vector data available on the head-up display. Existing flight procedures reflect a dependence on attitude instrument flight.

The role of the non-flying pilot

There is a need to ensure that the procedures developed in the previous two subsections make proper use of the pilot not flying (PNF). Obviously, this applies to transport airplanes only.

Can procedures be developed to allow the PNF to use a HUD to monitor the other pilot or automatic systems?

Research issues

There are a number of research issues which require further development.

Flight research vehicle

Most of the HUD research to date has been conducted in ground-based simulators. These allow for control of the experimental environment and permit reliable data recording. Many of the research issues discussed above do not lend themselves easily to such simulation but require actual flight conditions. Such issues include unusual attitude recognition and recovery, interference of the HUD symbols with real-world cues, and visual accommodation, to name a few. For these issues, the only appropriate research vehicle is a real airplane – in flight.

What is needed is an agile aircraft with good visibility and representative performance to act as a surrogate. The airplane must be capable of performing disorienting maneuvers to demonstrate the display's capability in unusual-attitude recovery. A HUD-equipped military trainer is recommended.

Also needed is an aircraft which can perform repeated instrument approaches and navigation tasks. This aircraft need not have the agility of the 'unusual attitude' airplane, but the approach speed range should be of the order of 135–150 knots. This aircraft should have two crew in order to validate some of the procedural issues applying to transports. A business jet would be recommended.

Both of the preceding aircraft types should have a HUD with a symbol generator capable of being rapidly reprogrammed with new symbols.

The number of such vehicles is limited at present. The NT-33 variable-stability aircraft presently has this capability, but is scheduled for retirement. The NT-38 FISP aircraft had this capability, but has been demodified. Flight Visions operated a surrogate single-engine airplane with a programmable HUD, but this too has been demodified. At this writing, the University of Maryland is operating a Cessna 421 with a HUD to develop enhanced vision systems.

The NT-33's planned replacement, Variable Stability Inflight Simulator Test Aircraft (VISTA), is another likely candidate, but at present there are no definite plans to incorporate a programmable HUD in VISTA.

Desktop prototyping

The development of a desktop prototyping tool (which can provide dynamic motion) is another task which has great potential payoff. This tool can be used to develop symbology and then to provide a data file to ensure configuration control.

The desktop workstation should be PC-based with source code available. The workstation should have the following features:

- able to draw display symbology;
- include symbol drive laws in definition;
- able to show dynamic motion;
- able to generate paper copy of symbology;
- able to generate standard data package.

The following are desirable features:

- able to compile program for airplane or simulator;
- able to show dynamic motion using a joystick.

The generation of a standard display data package is an essential feature of any display program. A standard display data interchange format is needed to describe each symbol element: shape, location, length, orientation, occlusion logic, masking logic, scaling, and drive parameters.

In addition, the use of a desktop PC for evaluation pilot practice and training could reduce the number of flight sorties (or simulator sessions) for the pilot to become familiar with the HUD symbology.

Configuration control

Recent HUD experiments have had difficulties with maintaining control of the software configuration. Symbology is developed at one organization and forwarded to the simulator/flight research organization, usually as drawings. These are scaled and entered by hand into the new symbol generator. The final check is usually a flight evaluation by one of the researchers. Often discrepancies arise during the course of the experiment, negating the evaluations by one or more of the evaluation pilots.

The use of the prototyping tool described in the previous subsection could minimize this difficulty by providing a medium for transferring a set of symbols from one computer to another.

Recommendations

There are a number of design recommendations stated within the context of this document. It seems superfluous to restate them as 'recommendations.' Likewise, there are many issues which are still unresolved. Clearly, these issues should be investigated and resolved.

Design philosophy

Perhaps the most important recommendation is to have a rational design philosophy when developing head-up displays. The information to be displayed on the HUD must be tailored to the pilot's needs. The choice of specific symbols should be relegated to a secondary role. In the past, too much attention has been devoted to micro-standardizing the symbols. The development of the symbol sets must be tailored to the mission, to the aircraft, and to the cockpit environment. Problems in the past have been the result of poor symbology choices, not the lack of standardization.

Display evaluation

Following the development of the HUD and the symbology, a careful evaluation of the HUD in a mission-related context is essential. The evaluation pilots must thoroughly exercise the HUD in all anticipated phases of flight. This evaluation must consider the effect of system failures.

HUD research aircraft

The continuing need for an aerial vehicle to study the issues and conduct evaluations prior to design freeze can not be overstated. At this writing, there are only three such aircraft in the United States, none of which is likely to be available beyond 1994.

References

(1)   Egan, D. E. and Goodson, J. E. *Human Factors Engineering for Head-Up Displays: A Review of Military Specifications and Recommendations for Research* (Pensacola, Florida: Naval Aeromedical Research Laboratory, 1978), NAMRL Monograph-23

(2)   Haines, R. F. *Selected Research Issues and Abbreviated Discussion Related to Head-Up Displays* (Moffett Field, California: National Aeronautics and Space Administration, June 1979), HUD Report 3

(3)   Walters, D. J. 'The electronic display of primary flight data', in *Problems of the Cockpit Environment* (Paris: Advisory Group for Aeronautical Research and Development, 1968), Paper 28, AGARD CP-55

(4)   Newman, R. L. *Improvement of Head-Up Display Standards. II. Evaluation of Head-Up Displays to Enhance Unusual Attitude Recovery* (Wright-Patterson AFB, Ohio: Air Force Wright Aeronautical Laboratory, 1987), AFWAL TR-87-3055. Vol. II

(5)   Eksuzian, D. J. *et al. TRISTAR I: Evaluation Methods for Testing Head-Up Display Flight Symbology* (Moffett Field, California: Tri-Service Flight Symbology Working Group, in preparation), FSWG TR-91-01

(6)   *Aircraft Accident Report: China Airlines B-747SP, N-4522V, 300 Nautical Miles Northwest of San Francisco, California, February 19, 1985* (Washington: National Transportation Safety Board, 1986), AAR-86-03

(7)   Newman, R. L. *Operational Problems Associated with Head-Up Displays During Instrument Flight* (Wright-Patterson AFB, Ohio: Air Force Aeromedical Research Laboratory, 1980), AFAMRL TR-80-116

(8)   *Military Standard, Electronically or Optically Generated Displays for Aircraft Control or Combat Cue Information* (Philadelphia, Pennsylvania, Naval Publications and Forms Center, 1975), MIL-STD-884C

(9)   Newman, R. L. *Symbology for the FV-2000/KA Head-Up Display* (San Marcos, Texas: Crew Systems, 1991), TR-91-10A

(10)   *F-15 Spatial Disorientation* (Langley AFB, Virginia: First Tactical Fighter Wing, ca. 1986), Videotape briefing

(11)   Hankey, W. L., Miller, L. E. and Scherr S. J. *Use of Quaternions in Flight Mechanics* (Wright-Patterson AFB, Ohio: Air Force Wright Aeronautical Laboratory, 1984), AFWAL TR-84-3045

(12)   Middleton, D. B., Srivatsan, R., and Person, L. H. 'Takeoff performance monitoring system display options', in *Proceedings of the AIAA/AHS Flight Simulation Technologies Conference, Hilton Head* (Washington: American Institute of Aeronautics and Astronautics, 1992), pp. 57–67

(13)   Sanford, B. D. 'Head-up displays: effects of information location on the processing of superimposed symbology', Thesis, San Jose State University, 1992

(14)   Bitton, D. F. and Evans, R. H. *Report on Head-Up Display Symbology Standardization*

(Randolph AFB, Texas: Air Force Instrument Flight Center, 1990), AFIFC TR-91-01

(15) 'Panel discussion on situational awareness', *SAE Aerotech'92 Meeting* (Anaheim, California: Society of Automotive Engineers, 1992)

(16) *T-38 Head-Up Display (HUD) Avionics System Manual* (Wright-Patterson AFB, Ohio: 4950 Test Wing, 1991)

(17) Ivins, M. 'Space Shuttle applications', in *Proceedings of the Flight Operations Symposium, Vancouver* (Redmond, Washington: Sundstrand Data Control, 1979), Vol. II, pp. 104–117; Vol. IIA, section 6

(18) Roscoe, S. N. 'Designed for disaster', *Human Factors Society Bulletin*, **29**, June 1986, 1–2

(19) Roscoe, S. N. 'Spatial misorientation exacerbated by collimated virtual flight display', *Information Display*, September 1986, 27-28

(20) Roscoe, S. N., 'The trouble with HUDs and HMDs'. *Human Factors Society Bulletin*, **30**, July 1987, 1-2

(21) Iavecchia, J. H. *The Potential for Depth Perception Errors in Piloting the F-18 and A-6 Night Attack Aircraft* (Warminster, Pennsylvania: Naval Air Development Center, 1987), NADC 87037-20

12 Glossary

One of the problems in head-up display literature has been a lack of standardization of words and abbreviations. Several different words have been used for the same concept: flight path angle, flight path marker, velocity vector, and total velocity vector all refer to the same thing.

In other cases, the same word has been used with two different meanings, such as binocular field of view.

This glossary presents HUD-related definitions grouped according to functional groups. These groups are Optical definitions, Symbology definitions, Systems definitions and Weapons definitions.

Optical definitions

achromatic Corrected to have the same focal length for two selected wavelengths.

accommodation A change in the thickness of the lens of the eye (which changes the eye's focal length) to bring the image of an object into proper focus on the retina. Accommodation describes the adjustments to distance which are internal to the eye. Vergence describes the relative pointing differences between the two eyes.

alert eye reference point (AERP) The location of the pilot's eye when he is looking for critical external visual cues. The AERP is

225

usually assumed to be somewhat forward of the *design eye reference point* (DERP). For fighter aircraft, the AERP may be above the DERP.

aperture stop   An internal limitation on optical rays. *See exit pupil.*

astigmatism   Refractive error due to unequal refraction of light in different meridia caused by nonuniform curvature of the optical surfaces of the eye, especially the cornea.

binocular   Vision using both eyes.

binocular instantaneous field of view (IFOV)   The field of view visible to both left and right eyes. Two binocular IFOVs can be described: combined IFOV and intersecting IFOV. Figure 12.1 illustrates the difference between combined and intersecting IFOVs.

boresight   The reference axis looking forward through an optical assembly or other non-visual sensor; the view with no directional adjustment. As a verb, to align a system with the reference axis of the airplane.

brightness   The subjective attribute of light sensation by which a stimulus appears more or less intense (*1*).

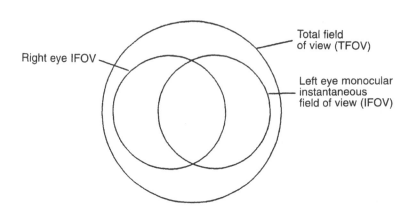

Right eye monocular IFOV

Combined binocular IFOV

Intersecting binocular IFOV

Left eye monocular IFOV

Figure 12.1   Binocular and monocular fields of view

226

catadioptric Describing an optical system with an odd number of reflecting surfaces.

candela (cd) The intensity of blackbody radiation from a surface of $1/60\,cm^2$ at $2045\,K$.

chromatic aberration An error in which a lens has different focal lengths for different wavelengths of light.

collimation The act of making rays of light travel in parallel lines.

collimator The optical components used to collimate the display image.

combined binocular IFOV The envelope of both left and right eye monocular IFOVs. This is the field of view visible to both eyes. It is called **ambinocular IFOV** by some authorities and **binocular IFOV** by others. The use of the adjective 'combined' is recommended. The IFOV which is visible to one eye, but not both is included in the combined IFOV. Figure 12.1 illustrates the difference between combined and intersecting IFOVs.

combiner The component located in the pilot's forward field of view providing superposition of the symbology on the external field of view.

contrast The difference in luminance between two areas in a display.

contrast ratio The ratio of display symbology brightness to the external visual cue brightness. Contrast ratio must specify the ambient brightness level.

conventional collimator *See refractive collimator.*

convergence The shifting of an observer's eyes inward to view a nearby object: i.e. crossing the observer's eyes.

convergent disparity The horizontal component of disparity making the optical rays appear to emanate from a point closer than infinity.

dark focus The point of accommodation of the eye in the absence of visual stimuli. The dark focus is of the order of $1\,m$ in most persons. *See empty-field myopia.*

design eye reference point (DERP) The location of the pilot's eye used to calculate fields of view and to make other comparisons between HUDs.

diffraction collimator A collimator using one or more diffraction gratings for collimation (and often for superposition as well). Since the diffraction gratings are usually produced using holograms, these are sometimes referred to as **holographic collimators**.

diopter The reciprocal of the focal length (in meters) of a lens.

diplopia A condition in which a single object appears as two objects because the left and right eyes' images do not fall on corresponding portions of the retinas.

dipvergence The shifting of an observer's eyes vertically, one up and

227

one down.

dipvergent disparity   The vertical component of disparity.

disparity   Misalignment of the images or light rays seen by each eye.

displacement error   The difference in apparent position of a real world visual cue caused by optical effects (such as refraction) when viewed through the combiner.

distortion   Variation in apparent geometry of real-world objects when viewed through the combiner.

divergence   The shifting of an observer's eyes outward.

divergent disparity   The horizontal component of disparity, making the rays appear to emanate from a point further than optical infinity.

double dision   *See diplopia.*

empty-field myopia   A situation where the resting focus of the eye moves to a near point in the absence of visual stimuli.

exit pupil   A small disk containing all of the light collected by the optics from the entire FOV. Figure 12.2 shows a simple optical system. The aperture stop is shown by P_0. The rays of light passing through the system will be limited by either the edges of one of the components or by the internal aperture, P_0. The image of P_0 on the entrance side is the entrance pupil, P_1; that on the exit side is the exit pupil, P_2. All rays that pass through P_0 must also pass through the entrance and exit pupils (2). By locating the observer's eyes within the exit pupil, the maximum FOV is obtained. As the observer's eyes move back from the exit pupil, the IFOV becomes smaller, although the TFOV is available by moving the eye's transverse to the optical axis.

eye reference point (ERP)   *See design eye reference point.*

eye relief   The distance from the HUD combiner to the exit pupil.

eyebox   A three-dimensional envelope within which the pilot's eyes are assumed to be. This is sometimes called the **eye motion box**.

field of regard (FOR)   The spatial angle in which a sensor can view.

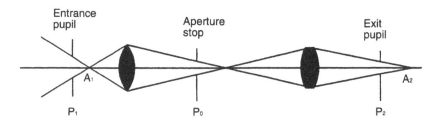

Figure 12.2   Aperture stop and entrance and exit pupils

228

For helmet-mounted displays, the spatial angle in which the display can present usable information.

field of view (FOV)   The spatial angle in which the symbology can be displayed measured laterally and vertically.

fixed combiner   A combiner fixed in the pilot's view.

foot-lambert (FL)   A unit of illuminance equal to one lumen per square foot.

hyperopia   A situation where the image of the eye's lens falls behind the retina, making it difficult to focus on nearby objects. Hyperopia is sometimes called **far-sightedness**.

illuminance   The amount of light intercepting a surface.

image intensifier (I^2)   A device to amplify light intensity by allowing the light to strike a screen which emits several photons for each photon from the original light source.

instantaneous field of view (IFOV)   The spatial angle in which the symbology is visible from a single eye position. The IFOV is the spatial angle of the collimator exit aperture as seen from the eye.

intensity   A measure of the rate of energy transfer by radiation. For a point-source emitter, the units of intensity are watts per steradian. For a surface receiving incident flux, the units of intensity are watts per square meter. For an extended source (one with finite dimensions as opposed to a point source), intensity is expressed in terms of energy per unit solid angle per unit area, or watts per steradian per square meter. In photometry, special units are often used to account for the spectral sensitivity of the eye. The intensity of a light source is sometimes measured in candelas which is based on blackbody radiation at a specified temperature. *See Candela.*

intersecting binocular IFOV   The envelope within the combined binocular IFOV which is common to both left- and right-eye monocular IFOVs. This is the FOV in which the symbology is visible to both eyes simultaneously. This is called **binocular IFOV** by some authorities. The use of the adjective 'intersecting' is recommended. The use of the adjective 'simultaneous' is not recommended. The IFOV which is visible to one eye, but not both is not included in the intersecting IFOV. Figure 12.1 illustrates the difference between combined and intersecting IFOVs. *See overlap.*

knothole effect   The apparent limitation of the TFOV by the exit aperture. This is an analogy of the TFOV which is the world beyond the 'knothole' and the IFOV is the 'knothole.' By shifting one's eye, the view of the real world beyond the 'knothole' can be viewed, though not all at once. Gibson(*3*) calls this the 'porthole.'

line of sight (LOS)   A line from the pilot's eyes in the direction of viewing.

line width   The width at 50% of peak luminance of the line luminance distribution.

lumen   A unit of luminous flux equal to one candela per steradian.

luminance   Luminous flux reflected or transmitted by a surface per unit solid angle of projected area in a given direction. The unit of measurement is the foot-lambert. In the SI systems the unit is the candela per square meter (cd/m^2).

monocular combiner   A combiner intended to be viewed with one eye.

monocular IFOV   The spatial angle in which the symbology is visible viewed from a single eye (left eye, right eye, or single ERP) position.

myopia   A situation where the image of the eye's lens falls in front of the retina, making it difficult to focus on objects at a distance. Myopia is sometimes called **near-sightedness**.

optical axis   The axis of symmetry of an optical system (*4*).

optical infinity   Located at such a distance that rays of light appear parallel.

overlap   The lateral angle subtended by the intersecting binocular IFOV.

photon   The fundamental quantum of light energy.

real image   An image formed when the rays from an external object meet at an image point. A real image may be recorded by placing a photographic film at this point (*2*). Real images are formed on the opposite side of the lens from the objects they represent. Figure 12.3 shows the geometry of real and virtual images.

reflective collimator   A collimator using mirrors (perhaps in conjunction with lenses) for collimation (and often for superposition as well), i.e. using the principle of reflection.

refractive collimator   A collimator using only lenses for collimation, i.e. using the principle of refraction. Refractive collimators are sometimes referred to as 'conventional' collimators.

resolution   The ability to distinguish to fine detail. Resolution can be expressed in terms of the separation required to detect two objects (lines or points) or in terms of numbers of lines or points per degree of the FOV. Some displays are described in terms of the number of lines or points across the display. Resolution has also been described in terms of equivalent visual acuity: e.g. a resolution of 2 arc min could be described as 20/40. *See **Snellen visual acuity**.*

Snellen visual acuity   Visual acuity measured by recognition of standard letters. The observer's task is to recognize (i.e. read) the letters. The 'standard' visual acuity is 1 arc min (line width). The result is usually expressed in terms of the observer's acuity relative to this nominal value as a fraction whose numerator is 20. For example,

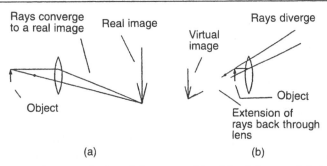

Figure 12.3 **Real and virtual images: (a) object beyond focal point results in a real image; (b) object within focal point results in a virtual image**

20/200 implies a visual acuity of 10 arc min and that the observer can read at 20 ft the letter that the 'standard' observer can at 200 ft.

spatial frequency For a periodic visual target (such as a pattern of equally spaced bars), the reciprocal of the spacing between the bars (i.e. the width of one cycle – one dark bar plus one light bar), generally expressed in cycles/mm or cycles/deg.

stowable combiner A combiner that can be deployed for use or retracted out of view.

total field of view (TFOV) The total spatial angle within which symbology can be viewed. When a HUD is viewed from the exit pupil, symbology within the TFOV can be seen. As the observer moves back, only the symbology which can be seen through the exit pupil is visible. The angle restricted by the exit pupil is the IFOV. The area covered by the IFOV may not be the entire display. By moving his head, the pilot may be able to see more symbology. The TFOV represents the total symbology available by moving the eye position.

transmittance of combiner The percentage of ambient light from an external source passing through the combiner. The wavelength spectrum of the light from the external source must be specified. Normally, the spectrum of sunlight is usually assumed.

vergence The angle between light rays; the angle between the eyes of an observer. When referring to the angle of the observer's eyes, the convention measures the angle looking from the observer toward the source of the light rays.

vignetting Partial loss of illumination caused by some of the light rays being blocked by the aperture stop.

visual acuity The ability of an observer to distinguish fine patterns. Visual acuity can be expressed in terms of the angular separation required to see that two or more objects are separate. It can be expressed in terms of the angular size necessary to detect a small target. Visual acuity has also been expressed in terms of reading standard letters or determining the orientation of small symbols. The most commonly used of these are the Snellen letters. *See **Snellen visual acuity**.*

visual disparity   The difference in apparent position of an image as presented to each eye.

virtual image   An image which can be seen by an observer, but is not a real image. A virtual image is formed when the projection of the rays (from an external object) cross, although the rays themselves do not (2). Virtual images are formed on the same side of the lens as the objects they represent. Figure 12.3 shows the geometry of real and virtual images.

windshield combiner   An area of the windshield which functions as the combiner.

Symbology definitions

absolute altitude   The altitude above the terrain.

aircraft coordinates   A coordinate system with the origin at the aircraft center of gravity. For displays, the convention is x lying along the lateral axis, y along the vertical axis, and z along the longitudinal axis. The sign convention is positive right, up, and forward.[1]

aircraft reference symbol (ARS)   The cue by which the pilot flies the airplane. The ARS can be the pitch marker, the flight path marker, or the climb–dive marker. It is used relative to the pitch ladder. Secondary cues (such as angle-of-attack error) are referenced to the ARS.

airspeed   The magnitude of the speed with which the aircraft moves through the air.

airspeed, calibrated   *See **calibrated airspeed**.*

airspeed, indicated   *See **indicated airspeed**.*

airspeed, true   *See **true airspeed**.*

air-mass symbols   Flight path symbols defined using the air-mass velocity vector. *See* definitions for ***climb-dive marker**, **flight path angle**, **flight path marker**,* and ***velocity vector**.*

---

[1]This sign convention will usually be different from the sign convention used by the aircraft designer. The typical airframe design convention is x, y, and z axes lying along the longitudinal, lateral, and vertical axes. The z axis sign convention is usually positive down.

alphanumeric information   Information presented as letters and numerical digits, such as text messages.

altitude   The height of the aircraft above sea level or some other reference.

altitude, barometric   *See barometric altitude.*

altitude, radar   *See radar altitude.*

analog information   Information presented as a continuously moving symbol, such as the hands on a watch, as opposed to discrete information.

angle of attack (AOA or α)   The angle between an aircraft longitudinal reference (FRL or ACRL) and the air velocity vector projected on the plane defined by the aircraft longitudinal reference and the aircraft vertical axis.

angle of sideslip (β)   The angle between the aircraft longitudinal reference (FRL or ACRL) and the air velocity vector projected on the plane defined by the aircraft longitudinal reference and the aircraft lateral axis. β is the left-right equivalent of α.

articulation   The canting of pitch ladder lines to indicate the nearest horizon.

aspect ratio   The ratio of horizontal to vertical dimension of a display.

Augie arrow   A roll-referenced symbol consisting of an arrow referenced to the flight path marker. The Augie arrow automatically appears during unusual attitudes and indicates the roll attitude to aid recovery (5).

bank   The angle between local vertical and the plane defined by the aircraft's vertical and longitudinal axes.

barometric altitude   The altitude calculated from measuring the ambient static pressure through the pitot-static system.

bendy bars   Articulated pitch ladder lines indicating the direction to the nearest horizon.

cage   To constrain the flight path marker to the center of the field of view.

calibrated airspeed (CAS)   Indicated airspeed corrected for pitot-static system position error.

climb–dive marker (CDM)   The symbol showing the aircraft flight path angle, i.e. the velocity vector constrained laterally.

climb–dive marker, air-mass   The climb–dive marker defined using the air-mass velocity vector.

climb–dive marker, inertial   The climb–dive marker defined using the inertial velocity vector.

coding characteristics   Readily identifiable attributes associated with a symbol by means of which symbols can be differentiated; i.e. size, shape, color, etc.

combined steering cue A multiple-axis steering cue which, when followed, will place the aircraft on a trajectory to intercept and maintain a preselected computed path through space.

compression An angular relation where an angle within the display corresponds to a greater angle in the real world. Compressed scales can not be conformal.

conformal display A HUD in which the symbols appear to overlie the objects they represent.

contact analog A display which is a presentation of the real world. Note a contact analog format need not be conformal.

course deviation An indication of aircraft displacement (left–right) from a desired track (VOR or TACAN radial, ILS localizer, INS track, etc.).

deviation An indication of aircraft displacement (left–right, up–down) from a desired track.

deviation box An indication of aircraft displacement (left–right, up–down, or both) from a desired track. Normally shown as a box or circle, the steering box shows the displacement compared to a maximum or nominal displacement (such as the ILS Category II limits).

digital information Quantitative information presented as numerical digits, such as an automobile odometer or digits on a watch. Digital information uses the numbers to show the magnitude of the information and will change as the source information changes.

directed decision cue A displayed command directing the pilot to a specific action, such as 'SHOOT,' 'GO AROUND,' or 'BREAKAWAY.'

direction cue A symbol depicting the location of a particular line of position (LOP), such as VOR radials or runway centerline extensions.

discrete information Information presented in defined steps or intervals, such as the digits on a digital watch, as opposed to analog information.

display coordinates A coordinate system oriented with the display. The origin is at the design eye reference point. The convention is x and y lying transverse to the display boresight and z lying along the boresight. The x axis is horizontal and y vertical.

display reference The orientation of the angular information in a display reference to the information in the real world.

DME A symbol showing the distance in nautical miles to a TACAN or DME navigation station. Also the distance-measuring equipment itself.

embedded symbol A symbol embedded in the raster image.

error information   Information presented which enables the user to assess the deviation of some parameter from its desired value without requiring attention to a numerical value, such as left/right ILS deviation.

fixed aircraft reference (Θ)   A symbol which represents an extension of the fuselage reference line (FRL) or other longitudinal aircraft reference line (ACRL). The symbol indicates relative pitch and roll angles of the aircraft when compared to the horizon (either artificial or real world) or to a displayed pitch ladder. It is sometimes called the waterline or pitch marker. *See pitch marker* and *waterline.*

fixed symbol   A display symbol which is moved to correct for aircraft movement. The term 'fixed' is used rather than 'stabilized' or 'referenced' to avoid confusion and to emphasize that the image is being corrected for aircraft motion. *See screen-fixed, or world-fixed.*

flare cue   A symbol indicating the desired vertical flight path during the landing flare. The flare cue is usually a vertical steering cue.

flight director   Steering information which, when followed, will place the aircraft on a trajectory to intercept and maintain a preselected computed path through space.

flight path angle (FPA or γ)   The velocity vector component projected on the plane defined by the aircraft FRL (or ACRL) and the aircraft vertical axis. The FPA is the velocity vector constrained laterally.

flight path angle, air-mass   The FPA defined using the air-mass velocity vector.

flight path angle, inertial   The FPA defined using the inertial velocity vector.

flight path marker (FPM)   The symbol showing the aircraft velocity vector. The difference between FPM and velocity vector is that the FPM is used for direct aircraft control, while the velocity vector is not.

flight path marker, air-mass   The FPM defined using the air-mass velocity vector.

flight path marker, inertial   The FPM defined using the inertial velocity vector.

flyback   The return trace from the end of one raster image to the start of the next.

framing   An effect where vertical and horizontal lines and tape scales present a false 'pseudo-horizon' sense to the pilot.

framing reference   A display format which presents angular/attitude information oriented in the same direction as the display. Framing displays are intended to provide an orientation cue in the same perspective as the pilot's LOS. Examples of framing referenced displays are attitude indicators and HUD pitch ladders. *See non-framing reference.*

geometrical horizon   The pilot's LOS tangent to the surface of the earth (*6*).

ghost horizon   A line parallel to the horizon drawn near the edge of the field of view to indicate the nearest horizon.

ghost velocity vector   *See velocity vector, ghost.*

glideslope (GS)   The vertical reference for an instrument-landing system (ILS) approach generated by a ground-based navigation transmitted signal.

grid heading   The horizontal angle made with grid north.

groundspeed (GS)   The magnitude of the speed with which the aircraft moves with respect to the surface.

heading   The horizontal angle made by the longitudinal reference (FRL or ACRL) with a reference direction.

heading referenced   A symbol in which the angular elements rotate to compensate for changes in aircraft heading. The horizontal situation indicator (HSI) is an example.

heading scale compression   A form of compression in which the heading angles are compressed. Heading compression is quite common in fighter HUDs to prevent blurring of the heading scale. While a compressed heading scale will not be conformal, the balance of the HUD may be.

horizon, geometrical   *See geometrical horizon*

horizon line   A symbol indicating a horizontal reference or zero pitch. Hughes (*7*) makes the point of emphasizing that this may not overlie the 'true' horizon (the pilot's LOS tangent to the earth) at high altitude. Bowditch (*6*) defines several different horizons the sensible horizon (a horizontal plane passing through the eye of the observer), the geoidal horizon (a horizontal plane tangent with the geoid directly below the observer), the geometrical horizon (the observer's LOS tangent to the geoid), and the visible horizon (the demarcation between surface and sky). The difference between the geometrical horizon and the visible horizon is caused by atmospheric refraction and by the elevation of the terrain. The difference between the sensible horizon and the visible horizon is called the dip correction. *See geometrical horizon, sensible horizon,* or *visible horizon.*

horizon, sensible   *See sensible horizon*

horizon, visible   *See visible horizon*

inertial symbols   Flight path symbols defined using the inertial velocity vector. *See climb–dive marker, flight path angle, flight path marker,* or *velocity vector.*

indicated airspeed (IAS)   The airspeed calculated from the dynamic pressure of the impact air pressure from the pitot-static system. IAS is uncorrected for position error. *See **calibrated airspeed**.*

Klopfstein runway   A contact analog symbol presented as a perspective figure depicting the location of the runway (*8*). *See **synthetic runway**.*

le boule   The small attitude display resembling an attitude ball in the lower-left corner of the FOV.

lateral acceleration   The measure of the sideforces generated aerodynamically by sideslip.

lateral steering cue   Single-axis steering information which, when followed, will place the aircraft on a trajectory to intercept and follow a preselected computed ground track.

mach number   The ratio of the TAS to the ambient speed of sound.

magnetic heading   The horizontal angle made with magnetic north.

non-framing reference   A display format which presents angular/attitude information in a different orientation as the display. Examples of non-framing referenced displays are horizontal situation indicators (HSI's). In the case of an HSI, the pilot views the display facing forward, while the display represents the view from directly overhead. This requires the pilot to mentally rotate the display coordinates while viewing the display. *See **non-framing reference**.*

normal load factor   The ratio of the lift to the aircraft weight. Normal load factor is sometimes called **normal acceleration** and is referred to by pilots as '*g*'s'.

orange peel   A symbol consisting of a segment or an arc surrounding the flight path marker. The length of the arc indicates the pitch attitude (zero pitch is a 180° arc). The center of the arc is oriented to show the vertical (down) direction.

pitch attitude   The angle above or below the horizon made by the aircraft reference line. This is sometimes called **pitch angle**.

pitch index   A symbol on the HUD positioned at a predetermined pitch angle used to represent a desired flight path angle or pitch attitude.

pitch ladder   A set of pitch reference symbols showing increments of angles to the horizon. Some authorities (*9, 10*) refer to this as the **climb–dive ladder** since most HUDs do not use pitch as the primary aircraft symbol. The terms climb–dive ladder and pitch ladder are synonymous. We will use the term pitch ladder because of historic use and economy of syllables.

pitch marker   The symbol which shows the aircraft pitch when read against the pitch ladder. *See **waterline**.*

237

pitch reference frame One or more symbols which represent fixed angles in space and are used as references for aircraft pitch and flight path symbols.

pitch-referenced A symbol in which the angular elements move to indicate aircraft pitch. The pitch cue on the VAM is an example (*11*). A symbol in which the angular elements rotate to indicate aircraft pitch and bank, such as the pitch ladder on most HUDs, can be described as being both pitch- and roll-referenced.

pitch scale compression A form of compression in which the pitch angles are compressed, but roll angles are not. Pitch compression is sometimes called **gearing**.

pixel A dot composing one of a number of picture elements.

potential flight path (PFP) A cue, normally calculated from longitudinal aircraft acceleration, which shows the velocity vector achievable for the aircraft by balancing existing thrust and drag.

predictive information Information predicting the future condition or position of the aircraft or a system.

pull-up cue A symbol used to indicate an approaching pull-up requirement during air-to-ground weapon delivery.

qualitative information Information presented which enables the user to assess the status of the aircraft or system without requiring a numerical value.

quantitative information Information presented which enables the user to directly observe or extract a numerical value.

radar altitude Absolute altitude measured from the time for a radar signal to return. It is sometimes called **radio altitude**.

range A symbol showing the distance to a specified waypoint, ground location, or target.

raster A CRT image composed of a series of parallel lines which trace a path over the face of the image tube. These parallel lines are modulated to create the image. Raster lines are written even when no symbols are to be displayed. This is sometimes referred to as a **video image**.

raster/stroke Stroke symbols drawn during the flyback.

reference airspeed The desired airspeed on final approach to landing, normally 1.3 times the stall speed.

reference angle of attack The desired angle of attack on final approach to landing.

roll-referenced A symbol in which the angular elements rotate to indicate aircraft bank. A bank pointer or the Augie arrow (*5*) are examples of roll-referenced symbols. Previous literature has used the term **roll-stabilized** to denote this.

rollout guidance An indication of aircraft displacement (left–right) from the runway centerline used for instrument takeoffs and low visibility landings.

rollout steering cue   A lateral steering cue which, when followed during the takeoff or landing ground roll, will place the aircraft on a trajectory to intercept and follow the runway centerline.

runway distance remaining   A symbol showing the distance to the end of the runway.

runway symbol   A symbol depicting the location of the runway.

scales   Secondary symbol suites showing airspeed, altitude, and heading.

screen coordinates   A two-dimensional coordinate system with the origin at the center of the display screen. For HUDs, this is the center of the CRT or other image source. This coordinate system is used to define the signals to the CRT.

screen-fixed   A symbol in which the angular elements are not moved to correct for aircraft movement. An example is the gun cross on most fighter HUDs.

sensible horizon   A horizontal plane passing through the pilot's eye (6).

sensor search area   A symbol showing the areas of sensor coverage, such as radar or FLIR.

situation information   Information indicating present condition or position of the aircraft or a system.

speed command   Steering information which, when followed, will cause the aircraft to maintain a desired airspeed.

stair-stepping   Distortion caused by forcing a symbol to follow raster lines.

steering information   Information presented which shows the control inputs necessary to fly a particular trajectory, such as the flight director pointers during an ILS approach. Steering information differs from situation information by indicating the desired control inputs only and not the current aircraft condition or position. It is called **command** or **director information** in different publications.

stroke   Symbols which consists of cursive lines drawn on the face of the image tube. Stroke images are written only where symbols are to be displayed.

symbol   An individual representation of information.

symbology   The collection of symbols shown in a display.

symbol location   The term **fixed** has been adopted to indicate that the location of the symbol has been moved (on the screen) to compensate for aircraft motion and allow the symbol to overly a cue in the external visual scene. **World-fixed** means that the symbol is rotated/moved to compensate for aircraft motion. **Screen-fixed**

means that no compensation has been applied. Rigid could be used instead of fixed. The term **stabilized** has been avoided since it has meant both referenced and fixed in previous definitions. In the past, **roll-stabilized** has meant **roll-referenced** (in the proposed nomenclature). **World-stabilized** has meant **world-fixed** (in the proposed nomenclature). It is entirely feasible for a symbol to be, for example, world-referenced/screen-fixed. An example is the attitude reference, *le boule*.

symbol orientation   The term **reference** has been adopted to indicate how a symbol has been rotated to compensate for mis-alignment between the world and aircraft coordinates. **World-referenced** means that the symbol is rotated to compensate for differences between display coordinates and world coordinates. These differences could be caused by aircraft motion or, in the case of HMDs, by pilot head motion. These compensations are normally thought of as accounting for misalignment of all three axes. In fact, they are often applied to one or two axes only.

symbol reference   The point defining the origin of the symbol's coordinate system. The reference can be the center of rotation, such as the origin of the rotating deviation symbol on the FDI HUD (*12*). For tape scales, the reference is the lubber line or index against which the tape is read. For thermometer scales, the reference is usually the base of the thermometer. The reference point of a symbol can be another symbol. For most HUDs, the pitch ladder and climb–dive marker use the same reference point. The climb-dive marker is moved away from this reference point to indicate climb–dive angle.

synthetic runway   A contact analog symbol presented as a perspective figure depicting the location of the runway. This is often referred to as the Klopfstein runway. *See **Klopfstein runway**.*

tapering   Shortening of the pitch ladder lines as the angle from the horizon increases.

time to go   A symbol showing the predicted time of arrival at a preselected waypoint, ground location, or target.

true airspeed (TAS)   The actual aircraft speed through the air.

true heading   The horizontal angle made with true north.

unreferenced display   A display format which presents no angular information, such as an airspeed indicator or an altimeter. While the information may be useful in maintaining situational awareness, it is presented in scalar, not perspective format.

update rate   The rate at which the output data is recalculated.

velocity vector   The linear projection of the aircraft velocity originating at the aircraft center of gravity or some other well-defined location on the aircraft. The use of a location forward of the aircraft center of gravity is often used to provide pitch-rate quickening to the velocity vector symbol. Some HUD systems refer to the velocity vector as the **flight path marker**.

velocity vector, air-mass   The linear projection of the aircraft velocity through the air-mass. The inverse of the air-mass velocity vector is the relative wind.

velocity vector, ghost   A symbol, shown as a dashed version of the CDM, showing the location of the velocity vector.

velocity vector, inertial   The inertial velocity vector is the linear projection of the aircraft velocity relative to the ground. The inertial velocity vector is sometimes called the **ground-referenced velocity vector**.

vertical deviation   An indication of aircraft displacement (up–down) from a desired track (ILS glideslope, target altitude. etc.).

vertical steering cue   A single-axis steering cue which, when followed, will place the aircraft on a trajectory to intercept and follow a preselected vertical flight path, such as the ILS glideslope or target altitude.

vertical speed   The rate of ascent or descent, usually calculated from the rate of change of barometric altitude. Vertical speed is sometimes called **vertical velocity**.

visible horizon   The demarcation between the earth's surface and the sky (6).

warning information   Information intended to alert the pilot to abnormal or emergency conditions.

waterline   The symbol, usually shown by a winged W, which shows the fixed aircraft reference. The waterline implies that the symbol is fixed in the HUD FOV, while pitch marker does not carry that implication. *See pitch marker.*

waypoint   A symbol depicting the location of a particular navigation location.

world coordinates   A coordinate system fixed with respect to the earth. The location of the origin and the direction of the *x* and *y* axes depend on the mission. Normally, the *z* axis is vertical.

world-fixed   A symbol which is moved to correct for aircraft attitude or heading. Examples are the horizon line on the FDI HUD (*12*) or target designator symbols. With world-fixed symbols, they (the symbols) appear to be stationary relative to the outside visual cues. Some symbols may be fixed in only one or two axes. HUD pitch ladders are usually described as world-fixed, but this is not strictly true as they do not move to compensate for heading changes. They should properly be described as being pitch/roll fixed.

world-referenced   A symbol which is rotated to indicate for aircraft attitude or heading. World-referenced symbols present the same angular orientation as the pilot sees along his LOS. Non-framing referenced symbols rotate to preserve the same relative angular orientation as the aircraft turns. Some symbols compensate for aircraft motion along one or two axes. For example, the pitch ladder on most HUDs compensate for pitch and roll, but not for heading. The pitch symbols on a three-axis ADI are an example of a world-referenced symbol.

Systems definitions

aircraft reference line (ACRL)   A line defining a reference axis of the aircraft established by the manufacturer. *See fuselage reference line.*

business aircraft   A passenger aircraft with a gross takeoff weight less than 30 000 lb.

category I   Landing minima associated with conventional ILS approaches, typically 200 ft decision height (DH) and 1/2 mile visibility.

category II   ILS landing minima between 100 ft and 200 ft, typically 100 ft DH and 1/4 mile visibility. Category II minima were originally based on a requirement for sufficient visual cues for 'see-to-flare.'

category III   Landing minima below 100 ft. Category III landing minima are typically divided into category IIIa, IIIb, and IIIc. Category IIIa minima are typically 50 ft DH and 700 ft runway visual range. Category IIIa were originally based on sufficient visual cues for 'see-to-rollout.' Category IIIb were originally based on sufficient visual cues for 'see-to-taxi.' Category IIIc is true blind landing.

certification authority   The agency with the authority to determine airworthiness of the system. In the case of civil aircraft, the certification authority is the Federal Aviation Administration (FAA) or its foreign equivalent. In the case of public or military aircraft, this agency is the appropriate government or military organization. The certification authority will be responsible for minimum or maximum acceptable values for many of the HUD system specifications.

civil aircraft   An aircraft not operated by a government agency (*13*).

decision height (DH)   The lowest altitude permitted for continuing a precision landing approach without acquiring visual cues for landing. *See Category I, Category II,* and *Category III.*

display electronics   The electronic unit which produces the visible image of the symbols and which monitors the symbols.

display control panel (DCP) The assembly which houses the HUD controls, such as brightness, mode selection, etc.

electronic unit (EU) The assembly which consists of the signal processor, the symbol generator, and the display electronics. Electronic units may be combined into fewer physical units or they may be merged with other systems.

enhanced vision system (EVS) A system which uses visual or non-visual sensors (such as FLIR or MMWR) to augment the pilot's view of the external scene. Normally, enhanced vision implies simply displaying a sensor image with no sensor fusion or computer enhancement. *See synthetic vision.*

extremely improbable For civil aircraft, extremely improbable means less than once per billion hours (*14*). For military aircraft, extremely improbable means that the probability of occurrence cannot be distinguished from zero and that it is so unlikely that it can be assumed that this hazard will not be experienced in the entire fleet (*15*). The definitions of some reliability terms, such as 'extremely improbable,' etc., will be specified by the certification authority.

fail-obvious A display designed such that a single failure will allow the pilot to readily determine the failure and take appropriate action. The appropriate action may include switching the source of the data or using another display.

fail-operational A system designed such that a single failure will allow the system to continue operation with no loss in performance (*16*).

fail-passive A system designed such that a single failure will cause a system disconnect leaving the airplane in trim with no control hardover (*16*).

frame time The interval during which calculations are made by the signal processor.

fuselage reference line (FRL) A line defining a reference axis of the aircraft established by the manufacturer. *See aircraft reference line.*

glidepath intercept point (GPIP) The point on the runway where the final approach course and glidepath intersect the runway surface.

hands on collective and cyclic (HOCAC) The HOTAS philosophy applied to helicopters.

hands on throttle and stick (HOTAS) The operating philosophy which allows the pilot to control all essential mission related functions through control buttons on the control stick and throttle.

hands on throttle and yoke (HOTAY) The HOTAS philosophy applied to aircraft with a control yoke in place of a stick.

head-up display (HUD) A display which presents flight control symbols into the pilot's forward field of view. The symbols should be presented as a virtual image focused at optical infinity.

helmet-mounted display (HMD) A display, mounted on the pilot's helmet, which presents flight control symbols into the pilot's field of view.

image source The component providing the optical origin of the symbology, such as a cathode-ray tube (CRT) screen or laser source.

instrument meteorological conditions (IMC) Flight conditions precluding the use of the external visual scene to control the aircraft.

line-replaceable unit (LRU) System components intended to be replaced by line mechanics and repaired by support organizations.

mode The operational state of the display a selected group of display formats, input selections, and processing algorithms.

night-vision goggles (NVG) An image intensifier (I^2) system worn by a crewmember allowing viewing of objects at night.

operator The organization responsible for issuing the final HUD system specification and which will be the ultimate user of the equipment. The operator will have the final decision on specifications based on the recommendations contained in this document, subject to the airworthiness requirements set by the certification authority. Note: For military and public aircraft, the certification authority and the operator may be the same organization.

pilot display unit (PDU) The assembly consisting of the image source, the collimator, and the combiner.

primary flight reference (PFR) A display which displays information sufficient to maneuver the aircraft about all three axes and accomplish a mission segment (such as takeoff or instrument approach). The amount of data displayed obviously depends on the mission segment to be performed. As a guide, the data displayed in the basic 'T,' i.e. airspeed, pitch attitude, altitude, heading, and lateral deviation (or their substitutes) should be displayed in a primary flight reference. Other data which is critical for immediate use, such as glideslope deviation during a precision instrument approach, should be included for those mission segments where it is required. A PFR must have at least the reliability specified by the certification authority.

primary visual signal area (PVSA) The area of the instrument panel enclosed by 12 in arc centered on the intersection of the crewmember's vertical centerline plane and the top of the instrument panel (*17*).

public aircraft An aircraft operated by a government, including the military (*13*).

refresh rate   The rate at which the displayed image is redrawn.

sampling rate   The rate at which input data is sampled. Digital computers require a finite time interval (frame time) within which to accomplish the necessary calculations. As a result, the input data (and output signal) is changed at intervals. This introduces an artifact into the displayed symbols. The effect is different from (and generally more critical for handling qualities) than a pure time delay. *See frame time.*

signal processor   The electronic unit which performs any calculations, filtering, etc. of the raw data to generate parameters to be displayed. An example of such calculations is the calculation of the inertial velocity vector from the raw data of three velocities from the inertial platform.

symbol generator   The electronic unit which generates the actual symbols to be displayed on the HUD. The symbol generator converts the values of the variables into shapes and locations of symbol elements to be drawn on the display unit, usually a CRT.

synthetic vision system (SVS)   A system which uses visual or non-visual sensors to augment the pilot's view of the external scene. Normally, synthetic vision implies image enhancement, sensor fusion, computer or a means of tagging symbology to the image location in the display. *See enhanced vision system.*

tactical aircraft   An aircraft defined as Class IV in MIL-F-8785C. (*18*). Tactical aircraft also include aircraft used to train for tactical aircraft.

trainer aircraft   An aircraft designed or used for primary and basic training.

transport aircraft   An aircraft defined as Class III in MIL-F-8785C (*18*).

visual meteorological conditions (VMC)   Flight conditions allowing the use of the external visual scene to control the aircraft.

Weapons definitions

aiming reticle   A symbol used as a weapon aiming cue.

azimuth steering line (ASL)   A left–right steering cue used in air-to-ground weapon delivery.

bomb-fall line (BFL)   A symbol indicating the approximate trajectory of a weapon following release.

breakaway symbol   A symbol displayed at minimum weapon release range and/or reaching the minimum safe pullout altitude during air-to-ground weapon delivery. The breakaway symbol indicates the need for an immediate pull-up of the aircraft.

continuously computed impact line (CCIL) A symbol used to display the locus of bullet impact points, usually with bullet time-of-flight points indicated.

continuously computed impact point (CCIP) A symbol indicating the predicted impact point of a weapon.

gun cross A symbol indicating the gun boresight axis.

lead-compensating optical sight (LCOS) An aiming reticle showing the bullet impact point taking aircraft maneuvering, target motion, and target range in account

solution cue A symbol indicating a release solution for a computed weapon delivery.

standby reticle A backup display intended for manual aiming in the event of HUD or other system failure.

target aspect A symbol indicating the orientation of the target vehicle (aircraft, ship, or ground vehicle).

target designator A symbol showing the location of the target.

target range A symbol showing the range to the target.

target range rate A symbol showing the rate of change of the target range.

weapon boresight A symbol indicating the weapon boresight axis.

References

(1)   Boff, K. R. and Lincoln, J. E. (eds) *Engineering Data Compendium. Human Perception and Performance* (Wright-Patterson AFB, Ohio: Crew System Ergonomics Information Analysis Center, 1988)

(2)   Heavens, O. S. and Ditchburn, R. W. *Insight into Optics* (New York: Wiley, 1991)

(3)   Gibson, C. P., 'Binocular disparity and head-up displays', *Human Factors*, **22**, 1980, 435-444

(4)   Smith, W. J., 'Image formation, geometrical and physical optics', in *Handbook of Optics*, W. G. Driscol and W. Vaughan (eds) (New York: McGraw-Hill, 1978), Chapter 2

(5)   Newman, R. L. *Improvement of Head-Up Display Standards. II. Evaluation of Head-Up Displays to Enhance Unusual Attitude Recovery* (Wright-Patterson AFB, Ohio: Air Force Wright Aeronautical Laboratory, 1987), AFWAL TR-87-3055, Vol. II

(6)   Bowditch, N. *American Practical Navigator, An Epitome of Navigation* (Washington, DC, US Navy Hydrographic Office, 1986), Publication HO 9, pp. 384–387

(7)   Hughes, R. E. *The HUD Coloring Book: Recommendations Concerning Head-Up Displays* (Washington: Naval Air Systems Command, 1991)

(8)   Klopfstein, G. *Rational Study of Aircraft Piloting* (Paris: Thomson-CSF, ca. 1966); reprint of 1966 article in *Intrados*

(9)   Hall, J. R., Stephens, C. M. and Penwill, J. C. *A Review of the Design and Development of the RAE Fast-Jet Head-Up Display Format* (Bedford, England: Royal Aeronautical Establishment, 1989), RAE FM-WP(89)034

(10)   Bitton, D. F. and Evans, R. H. *Report on Head-Up Display Symbology Standardization* (Randolph AFB, Texas: Air Force Instrument Flight Center, 1990), AFIFC TR-

91-01

(11)   *Engineering Report, Delta Gamma Visual Landing System* (Redmond, Washington: Sundstrand Data Control, 1971), Report 070-0676-001

(12)   *FDI Model 1000 Head-Up Display System Specification* (Portland, Oregon: Flight Dynamics, February 1989), Report 404-0249

(13)   *Definitions and Abbreviations* (Washington, DC: Federal Aviation Administration, no date), Federal Aviation Regulations Part 1

(14)   *System Design Analysis* (Washington, DC: Federal Aviation Administration, 1988), FAA AC-25.1309-1A

(15)   *Military Standard: System Safety Program Requirements* (Philadelphia, Pennsylvania, Naval Publications and Forms Center, no date), MIL-STD-882C.

(16)   *Criteria for Approval of Category III Landing Weather Minima* (Washington, DC: Federal Aviation Administration, 1984), FAA AC-120-28C

(17)   *Crew Stations and Passenger Accommodations* (Wright-Patterson AFB: Ohio Aeronautical Systems Division, no date), AFSC DH-2-2

(18)   *Military Specification: Flying Qualities of Piloted Airplanes* (Philadelphia, Pennsylvania, Naval Publications and Forms Center, 1979), MIL-F-8785C

247

Appendix: HUD symbologies

The following HUD symbologies represent HUDs which are significant from a historical perspective or which are current production HUDs. Three aircraft HUDs (AV-8, F-14, and F-15) are included to show the development of follow-on HUDs from initial models.

The primary display elements (basic flight displays) for each HUD should be self-evident. Where required, the text indicates unusual features of each HUD.

A-7 HUD

The A-7 HUD (shown in Figure 13.1) was the first operational HUD in the US inventory. It does not display an aircraft pitch symbol (*1*). The airspeed and altitude scales are thermometer scales showing the airspeed from 0 to 99 knots and 0 to 999 ft. The hundreds of knots for airspeed and thousands of feet are shown digitally below the scales. Radar altitude may be substituted for barometric altitude.

The AOA error bracket is a 'fly-from' scale. While the A-7 HUD specification (*2*) called for a fly-to AOA bracket, anecdotal reports suggest that the manufacturer's project pilot changed the sense of the error to emphasize the angular relationship between AOA, pitch, and flight path.

A perspective single ILS cue shows localizer and glideslope

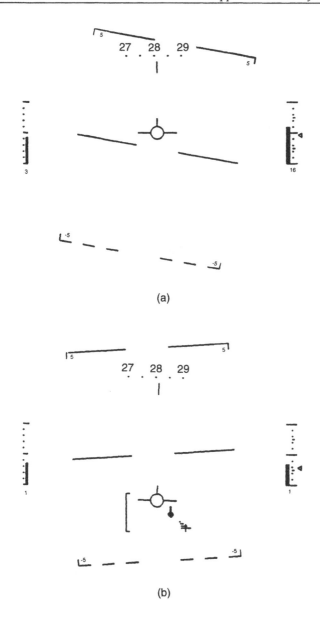

(a)

(b)

Figure 13.1   A-7D HUD symbology (2): (a) navigation mode; (b) landing mode

249

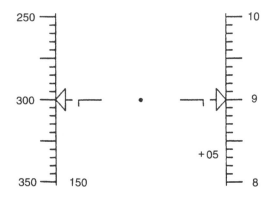

Figure 13.2   A-10 HUD symbology (*3*)

deviation. The flight director cue is the tadpole.

A-10 HUD

The A-10 HUD is typical of a HUD intended solely for weapon delivery. It displays neither an aircraft pitch symbol nor a flight path symbol (*3*). The airplane reference symbol (ARS) is fixed in the FOV (it does indicate aircraft roll.) Pitch is shown digitally below and to the right of the ARS (shown as +05 [degrees] in Figure 13.2). The depression angle in milliradians is shown below and to the left of the ARS.

A-320 HUD

The A-320 HUD (shown in Figure 13.3) was developed as an ILS approach monitor (*4*). The A-320 HUD does not display barometric altitude. The symbology for energy and airspeed error is reversed from the conventional HUD arrangement. The energy symbol (potential flight path) is a tape on the wing of the airplane reference symbol (ARS) and the airspeed error is a caret next to the ARS.

ILS deviation is shown as a box referenced to the flight path marker.

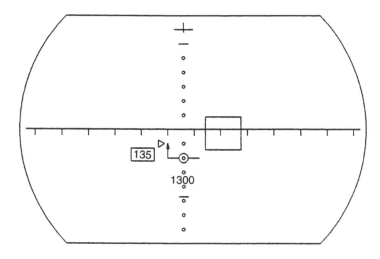

Figure 13.3 A-320 HUD symbology (4)

AV-8 HUD

The AV-8A HUD (5) is shown in Figure 13.4. The vertical scale on the left displays angle of attack. The horizontal scale above it shows airspeed and airspeed error. Altitude is shown digitally on the right with a vertical scale for vertical speed. Heading is displayed on the bottom. Sideslip is shown as a ball in a race at the bottom in the V/STOL mode.

The AV-8B HUD (shown in Figure 13.5) has a conventional arrangement of airspeed, altitude and heading (6). AOA and vertical speed are shown as vertical scales on the left and right below the digital airspeed and altitude. Sideslip is shown as a traditional ball scale at the bottom. Engine and nozzle parameters are shown digitally at the bottom left and right. The display of power is common in HUDs installed in V/STOL aircraft or in helicopters.

F-14 HUD

The F-14A HUD (7) shows vertical speed and radar altitude on the left and right of the FOV as shown in Figure 13.6. The cruise mode is compressed 4:1.

The F-14D HUD (shown in Figure 13.7) is conventional (8).

251

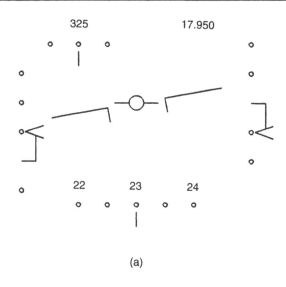

(a)

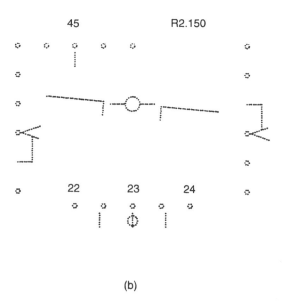

(b)

Figure 13.4 AV-8A HUD symbology (5): (a) fixed-wing (GEN mode); (b) V/STOL mode

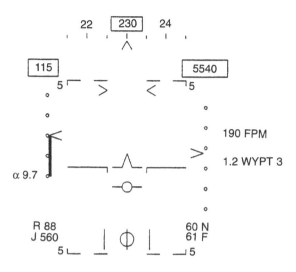

Figure 13.5   AV-8B HUD symbology (6)

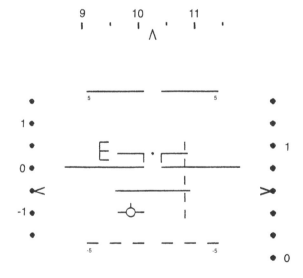

Figure 13.6   F-14A HUD symbology (7)

253

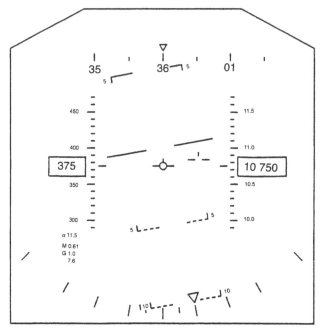

Figure 13.7   F-14D HUD symbology (8)

F-15 HUD

The F-15A HUD (9) is shown in Figure 13.8 and the F-15E HUD (10) is shown in Figure 13.9. Both are conventional in arrangement. During landing, the F-15A HUD has an AOA scale located inboard of the airspeed scale.

The F-15A uses vertical tapes for airspeed and altitude, while the F-15E uses digits only.

F-16 HUD

The F-16 HUD (shown in Figure 13.10) compresses the pitch ladder 2:1 at pitch attitudes above ±60° (11). The flight path symbol can be caged at pilot option.

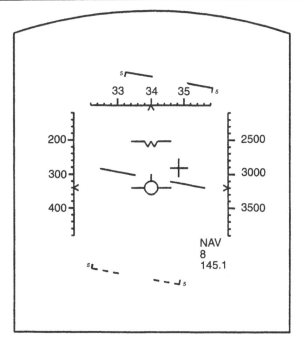

Figure 13.8   F-15A HUD symbology (*9*)

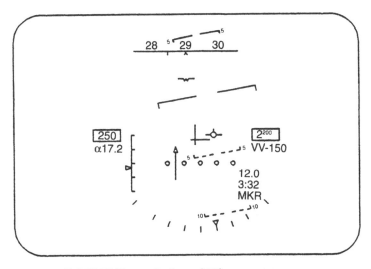

Figure 13.9   F-15E HUD symbology (*10*)

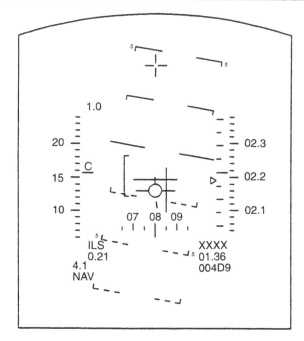

Figure 13.10   F-16 HUD symbology (*11*)

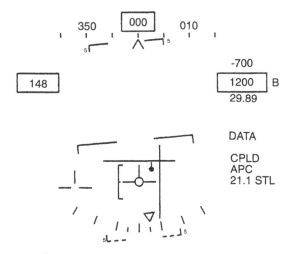

Figure 13.11   F-18 HUD symbology (*12*)

256

F-18 HUD

The F-18 HUD displays airspeed, altitude, and heading digitally (*12*). It is shown in Figure 13.11. Many later US Navy HUDs and HUDs developed for McDonnell-Douglas fighters show the F-18 heritage.

Flight Dynamics HUDs

FDI 1000 HUD

The Flight Dynamics 1000 HGS (certified in the B-727) was designed for Category IIIa use (*13*). Figure 13.12 shows the symbology. The airspeed and altitude are shown digitally. The heading ticks are conformal on the horizon line with a digital heading in the upper center. The airplane reference symbol is unconstrained laterally (i.e. it is an FPM). The pitch ladder rotates about the waterline.

The FDI 1000 HGS computes steering cues for the ILS approach and does not repeat the steering from the head-down flight director. The company emphasizes this by referring to their units as 'head-up guidance systems,' not as HUDs. Course-intercept symbology shows a rotating 'HSI-like' cue centered on the waterline.

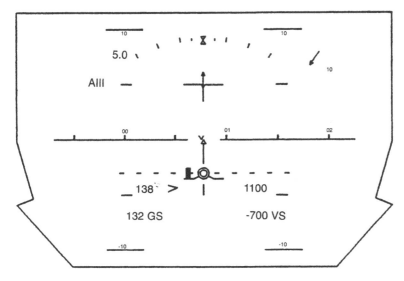

Figure 13.12   FDI 1000 HUD symbology (*13*)

FDI 2000 HUD

The FDI Model 2000 HGS is a development of the Model 1000. While also intended as a Category IIIa display, it has been approved for all flight regimes. Vertical tapes have been added to the airspeed and altitude scales to present trend information. The waterline deviation scale has been replaced with a partial HSI in the bottom of the FOV to improve orientation during course interception. While the HSI symbology appears quite cluttered, it actually occupies part of the FOV which is obscured by the aircraft nose and thus does not block the external visual scene. This can be seen in Figure 3.23.

The FDI 2000 HGS is certified in the B-737, although Category III approval has not yet been granted.

FV-2000 HUD

The Flight Visions FV-2000 is certified in the Beech A-100 King Air (*14*). This HUD (shown in Figure 13.13) displays aircraft pitch only. The pitch ladder is compressed full-time. The counter-pointers are unusual, displaying the digital values below the pointers.

The FV-2000 HUD is also certified in the Bell 230 helicopter. This HUD is similar to the King Air HUD, but adds a torque scale at the

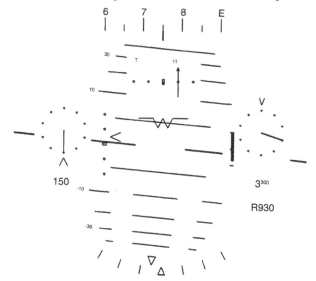

Figure 13.13   FV-2000 HUD fixed-wing symbology (*14*)

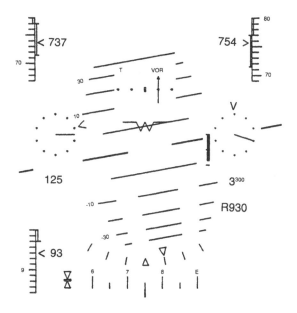

Figure 13.14   FV-2000 HUD helicopter symbology (*15*)

bottom left and separate engine temperature scales at the top left and right. The heading is also moved to the bottom above the roll scale. A collective cue is shown between the heading and the torque scales. Figure 13.14 shows the symbology (*15*).

The juxtaposition of the heading and roll scales at the bottom is potentially confusing. It appears to be a result of enforcing strict compliance with the basic T arrangement. Most civil HUDs have deviated from the basic T, using equivalent safety as a rationale (*16*).

MB-339C HUD

The MB-339C HUD was developed to be used during advanced weapons training (*17*). The HUD displays digits only for airspeed and counter-pointers for altitude. Radar altitude can be substituted for barometric altitude. This is indicated by a preceding 'R'. Figure 13.15 shows the symbology.

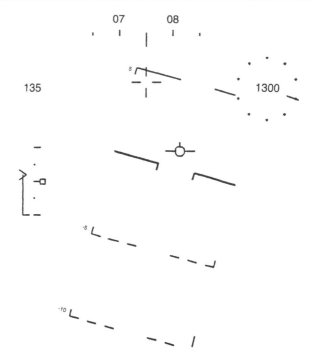

Figure 13.15   MB-339C HUD symbology (*17*)

McDonnell-Douglas HUD

The McDonnell-Douglas HUD displayed pitch information only (non-referenced pitch HUD). It was flown in several operational evaluations (*18*), but never became operational. The symbology is very similar to that shown in Figure 4.4.

MD-80 HUD

The MD-80 HUD (shown in Figure 13.16) was developed as a Category III monitor (*19*). It also allowed limited manual flight capacity. The single aircraft reference symbol is a highly augmented flight path symbol during the approach phase of flight and changes to show aircraft pitch during the missed approach climb.

ILS deviation is shown as a deviation box. A synthetic runway symbol is also shown to aid the flare and roll out.

260

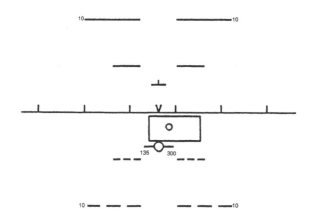

Figure 13.16   MD-80 HUD symbology (*19*)

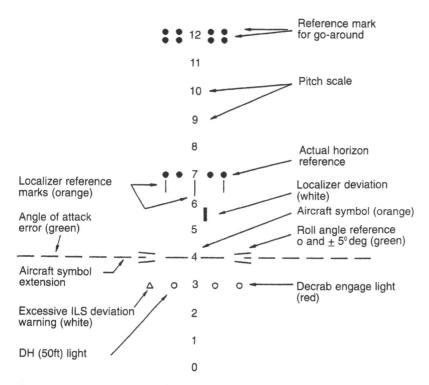

Figure 13.17   Mercure HUD symbology (*20*)

Mercure HUD

The Mercure HUD was also intended as a Category III monitor (*20*). It has sufficient cues to continue the approach in the event of an autoland failure below 50 ft. It is not suitable, nor was it intended for use during instrument flight.

The display (shown in Figure 13.17) makes use of a depressed pitch symbol to indicate the correct angle of attack when compared with the velocity vector.

Microvision

The Microvision HUD displayed an image of microwave transmitters located on the periphery of a runway. However, it never became

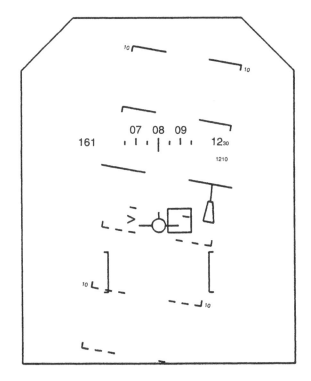

Figure 13.18   Mirage HUD symbology (*22*)

operational (*21*).

Mirage HUD

Figure 13.18 shows the Mirage symbology (*22*). The landing symbology is similar to PERSEPOLIS.

PERSEPOLIS HUD

The PERSEPOLIS HUD symbology (shown in Figure 13.19) was developed as a HUD allowing low visibility ILS approaches (*23*). The angle of attack error bracket is a fly-from scale. The Mirage symbology was developed from PERSEPOLIS.

Thomson TC-121

The Thomson-CSF HUD was the HUD showing the Klopfstein symbology (*24*). This is shown in Figure 2.1.

The Klopfstein symbology (*25*) combined air-mass angular information allowing precise control of airspeed/AOA and a contact analog runway allowing precise control of trajectory.

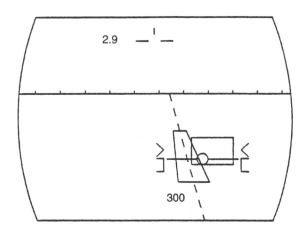

Figure 13.19   PERSEPOLIS experimental HUD symbology (*23*)

VAM-based HUDs

The Visual Approach Monitor was developed by Sundstrand Data Control. This HUD was an electromechanical display which presented images of incandescent wires in the FOV. The original version (VAM) displayed no roll information (*26*). Later derivatives incorporated roll information.

VAM

The Visual Approach Monitor HUD does not display an aircraft roll or any guidance. It displays a pitch reference to guide the landing glidepath in the absence of visual cues. If the flight path bar is placed over the touchdown point, the bar will be controlled to direct the airplane back to the desired glidepath (usually 3°, although other glidepath values could be set in the control panel).

A fast/slow airspeed error scale is shown on the HUD. The reference airspeed was set in the HUD control panel. Figure 13.20 shows the basic VAM symbology (*26*).

A radar-altitude-driven flare cue was offered as an option.

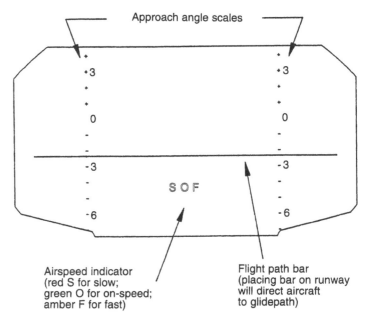

Figure 13.20   Visual Approach Monitor HUD symbology (*26*)

Light Line

The Light Line HUD was a modified VAM showing roll and pitch attitude and the velocity vector (*27*). It was installed in a T-38 in the late 1970s. The velocity vector represented a beam of light drawn in the direction of flight. The beam strobed to show airspeed error from the approach reference.

MARS HUD

The MARS HUD was installed operational in the mid-1970s in CH-3E and JC-130 mid-air retrieval systems (MARS) aircraft. This was a missionized display for recovering parachuted packages in mid-air. An inverted 'V' aiming symbol was overlaid on the parachute canopy. As the aircraft closed with the parachute, the symbol led the pilot to clear the canopy by the correct distance to engage a hook trailing below the aircraft (*28*).

References

(1)   *A-7D Flight Manual* (Washington: US Air Force, ca. 1984), TO-1A-7D-1
(2)   *Procurement Specifications for Display Set, Pilot Head-Up for a A-7D/E Airplane* (Dallas, Texas: Vought Aeronautics, 1967), Specification 204-16-19C
(3)   *A-10A Flight Manual* (Washington: US Air Force, ca. 1984), TO-1A-10A-1
(4)   *Manuel d'Exploitation A320 Partie Utilisation* (Paris: Air Inter, 1988), Section 227
(5)   *AV-8A Flight Manual* (Washington: Naval Air Systems Command, ca. 1984), NAVAIR-01-AV8A-1
(6)   *AV-8B Flight Manual* (Washington: Naval Air Systems Command, [1990]), NAVAIR A1-AV8BB-NFM-000
(7)   *F-14A Flight Manual* (Washington: Naval Air Systems Command, ca. 1984), NAVAIR-01-F14AAA-1
(8)   *F-14D Head Up Display (HUD) Format* (Bethpage, New York: Grumman Aerospace, 1985)
(9)   *F-15A Flight Manual* (Washington: US Air Force, ca. 1984), TO-1A-15A-1
(10)   *Literature Review of HUD Symbology* (Warrendale, Pennsylvania: Society of Automotive Engineers, 1991), SAE AIR-4654
(11)   *F-16A Flight Manual* (Washington: US Air Force, ca. 1984), TO-1A-16A-1
(12)   *F-18 Flight Manual* (Washington: Naval Air Systems Command, ca. 1984), NAVAIR-A1-F18AC-NFM-000
(13)   *FDI Model 1000 Head-Up Display System Specification* (Portland, Oregon: Flight Dynamics, February 1989), Report 404-0249
(14)   *Head-Up Displays for Corporate Aircraft* (Sugar Grove, Illinois: Flight Visions, ca. 1993)
(15)   *Introducing the First Head-Up Display for Your Helicopter* (Sugar Grove, Illinois: Flight Visions, ca. 1994)
(16)   'Issue of type certificate: normal, utility, acrobatic, commuter, and transport

category aircraft; manned free balloons, special classes of aircraft; aircraft engines; propellers', *Certification Procedures for Products and Parts,* (Washington, DC: Federal Aviation Administration, no date), Federal Aviation Regulations paragraph 21.21(b)(1)

(17) *MB-339C Aircraft Pilot's Guide* (Varese, Italy, Aermacchi, ca. 1993), PIPG01-9CB

(18) Therrien, R. L. 'Head-up display – a pilot's evaluation', *17th Annual Flight Safety Foundation Corporate Aircraft Safety Seminar, Washington* (Alexandria, Virginia: Flight Safety Foundation, 1972)

(19) *Head-Up Display for the DC-9 Super 80* (Long Beach, California: McDonnell-Douglas Aircraft, 1979)

(20) *Technical and Operational Description of CV-91AB* (Paris: Thomson-CSF, ca. 1980)

(21) *Head-Up Display* (Wright-Patterson AFB, Ohio: Air Force Flight Dynamics Laboratory, 1969), AFFDL Fact Sheet FS-69-57

(22) *Mirage 2000 Flight Manual* (Vaucresson, France: Avions Marcel Dassault-Breguet Aviation, ca. 1990), 1F-M2000-1-1

(23) Suisse, H. *Head-Up Display System: PERSEPOLIS Symbology* (Vaucresson, France: Avions Marcel Dassault-Breguet Aviation, 1979), DGT-16433

(24) *All Weather Approach and Landing Monitor, TC-121* (Paris: Thomson-CSF, no date)

(25) Klopfstein, G. *Rational Study of Aircraft Piloting* (Paris: Thomson-CSF, ca. 1966); reprint of 1966 article in *Intrados*

(26) *Visual Approach Monitor* (Redmond, Washington: Sundstrand Data Control, ca. 1977)

(27) *Light Line Head-Up Display System* (Redmond, Washington: Sundstrand Data Control, no date ca. 1978), Pilot Handbook

(28) Newman, R. L. *CH-3E (MARS) Head-Up Display Evaluation* (Yellow Springs, Ohio: Crew Systems, 1977), TR-77-02

Bibliography

The citations in this bibliography are listed on a year-by-year basis since this allows the reader to follow the chronological development of head-up displays more easily. Within each year, the references are listed alphabetically by author. References with no personal author follow at the end of each year's listing. References for which no publication date is available, or which are issued periodically, are grouped following the 1993 references.

Pre-1965

Lane, J. C. and Cumming, R. W. *The Role of Visual Cues in Final Approach to Landing* (Melbourne, Australia: Aeronautical Research Laboratories, 1955), HEN-1

Bentley, L. C. and Naish, J. M. *Means for Displaying Navigational Information to the Pilot of an Airplane* UK Patent 891255, July 1959

Lane, J. C. and Cumming, R. W. *Pilot Opinions and Practices on the Approach to Landing: A Questionnaire Survey Among Australian Civil and Military Pilots* (Melbourne, Australia: Aeronautical Research Laboratories, 1959), HER-1

Naish, J. M. *Simulation of Visual Flight with Particular Reference to Study of Flight Instruments* (Bedford, England: Royal Aircraft Establishment, 1960), CP-21663

Naish, J. M. *System for Presenting Steering Information During Visual Flight. Part I, The Position of the Presented Information* (Bedford, England: Royal Aircraft Establishment, 1961), RAE TN-IAP-1132

McLane, T. and Potter, E. F. *Development of an Advanced Approach and Landing Display* (Great Neck, New York: Sperry Gyroscope Co., 1962), CA-1245-0206

Naish, J. M. *System for Presenting Steering Information During Visual Flight. Part II, The Form of the Presentation* (Bedford, England: Royal Aircraft Establishment, 1962), RAE TN-IAP-1138

Baxter, J. R., 'Projected symbolic display – its application to all weather landing', in *15th IATA Technical Conference, Lucerne*, April 1963, WP-18

Mooney, P. F. 'Optically projected cockpit display for all-weather commercial operations', in *15th IATA Technical Conference, Lucerne*, April 1963, WP-88

Naish, J. M. 'Properties of a head-up display relevant to approach and landing', in *15th IATA Technical Conference, Lucerne*, April 1963, WP-106

Ramsey, W. E. and Momiyama, T. S. *Flight Test and Evaluation of the Sperry Head-Up Display Installed in an F-11A (F11F-1) Airplane* (Patuxent River, Maryland: NATC, 1963), NATC FT-2211-15R-63

Cane, P., 'Head-up display for the airlines', *Shell Aviation News*, no. 363, 1964, 16–19

Collins, L. 'Bendix Microvision', *Air Facts*, September 1964

Gold, T. *Flight Control System*, US Patent 3128623, 1964

Gold, T., 'Quickened manual flight control with external visual guidance', *IEEE Transactions on Aerospace and Navigational Electronics*, September 1964, 151–156

Johnson, R. K. and Momiyama, T. S. *Flight Test and Evaluation of the Spectocom Head-Up Display Installed in an A-5A Airplane* (Patuxent River, Maryland: NATC, 1964), NATC FT-2222-65R-64

Lambert, M., 'Head-up over the hills', *Flight International*, 22 October 1964, 709–713

Naish, J. M. *System for Presenting Steering Information During Visual Flight. Part III, The Influence of Errors and Limitations* (Bedford, England: Royal Aircraft Establishment, 1964), RAE TN-64026

Naish, J. M., 'Combination of information in superimposed visual fields', *Nature*, **202**, 1964, 641-646

Naish, J. M., 'The flight simulator in display research', Journal of The Royal Aeronautical Society, **68**, 1964, 653–659

Sviden, O. *Symbols and Control Laws for the Pole Track Head-Up Display* (Linköping, Sweden: SAAB, 1964), YK-37-64.B8

1965

Benson, A. J. 'Spatial disorientation in flight', in *A Textbook of Aviation Physiology*, Gillies, J. A. (ed.) (London: Pergamon Press, 1965), pp. 1086–1129

Bergstrom, B. *Multi-Task Performance in Simulated Flights with a Head-Up Display* (Linköping, Sweden: SAAB, 1965), YK-37-65.R1

Carel, W. L. *Pictorial Displays for Flight* (Culver City, California: Hughes Aircraft Co., 1965), TR-2732-01/40

Gold, T. and Workman, J. D. 'Research in the application of windshield projection displays to the all-weather landing task', *Journal of Aircraft* **2**, 1965, 328–336

Naish, J. M. 'Display research and its application to civil aircraft', *Journal of the Royal Aeronautical Society*, **69**, 1965, 662–669

Nordstrom, L. *Eye Level Flight Information by a Perspective Pole-Track* (Linköping, Sweden: SAAB, 1965), TN-58

1966

Bergstrom, B. 'Interpretability of symbols in a head-up display', in *6th Conference, Western European Association for Aviation Psychology, The Hague*, 1966

Fry, D. E., Burdin, K. and Green, M. R. *The Design and Flight Testing of a Take-off and Overshoot Director* (Bedford, England: Royal Aircraft Establishment, 1966), RAE TR-66083

Klopfstein, G. *Rational Study of Aircraft Piloting* (Paris: Thomson-CSF, ca. 1966); reprint of 1966 article in *Intrados*

Roscoe, S. N., Hasler, S. G. and Dougherty, D. J. 'Flight by telescope: making takeoffs and landings; the influence of image magnification; practice: and various conditions of flight', *Human Factors*, **8**, 1966, 13–40

1967

Behan, R. A. and Siciliani, F. A. 'Landing task and pilot acceptance of displays', *Journal of Aircraft*, **4**, 1967, 141–145

Bergstrom, B. *Interpretability Studies of Electronic Flight Instruments* (Linköping, Sweden: SAAB, 1967), SAAB TN-61

Stout, C. L. and Naish, J. M. 'Total system concept for Category III Operations', in *Proceedings 11th Symposium, Society of Experimental Test Pilots, Beverly Hills* (Lancaster, California: Society of Experimental

Test Pilots, 1967), pp. 79–105
Procurement Specifications for Display Set, Pilot Head-Up for a A-7D/E Airplane (Dallas, Texas: Vought Corp., 1967), Specification 204-16-19C

1968

DeBotton, I. 'Human factors evaluation of head-up display and flight performance by photography and data reduction methods', *Human Factors*, **10**, 1968, 41-52

Dekker, F. E. D. 'Head-Up Display Symbology', in *Problems of the Cockpit Environment* (Paris: Advisory Group for Aeronautical Research and Development, 1968), AGARD CP-55, Paper 23

Deliac, P. J., 'A collimator for head-up display piloting (CSF-193)', in *Problems of the Cockpit Environment* (Paris: Advisory Group for Aeronautical Research and Development, 1968), AGARD CP-55

Glover, J. H. *Visual Flight Landing Approach Aid* (Seattle, Washington: Boeing, 1968), D6-23712TN

Gold, T. and Deutschle, C. A. *Flight Simulation Study of Head-Up Displays for High-Speed Flight at Low Altitude* (Great Neck, New York: Sperry Rand Corp., 1968), SGD-4277-0190

Hyman, A. and Gold, T. 'Dynamic Visual Cues in Flying', *Current Developments in Optics and Vision* (Washington: NAS-NRC, 1968), pp. 3–21

Johnson, D. and Jones, R. W. 'The head-up display of approach information', in *Problems of the Cockpit Environment*, (Paris: Advisory Group for Aeronautical Research and Development, 1968), AGARD CP-55, Paper 20

Jullien, M. J. 'Elaboration et présentation d'information d'aide à l'atterrissage', in *Problems of the Cockpit Environment* (Paris: Advisory Group for Aeronautical Research and Development, 1968), AGARD CP-55, Paper 24

Ketchel, J. M. and Jenney, L. L. *Electronic and Optically Generated Aircraft Displays: A Study of Standardization Requirements* (Washington, Office of Naval Research, 1968), JANAIR 680505

Maureau, C. 'Head-up displays', in *The Impact of New Guidance and Control Systems on Military Aircraft Cockpit Designs* (Paris: Advisory Group of Aeronautical Research and Development, 1968), AGARD CP-312

St John, O. B. 'All-weather landing', *Shell Aviation News*, No. 364, 1968, 2–11

Schultz, W. C., 'Problems of information transfer in the modern jet cockpit', in *Problems of the Cockpit Environment* (Paris: Advisory Group for Aeronautical Research and Development, 1968), AGARD CP-55

Schultz, W. C. *Problems of Information Transfer in the Modern Jet Cockpit* (Buffalo, New York: Cornell Aeronautical Laboratory, 1968), CAL-IH-2235-B-1

Walters, D. J., 'The electronic display of primary flight data', in *Problems of the Cockpit Environment* (Paris: Advisory Group for Aeronautical Research and Development, 1968), AGARD CP-55, Paper 28

Wanner, J.-C. L. 'Présentation des informations nécessaires pour le décollage et l'atterrissage', in *Takeoff and Landing* (Paris: Adsvisory Group for Aeronautical Research and Development, 1968), AGARD CP-160, Paper 18

A Comparison of Electronic World and Flight Director World Head-Up Displays: Their Installation and Philosophy (Rochester, England: Elliott Brothers, 1968), ADD-229

Head-Up Display (Wright-Patterson AFB, Ohio: Air Force Flight Dynamics Laboratory, 1968), Fact Sheet FS-68-28

1969

Armstrong, D. B. *The Value of a Head-Up Display When Landing a Large Aircraft* (Bedford, England: Royal Aircraft Establishment, 1969), RAE TR-69236

Gold, T. and Potter, E. F. 'Visual suitability – a primary factor in head-up displays', *Sperry Rand Engineering Review*, 1969, 37–43

Kraft, C. L. and Elworth, C. L. 'Night visual approaches', *Air Line Pilot*, June 1969, 20–22

Naish, J. M. and Von Wieser, M. F., 'Human factors in the all-weather approach', *Shell Aviation News*, No. 374, 1969, 2–11

Singleton, W. T. 'Display design: principles and procedures', *Ergonomics*, **12**, 1969, 519–531

Sleight, G. R. and Lewis, C. J. G. *Practical Experience with Electronic Head-Up Displays in Transport Aircraft* (Rochester, England: Elliott, 1969), Report 29/11/2/BO5

80 Series Head-Up Display Fitted to McDonnell-Douglas DC-9-20 (Rochester, England: Marconi-Elliott, 1969)

Head-Up Display (Wright-Patterson AFB, Ohio: Air Force Flight Dynamics Laboratory, 1969), Fact Sheet FS-69-58

Head-Up Display (Wright-Patterson AFB, Ohio: Air Force Flight Dynamics Laboratory, 1969), Fact Sheet FS-69-59

Head-Up Display (Wright-Patterson AFB, Ohio: Air Force Flight Dynamics Laboratory, 1969), Fact Sheet FS-69-60

Head-Up Display (Wright-Patterson AFB, Ohio: Air Force Flight Dynamics Laboratory, 1969), Fact Sheet FS-69-62

1970

Gold, T. and Hyman, A. *Visual Requirements Study for Head-Up Displays* (Great Neck, New York: Sperry Rand Corp., 1970), JANAIR 680712

Kane, R. S. *Study and Analysis of Requirements for Head-Up Display (HUD)* (Washington: National Aeronautics and Space Administration, 1970), NASA CR-66912

Lowe, J. R. *Flight Path Angle Display Study* (Long Beach, California: McDonnell-Douglas Corp., 1970), MDC-J0812

Naish, J. M. 'Control gains in head-up presentation', in *Proceedings of 6th Annual Conference on Manual Control, Wright-Patterson AFB*, April 1970, pp. 19–46

Naish, J. M. *Flight Tests of the Head-Up Display (HUD) in DC-9-20, Ship 382* (Long Beach, California: McDonnell-Douglas Aircraft, 1970), MDC-J0878

Naish, J. M. *Properties and Design of the Head-Up Display* (Long Beach, California: McDonnell-Douglas Aircraft, 1970), MDC-J1409

Sherr, S. *Fundamentals of Display System Design* (New York: Wiley, 1970)

Technical Description of the Visual Landing System (Redmond, Washington: United Data Control, 1970), Document 060-0483-001A

Visual Landing Aid System (Wright-Patterson AFB, Ohio: Air Force Flight Dynamics Laboratory, 1970), Fact Sheet FS-70-61

1971

Benson, A. J. (ed.) *The Disorientation Incident* (Paris: Advisory Group for Aeronautical Research and Development, 1971), AGARD CP-95

Beranovsky, M. 'Electronic head-up display at pilot's eye level, Zravodaj Vzlu (Czechoslovakia)', No. 6, 1971, 5-17; NASA TT-F-17390

Dobie, T. G. 'The disorientation accidents – philosophy of instrument flying training', *The Disorientation Incident*, Benson, A. J. (ed.) (Paris: Advisory Group for Aeronautical Research and Development, 1971), AGARD CP-95, Paper A15

Driscoll, N. 'Avionics integration – the pilot's part', in *Proceedings 15th Symposium, Society of Experimental Test Pilots, Beverly Hills* (Lancaster, California: Society of Experimental Test Pilots, 1971), pp. 189–197

Foxworth, T. G. and Newman, R. L. *A Pilot's Look at Aircraft Instrumentation* (New York: American Institute of Aeronautics and

Astronautics, 1971), AIAA Paper 71-787

Frieberg, U. 'Basic about scale one-to-one head-up display', in *Proceedings 15th Symposium, Society of Experimental Test Pilots, Beverly Hills* (Lancaster, California: Society of Experimental Test Pilots, 1971), pp. 77–85

Jenney, L. L., Malone, T. B. and Schweickart, G. A. *Head-Up Displays: A Study of Their Applicability in Civil Aviation* (Washington: National Aeronautics and Space Administration, 1971), NASA CR-117135

Larribiere and Lacombe, 'Exploitation des Minima categorie IIIA à Air Inter' (Exploitation of Category IIIA Minima at Air Inter), in *Colloquium on Aeronautical Meteorology, Paris,* May 1971, Paper 9

Naish, J. M., 'Information transfer in all-weather operations', *Shell Aviation News*, No. 396, 1971, 8–10

Semple, C. A. *et al. Analysis of Human Factors Data for Electronic Flight Display Systems* (Wright-Patterson AFB, Ohio: Air Force Flight Dynamics Laboratory, 1971), AFFDL TR-70-174

Tyler, P. E. and Furr, P. A. 'Disorientation, "fact and Fancy"', in *The Disorientation Incident,* Benson, A. J. (ed.) (Paris: Advisory Group for Aeronautical Research and Development, 1971), AGARD CP-95, Paper A4

Engineering Report, Delta Gamma Visual Landing System (Redmond, Washington: Sundstrand Data Control, 1971), Report 070-0676-001

1972

Augustine, W. L. *Head-Up Display Area Survey* (Wright-Patterson AFB, Ohio: Air Force Flight Dynamics Laboratory, 1972), AFFDL TM-72-11-FGR

Berjal, M. *Experimental Testing of Flight Control Head-Up Displays* (Paris: Air France, 1972)

Gold, T. and Perry, R. F. *Visual Requirements Study for Head-Up Displays* (Great Neck, New York: Sperry Rand Corp., 1972), JANAIR 700407

Larry, C. and Elworth, C. L. *The Effects of Pilot Age, Lighting, and Head-Down Time on Visual Accommodation* (Seattle, Washington: Boeing, 1972), D162-10378-1

Lincoln, R., Palmer, E. A. and Wempe, T. E. *Effect of Pictorial Display Configuration on the Frequency of Control Reversals During Aircraft Landing Approaches* (Moffett Field, California: National Aeronautics and Space Administration, 1972), NASA TM-X-62191

Naish, J. M. 'Factors affecting head-up display design', in *8th Annual Symposium on Human Factors in Electronics, Palo Alto,* May 1972

Naish, J. M. 'A conformal head-up display for the visual approach', in

Proceedings of the 8th Annual Conference on Manual Control, Ann Arbor (Cambridge, Massachusetts: Massachusetts Institute of Technology, 1972), pp. 159–174

Naish, J. M. 'Application of the head-up display (HUD) to a commercial jet transport', *Journal of Aircraft*, **9**, 1972, 530–536

Palmer, E. A. *Night Visual Approaches – Pilot Performance With and Without a Head-Up Display* (Moffett Field, California: National Aeronautics and Space Administration, 1972), NASA TM-X-62188

Reising, J. M. and Augustine, W. L. *Evaluation of the Thomson-CSF CV-91 and Observation of the TC-121 Displays*, (Wright-Patterson AFB, Ohio: Air Force Flight Dynamics Laboratory, 1972), TM-72-9-FGR

Smith, J. H. 'The evolution of head-up displays', *Interavia*, **27**, 1972, 858–860

Therrien, R. L. 'Head-up display – a pilot's evaluation', in *17th Annual Flight Safety Foundation Corporate Aircraft Safety Seminar, Washington*, April 1972

Von Wieser, M. F. 'Operating a head-up display', *Shell Aviation News*, No. 411, 1972, 14–19

A-7E Nav/Weapon Delivery System (Dallas, Texas: Vought Corp., 1972)

Farrand Ultra-Wide Field of View Head-Up Display (Wright-Patterson AFB, Ohio: Air Force Flight Dynamics Laboratory, 1972), Fact Sheet FS-72-68

McDonnell-Douglas F-15 Head-Up Display (Wright-Patterson AFB, Ohio: Air Force Flight Dynamics Laboratory, 1972), Fact Sheet FS-72-67

Military Specification: Display, Head-Up, General Specification for (Philadelphia, Pennsylvania: Naval Publications and Forms Center, 1972), MIL-D-81641(AS)

Theory of Operation, Visual Approach Monitor Utilizing a Vertical Gyro and Pitot-Static Inputs (Redmond, Washington: Sundstrand Data Control, 1972), Document 020-0026-001

1973

DeBellis, W. B. *Flight Information Scale Test for Heads-Up and Panel Mounted Displays* (Aberdeen, Maryland: Aberdeen Proving Ground, 1973), HEL-TM-22-73

DeCelles, J. L., Burke, E. J. and Burroughs, K. L. 'A real world situation display for all-weather landing', in *Crew System Design*, Cross, K. D. and McGrath, J. J. (eds), (Santa Barbara, California: Anacapa Sciences, 1973), pp. 255–263

Foxworth, T. G. *A new concept of flying: flying the TC-121 all-weather head-up display* (Egham, England: International Federation of Air Line

274

Pilots Associations, 1973)

Harris, R. L. and Hewes, D. E. *An Exploratory Simulation Study of a Head-Up Display for General Aviation Lightplanes*, (Hampton, Virginia: National Aeronautics and Space Administration, 1973), NASA TN-D-7456

Hoerner, F. C. 'V/STOL terminal guidance head-up displays: a real world evaluation', in *Crew System Design*, Cross, K. D. and McGrath, J. J. (eds) Santa Barbara, California: Anacapa Sciences, 1973), pp. 273-274

McCloskey, St J. *Flying the TC-121, A Visit to Bretigny to Fly the Thomson-CSF Head-Up Display* (Egham, England: International Federation of Air Line Pilots Associations, 1973), Document 74C95

McGrath, I. L. *Trident All Weather Operations* (London: British European Airlines, 1973)

Mackie, R., 'The jet turbine aircraft in the Canadian Arctic', paper presented at *Canadian Aeronautics and Space Institute Symposium on Aircraft Operations in the Canadian Arctic, Edmonton* (Edmonton, Alberta: Pacific Western Airlines, 1973)

Opittek, E. W. *Head-Up Display Study* (Wright-Patterson AFB, Ohio: Air Force Avionics Laboratory, 1973), AFAL TR-73-215

Parks, D. P., Hayashi, M. M. and Fries, J. R. *Development of an Independent Altitude Monitor Concept* (Seattle, Washington: Boeing, 1973), FAA RD-73-168

Wanner, J.-C. L. 'Piloting techniques and flying qualities of the next generation of aircraft', *Aeronautical Journal*, **77**, 1973, 593–605

Weener, E. F., Howe, R. M. and Pew, R. W. 'Effects of visual flight display on altitude tracking performance in a flight simulator', in *Proceedings 9th Annual Conference on Manual Control, Cambridge* (Cambridge, Massachusetts: Massachusetts Institute of Technology, 1973), pp. 3–8

Wilckens, V. 'Improvements in pilot/aircraft integration by advanced contact analog displays', in *Proceedings of the 9th Annual Conference on Manual Control, Cambridge* (Cambridge, Massachusetts: Massachusetts Institute of Technology, 1973), pp. 175–192

Cahier des Charges du Collimateur TH-CSF Type 193M (Paris: Thomson-CSF, 1973), AVG/OP-73/169C

Special Study Report on Approach and Landing Accident Prevention (Washington: National Transportation Safety Board, 1973) NTSB AAS-73-2

1974

Behm, D. 'HUD: radar and air-to-air modes', *McDonnell-Douglas Product Support Digest*, **21**, 1974, 11–12

Geddes, J. P., 'Avionics and the Corsair', *Interavia*, **19**, October 1974, 1015–1018

Gold, T. and Walchli, R. M. *Head-Up Display for All-Weather Approach and Landing of Tilt-Wing V/STOL Aircraft* (New York: American Institute of Aeronautics and Astronautics, 1974), AIAA Paper 74-952

Harris, R. L. *Simulation and Flight Evaluation of a Heads-Up Display for General Aviation* (Warrendale, Pennsylvania: Society of Automotive Engineers, 1974), SAE Paper 740347

Hutchinson, J. E. 'The approach hazard', *Shell Aviation News*, No. 426, 1974, 10–15

Plummer, C. 'HUD ... basic symbology, hardware, and navigation modes', *McDonnell-Douglas Product Support Digest*, **21**, 1974, 8–10

Pursel, R. H. *An Evaluation of a Microwave Runway Perspective Independent Landing Monitor* (Atlantic City, New Jersey: Federal Aviation Administration, 1974), FAA-RD-73-201; FAA-NA-73-95

Riordan, R. H. 'Monocular visual cues and space perception during the approach to landing', *Aerospace Medicine*, **45**, 1974, 766–771

Ropelewski, R. R. 'Viggen designed to ease pilot workload', *Aviation Week*, 1 May, 1974, 42–49

Sorum, D. R. and Fister, B. L. *C-5 Visual Approach Monitor* (Scott ABF, Illinois: Miltary Airlift Command, 1974) MAC-OTO-15-2-73

Weener, E. F. *The Effects of Simulator Dynamics on Pilot Response* (Moffett Field, California: National Aeronautics and Space Administration, 1974), NASA CR-132459

A-7D Navigation/Weapon Delivery System (Dallas, Texas: Vought Aeronautics, 1974), Report 2-14000/4R-10

The Requirement for VAM (Redmond, Washington: Sundstrand Data Control, 1974)

1975

Crews, L. L. and Hall, C. H. *A7D/E Aircraft Navigation Equations* (China Lake, California: Naval Weapons Center, 1975), NWC TN-404-176

Cronn, F. W. and Palmer, E. A. *Comparison of Two Head-Up Displays in Simulated Standard and Noise Abatement Night Visual Approaches* (Moffett Field, California: National Aeronautics and Space Administration, 1975), NASA TM-X-3264

Doucette, A. R. 'F-14 aircraft head up display', in *Proceedings National*

Aerospace Electronics Conference (NAECON '75), Dayton, (New York: Institute of Electrical and Electronics Engineers, 1975), pp. 594–600

Dwyer, J. H. and Palmer, E. A. *Three Methods of Presenting Flight Vector Information in a Head-Up Display During Simulated STOL Approaches* (Moffett Field, California: National Aeronautics and Space Administration, 1975), NASA TM-X-3273

Hutchinson, J. E. 'Velocity vector – the logical solution – aircraft guidance HUD', *Shell Aviation News,* No. 427, 1975, 6-10

Kirschner, R. K. *The Light-Line Head-Up Display: A Unique Three Dimensional Display Cue* (Redmond, Washington: Sundstrand Data Control, 1975)

Lavernhe, J. 'A new pilot head-up display – medical and physiological considerations', *Revue de Medicine Aeronautique et Spatiale,* **14,** 1975, 3–ff.

Orrick, W. P. and York, P. E. *Head-Up Display Symbology* (Warminster, Pennsylvania: Naval Air Development Center, 1975), NADC 75267-40

Walchli, R. M. *et al. Flight Evaluation of a Head-Up Display with Real World Overlay for Instrument Approach and Landing of V/STOL Aircraft* (Patuxent River, Maryland: Naval Air Test Center, 1975), NATC TR-SY-23R-75

Approche Automatique Mode Land, Periode Transitore de 1 Avril 75 au 12 Octobre 75 (Paris: Air Inter, 1975)

AV-8A Head Up Display Modification Specification (St Louis, Missouri: McDonnell-Douglas Aircraft, 1975), MDC-A3589

Military Standard: Electronically or Optically Generated Displays for Aircraft Control or Combat Cue Information (Philadelphia, Pennsylvania: Naval Publications and Forms Center, 1975), MIL-STD-884C

The Peri-HUD (Rochester, England: Marconi–Elliott, 1975)

1976

Barnette, J. F. *Role of Head-Up Display in Instrument Flight* (Randolph AFB, Texas: Air Force Instrument Flight Center, 1976), AFIFC LR-76-2

Barnette, J. F. and Intano, G. P. *Determining the Utility of Expanded Pitch Scale and Flightpath Angle as Display Parameters* (Randolph AFB, Texas: Air Force Instrument Flight Center, 1976), AFIFC TR-76-4

Doucette, A. R. 'Design decisions for a head-up display', *IEEE Spectrum,* **13,** 1976, 28–32

Egan, D. E. 'Research toward improving the performance of pilots using head-up displays', in *Proceedings of the Carrier Landing*

Performance Conference, Norfolk, April 1976, pp. 117–131

Eisele, J. E., Willeges, R. C. and Roscoe, S. N. *The Isolation of Minimum Sets of Visual Image Cues Sufficient for Spatial Orientation During Aircraft Landing Approaches* (Champaign, Illinois: University of Illinois, 1976), ARC-76-16/ONR-76-3

Ellis, S. M. *Head-Up Display Units and Optical Devices* US Patent 3936148, 1976

Ertzgaard, J. H. *IFALPA Flight Test Report: Thomson-CSF TC-121* (Egham, England: International Federation of Air Line Pilots Associations, 1976), L76C228

Fuller, H. V. and Outlaw, B. K. E. *Description of a Landing Site Indicator (LASI) for Light Aircraft Operation* (Hampton, Virginia: National Aeronautics and Space Administration, 1976), NASA TM-X-72811

Gallaher, P. D., Hunt, R. A. and Williges, R. C. *A Regression Analysis to Generate Aircraft Predictor Information* (Washington: National Aeronautics and Space Administration, 1976), NASA TM-X-73170

Harris, R. L., Goode, M. W. and Yenni, K. R. *Simulation and Flight Evaluation of a Head-Up Display Landing Aid for General Aviation* (Hampton, Virginia: National Aeronautics and Space Administration, 1976), NASA TP-1276

Hillman, R. E. and Wilson, J. W. 'Investigation into the optimum use of advanced displays in future transport aircraft', *Aeronautical Journal,* **80**, 1976, 377–384

Kama, W. N., Martin, W. L., and Kuperman, G. G. 'The effect of HUD symbology size on operator performance under various luminance conditions', in paper presented at *5th Symposium on Psychology in the Air Force,* April 1976

Karmarker, J. S. and Sorenson, J. A. *Information and Display Requirements for Independent Landing Monitors* (Washington: National Aeronautics and Space Administration, 1976), NASA CR-2687

Klopfstein, G. 'Rational study of aircraft piloting', in *Proceedings 3rd Advanced Aircrew Display Symposium,* Patuxent River, May 1976, pp. 231–248

Swartz, W. F., Condra, D. M. and Madero, R. P. *Pilot Factors Considerations in See-to-Land* (Wright-Patterson AFB, Ohio: Air Force Flight Dynamics Laboratory, 1976), AFFDL TR-76-52

Tapia, M. H. and Intano, G. P. *Light-Line Visual Landing Head-Up Display (HUD) Evaluation, Phase I* (Randolph AFB, Texas: Air Force Instrument Flight Center, 1976), AFIFC TR-76-1

Terhune, G. J. *TC-121 and Other HUD Mismatch with Runway* (Washington: Air Line Pilots Association, 1976)

Bendix Micro HUD (Wright-Patterson AFB, Ohio: Air Force Flight Dynamics Laboratory, 1976), Fact Sheet FS-76-01

Critical Item Development Specification for Head-Up Display (Hagerstown, Maryland: Fairchild Aircraft, 1976), Specification 16OS417001B
Head-Up Display Evaluation (Hickam AFB, Hawaii: 6594th Test Group, 1976), LTR-76-8
Head-Up Displays (Redmond, Washington: Sundstrand Data Control, 1976)
System Specification: Head-Up Display (HUD) Air Retrieval System (Redmond, Washington: Sundstrand Data Control, 1976), 070-0936-001B

1977

Bateman, C. D. 'A review of some recent undershoot accidents and incidents: five year period July 1972 to 1977', in *Proceedings of the International Head-Up Display Symposium, Vancouver*, (Redmond, Washington: Sundstrand Data Control, 1977), pp. 27–33
Carel, W. L. *Advanced Contact Analog Symbology* (Culver City, California: Hughes Aircraft Co., 1977), D-7123
Chisum, G. T. and Morway, P. E. 'Effect of virtual image projection distance on the accommodative response of the eye', *Aviation, Space, and Environmental Medicine*, **48**, 1977, 819–823
Coonrod, J. F. and Ernstoff, M. N., 'Advanced head-up display technology – the integrated HUD', in *Proceedings National Aerospace Electronics Conference (NAECON '77)*, Dayton (New York: Institute of Electrical and Electronics Engineers, 1977), pp. 981–990
Ernst, H. L. 'YC-14 VAM/HUD program experience', in *Proceedings of the International Head-Up Display Symposium, Vancouver* (Redmond, Washington: Sundstrand Data Control, 1977), pp. 46–55
Green, G. N. *Head-Up Display Symbology* (Bedford, England: Royal Aircraft Establishment, 1977), RAE TN-77050
Haines, R. F. 'FAA/NASA head-up display program', in *Proceedings of the International Head-Up Display Symposium, Vancouver* (Redmond, Washington: Sundstrand Data Control, 1977), pp. 82–91
Kiltz, R. M., 'Fundamentals of HUD Technology', in *Proceedings of the International Head-Up Display Symposium, Vancouver* (Redmond, Washington: Sundstrand Data Control, 1977)
Long, M. G. 'Considerations in the simulation of head-up displays', in *Proceedings of the International Head-Up Display Symposium, Vancouver* (Redmond, Washington: Sundstrand Data Control, 1977), pp. 62–73
Mazza, J. D. *A Comparison of Integrated and Conventional Cockpit Warning Systems*, Thesis, Naval Postgraduate School, 1977
Newman, R. L. *CH-3E (MARS) Head-Up Display Evaluation* (Yellow

Springs, Ohio: Crew Systems, 1977), TR-77-02

Newman, R. L. 'Head-up displays: crew procedures and training implications', in *Proceedings of the International Head-Up Display Symposium, Vancouver* (Redmond, Washington: Sundstrand Data Control, 1977), pp. 74–81

Penwill, J. C. *A Simulator Study to Examine the Problems of Manual Landings in Cat 3 Conditions* (Bedford, England: Royal Aircraft Establishment, 1977), RAE TM-FS-149

Ribiere, R. *Analysis of Civilian Aircraft Flight Safety in the Approach and Landing* (Paris: Thomson-CSF, 1977)

Short, D. C. 'Operational briefing', in *Proceedings of the International Head-Up Display Symposium, Vancouver* (Redmond, Washington: Sundstrand Data Control, 1977), pp. 33–42

Terhune, G. J. 'How an airline pilot would use HUD', in *Proceedings of the International Head-Up Display Symposium, Vancouver* (Redmond, Washington: Sundstrand Data Control, 1977), pp. 92–110

Les Approches de Precision de Categorie III à la Compagnie Air Inter (Paris: Air Inter, 1977)

System Specification: Visual Approach Monitor for the B-737 Aircraft System No. 960-2008 (Redmond, Washington: Sundstrand Data Control, 1977), 060-1624

1978

Augustine, W. L. *et al.* 'A head-up display for drone recovery', in *Proceedings of the 14th Annual Conference on Manual Control, Los Angeles* (Washington: National Aeronautics and Space Administration, 1978), NASA CP-2060, pp. 381–394

Borodin, V. T. and Rylskii, G. I. *Piloting and Control Systems for Airplanes and Helicopters* (Moscow: Izdatel'stvo Mashinostroenie, 1978)

Brown, A. D., Penwill, J. C. and Packwood, R. J. *A Preliminary Simulator Evaluation of a Monocular HUD as an All-Weather Approach Aid* (Bedford, England: Blind Landing Experimental Unit, 1978), BLEU TM-FS-229

Clement, W. F. *Potential Control Display Investigations for V/STOL Terminal Operations: Vol. III, Head-Up Display Requirements* (Warminster, Pennsylvania: Naval Air Development Center, 1978), NADC 77030-30

DeCelles, J. L. and Terhune, G. J. *A HUD Symbology for Civil Transport Aircraft* (Washington: Air Line Pilots Association, 1978)

Egan, D. E. and Goodson, J. E. *Human Factors Engineering for Head-Up Displays: A Review of Military Specifications and Recommendations for*

Research (Pensacola, Florida: Naval Aeromedical Research Laboratory, 1978), Monograph 23

Foxworth, T. G. 'Head-up displays' *Journal of the British Air Line Pilots Association*, **39**, July 1978, 5–7

Gibson, C. P. *Collimation and the Human Visual System – A Review and Literature Search* (Bedford, England: Royal Aircraft Establishment, 1978), RAE TM-FS-173

Guercio, J. G. and Haines, R. F. *A Preliminary Study of Head-Up Display Assessment Techniques. II. HUD Symbology and Panel Information Search Time* (Moffett Field, California: National Aeronautics and Space Administration, 1978), NASA TM-78536; NASA HUD Report 3

Haines, R. F. *Project Plan for Joint FAA/NASA Head-Up Display Concept Evaluation* (Moffett Field, California: National Aeronautics and Space Administration, 1978), NASA TM-78512; NASA HUD Report 1

Haines, R. F. *Preliminary Study of Head-Up Display Assessment Techniques. I. Viewing Duration of Instrument Panel and HUD Symbology Using a Recall Methodology* (Moffett Field, California: National Aeronautics and Space Administration, 1978), NASA TM-78517; NASA HUD Report 2

Iavecchia, J. H., Iavecchia, H. P. and Roscoe, S. N. *The Moon Illusion: Apparent Size and Accommodation Distance* (Champaign, Illinois: University of Illinois, 1978), Eng Psy-78-4/AFOSR 78-3

Jensen, R. H. 'The effects of prediction, quickening, frequency separation, and percent of pursuit in perspective displays for low-visibility landing', in *Proceedings of the 22nd Annual Meeting of the Human Factors Society, Detroit* (Santa Monica, California: Human Factors Society, 1978), pp. 208–212

Lebacqz, J. V., Radford, R. C. and Beilman, J. L. *An Experimental Investigation of Control–Display Requirements for a Jet-Lift VTOL Aircraft in the Terminal Area* (Buffalo, New York: Calspan Corp., 1978), AK-58985-F-1

Lowe, J. R. *Improving the Accuracy of HUD Approaches with a New Control Law* (New York: American Institute of Aeronautics and Astronautics, 1978), AIAA Paper 78-1494

Newman, R. L. 'KC-135 boom operator's head-up display', *Journal of Aircraft*, **15**, 1978, 124–126

Schiff, B. 'Poor man's autothrottle', *Aircraft Owners and Pilots Association Pilot*, January 1978, pp. 55–57

Short, D. C. 'Head-up display in operation', *Flight Operations*, March 1978, pp. 25–29

Prime Item Development Specification for the F-16 Head-Up Display Set, CDRL-ELIN-A008 (Fort Worth, Texas: General Dynamics, 1978),

Specification 16ZE017C

979

Berg, A. 'Diffraction HUD concept', in *Proceedings of the Flight Operations Symposium, Vancouver* (Redmond, Washington: Sundstrand Data Control, 1979), Vol. II, pp. 59–76; Vol. IIA, section 3

Brown, A. D. and Gurney, D. J. 'Manual landings in Category 3 conditions', *Aeronautical Journal*, **83**, 1979, 296–305

Chisum, G. T. and Morway, P. E. *Visual Accommodation Responses in a Virtual Image Environment* (Warminster, Pennsylvania: Naval Air Development Center, 1979), NADC 79216-60

Chorley, R. A. and St. Leger Searle, S. M. 'Use of diffractive optical elements in head-up displays in aircraft', *Conference on Electronic Displays 1979, London*, September 1979, pp. 11–ff

DeCelles, J. L. and Terhune, G. J. 'Flight instrumentation requirements for all-weather approach and landing', in *Proceedings 1979 Air Transportation Conference, New Orleans*, April 30–May 3 1979, pp. 153–164

Fadden, D. N. and Weener, E. F. 'Computer generated displays as primary flight instruments', in *New Technology and Aviation Safety, Proceedings 32nd International Air Safety Seminar, Flight Safety Foundation, London*, October 1979, pp. 127–133

Fisher, E. *The Role of Cognitive Switching in Head-Up Displays* (Moffett Field, California: National Aeronautics and Space Administration, 1979), NASA CR-3137; NASA HUD Report 5

Frank, L. H. *Comparison of Specifications for Head-Up Displays in the Navy A-4M, A-7E, AV-8A, and F-14A Aircraft* (Pensacola, Florida: Naval Aeromedical Research Laboratory, 1979), SR-79-6

Haines, R. F. 'FAA/NASA HUD study', in *Proceedings of the Flight Operations Symposium, Vancouver* (Redmond, Washington: Sundstrand Data Control, 1979), Vol. I, pp. 38–69; Vol. IA, section 2

Haines, R. F. and Guercio, J. G. 'A comparison of information transfer from an instrument panel and symbolic display containing an equivalent amount of information', in *Proceedings of the 1979 Meeting of the Aerospace Medical Association, Washington*, May 1979, pp. 37–38

Haines, R. F. *Selected Research Issues and Abbreviated Discussion Related to Head-Up Displays* (Moffett Field, California: National Aeronautics and Space Administration, 1979), NASA HUD Report 8

Jeffley, R. K. and Jewell, W. F. *Development of a CTOL Pilot Technique Measurement Scheme for a Real-Time Simulator Environment* (Moffett

Bibliography

Field, California: National Aeronautics and Space Administration, 1979), NASA CR-152294; NASA HUD Report 9

Heft, E. L. and Newman, R. L., 'Using a head-up display for mid-air retrieval systems', in *Proceedings of the Flight Operations Symposium, Vancouver* (Redmond, Washington: Sundstrand Data Control, 1979), Vol. II, pp. 76–93; Vol. IIA, section 4

Hoerner, F. C. 'HUD military aspects', in *Proceedings of the Flight Operations Symposium, Vancouver* (Redmond, Washington: Sundstrand Data Control, 1979), Vol. II, pp. 53–58, 117–145

Ivins, M. 'Space Shuttle applications', in *Proceedings of the Flight Operations Symposium, Vancouver* (Redmond, Washington: Sundstrand Data Control, 1979), Vol. II, pp. 104–117; Vol. IIA, section 6

Juergens, R. A. 'F/A-18 Hornet display system', in *Proceedings National Aerospace Electronics Conference (NAECON'79), Dayton* (New York: Institute of Electrical and Electronics Engineers, 1979), pp. 434–442

Kiltz, R. M. 'HUDs: an overview of progress', in *Proceedings of the Flight Operations Symposium, Vancouver* (Redmond, Washington: Sundstrand Data Control, 1979), Vol. I, pp. 10–38; Vol. IA, section 1

Lebacqz, J. V. *Survey of Helicopter Control/Display Investigations for Instrument Decelerating Approaches* (Moffett Field, California: National Aeronautics and Space Administration, 1979), NASA TM-78565; NASA HUD Report 15

Moroney, W. F., Pruitt, R. and Lau, C. 'Utilization of energy maneuverability data in improving in-flight performance and performance in air combat maneuvering', in *Proceedings of 23rd Annual Meeting of the Human Factors Society, Boston* (Santa Monica, California: Human Factors Society, 1979), pp. 503–507

Naish, J. M. *Review of Some Head-Up Display Formats* (Moffett Field, California: National Aeronautics and Space Administration, 1979), NASA TP-1499; NASA HUD Report 4

Owens, D. A. 'The Mandelbaum effect: evidence for an accommodative bias toward intermediate viewing distances', *Journal of the Optical Society of America*, **69**, 1979, 646–651

Oliver, J. G. *A Report on the TC-125 Head-Up Display* (Washington: Air Line Pilots Association, 1979)

Peer, Y. 'Flight testing the Kfir', *Society of Experimental Test Pilots Technical Review*, **14**, 1979, pp. 26–37

Pekich, H. 'Boom operator HUD', in *Proceedings of the Flight Operations Symposium, Vancouver* (Redmond, Washington: Sundstrand Data Control, 1979), Vol. II, pp. 1–27; Vol. IIA, section 4

Roland-Billecart, A. and Deschamps, J. G. 'Operational experience with HUD in CAT III', in *Proceedings of the Flight Operations Symposium,*

Vancouver (Redmond, Washington: Sundstrand Data Control, 1979), Vol. I, pp. 122–153

Roscoe, S. N. *Ground Referenced Visual Orientation with Imaging Displays* (Champaign, Illinois: University of Illinois, 1979), TR-Eng Psy-79-4/AFOSR-79-4

Roscoe, S. N. 'When day is done and shadows fall, we miss the airport most of all', *Human Factors*, **21**, 1979, 721–731

Schilling, R. 'Operational requirements for CAT III and HUDs on DC-9-80', in *Proceedings of the Flight Operations Symposium, Vancouver* (Redmond, Washington: Sundstrand Data Control, 1979), Vol. II, pp. 1–27; Vol. IIA, section 1

Shawler, W. H. 'Night/adverse weather A-10 evaluator program', *Society of Experimental Test Pilots Technical Review*, **14**, 1979, pp. 27–30

Smith, R. H., Geddes, N. D. and Honaker, J. *A Phase Angle Design Criteria for Dynamic Fidelity of Manned Aircraft Simulators* (Beavercreek, Ohio: System Research Laboratories, 1979)

Smith, R. H. and Geddes, N. D. *Handling Quality Requirement for Advanced Aircraft Design: Longitudinal Mode* (Wright-Patterson AFB, Ohio: Air Force Flight Dynamics Laboratory, 1979), AFFDL TR-78-154

Smith, W. D. 'Boeing HUD development', in *Proceedings of the Flight Operations Symposium, Vancouver* (Redmond, Washington: Sundstrand Data Control, 1979), Vol. I, pp. 69–97

Suisse, H. *Head-Up Display System – PERSEPOLIS Symbology* (Vaucresson, France: Avions Marcel Dassault-Breguet Aviation, 1979), DGT-16433

Terhune, G. J. 'Flight guidance data required in CAT III HUD', in *Proceedings of the Flight Operations Symposium, Vancouver*, (Redmond, Washington: Sundstrand Data Control, 1979), Vol. II, pp. 27–52; Vol. IIA, section 2

Terhune, G. J. *Report to ALPA on PERSEPOLIS Simulations* (Washington: Air Line Pilots Association, 1979)

Terhune, G. J. *Report to ALPA on TC-125 Simulations* (Washington: Air Line Pilots Association, 1979)

Uhlin, J. G. 'Experience from testing the Viggen electronic systems utilizing existing computer capacity', in *Proceedings of the 10th Annual Symposium, Society of Flight Test Engineers, Las Vegas* September 1979

Woodburn, P. 'Are we being HUDwinked', in *Proceedings of the Flight Operations Symposium, Vancouver* (Redmond, Washington: Sundstrand Data Control, 1979), Vol. I, pp. 97–122

AH-1S Cobra Attack Helicopter Head-Up Display System Description (San Jose, California: Kaiser Electronics, 1979), Brochure 78-3945

'Head-up displays, the tide has turned', *Air Line Pilot*, October 1979, 30–31

Head-Up Display for the DC-9 Super 80 (Long Beach, California, Douglas Aircraft, 1979)

Head-Up Display for the DC-9 Super 80 (Redmond, Washington: Sundstrand Data Control, 1979)

'KC-135s get "heads-up" research – head-up displays in midair refueling', *Aviation Engineering and Maintenance*, **3**, March 1979, 43–45

Military Specification: Flying Qualities of Piloted Airplanes (Philadelphia, Pennsylvania: Naval Publications and Forms Center, 1979), MIL-F-8785C

Programme Simulateur – Approche Automatique Mode Land (Paris: Air Inter, 1979)

'A word from the Navy', *ALPA Head-Up Display Newsletter*, January 1979, pp. 4-5

1980

Adamson, J. C., Born, G. J. and Dukes, T. A. *A Simulator Study of Control and Display Augmentations for Helicopters* (Princeton, New Jersey: Princeton University, 1980), NASA CR-163451

Berry, D. T. *et al. A Summary of an In-Flight Evaluation of Control System Pure Time Delays During Landing Using the F-8 DFBW Airplane* (New York: American Institute of Aeronautics and Astronautics, 1980), AIAA Paper 80-1626

Bray, R. S. A *Head-Up Display Format for Application to Transport Aircraft Approach and Landing* (Moffett Field, California: National Aeronautics and Space Administration, 1980), NASA TM-81199; NASA HUD Report 11

DeCelles, J. L. *et al. The CAT III Crisis* (Washington: Air Line Pilots Association, 1980)

Fisher, E., Haines, R. F. and Price, T. A. *Cognitive Issues in Head-Up Displays* (Moffett Field, California: National Aeronautics and Space Administration, 1980), NASA TP-1711; NASA HUD Report 7

Frazier, M. L. and Milam, D. W. *A Synopsis of Pilot Comments on One-Time F-16 FSD Qualification/Familiarization Flights* (Edwards AFB, California: Air Force Flight Test Center, 1980)

Frazier, M. L. 'Canopy induced displacement evaluation (visual displacement of targets for fighter aircraft)', in *Proceedings 24th Annual Meeting Human Factors Society, Los Angeles* (Santa Monica, California: Human Factors Society, 1980), pp. 552–556

Gibson, C. P. 'Binocular disparity and head-up displays', *Human Factors*, **22**, 1980, 435–444

Haines, R. F., Fisher, E. and Price, T. A. *Head-Up Transition Behavior of Pilots with and without Head-Up Display in Simulated Low-Visibility Approaches* (Moffett Field, California: National Aeronautics and Space Administration, 1980), NASA TP-1720; NASA HUD Report 10

Herron, E. 'A case for early objective evaluation of candidate display formats of head-up displays based on pilot performance experiments', in *Proceedings 24th Annual Meeting, Human Factors Society* (Santa Monica, California: Human Factors Society, 1980), pp. 529–533

Lambert, M. 'Mirage 2000 headup display', *Flight International*, 12 April 1980, p. 1124

Lowe, J. R. and Hamilton, F. W. 'The DC-9 Super 80 compensated-control HUD', *DC Flight Approach*, **34**, 1980, 7–11

Lumsden, R. B. *The Role of HUD in Economical Category 3 Operations* (Bedford, England: Blind Landing Experimental Unit, 1980), BLEU TM-FS-333

Malinski, E., 'The HUD optoelectronic projection indicator system', *Technika Lotnicza i Astronautyczna*, **35**, July 1980, 24–29

Malinski, E. 'Elektroniczno-optyczne systemy wskaszan proekcyjnch/HUD III', *Technika Lotnicza i Astronautycczena*, **35**, August/September 1980, 17–20

Monagan, S. J. and Smith, R. E. 'Head-up display flight tests', in *Proceedings 24th Symposium, Society of Experimental Test Pilots, Beverly Hills* (Lancaster, California: Society of Experimental Test Pilots, 1967), pp. 75–87

Naish, J. M. and Miller, D. L. *Experimental Evaluation of Head-Up Displays* (Moffett Field, California: National Aeronautics and Space Administration, 1980), NASA TP-1550

Naish, J. M. *Head-Up Display in the Non-Precision Approach* (Moffett Field, California: National Aeronautics and Space Administration, 1980), NASA TM-81167; NASA HUD Report 12

Newman, R. L. *Operational Problems Associated with Head-Up Displays During Instrument Flight* (Wright-Patterson AFB, Ohio: Air Force Aeromedical Research Laboratory, 1980), AFAMRL TR-80-116

Obermeier, E. K. 'Tornado – avionic development testing', in *Flight Test in the Eighties, Proceedings 11th Annual Symposium, Society of Flight Test Engineers, Atlanta* August 1980

Randle, R. J., Roscoe, S. N. and Petit, J. C. *Effects of Magnification and Visual Accommodation on Aimpoint Estimation in a Simulated Landing Task* (Moffett Field, California: National Aeronautics and Space Administration, 1980), NASA TP-1635

Roscoe, S. N. and Eisele, J. E. 'Integrated flight displays', in *Aviation Psychology*, Roscoe, S. N. (ed.) (Ames, Iowa: Iowa State University

Press, 1980), pp. 48–61

Schifflet, S. G. *Evaluation of a Pilot Workload Assessment Device to Test Alternate Display Formats and Control Handling Qualities* (Patuxent River, Maryland: Naval Air Test Center, 1980), NATC SY-33R-80

Steenblik, J. W., 'The future of HUD is looking up', *Air Line Pilot*, February 1980, 6–10

Stonehouse, D. 'Evolution of the airborne display', *Electronic Engineering (London)*, **52**, Mid-Oct 1980, 29–45

Terhune, G. J. *Report on Douglas DC-9-10 HUD* (Washington: Air Line Pilots Association, 1980)

Terhune, G. J. and DeCelles, J. L. *PERSEPOLIS HUD* (Washington: Air Line Pilots Association, 1980)

Wewerinke, P. H. 'The effect of visual information on manual approach and landing', in *Proceedings 16th Annual Conference on Manual Control*, May 1980

F-16 Avionics: Block 10 Changes (Fort Worth, Texas: General Dynamics, 1980), 16PR1467B

1981

Adam, E. C. *F/A-18 'Hornet' - One Man Operability* (New York: American Institute of Aeronautics and Astronautics, 1981), AIAA Paper 81-2266

Bennett, P. J. *The Head-Up Display of Power Margin in Harrier and AV-8B Aircraft* (Bedford, England: Royal Aircraft Establishment, 1981), RAE TM-FS-439

Berry, R. L. 'The application of diffraction optics to the LANTIRN head-up display', in *Proceedings 5th Advanced Aircrew Display Symposium, Patuxent River*, September 1981, pp. 163–175

Bray, R. S. and Scott, B. C. *A Head-Up Display Format for Low Visibility Approach and Landing* (New York: American Institute of Aeronautics and Astronautics, 1981), AIAA Paper 81-0130

Dopping-Hepenstal, L. L. 'Head-up displays. The integrity of flight information', *IEE Proceedings, Part F: Communications, Radar and Signal Processing*, **128**, 1981, 440–442

Enevoldson, E. K. and Horton, V. W. 'Light bar attitude indicator', in *Proceedings 5th Advanced Aircrew Display Seminar, Patuxent River*, September 1981, pp. 251–261

Ernstoff, M. N. *Study and Development of an Integrated Head-Up Display* (Wright-Patterson AFB, Ohio: Air Force Wright Aeronautical Research Laboratory, 1981), AFWAL TR-81-1042

Hobe, G. A. *et al. Government Furnished Cockpit Instruments and Displays*

Study (Wright-Patterson AFB, Ohio: Aeronautical Systems Division, 1981), Project 81-015-DAY

Jarvi, D. *Investigation of Spatial Disorientation of F-15 'Eagle' Pilots* (Wright-Patterson AFB, Ohio: Aeronautical Systems Division, 1981), ASD TR-81-5016

Lauber, J. K., Bray, R. S. and Scott, B. C. 'An evaluation of head-up displays in civil transport operations', in *Aircraft Safety and Operating Problems* (Moffett Field, California: National Aeronautics and Space Administration, 1981), pp. 197–199

Leitner, E. F. and Haines, R. F. *Magnitude of Visual Accommodation to a Head-Up Display* (Moffett Field, California: National Aeronautics and Space Administration, 1981), NASA TP-1796; NASA HUD Report 14

Lowe, J. R. and Ornelas, J. R. 'Applications of head-up displays in commercial transport aircraft', *4th Digital Avionics Systems Conference, St Louis,* November 1981, pp. 409–414

Lumsden, R. B. and Penwill, J. C. *Manual Landings Using Head-Up Display in Category 3 Conditions* (Bedford, England: Royal Aircraft Establishment, 1981), RAE TM-FS-373

Lumsden, R. B. *et al.* *The Economic Category 3 Programme* (Bedford, England: Royal Aircraft Establishment, 1981), RAE TR-81025

Miller, M. and Aretz, A. J. 'Software considerations in the design of computer generated flight displays', in *Proceedings of the National Aerospace and Electronics Conference (NAECON '81), Dayton* (New York: Institute of Electrical and Electronics Engineers, 1981), pp. 544–548

Newman, R. L. and Welde, W. L. 'Head-up displays in operation – some unanswered questions', in *Proceedings: 1st Symposium on Aviation Psychology, Columbus* (Columbus, Ohio: Ohio State University, 1981)

Newman, R. L. 'Head-up displays operational problems', in *Proceedings 5th Advanced Aircrew Display Symposium, Patuxent River,* September 1981, pp. 241–250

Norton, P. S. *et al.* 'Findings and recommendations of the cockpit design subcommittee', in *Proceedings, Test Pilots' Aviation Safety Workshop, Monterey* (Lancaster, California: Society of Experimental Test Pilots and New York: American Institute of Aeronautics and Astronautics, 1981), pp. 19–47

Person, L. H. and Steinmetz, G. 'Systems integration of primary flight information' in *Proceedings 5th Advanced Aircrew Display Symposium, Patuxent River,* September 1981, pp. 89–103

Roscoe, S. N., Corl, L. and Jensen, R. H. 'Flight display dynamics revisited', *Human Factors,* **23**, 1981, 341–353

Schifflet, S. G., Linton, P. M. and Spicuzza, R. J. 'Evaluation of a pilot workload assessment device to test alternate display formats and control handling qualities' in *Proceedings 5th Advanced Aircrew Display*

Symposium, Patuxent River, September 1981, pp. 117–128

Smith, R. E. 'Display evaluation flight test', in *Proceedings 5th Advanced Aircrew Display Symposium, Patuxent River,* September 1981, pp. 104-116

Terhune, G. and DeCelles, J. L. 'Information requirements for pilot supervision of automatic landing in low visibility conditions', in *Proceedings 5th Advanced Aircrew Display Symposium, Patuxent River,* September 1981, pp. 129–137

Tills, A. D., Doolittle, J. H. and Woods, N. R. *A-7K Qualification Test and Evaluation, Vol. III. Limited Armament and Avionics Systems Evaluation* (Edwards AFB, California: Air Force Flight Test Center, 1981), AFFTC TR-81-22

Tkach, M. J. 'F/A-18 weapon system development', *Canadian Aeronautics and Space Journal,* **27**, 1981, 242–252

Watler, J. F. and Logan, W. B. 'The maneuvering flight path display – a flight trajectory solution display concept', in *Proceedings of the National Aerospace and Electronics Conference (NAECON '81), Dayton,* (New York: Institute of Electrical and Electronics Engineers, 1981), pp. 1254–1260

F-16 Avionics System Manual, Block 15B (Fort Worth, Texas: General Dynamics, 1981), Document 16PR1624A

F-16 Avionics System Manual, Block 25B (Fort Worth, Texas: General Dynamics, 1981), Document 16PR3927A

Technical Description: AN/AVQ-24B A-4M HUDWAC System (Rochester, England: Marconi-Elliott, 1981)

1982

Bakker, J. T. 'Effect of control system delays on fighter flying qualities', in *Symposium on Criteria for Handling Qualities of Military Aircraft, Fort Worth,* April 1982, Paper 19

Barnes, G. R., Turnipseed, G. T. and Guedry, F. E. *Effects of Character Stroke Width on the Visibility of a Head-Coupled Display* (Pensacola, Florida: Naval Aeromedical Research Laboratory, 1982), NAMRL-1297

Bick, F. J. 'Advances in control/display systems for army helicopters', in *Proceedings Behavioral Objectives in Aviation Automated Systems Symposium, SAE Aerospace Congress and Exposition, Anaheim* October 1982, pp. 127–132

Gard, J. H. 'Holographic HUDs de-mystified', in *Proceedings National Aerospace Electronics Conference (NAECON '82), Dayton* (New York: Institute of Electrical and Electronics Engineers, 1982), pp. 752–759

Hamilton, F. W. 'Development and certification of a commercial head-up display', in *Proceedings 26th Symposium, Society of Experimental Test Pilots, Beverly Hills* (Lancaster, California: Society of Experimental Test Pilots, 1982), pp. 123–130

Hall, J. R. *et al. NATC/McDonnell-Douglas Aircraft Visit to RAE Bedford to Discuss AV-8B Head-Up Display Formats* (Bedford, England: Royal Aircraft Establishment, 1982), RAE TM-FS(B)490

Hull, J. C., Gill, R. T. and Roscoe, S. N. 'Locus of the stimulus to visual accommodation: where in the world or where in the eye?', *Human Factors*, **24**, 1982, 311–319

Jauer, R. A. and Quinn, T. J. *Pictorial Formats. Volume I. Format Development* (Wright-Patterson AFB, Ohio: Air Force Wright Aeronautical Research Laboratory, 1982), AFWAL TR-81-3156-VOL-1

Jewell, W. F. 'Application of a pilot control strategy identification technique to a joint FAA/NASA ground-based simulation of head-up displays for CTOL aircraft', in *Proceedings 16th Annual Conference on Manual Control*, July 1982, pp. 395–409

Koonce, J. M. and Moroze, M. L. 'The effects of stress on processing abstract information by aircraft pilots', in *Proceedings Behavioral Objectives in Aviation Automated Systems, Aerospace Congress, Anaheim*, October 1982, pp. 9–11

Lauber, J. K. *et al. An Operational Evaluation of Head-Up Displays for Civil Transport Operations. NASA/FAA Phase III Final Report* (Moffett Field, California: National Aeronautics and Space Administration, 1982), NASA TP-1815; HUD Report 16

Lumsden, R. B. *Further Low Visibility Approach and Landing Operations in Cat III Conditions Including the Use of HUD and Decision Heights Below 50 ft* (Bedford, England: Royal Aircraft Establishment, 1982), RAE TM-FS-484

Lumsden, R. B. and Brown, T. *Military Fixed Wing Low Visibility Approach and Landing* (Bedford, England: Royal Aircraft Establishment, 1982), RAE TM-FS-488

McCormack, L. B. and George, F. L. 'Impact of display dynamics on flying qualities', in *Proceedings National Aerospace Electronics Conference (NAECON '82), Dayton* (New York: Institute of Electrical and Electronics Engineers, 1982)

Martin, W. L. *et al. Night Attack Workload Steering Group* (Wright-Patterson AFB, Ohio: Aeronautical Systems Division, 1982), ASD TR-82-5002

Penwill, J. C. *A Flight Simulator Assessment of a 1:1 Head-Up Display Format for the Jaguar* (Bedford, England: Royal Aircraft Establishment, 1982), RAE TM FS(B)497

Penwill, J. C. and Wills, C. D. *A Flight Trial Assessment of Several Head-Up Display Formats with Unity Pitch Attitude Scaling* (Bedford, England: Royal Aircraft Establishment, 1982), RAE TM-FS(B)476

Quinn, T. J. *Pictorial Formats. Volume III. Literature Review* (Wright-Patterson AFB, Ohio: Air Force Wright Aeronautical Research Laboratory, 1982), AFWAL TR-81-3156-VOL-3

Reising, J. M. and Calhoun, G. L. 'Color displays in the cockpit: who needs them', in *Proceedings 26th Annual Meeting Human Factors Society* (Santa Monica, California: Human Factors Society, 1982), pp. 446–449

Schmidt, V. P. 'Factors affecting the allocation of attention and performance in cross-monitoring flight information displays', in *Advanced Avionics and the Military Aircraft Man/Machine Interface* (Paris: Advisory Group for Aeronautical Research and Development, 1982), AGARD CP-329, paper 20

Smith, R. E. and Bailey, R. E. 'Effect of control system delays on fighter flying qualities', in *Symposium on Criteria for Handling Qualities of Military Aircraft, Fort Worth* (Paris: Advisory Group for Aeronautical Research and Development, 1982), Paper 18

Taylor, R. M. 'Human factor aspects of aircraft head-up display symbology: the presentation of attitude information', in *Proceedings, Electronic Displays and Information Display Systems Conference, London, October 1982*, pp. 41–61

Wagner, D. P. *et al. An Analysis of an Aircraft Head-Up Display Using Reliability and Risk Analysis Methodology* (Knoxville, Tennessee: JBF Associates, 1982), JBFA-107-82

Wieder, R. L. and Thurlow, N. E. 'TF/TA by means of integrated FLIR and radar sensors – terrain following/terrain avoidance displays using forward looking infrared imagery', in *Proceedings of the National Aerospace and Electronics Conference (NAECON '82), Dayton* (New York: Institute of Electrical and Electronics Engineers, 1982), pp. 1270–1276

Williams, L. J. 'Cognitive load and the functional field of view', *Human Factors*, **24**, 1982, 683–692

F-16 Avionics: Block 15B Improvements (Fort Worth, Texas: General Dynamics, 1982X), Document 16PR1628E

Holographic Head-Up Display for Transport Aircraft (Portland, Oregon: Flight Dynamics, 1982)

Minimum Performance Standards for Airborne Multipurpose Electronic Displays (Warrendale, Pennsylvania: Society of Automotive Engineers, 1982), SAE AS-8034

Prime Item Development Specification for the 1667 Improved A-10 Head-Up Display for the LANTIRN Program (Rochester, England: Marconi

Avionics, 1982), Document 29/1186/1/P01/B

1983

Blomberg, R. D. and Pepler, R. D., 'Performance evaluation of electronic flight instruments', in *Proceedings of the 2nd symposium on Aviation Psychology, Columbus* (Columbus, Ohio: Ohio State University, 1983), pp. 17–25

Boucek, G. P., Pfaff, T. A. and Smith, W. D. *The Use of Holographic Head-Up Display of Flight Path Symbology in Varying Weather Conditions* (Warrendale, Pennsylvania: Society of Automotive Engineers, 1983), SAE Paper 831445

Desmond, J. P. *A Holographic Head-Up Display for Low Visibility Landing Operations* (Warrendale, Pennsylvania: Society of Automotive Engineers, 1983), SAE Paper 831451

Detro, S. D. and Bateman, R. P. 'The impact of display size on continuous and discrete anticipatory cues (head-up display symbology for fighter aircraft weapons delivery)', in *Proceedings of the National Aerospace and Electronics Conference, Dayton (NAECON '83)* (New York: Institute of Electrical and Electronics Engineers, 1983), Volume 2, pp. 1147–1150

Genco, L. V. 'Optical interactions of aircraft windscreens and HUDs', in *Optical and Human Performance Evaluation of HUD Systems Design* (Wright-Patterson AFB, Ohio: Air Force Aeromedical Research Laboratory, 1983), AFAMRL TR-83-95; ASD TR-83-5019

Genco, L. V. 'Visual effects of F-16 canopy/HUD (head up display) integration', in *Proceedings Conference on Aerospace Transparent Materials and Enclosures, Dayton* (Dayton, Ohio: University of Dayton, 1983), pp. 793–807

Ginsburg, A. P., Martin, W. L. and Self, H. C. 'Contrast sensitivity performance assessment of HUD display systems', in *Proceedings of the 2nd Symposium on Aviation Psychology, Columbus* (Columbus, Ohio: Ohio State University, 1983), pp. 473–480

Hawkins, J. S., Reising, J. M. and Gilmour, J. D. 'Pictorial format display evaluation', in *Proceedings of the National Aerospace and Electronics Conference, (NAECON '83), Dayton* (New York: Institute of Electrical and Electronics Engineers, 1983), pp. 1132–1138

Himmelberg, M. R. and Wallis, R. A. 'Low altitude navigation and targeting infrared system for night (LANTIRN)', in *Proceedings of the 5th Digital Avionics Systems Conference, Seattle*, October/November 1983

Hussey, D. W. 'Wide angle raster head-up display design and

application to future single seat fighters', in *Impact of Advanced Avionics Technology on Ground Attack Weapon Systems, Aghios-Andreas, Greece* (Paris: Advisory Group for Aeronautical Research and Development, 1983)

Iavecchia, J. H., Iavecchia, H. P. and Roscoe, S. N. 'The Moon illusion revisited', *Aviation, Space, and Environmental Medicine*, **54**, 1983, 39–46

Kraus, J. M. *Flight Dynamics Model 1000 Head-Up Display Basic Pilot Training Manual* (Portland, Oregon: Flight Dynamics, 1983), Document 404-0071

Liebowitz, H. W., Shupert, C. L. and Post, R. B. 'Two modes of visual processing: implications for spatial orientation', in *Peripheral Vision Horizon Display (PVHD), Proceedings of a Conference, Edwards AFB* (Washington: National Aeronautics and Space Administration, 1983), NASA CP-2306, pp. 41-44

Lowe, J. R. and Ornelas, J. R. 'Applications of head-up displays in commercial transport aircraft', *Journal of Guidance, Control, and Dynamics*, **6**, 1983, 77–83

Martin, W. L. (ed.) *Optical and Human Performance Evaluation of HUD Systems Design* (Wright-Patterson AFB, Ohio: Air Force Aeromedical Research Laboratory, 1983), AFAMRL TR-83-95; ASD TR-83-5019

Moroze, M. L. and Koonce, J. M. 'A comparison of analog and digital scales for use in heads-up displays', in *Proceedings 27th Annual Meeting Human Factors Society, Norfolk* (Santa Monica, California: Human Factors Society, 1983), Volume 2, pp. 938–940

Payne, J. M. *Comparison of the Longitudinal Flying Qualities of an Optimal Pilot Model, A Ground-Based Simulator, and an Airborne Simulator* (Wright-Patterson AFB, Ohio: Air Force Institute of Technology, 1983), AFIT GAE/AA/83S-5

Penwill, J. C. and Henson, J. M. *Flight Simulator Assessments of a 1:1 Head-Up Display Format for the Jaguar* (Bedford, England: Royal Aircraft Establishment, 1983), RAE TM-FS(B)520

Schmider, D. E. and Weathersby, M. R. 'Detection performance in clutter with variable resolution', *IEEE Transactions on Aerospace and Electronic Systems*, **AES-19**, 1983

Scott, B. C. *et al. Installation, Validation, and Flight Evaluation of the Federal Aviation Administration's Head-Up Display System* (Moffett Field, California: National Aeronautics and Space Administration, 1983), NASA TM-85255; FAA CT-82-92

Sexton, G. A. *Crew Systems and Flight Station Concepts for a 1995 Transport Aircraft* (Washington: National Aeronautics and Space Administration, 1983), NASA CR-166068

Simon, B. 'Le combine de visualisation (combined visualization)', in

AGARD Advanced Concepts for Avionics/Weapon System Design, Development and Integration (Paris: Advisory Group for Aeronautical Research and Development, 1983)

Simonelli, N. M. 'The dark focus of the human eye and its relationship to age and visual defect', *Human Factors*, **25**, 1983, 85–92

Summers, L. G. and Miller, J. I. *Primary Flight Display, A Step Beyond EADIs* (Warrendale, Pennsylvania: Society of Automotive Engineers, 1983), SAE Paper 831533

Swortzel, F. R. and Bennett, W. S. 'AFTI/F-16: an integrated system approach to combat automation', in *AGARD Advanced Concepts for Avionics/Weapon System Design, Development, and Integration* (Paris: Advisory Group for Aeronautical Research and Development, 1983)

Task, H. L. Measurement of HUD (head-up display) optical quality', in *Optical and Human Performance Evaluation of HUD Systems Design* (Wright-Patterson AFB, Ohio: Air Force Aeromedical Research Laboratory, 1983), AFAMRL TR-83-95, pp. 11–19; ASD TR-83-5019

Vallance, C. H. 'The approach to optical systems designs for aircraft head-up displays', in *Proceedings Optical System Design, Analysis, and Production, Geneva*, April 1983, pp. 15-25

Wurfel, H.-G. and Leuthauser, D. A. *F-16 Wide Field of View (WFOV) Head-Up Display (HUD) Evaluation* (Edwards AFB, California: Air Force Flight Test Center, 1983), AFFTC TR-83-13

'Alpha Jet – further version for the international market', *Dornier-Post*, No. 2, 1983, 31–33

F-18 Head-Up Display/Multipurpose Display Group System Description (San Jose, California: Kaiser Electronics, 1983), C78-3514

Proceedings of the HUD/Instruments Conference, Langley AFB (Langley AFB, Virginia: Tactical Air Command, 1983)

Symbol Display Format (Culver City, California: Hughes Aircraft Co., 1983), Document 7-319800002

System Description for FDI Model 1000 Head-Up Display (Portland, Oregon: Flight Dynamics, 1983), Document 404-0097

1984

Brandenstein, D. C. 'Space Shuttle night landing', in *Proceedings 28th Symposium, Society of Experimental Test Pilots, Beverly Hills* (Lancaster, California: Society of Experimental Test Pilots, 1984), pp. 257–281

Carr, G. P. and Montemedo, M. D. (eds) *Aerospace Crew Station Design* (Amsterdam: Elsevier, 1984)

Carr, L. A. *Presentation of Radar Altitude Information on the HUD* (Warrendale, Pennsylvania: Society of Automotive Engineers, 1984),

SAE Paper 841464

Desmond, J. P. and Ford, D. W. 'Certification of a holographic head-up display system for low visibility landings', in *Proceedings of the AIAA/IEEE 6th Digital Avionics Systems Conference, Baltimore*, December 1984, pp. 441–446

Gawron, V. J. and Knotts, L. H. 'A preliminary flight evaluation of the peripheral vision display using the NT-33 aircraft', in *Proceedings of the 28th Annual Meeting Human Factors Society* (Santa Monica, California: Human Factors Society, 1984), pp. 539–541

Heimple, H. H. and McMonagle, D. R. 'Flight test techniques for the advanced fighter technology integration (AFTI) F-16', *Society of Experimental Test Pilots Cockpit*, **19**, Oct–Dec 1984, pp. 4–19

Herlt, S. M. *et al. Comparison of the Effects of Pure and Equivalent Time Delays on Approach and Landing Handling Qualities* (Edwards AFB, California: Air Force Test Pilots School, 1984), USAFTPS TR-83B-1-2

Knotts, L. H., Ball, J. and Parrag, M. *Test Pilot School: Flight Syllabus and Background Material for the NT-33A Research Aircraft* (Buffalo, New York: Calspan Corp., 1984)

Kyle, W. D. 'Holographic head-up display gives military transport pilots see-through accuracy', *Defense Systems Review and Military Communications*, **2**, September 1984, pp. 29–32

Lovering, P. B. and Andes, W. S. *Head-Up Display Symbology and Mechanization Study* (Wright-Patterson AFB, Ohio: Aeronautical Systems Division, 1984), ASD TR-84-5023

Lovering, P. B. and Andes, W. S. 'The HUD as a primary flight instrument', in *Proceedings 3rd Aerospace Behavioral Engineering Technology Conference, Long Beach*, October 1984, pp. 33–36

Lowe, J. R. *Conformal Head-Up Display*, US Patent 4454496, 1984

Malcomb, R., 'Pilot disorientation and the use of a peripheral vision display', *Aviation, Space, & Environmental Medicine*, 1984, pp. 231–238

Menu, J. P. and Brun, J. 'Méthodologie d'étude de la transition tête haute tête basse' (A methodology for studying the head up–head down transition), *Medecine Aeronautique et Spatiale*. **23**, 1984, 230–233

Mitchell, D. G. and Hoh, R. H. 'Integrating handling qualities and displays', in *Proceedings of the National Aerospace and Electronics Conference (NAECON '84), Dayton* (New York: Institute of Electrical and Electronics Engineers, 1984), p. 470

Newman, R. L. *Evaluation of MD-80 HUD* (Yellow Springs, Ohio: Crew Systems, 1984), TM-84-01

Newman, R. L. *Evaluation of FDI HUD* (Yellow Springs, Ohio: Crew Systems, 1984), TM-84-03

Newman, R. L. and Foxworth, T. G. *A Review of Head-Up Display*

Specifications (Wright-Patterson AFB, Ohio: Aeronautical Systems Division, 1984), ASD TR-84-5024

Powers, B. G. *Space Shuttle Pilot-Induced-Oscillation Research Testing* (Washington: National Aeronautics and Space Administration, 1984), NASA TM-86034

Roscoe, S. N. 'Judgments of size and distance with imaging displays', *Human Factors*, **26**, 1984, 617–629

Statler, I. C. 'Military pilot ergonomics', in *Proceedings AGARD Symposium on Human Factors Considerations in High Performance Aircraft, Williamsburg* (Paris: Advisory Group for Aeronautical Research and Development, 1984), AGARD CP-371

Steenblik, J. W. 'The caret, the worm, and the flat-footed duck', *Air Line Pilot*, March 1984, 6–11, 38–39

Stoliker, F. N. *Technical Evaluation: Report on the FDP Symposium on Flight Test Techniques* (Paris: Advisory Group for Aeronautical Research and Development, 1984), AGARD AR-208

Taylor, R. M. 'Some effects of display format variables on the perception of aircraft spatial orientation', in *Proceedings AGARD Symposium on Human Factors Considerations in High Performance Aircraft, Williamsburg* (Paris: Advisory Group for Aeronautical Research and Development, 1984), AGARD CP-371

Warren, R., Genco, L. V. and Connon, T. R. *Horizontal Diplopia Thresholds for Head-Up Displays* (Wright-Patterson AFB, Ohio: Air Force Aeromedical Research Laboratory, 1980), AFAMRL TR-84-18

Warwick, G. 'Military avionics – increasing integration at all levels', *Flight International*, 15 December 1984, 1635–1641

Weintraub, D. J., Haines, R. F. and Randle, R. J. 'The utility of head-up displays – eye focus versus decision times', in *Proceedings 28th Annual Meeting, Human Factors Society* (Santa Monica, California: Human Factors Society, 1984), pp. 529–533

Wurfel, H. G. F. 'F-16 and A-10 diffraction optics head up display (HUD) flight test evaluation', in *Proceedings of the Flight Mechanics Panel Symposium, Lisbon* (Paris: Advisory Group for Aeronautical Research and Development, 1984)

A-6F Head-Up Display (HUD) Format (Bethpage, New York: Grumman Aerospace, 1984), Specification AV-128SCS-95G

Military Specification: Displays, Airborne, Electronically–Optically Generated (Philadelphia, Pennsylvania: Naval Publications and Forms Center, 1984), MIL-D-87213; (Wright-Patterson AFB, Ohio: Aeronautical Systems Division, 1987), AFGS-87213A

Military Standard: Human Factors Engineering Design Criteria for Helicopter Cockpit Electro-Optical Display Symbology (Philadelphia, Pennsylvania: Naval Publications and Forms Center, 1984), MIL-STD-1295A

1985

Adams, K. A. *The Interactive Generation of Alphanumerics and Symbology with Designs on the Future* (Wright-Patterson AFBL Ohio: Air Force Institute of Technology, 1985), AFIT-GCS-MA-85J-2

Augustine, W. L. and Simmons, C. D. *Criteria to be Considered for Approving the Head-Up Display as the Primary Flight Instrument* (Wright-Patterson AFB: Ohio: Aeronautical Systems Division, 1985)

Doten, F. S. 'Northrop's surrogate trainer (simulating AH-64A helicopter)', in *Proceedings 29th Symposium, Society of Experimental Test Pilots, Beverly Hills* (Lancaster, California: Society of Experimental Test Pilots, 1985), pp. 67–92

Golovcsenko, I. V. and Balazs, A. J. 'Embedded training avionics integration', in *Proceedings of the National Aerospace and Electronics Conference (NAECON '85), Dayton* (New York: Institute of Electrical and Electronics Engineers, 1985), Volume 2, pp. 1120–1124

Iavecchia, J. H. *Response Biases with Virtual Imaging Displays* (Warminster, Pennsylvania: Naval Air Development Center, 1985), NADC 85165-60

Innocenti, M. *Interaction Between Display Dynamics and Handling Qualities in Manual Control Tasks*, (Washington: American Institute of Aeronautics and Astronautics, 1985), AIAA Paper 85-1805

Konnce, J. M., Gold, M. and Moroze, M. 'Comparison of novice and experienced pilots using analog and digital flight displays', in *Proceedings, 3rd Symposium on Aviation Psychology, Ohio State University*, (Columbus, Ohio: Ohio State University, 1985), pp. 143–149

Kyle, W. D. *Head-Up Displays for General Aviation* (Warrendale, Pennsylvania: Society of Automotive Engineers, 1985), SAE Paper 850902

Lowe, J. R. *Conformal Head-Up Display* US Patent 4554545, 1985

McNaughton, G. B. 'Vision in spatial disorientation (SDO) and loss of aircraft attitude or control awareness', in *Proceedings 3rd Symposium on Aviation Psychology, Columbus* (Columbus, Ohio: Ohio State University, 1985), pp. 25–38

Matthes, G. W. 'LANTIRN flight test – opening the night window – low altitude navigation and targeting infrared system for night', *Society of Experimental Test Pilots Cockpit*, 4th Quarter 1985, 5–20

Menu, J. P., Amalberti, R. and Santucci, G. 'Data displays in modern aircraft', *Medicine Aeronautique et Spatiale*, **24**, 2nd Quarter 1985, 104–106

Menu, J. P. *et al.* 'La collimation intermédiaire: description – buts – premiers résultats' (Intermediate collimation: description – goals – initial results), *Medecine Aeronautique et Spatiale*, **24**, 1985, 158–161

Monaco, W. A. and Hamilton, P. V. 'Visual capabilities related to fighter aircrew performance in the F-14 and adversary aircraft', in *Medical Selection and Physiological Training of Future Fighter Aircrew* (Paris: Advisory Group for Aeronautical Research and Development, 1985), AGARD CP-396

Morris, A. *et al.* 'Vision test battery threshold and response time as predictors of air-to-air visual target acquisition in F-14 and adversary aircraft', in *AGARD Medical Selection and Physiological Training of Future Fighter Aircrew* (Paris: Advisory Group for Aeronautical Research and Development, 1985), AGARD CP-396

Newman, R. L. *HUD Evaluation Flight in NT-33* (Yellow Springs, Ohio: Crew Systems, 1985), TM-85-13

Roscoe, S. N. 'Bigness is in the eye of the beholder', *Human Factors*, **27**, 1985, 615–636

Schmidt, B. L. and Schilling, R. *Swissair MD-81: Three Winters of CAT 3* (Zurich: Swissair, 1985)

Smith, W. L. *The Integrated Digital Avionics System for the F-20 Tigershark* (Warrendale, Pennsylvania: Society of Automotive Engineers, 1985), SAE Paper 851850

Weintraub, D. J., Haines, R. F. and Randle, R. J. 'Runway to HUD transitions monitoring eye focus and decision times', in *Proceedings 29th Human Factors Society Annual Meeting, Baltimore* (Santa Monica, California: Human Factors Society, 1985), Volume 1, pp. 615–619

Aircraft Attitude Awareness Workshop, Wright-Patterson AFB (Wright-Patterson AFB, Ohio: Air Force Wright Research and Development Center, 1985), WRDC TR-85-7009; ASD TR-85-5020

F-14D Head-Up Display Format (Bethpage, New York: Grumman Aerospace, 1985)

Flight Instrumentation Conference, Pentagon (Washington: US Air Force, 1985)

Head-Up Display System, Model 9000A (Grand Rapids, Michigan: Jet Electronics and Technology, 1985)

Indicator Group, Head-Up Display OD-(*)/AVQ, Design Control Specification for F-14D and A-6E Upgrade Weapon Systems (Bethpage, New York: Grumman Aerospace, 1985) Specification A55DCVAD051

'Jaguar hit trees', *Flight International*, 19 July 1985, 16

1986

Armando, A. and Spinoni, M. *Use of Aeritalia Flight Simulator for the Development of the AM-X Weapon System* (Turin, Italy: Aeritalia SpA, 1986)

Bailey, R. E. *Effect of Head-Up Display Dynamics on Fighter Flying Qualities,* (Washington: American Institute of Aeronautics and Astronautics, 1985), AIAA Paper 86-2206

Bailey, R. E. *Investigation of Head-Up Display Dynamic Response and Symbol Accuracy Requirements* (Buffalo, New York: Calspan Corp., 1986), Report 7205-14

Dana, W. H., Smith, W. B. and Howard, J. D. 'Pilot vehicle interface on the advanced fighter technology integration F-16', in *Proceedings of the 1986 National Aerospace and Electronics Conference (NAECON '86), Dayton,* (New York: Institute of Electrical and Electronics Engineers, 1986), Volume 2, pp. 595–607

Desmond, J. P. *Improvements in Aircraft Safety and Operational Dependability from a Projected Flight Path Guidance Display* (Warrendale, Pennsylvania: Society of Automotive Engineers, 1986), SAE Paper 861732

Edwards, R. E., Way, T. C. and Honsby, M. E. 'Development of pictorial formats for beyond-visual-range air-to-air engagements', in *Proceedings of the National Aerospace and Electronics Conference (NAECON '86), Dayton* (New York: Institute of Electrical and Electronics Engineers, 1986), pp. 1355–1361

Frieberg, U. and Holmström, S. 'An ordinary 3-axis horizon instrument which every pilot likes — can it be misleading and dangerous? The answer is Yes', in *Proceedings 30th Symposium, Society of Experimental Test Pilots, Beverly Hills* (Lancaster, California: Society of Experimental Test Pilots, 1986), pp. 187–199

Georges, J.-F. *Flying Head-Up* (Vaucresson, France: Avions Marcel Dassault–Breguet Aviation, 1986)

Guttman, J. *Evaluation of the F/A-18 Head-Up Display for Recovery from Unusual Attitudes* (Warminster, Pennsylvania: Naval Air Development Center, 1986), NADC 86157-60

Hutchinson, J. E. *The Advantages of a Primary Flight Display* (Warrendale, Pennsylvania: Society of Automotive Engineers, 1986), SAE Paper 861730

Kessler, G. and Huff, R. *A-6F Airplane Power Approach Systems Development and Analysis* (Patuxent River, Maryland: Naval Air Test Center, 1986), NATC SA-118R-86

Kinsley, S. A., Warner, N. W. and Gleisner, D. P. *A Comparison of Two Pitch Ladder Formats and an ADI Ball for Recovery from Unusual Attitudes* (Warminster, Pennsylvania: Naval Air Development Center, 1986), NADC 86012-60

Menu, J. P. 'Head-up/head-down transition – measurement of transition times', *Aviation, Space, and Environmental Medicine,* **57,** 1986, 218–222

Millard, S. W. *Space Shuttle Performance with a Heads-Up Display* (Washington: American Institute of Aeronautics and Astronautics, 1986), AIAA Paper 86-0193

Newman, R. L. *Flight Evaluation of JET HUD in Pilatus PC-9* (Yellow Springs, Ohio: Crew Systems, 1986), TM-86-15A

Newman, R. L. *The Head-Up Display as a Primary Flight Reference* (Yellow Springs, Ohio: Crew Systems, 1986), TM-86-22

Norman, J. and Ehrlich, S. 'Visual accommodation and virtual image displays: target detection and recognition', *Human Factors*, **28**, 1986, 135–151

Oliver, J. G. *The Advantage of Flightpath-Oriented Situation Displays During Microburst Encounters* (Warrendale, Pennsylvania: Society of Automotive Engineers, 1986), SAE Paper 861733

Roscoe, S. N. 'Designed for disaster', *Human Factors Society Bulletin*, **29**, June 1986, 1–2

Roscoe, S. N. *Human Factors Affecting Pilot Performance in Vertical and Translational Instrument Flight* (Las Vegas, New Mexico: New Mexico State University, 1986), BEL-86-1/ONR-86-1

Roscoe, S. N. 'Spatial misorientation exacerbated by collimated virtual flight display', *Information Display*, September 1986, 27–28

Sexton, G. A. 'A new meaning to "flying the desk"', in *Proceedings National Aerospace Electronics Conference (NAECON '86), Dayton* (New York: Institute of Electrical and Electronics Engineers, 1986), Vol. 2, pp. 360–366

Trousdale, D. M. *Flying the Flight Dynamics HUD: Windshear Symbology* (Washington: Air Line Pilots Association, 1986)

Vallance, C. H. 'Head-up displays – an evolving technology for pilots', *GEC Review*, **2**, 1986, pp. 37–41

Vallance, C. H. 'Testing and development of holographic HUD systems', in *Proceedings 17th Annual Symposium, Society of Flight Test Engineers: Flight Testing – The Continuing Challenge, Washington*, August 1986

F-16C/D Avionics System Manual (Block 30) (Fort Worth, Texas: General Dynamics, 1986), Document 16PR4390

Flight Deck, Head-Up Displays (Warrendale, Pennsylvania: Society of Automotive Engineers, 1986), SAE ARP-4102/8; revised 1988

HUD 9000A Product Description (Grand Rapids, Michigan: Jet Electronics and Technology, 1986), FSCM 25583

Prime Item Development Specification for the 1665 F-16 Head-Up Display Set (Fort Worth, Texas: General Dynamics, 1986), Specification 16ZE235G

Specification for Head-Up Display Set AN/AVQ-24B (Rochester, England: GEC Avionics, 1986), EA-017-0041-C05, Revision E

1987

Abbott, T. A., Nataupsky, M. and Steinmetz, G. G. *Effects of Combining Vertical and Horizontal Information into a Primary Flight Display* (Hampton, Virginia: National Aeronautics and Space Administration, 1987), NASA TP-2783

Bailey, R. E. *et al. Effect of Time Delay on Manual Flight Control During In-Flight and Ground Simulation* (Washington: American Institute of Aeronautics and Astronautics, 1987), AIAA Paper 87-2370

Copeland, H. W. and Hoffman, S. K. *The High Technology Test Bed Program – An Overview* (Warrendale, Pennsylvania: Society of Automotive Engineers, 1987), SAE Paper 872312

Desmond, J. P. 'HUD guidance improves landing performance', *Aerospace Engineering*, **7**, July 1987, 49–53

Guttman, J. and Lindsey, N. J. *F-14D Display/Spin Study* (War minster, Pennsylvania: Naval Air Development Center, 1987), NADC-87178-60

Haber, R. N. 'Why low-flying fighter planes crash: perceptual and attentional factors in collisions with the ground', *Human Factors*, **29**, 1987, 519–532

Hannan, M. D., Herod, A. H. and McClure, A. R. *F-15E Human Engineering Design Approach Element* (St Louis, Missouri: McDonnell-Douglas, 1985), MDC-A9606B; revised 1987

Hawkins, F. H. 'Displays and controls', in *Human Factors in Flight* (Brookfield, Vermont: Gower Publishing, 1987)

Henson, J. M. N. *A Review of the Development of the Fast Jet Head-Up Display Drive Laws and Symbology Suite* (Bedford, England: Royal Aircraft Establishment, 1987), RAE TM-FS(F)-657

Iavecchia, J. H. *The Potential for Depth Perception Errors in Piloting the F-18 and A-6 Night Attack Aircraft* (Warminster, Pennsylvania: Naval Air Development Center, 1987)

Kama, W. N. and Kuperman, G. G. *Effect of HUD (Head-Up-Display) Symbology Size on Operator Performance under Various Luminance Conditions* (Wright-Patterson AFB, Ohio: Armstrong Aeromedical Research Laboratory, 1987), AAMRL TR-88-021

McCormack, L. B., Detroit, M. J. and See, D. N. 'Improving pilot–vehicle integration using cockpit display dynamics', in *Proceedings of the National Aerospace and Electronics Conference (NAECON '87), Dayton* (New York: Institute of Electrical and Electronics Engineers, 1987), pp. 530–536

Mann, T. L. *Autonomous Landing Guidance Concept – The Effects of Video and Symbology Dynamics on Pilot Performance* (Warrendale, Pennsylvania: Society of Automotive Engineers, 1987), SAE

Paper 872390

Newman, R. L. *Evaluation of the FDI Head-Up Display* (Yellow Springs, Ohio: Crew Systems, 1987), TM-87-04

Newman, R. L. *Improvement of Head-Up Display Standards. I. Head-Up Display Design Guide* (Wright-Patterson AFB, Ohio: Air Force Wright Aeronautical Laboratory, 1987), AFWAL TR-87-3055, Vol. 1

Newman, R. L. *Improvement of Head-Up Display Standards. II. Evaluation of Head-Up Displays to Enhance Unusual Attitude Recovery* (Wright-Patterson AFB, Ohio: Air Force Wright Aeronautical Laboratory, 1987), AFWAL TR-87-3055, Vol. 2

Newman, R. L. *Improvement of Head-Up Display Standards. III. An Evaluation of Head-Up Display Safety* (Wright-Patterson AFB, Ohio: Air Force Wright Aeronautical Laboratory, 1987), AFWAL TR-87-3055, Vol. 3

Newman, R. L. 'The HUD and spatial disorientation: reply to Roscoe', *Human Factors Society Bulletin*, October 1987, 3–5

Newman, R. L. and Bailey, R. E. *Improvement of Head-Up Display Standards. IV. Head-Up Display Dynamics Flight Tests* (Wright-Patterson AFB, Ohio: Air Force Wright Aeronautical Laboratory, 1987), AFWAL TR-87-3055, Vol. 4

Newman, R. L. and Bailey, R. E. *Improvement of Head-Up Display Standards. V. Head-Up Display ILS Accuracy Flight Tests* (Wright-Patterson AFB, Ohio: Air Force Wright Aeronautical Laboratory, 1987), AFWAL TR-87-3055, Vol. 5

Papa, R. M. and Stoliker, J. R. 'Pilot workload assessment – a flight test approach', in *The Man–Machine Interface in Tactical Aircraft Design and Combat Automation* (Paris: Advisory Group for Aeronautical Research and Development, 1987), AGARD CP-425, Paper 8

Penwill, J. C. *The Presentation of Pitch Bars in Head-Up Displays – A Flight Simulation Study* (Bedford, England: Royal Aircraft Establishment, 1987), RAE TR-87024

Roscoe, S. N. 'The trouble with HUDs and HMDs', *Human Factors Society Bulletin*, July 1987, 1–3

Roscoe, S. N. 'The trouble with virtual images revisited', *Human Factors Society Bulletin*, November 1987, 3–5

Roscoe, S. N. and Couchman, D. H. 'Improving visual performance through volitional focus control', *Human Factors*, **29**, 1987, 311–325

Taylor, R. M. 'Attitude awareness from aircraft head-up displays', in *Proceedings 4th International Symposium on Aviation Psychology, Columbus* (Columbus, Ohio: Ohio State University, 1987)

Way, T. C. *et al. Multi-Crew Pictorial Format Display Evaluation* (Wright-Patterson AFB, Ohio: Air Force Wright Aeronautical Laboratory, 1987), AFWAL TR-87-3047

Weintraub, D. J. 'HUDs, HMDs, and common sense, polishing virtual images', *Human Factors Society Bulletin*, October 1987, 1–3

Zenyuh, J. P. *et al.* 'Advanced head-up display (HUD) symbology aiding unusual attitude recovery', in *Proceedings 31st Annual Meeting, Human Factors Society* (Santa Monica, California: Human Factors Society, 1987), pp. 1067–1071

1988

Agneessens, D. 'General operational and training visual concerns', in *Visual Effects in the High Performance Aircraft Cockpit*, (Paris: Advisory Group for Aeronautical Research and Development, 1968), AGARD LS-156

Boettcher, K., Schmidt, D. K. and Case, L. *Display Systems Dynamics Requirements for Flying Qualities* (Wright-Patterson AFB, Ohio: Air Force Wright Aeronautical Laboratory, 1988), AFWAL TR-88-3017

Brown, S. E. *et al.* *Head-Up Display for Automobile*, US Patent 4740780, 1988

Carr, L. A. *An Evaluation of Three Linear Scale Radar Altimeter Displays* (Wright-Patterson AFB: Ohio: Aeronautical Systems Division, 1988), ASD TR-87-5005

Garg, S. and Schmidt, D. K. *Cooperative Synthesis of Control and Display Augmentation for a STOL Aircraft in the Approach and Landing Task* (Washington: American Institute of Aeronautics and Astronautics, 1988), AIAA Paper 88-4182

Green, H. B. 'Manual Cat IIIa with a HUD: requirements and testing', in *Proceedings 32nd Annual Symposium, Society of Experimental Test Pilots, Beverly Hills* (Lancaster, California: Society of Experimental Test Pilots, 1988), p. 223

Hasenbein, K. P. *et al.* *NT-33A Have Infidelity II. Effects of Aircraft Response Time Delays in Ground Based Simulations and In-Flight Operations* (Edwards AFB, California: Air Force Test Pilot School, 1988), USAFTPS TR-87B-S02

Hickl, H. 'Cockpit design – experience gained from modern fighter aircraft evaluation', paper presented at *20th Annual European Symposium, Society of Experimental Test Pilots, Linköping* (Lancaster, California: Society of Experimental Test Pilots, 1988)

Holbrook, M. E. *Development, Analysis, and Flight Test of the Lockheed Aeronautical System Company HTTB HUD* (Washington: American Institute of Aeronautics and Astronautics, 1988), AIAA Paper 88-4511

Iavecchia, J. H., Iavecchia, H. P. and Roscoe, S. N. 'Eye accommodation to head-up virtual images', *Human Factors*, **30**, 1988, 689–702

Iino, T., Otsuka, T. and Suzuki, Y. *Development of Heads-Up Display for a Motor Vehicle* (Warrendale, Pennsylvania: Society of Automotive Engineers, 1988), SAE Paper 880217

Isao, I. 'Trends and problems of head-up displays', *Journal of the Japan Society for Aeronautical and Space Sciences*, **36**, 1988, 30–35

Johnson, T. 'The how and the why of the HUD', *Professional Pilot*, June 1988, 58–62

Konicke, M. L. *747-400 Flight Displays Development* (Washington: American Institute of Aeronautics and Astronautics, 1988), AIAA Paper 88-4439

Meehan, J. W. and Triggs, T. J. 'Magnification effects with imaging displays depend on scene content and viewing condition', *Human Factors*, **30**, 1988, 487–494

Middleton, D. B., Srivatsan, R. and Person, L. H. *Simulator Evaluation of Takeoff Performance Monitoring Displays* (Washington: American Institute of Aeronautics and Astronautics, 1988), AIAA Paper 88-4611

Newman, R. L. 'The HUD in spatial disorientation', paper presented at *20th Annual European Symposium, Society of Experimental Test Pilots, Linköping*, (Lancaster, California: Society of Experimental Test Pilots, 1988)

Penwill, J. C. and Wills, C. D. *A Flight Evaluation of HUD Pitch Ladders Suitable for High Pitch Rates* (Bedford, England: Royal Aircraft Establishment, 1988), RAE TR 88014

Previc, F. H. *Towards a Physiologically Based HUD Symbology* (Brooks AFB, Texas: Air Force School of Aerospace Medicine, 1988), AFSAM TR-88-23

Reising, J., Zenyuh, J. and Barthelemy, K. 'Head-up display symbology for unusual attitude recovery', in *Proceedings of the IEEE National Aerospace and Electronics Conference (NAECON '88), Dayton* (New York: Institute of Electrical and Electronics Engineers, 1988), Volume 3, pp. 926–930

Sexton, G. A. *et al. An Evaluation of Flight Path Formats Head-Up and Head-Down* (Washington: National Aeronautics and Space Administration, 1988), NASA CR-4176

Steinmetz, G. G. *Development and Evaluation of an Airplane Electronic Display Format Aligned with the Inertial Velocity Vector*, (Hampton, Virginia: National Aeronautics and Space Administration, 1988), NASA TP-2648

Stephens, C. M. and Penwill, J. C. *RAE Bedford Technical Evaluation of the Variable Geared Ladder* (Bedford, England: Royal Aircraft Establishment, 1988), RAE FM-WP(88)007

Stokes, A. F. and Wickens, C. D. 'Aviation displays', in *Human Factors in Aviation* Wiener, E. L. and Nagel, D. C. (eds), (New York: Academic Press, 1988), pp. 387–431

Taylor, R. M. 'Aircraft attitude awareness from visual displays', *Displays: Technology and Applications*, **9**, April 1988, 65–75

Wells, M. J., Osgood, R. K. and Venturino, M. 'Using target replacement performance to measure spatial awareness in a helmet-mounted simulator', in *Proceedings 32nd Annual Human Factors Society Meeting, Anaheim* (Santa Monica, California: Human Factors Society, 1988), pp. 1429–1433

Wood, R. B. and Hayford, M. J. 'Holographic and classical head-up display technology for commercial and fighter aircraft', in *Holographic Optics: Design and Applications, Proceedings of the Meeting, Los Angeles*, January 1988, pp. 36–52

Aerospace Recommended Practice: Flight Deck, Head-Up Displays (Warrendale, Pennsylvania: Society of Automotive Engineers, 1988), SAE ARP-4102/8

Manuel d'Exploitation A320 Partie Utilisation (Paris: Air Inter, 1988), Section 227

Visual Effects in the High Performance Aircraft Cockpit (Paris: Advisory Group for Aeronautical Research and Development, 1988), AGARD LS-156

1989

Bailey, R. E. 'Effect of head-up display dynamics on fighter flying qualities', *Journal of Guidance, Control, and Dynamics*, **12**, 1989, 514–520

Brickner, M. S. and Foyle, D. C. 'Field of view effects on a simulated flight task with head-down and head-up sensor imagery displays', in *Proceedings of the 34th Annual Meeting, Human Factors Society* (Santa Monica, California: Human Factors Society, 1989), pp. 1567–1571

Deaton, J. E. *et al. Effect of Windscreen Bows and HUD Pitch Ladder Format on Pilot Performance during Simulated Flight* (Warminster, Pennsylvania: Naval Air Development Center, 1989), NADC 89084-60

Edelman, D. V. *Category IIIB, Fail Passive or Fail Operational* (Washington: Air Line Pilots Association, 1989)

Ercoline, W. R. *et al.* 'Effect of variations in head-up display pitch ladder representations on orientation recognition', in *Proceedings of the 33rd Human Factors Society Annual Meeting, Denver* (Santa Monica, California: Human Factors Society, 1989), Volume 2, pp. 1401–1405

Gard, J. H. *HUDs in Tactical Cockpits: A Basic Guide Book* (San Jose,

California: Kaiser Electronics, 1989)

Gawron, V. J. *et al.* 'Comparison of time delay during in-flight and ground simulation', in *Proceedings of the 33rd Human Factors Society Annual Meeting* Denver, (Santa Monica, California: Human Factors Society, 1989), pp. 121–123

Hall, J. R., Stephens, C. M. and Penwill, J. C. *A Review of the Design and Development of the RAE Fast-Jet Head-Up Display Format* (Bedford, England: Royal Aircraft Establishment, 1989), RAE FM-WP(89)034

Hall, J. R. and Penwill, J. C. *RAE Fast-Jet HUD Format – Specification Issue 2 (Display Tailored for T4 Harrier XW175)*, (Bedford, England: Royal Aircraft Establishment, 1989), RAE FM-WP(89)-064

Hameluck, D. and Stager, P. 'Instrument scanning and subjective workload with the peripheral vision horizon display', in *Proceedings of the 33rd Human Factors Society Annual Meeting, Denver* (Santa Monica, California: Human Factors Society, 1989), pp. 18–22

Hutchinson, J. E. *The Hybrid Landing System – An Airline Pilot's View*, (Warrendale, Pennsylvania: Society of Automotive Engineers, 1989), SAE Paper 892377

Kimchi, R., Rubin, Y. and Gopher, D. 'Attention in dichoptic and binocular vision', in *Proceedings of the 33rd Human Factors Society Annual Meeting, Denver* (Santa Monica, California: Human Factors Society, 1989) pp. 1435–1439

Koehler, R., Buchacker, E. and Biezad, D. J. 'GRATE: a new flight test tool for flying qualities evaluation', in *Flight Test Techniques* (Paris: Advisory Group for Aeronautical Research and Development, 1989)

Oliver, J. G. *A Final Report on the FAA Low Visibility Simulation* (Warrendale, Pennsylvania: Society of Automotive Engineers, 1989), SAE Paper 892376

Penwill, J. C. *The Zenith and Nadir Symbols of the Pitch Ladder for the RAE Head-Up Display Fast-Jet Format* (Bedford, England: Royal Aircraft Establishment, 1989), RAE TR 89020

Roscoe, S. N. 'The eyes prefer real images', in *Aviation Psychology*, Jensen, R. H. (ed.) (Brookfield, Vermont: Gower Publishing, 1989), pp. 231–239

Roust, L. M. *Evaluation of Head-Up Display Formats for the F/A-18 Hornet*, Thesis, Naval Postgraduate School, 1989

Sojourner, R. J. *Head-Up Display in the Automobile Environment*, Thesis, Air Force Institute of Technology, 1989

Steenblik, J. W. 'Alaska Airlines HGS', *Air Line Pilot*, December 1989, 9–13, 48

Stinnett, T. A. 'Human factors in the super cockpit', in *Aviation Psychology*, Jensen, R. H. (ed.) (Brookfield, Vermont: Gower Publishing, 1989), pp. 1–37

Weihrauch, M., Maloney, G. G. and Goesch, T. C. *The First Head-Up Display Introduced by General Motors* (Warrendale, Pennsylvania: Society of Automotive Engineers, 1989), SAE Paper 890288

Yokoi, R. and Matsubara, K. 'Two effective methods of approach and landing by visual display', *SAE Transactions, Journal of Aerospace*, **98**, 1989, 214–220

FDI Model 1000 Head-Up Display System Specification (Portland, Oregon: Flight Dynamics, 1989), Report 404-0249

Military Standard: Aircraft Display Symbology (Philadelphia, Pennsylvania: Naval Publications and Forms Center, 1989), MIL-STD-1787A

Proceedings of International Conference on Hybrid All Weather Landing Systems (Washington: Air Line Pilots Association, 1989)

Synthetic Vision Technology Demonstration Program. Report on the Certification Study Team Meeting (College Park, Maryland: University of Maryland, 1989), URF-89-1803

1990

Bitton, F. and Evans, R. *Report on Head-Up Display Symbology Standardization* (Randolph AFB, Texas: Air Force Instrument Flight Center, 1990), AFIFC TR-91-01

Collins, P. and MacRae, J. 'Fast Jet format and night attack using electro-optical sensors', paper presented at *22nd European Symposium, Society of Experimental Test Pilots, Arles* (Lancaster, California: Society of Experimental Test Pilots, 1990)

Deaton, J. E. *et al. Enhanced HUD Symbology Associated with Recovery from Unusual Attitudes* (Warrendale, Pennsylvania: Society of Automotive Engineers, 1990), SAE Paper 901919

Deaton, J. E. *et al.* 'Evaluation of the Augie arrow HUD symbology as an aid to recovery from unusual attitudes', in *Proceedings of the 34th Annual Meeting of the Human Factors Society, Orlando* (Santa Monica, California: Human Factors Society, 1990), pp. 31–35

Desmond, J. P. and Hansen, R. C. 'Flight-path display can improve safety, operational efficiency', *ICAO Journal*, **45**, March 1990, 14–18

Dryden, J. B. 'Joe Bill answers his mail', *Code One*, 5, April 1990, 16–20

Dryden, J. B. and Tapia, M. H. 'Breakout ... with confidence', *Code On*, 5, July 1990, 10–15

Edelman, D. V. *HUD Potential for Wide-Bodied Air Carrier Aircraft* (Warrendale, Pennsylvania: Society of Automotive Engineers, 1990), SAE Paper 901832

Ercoline, W. R. and Gillingham, K. K. 'Effects of variations in head-up display airspeed and altitude representations on basic flight performance', in *Proceedings of the 34th Annual Meeting of the Human Factors Society, Orlando* (Santa Monica, California: Human Factors Society, 1990), pp. 1547–1551

Garg, S. and Schmidt, D. K. 'Cooperative synthesis of control and display augmentation in approach and landing', *Journal of Guidance, Control, and Dynamics*, **13**, 1990, 466–475

Goesch, T. C. 'Head-up displays hit the road', *Information Display*, July/August 1990, 10–13

Hansen, R. *Head-Up Guidance System* (Warrendale, Pennsylvania: Society of Automotive Engineers, 1990), SAE Paper 901834

Hughes, T. C., Dudley, R. and Lovering, P. *A Comparison of Alternative Head-Up Display Symbol Sets During Approach and Landing, Navigation, and Ususual Attitude Recovery Tasks* (Wright-Patterson AFB, Ohio: Aeronautical Systems Division, 1990), CSEF TR-90-IFC-001

Johnson, T. *Alaska Airlines Experience with HGS-1000 Head-Up Guidance System* (Warrendale, Pennsylvania: Society of Automotive Engineers, 1990), SAE Paper 901828

Jones, D. R. and Burley, J. R. *Qualitative Evaluation of a Conformal Velocity Vector Display for Use at High Angles-of-Attack in Fighter Aircraft* (Hampton, Virginia: National Aeronautics and Space Administration, 1990), NASA TM-102629

Lintern, G., Roscoe, S. N. and Sivier, J. E. 'Display principles, control dynamics, and environmental factors in pilot training and transfer', *Human Factors*, **32**, 1990, 299–317

Long, H. A. *HUD Potential for Narrow-Bodied Air Carrier Aircraft* (Warrendale, Pennsylvania: Society of Automotive Engineers, 1990), SAE Paper 901831

Merrick, V. K., Farris, G. G. and Vanags, A. A. *Head Up Display Format for Application to V/STOL Aircraft Approach and Landing* (Moffett Field, California: National Aeronautics and Space Administration, 1990), NASA TM-102216

Newman, R. L. *Cockpit Situational Awareness: A Flight Experiment* (Yellow Springs, Ohio: Crew Systems, 1990), TR-90-04

Newman, R. L. *Flight Evaluation of Flight Visions Head-Up Display* (Yellow Springs, Ohio: Crew Systems, 1990), TM-90-06

Penwill, J. C. and Hall, J. R. *A Comparative Evaluation of Two HUD Formats by All Four Nations to Determine the Preferred Pitch Ladder Design for EFA* (Bedford, England: Royal Aircraft Establishment, 1990), RAE FM-WP(90)022

Sojourner, R. J. and Antin, J. F. 'The effects of a simulated head-up display speedometer on perceptual task performance', *Human Factors*, 3, 1990, 329–339

Steenblik, J. W. 'Holy hybrid, birdman', *Air Line Pilot*, February 1990,

10–14

Stokes, A., Wickens, C. and Kite, K. *Display Technology – Human Factors Concepts* (Warrendale, Pennsylvania: Society of Automotive Engineers, 1990), SAE R-102

Way, T. C. *et al. 3-D Imagery Cockpit Display Development* (Wright-Patterson AFB, Ohio: Wright Research and Development Center, 1990), WRDC TR-90-7003

Yenni, K. R. *Flight Tests of a Helmet Mounted Display Synthetic Vision Systems* (Washington: American Institute of Aeronautics and Astronautics, 1990), AIAA Paper 90-1270

'The A320 head-up display', paper presented at *Sixth Performance and Operations Conference* (Montreal: International Air Transport Association, 1990)

Proceedings, Head-Up Display Symposium (Seattle, Washington: Boeing, 1990)

Human Interface Design Methodology for Integrated Display Symbology (Warrendale, Pennsylvania: Society of Automotive Engineers, 1990), SAE ARP-4155

SZD-55-1 HUDIS Heads Up Display System User's Manual (Hilton Head, SC: Solaire Performance Sailplanes, 1990)

'Through the looking glass', *Avionics Review*, June 1990, 4

1991

Arbon, E. *et al. Head-Up Guidance System Technology (HGST) – A Powerful Tool for Accident Prevention* (Alexandria, Virginia: Flight Safety Foundation, 1991), FSF/SP-91/01

Dahlstedt, S. V. R. 'Up/down in (im)possible flight attitude indicators', in *Proceedings 35th Annual Meeting of the Human Factors Society, San Francisco* (Santa Monica, California: Human Factors Society, 1991)

Ercoline, W. R. and Weinstein, L. S. *The Utility of Analog Vertical Velocity Information During Instrument Flight with the Head-Up Display*, Krug Life Sciences briefing to Cockpit Display Working Group, Wright Patterson AFB, July 1991

Foyle, D. C., McCann, R. S. and Sanford, B. D. 'Superimposed information displays: attentional deficits and potential solutions', in *Proceedings at 32nd Meeting of the Psychonomic Society, San Francisco*, November 1991

Foyle, D. C., Stanford, B. D. and McCann, R. S. 'Attentional issues in superimposed flight symbology', in *Proceedings of the 6th International Symposium on Aviation Psychology, Columbus* (Columbus, Ohio: Ohio State University, 1991), pp. 577-582

Geiselman, E. E. *An Integration of Aircraft Attitude Display Symbology Structures*, Thesis, University of Dayton, 1991

Huff, R. W. and Kessler, G. K. 'Enhanced displays, flight controls, and guidance systems for approach and landing', in *Aircraft Ship Operations, Seville* (Paris: Advisory Group for Aeronautical Research and Development, 1991), AGARD CP-509

Hughes, R. E. *The HUD Coloring Book: Recommendations Concerning Head-Up Displays* (Washington: Naval Air Systems Command, 1991)

Hutchinson, J. E. 'Taking a look ahead', *Flight International*, 15 May 1991, 32–34

Larish, I. A. and Wickens, C. D. *Divided Attention with Superimposed and Separated Imagery: Implications for Head-Up Displays* (Champaign, Illinois: University of Illinois, 1991), ARL-91-4/NASA HUD-91-1

Larish, I. A. and Wickens, C. D. 'Attention and HUDs: flying in the dark', in *Digest of Technical Papers, Society for Information Display 1991 International Symposium* (New York: Society for Information Display, 1991), pp. 461–464

McFarland, R. H. 'The appropriate concern for possible aberrations in landing guidance signals', in *Proceedings of the 6th International Symposium on Aviation Psychology, Columbus* (Columbus, Ohio: Ohio State University, 1991), 235–240

Menu, J. P. 'Advanced concepts for the next-generation aircraft', in *Proceedings of the Society for Information Display Conference, Anaheim* (New York: Society for Information Display, 1991), paper 24.1

Newman, R. L. and Haworth, L. A. 'Flight test techniques for display evaluation', paper presented at *23rd European Society of Experimental Test Pilots Symposium, Bath* (Lancaster, California: Society of Experimental Test Pilots, 1991)

Newman, R. L. *Symbology Flight Test Report FVI Model FV-2000 Head-Up Display* (San Marcos, Texas: Crew Systems, 1991), TR-91-10A

Newman, R. L. *Symbology for the FV-2000/KA Head-Up Display* (San Marcos, Texas: Crew Systems, 1991), TR-91-11

Pearson, D. A. 'Flat-panel display dynamic control panel for head-up displays', in *Proceedings of the Society for Information Display Conference, Anaheim* (New York: Society for Information Display, 1991), paper 8.1

Reising, J. M., Barthelemy, K. and Hartsock, D. C. *Unusual Attitude Recoveries Using a Pathway in the Sky (Pilot HUD Tests)*, AIAA Paper 91-2927, 1991

Sheehy, J. B. and Gish, K. W. 'Virtual image displays: is redesign really necessary', in *Proceedings of the Society for Information Display Conference, Anaheim* (New York: Society for Information Display, 1991), paper 15.4

Steenblik, J. W. 'The diamond, the shark, and the inverted Christmas tree', *Air Line Pilot*, December 1991, 28–31

Weinstein, L. F. and Ercoline, W. R. 'The standardization of head-up display symbology', in *Proceedings of the 6th International Symposium on Aviation Psychology, Columbus* (Columbus, Ohio: Ohio State University, 1991), pp. 210–215

Weinstein, L. F. and Ercoline, W. R. 'HUD climb/dive ladder configuration and unusual attitude recovery', in *Proceedings 35th Annual Meeting of the Human Factors Society, San Francisco* (Santa Monica, California: Human Factors Society, 1991), pp. 12–17

Wright, B. A. and Hoobler, M. A. *Standardized Head-Up Display Symbology Evaluation* (Edwards AFB, California: Air Force Flight Test Center, 1991), AFFTC TR-91-04

Head-Up Displays (Edinburgh: GEC Ferranti, 1991), DSD 911110

T-38 Head-Up Display (HUD) Avionics System Manual (Wright-Patterson AFB, Ohio: 4950 Test Wing, 1991)

1992

Adam, C. *Certification and Proof of Concept Procedures for New Technology* (Warrendale, Pennsylvania: Society of Automotive Engineers, 1992), SAE Paper 921934

Andre, A. D. 'Quantitative layout analysis for cockpit display systems', presented at *1992 International Symposium, Society for Information Display, Boston* (New York: Society for Information Display, 1992), paper 34.2

Bailey, R. E. *et al. Evaluation of Proposed USAF HUD Standard, Session 2* (Buffalo, New York: Calspan Corp., 1992), Report 7738-14

Batson, V. M., Harris, R. L. and Houck, J. A. 'Effect of display parameters on pilots' ability to approach, flare and land', in *Proceedings of the AIAA/AHS Flight Simulation Technologies Conference, Hilton Head*, August 1992, pp. 332–337

Connor, S. A., Krone, N. J. and Connor, G. L. *Enhanced Vision Systems Pilot Performance and Workload* (Warrendale, Pennsylvania: Society of Automotive Engineers, 1992), SAE Paper 921969

Deaton, J. E. *et al.* 'Enhanced HUD symbology associated with recovery from unusual attitudes', *Society of Experimental Test Pilots Cockpit*, April–June 1992, pp. 4–12

Demonsthanes, T. A., Dillard, A. E. and Long, H. A. *Situation vs Command Guidance Symbology for Hybrid Landing Systems Applications* (Warrendale, Pennsylvania: Society of Automotive Engineers, 1992), SAE Paper 921967

Dryden, J. B. 'Flying through the glass', *Code One*, April 1992, 12–15

Dryden, J. B., 'Doing it (effectively) in the dark', in *Digest of Technical Papers 1992 International Symposium,, Society for Information Display, Boston* (New York: Society for Information Display, 1992), paper 16.6

Foyle, D. C., Kaiser, M. K. and Johnson, W. W. 'Visual cues in low-level flight: implications for pilotage, training, simulation, and enahnced/synthetic vision systems', *American Helicopter Society 448th Annual Forum*, Vol. 1, 1992, 253–260

Foyle, D. C. *et al. Enhanced/Synthetic Vision Systems: Human Factors Research and Implications for Future Systems* (Warrendale, Pensylvania: Society of Automotive Engineers, 1992), SAE Paper 921968

Groves, D. J. and Horowitz, A. D. 'Projection distance issues in automotive HUD implementation', in *Digest of Technical Papers 1992 International Symposium, Society for Information Display, Boston* (New York: Society for Information Display, 1992), paper 46.3

Hall, J. R. 'The design and development of the new RAF standard HUD format', in *Combat Automation for Airborne Weapon Systems: Man/Machine Interface Trends and Technologies, Edinburgh* (Paris: Advisory Group for Aeronautical Research and Development 1992), paper 11

Harris, R. L. *Piloted Studies of Enhanced or Synthetic Vision Display Parameters* (Warrendale, Pennsylvania: Society of Automotive Engineers, 1992), SAE Paper 921970

Hopkins, H. 'Through the looking glass', *Flight International*, 3 June 1992, 27–30

Kenyon, R. V. 'Wide-field-of-view displays: how much is enough', in *Digest of Technical Papers 1992 International Symposium, Society for Information Display, Boston* (New York: Society for Information Display, 1992), paper 16.2

Kruk, R. V. *Issues Associated with Enhanced Vision Systems* (Warrendale, Pennsylvania: Society of Automotive Engineers, 1992), SAE Paper 921935

Mages, J. G. *Enhanced Vision in Commercial Air Carrier Operations*, SAE Paper 921932, 1992

Martin-Emerson, R. and Wickens, C. D. 'The vertical visual field and implications for the head-up display', in *Proceedings 36th Annual Meeting of the Human Factors Society, Atlanta* (Santa Monica, California: Human Factors Society, 1992), pp. 1408–1412

Meehan, J. W. and Triggs, T. J. 'Apparent size and distance in an imaging display', *Human Factors*, **34**, 1992, 303–311

Middleton, D. B., Srivatsan, R. and Person, L. H. 'Takeoff performance monitoring system display options', in *Proceedings of the AIAA/AHS Flight Simulation Technologies Conference, Hilton Head*, August 1992, pp.

57–67

Nagati, M. G., Fulton, C. L. and Mirsafian, S. *A Guidance Display System for Single Pilot Operation* (Washington: American Institute of Aeronautics and Astronautics, 1992), AIAA Paper 92-4196

Sanford, B. D. *Head-Up Displays: Effect of Information Location on the Processing of Superimposed Symbology* Thesis, San Jose State University, 1992

Smith, G., Meehan, J. W. and Day, R. H. 'The effect of accommodation on retinal image size', *Human Factors*, **34**, 1992, 289–301

Todd, J. R., Hester, R. B. and Summers, L. G. *Seeing Through the Weather: Enhanced/Synthetic Vision Systems for Commercial Transports* (Warrendale, Pennsylvania: Society of Automotive Engineers, 1992), SAE Paper 921973

Tucker, R. R. *et al. Synthetic Vision System Technology Demonstration Results to Date* (Warrendale, Pennsylvania: Society of Automotive Engineers, 1992), SAE Paper 921971

Weinstein, L. F. and Ercoline, W. R. 'The standardization of head-up display symbology for the reduction of spatial disorientation', in *Proceedings 63rd Annual Scientific Meeting, Aerospace Medical Association, Miami Beach,* May, 1992

Weinstein, L. F., Ercoline, W. R. and Bitton, D. F. 'The utility of a ghost horizon and climb/dive ladder tapering on a head-up display', in *Proceedings 36th Annual Meeting, Human Factors Society, Atlanta* (Santa Monica, California: Human Factors Society, 1992), pp. 48–51

Weinstein, L. F., Ercoline, W. R. and Evans, R. H. *The Utility of Analog Vertical Velocity Information During Instrument Flight with a Head-Up Display (HUD)* (Brooks AFB, Texas: Armstrong Laboratory, 1992), AL-TP-1992-0021

Weintraub, D. J. and Ensing, M. J. *Human Factors Issues in Head-Up Display Design: The Book of HUD* (Wright-Patterson AFB, Ohio: Crew System Ergonomics Information Analysis Center, 1992), CSERIAC SOAR-92-2

Wood, R. B. 'Holographic head-up displays', in *Electro-Optical Displays*, M. A. Karim (ed.), (Dekker: New York, 1992), pp. 337–415

FDI Model 2300, Head Up Guidance System (HGS). System Description for the Boeing 737-400 (Hybrid Operations) (Portland, Oregon: Flight Dynamics, 1992), Report 9602-0013

Mechanization of the Instrument Flight Standardization Head-Up Display (HUD) Symbology (Wright-Patterson AFB, Ohio: Aeronautical Systems Division, 1992), CSEF TR-92-IFS-0001

Proceedings of the 7th Plenary Session of the Synthetic Vision Certification Issues Study Team, Williamsburg, June 1992

313

1993

Adam, E. C. 'Head-up displays vs helmet-mounted displays: the issues', in *Digest of Technical Papers, 1993 International Symposium, Society for Information Display, Seattle* (New York: Society for Information Display, 1993), pp. 429–432; paper 28.1

Advani, S. K. *et al. What Optical Cues Do Pilots Use to Initiate the Landing Flare of a Piloted Simulator Experiment* (Washington: American Institute of Aeronautics and Astronautics, 1993), AIAA Paper 93-3961

Bailey, R. and Knotts, L. *Flight and Ground Simulation Evaluation of the Proposed USAF Head-Up Display Standard* (Washington: American Institute of Aeronautics and Astronautics, 1993), AIAA Paper 93-3605

Bailey, R. E. and Parrag, M. L. 'Lessons learned in head-up display flight testing', in *Looking Ahead, International Symposium on Head-Up Display, Enhanced Vision, Virtual Reality, Amsterdam,* October 1993, Paper i, pp. 93–99

Barber, A. and Farrell, L. 'The Canadair Regional Jet head-up guidance programme', in *Looking Ahead, International Symposium on Head-Up Display, Enhanced Vision, Virtual Reality, Amsterdam,* October 1993, Paper 8, pp. 55–62

Burgess, M. *Synthetic Vision. What Has Been Accomplished and What is Next?* (Washington: American Institute of Aeronautics and Astronautics, 1993), AIAA Paper 93-3977

Cardullo, F. and George, G. *Transport Delay Compensation: An Inexpensive Alternative to Increasing Image Generator Update Rate* (Washington: American Institute of Aeronautics and Astronautics, 1993), AIAA Paper 93-3563

Chandya, D. and Weintraub, D. J. 'Designing head-up display symbology for unusual attitude recovery', in *Proceedings 7th International Symposium on Aviation Psychology, Columbus* (Columbus, Ohio: Ohio State University, 1993)

Cox, W. J. *Evaluation of Situation Versus Command Guidance Symbology in Hybrid Landing System Applications* (Washington: Federal Aviation Administration, in preparation)

Dorighi, N. S., Ellis, S. R. and Grunwald, A. J. 'Perspective format for a primary flight display (ADI) and its effect on pilot spatial awareness', in *Proceedings 37th Annual Meeting of the Human Factors and Ergonomics Society, Seattle* (Santa Monica, California: Human Factors and Ergonomics Society, 1993), pp. 88–92

Eksuzian, D. J. *et al. TRISTAR I: Tri-Service Symbology Test and Research,* (Moffett Field, California: Tri-Service Flight Symbology Working Group, to be published shortly), FSWG TR-91-01

314

Foyle, D. C. *et al.* 'Attentional effects with superimposed symbology: implications for head-up displays (HUD)', in *Proceedings 37th Annual Meeting of the Human Factors and Ergonomics Society, Seattle* (Santa Monica, California: Human Factors and Ergonomics Society, 1993), pp. 1340–1344

Haworth, L. A. and Newman, R. L. *Techniques for Evaluating Flight Displays* (Moffett Field, California: Army Aeroflightdynamics Directorate, 1993), USAAVSCOM TR-92-A-006; NASA TM-103947

Higgens K. 'EVS/HUD, manufacturer's viewpoint', in *Looking Ahead, International Symposium on Head-Up Display, Enhanced Vision, Virtual Reality, Amsterdam,* October 1993, Paper 9, pp. 63–67

Hoagland, D. 'HUD symbology improvements program', paper presented at *Display Conference, Edwards AFB* March–April 1993

Kaiser, K. 'The HUD experience of Alaska Airlines', in *Looking Ahead, International Symposium on Head-Up Display, Enhanced Vision, Virtual Reality, Amsterdam,* October 1993

Knoll, P. M. *et al.* 'Head-up display for automotive use', in *Digest of Technical Papers, 1993 International Symposium, Society for Information Display, Seattle* (New York: Society for Information Display, 1993), Paper 42.1

Lay, L. W., McCauley, S. G. and Nagati, M. G. *Evaluation of a Follow-Me-Box Heads Up Display for General Aviation* (Washington: American Institute of Aeronautics and Astronautics, 1993), AIAA Paper 93-4020

Liggett, K. K., Reising, J. M. and Hartsock, D. C. 'Failure indications on a head-up display', in *Proceedings 7th International Symposium on Aviation Psychology, Columbus* (Columbus, Ohio: Ohio State University, 1993)

McCann, R. S., Foyle, D. C. and Johnson, J. C. 'Attentional limitations with head-up displays', in *Proceedings 7th International Symposium on Aviation Psychology, Columbus* (Columbus, Ohio: Ohio State University, 1993), pp. 70–75

Martin-Emerson, R. *Conformal Symbology and the Head-Up Display* Thesis, University of Illinois, August 1993

Metalis, S. A. 'Assessment of pilot situational awareness: measurement via simulation', in *Proceedings 37th Annual Meeting of the Human Factors and Ergonomics Society, Seattle,* (Santa Monica, California: Human Factors and Ergonomics Society, 1993), pp. 113–117

Newman, R. L. *Flight Test Report. Flight Visions FV-2000/KA HUD Installed in a Beechcraft BE-A100* (San Marcos, Texas: Crew Systems, 1993), TR-93-09

Newman, R. L. *Head-Up and Helmet-Mounted Display Glossary* (San Marcos, Texas: Crew Systems, 1993), TR-93-11

Newman, R. L. and Standiford, S. N. *HUD Training: Training Pilots to Fly HUDs or Using HUDs to Train Pilots to Fly* (Washington: American Institute of Aeronautics and Astronautics, 1993), AIAA Paper 93-3971

Rogers, S. P. and Myers, L. D. 'Development of an intelligent system to aid in avionics display design', in *Proceedings, AIAA/IEEE Digital Avionics Systems Conference, Fort Worth,* October 1993, pp. 160–166

Roscoe, S. N. 'Visual orientation: facts and hypotheses', *International Journal of Aviation Psychology,* **3,** 221–229

Sanford, B. D. *et al.* 'Head-up displays: effect of information location on the processing of superimposed symbology', *Proceedings 7th International Symposium on Aviation Psychology, Columbus,* (Columbus, Ohio: Ohio State University, 1993), pp. 81–87

Turner, A. D. and Hattendorf, P. E. *Standardized Head-Up Display Symbology Evaluation* (Edwards AFB, California: Air Force Flight Test Center, 1993), AFFTC TR-92-15

Weinstein, L. F. and Ercoline, W. R. 'Procedures and metrics for aircraft cockpit display evaluations', in *Proceedings 37th Annual Meeting of the Human Factors and Ergonomics Society, Seattle* (Santa Monica, California: Human Factors and Ergonomics Society, 1993), pp. 1201–1205

Weinstein, L. F. *et al. Standardization of Aircraft Control and Performance Symbology on the USAF Head-Up Display* (Brooks AFB, Texas: Armstrong Laboratory, 1993), AL/CF TR-1993-0088

Beechcraft King Air A100 Landplane Flight Manual Supplement for Flight Visions Head-Up Display, Model FV-2000 (Sugar Grove, Illinois: Flight Visions, 1993), Document 9210-023A

Display Characteristics of HUDs Used in Civil Transport Aircraft (Warrendale, Pennsylvania: Society of Automotive Engineers, 1993), SAE ARP 4742

Literature Review of HUD Symbology (Warrendale, Pennsylvania: Society of Automotive Engineers, 1993), SAE AIR 4654

No date

80 Series Head-Up Display System for Transport Aircraft (Rochester, England: Marconi-Elliott, no date)

A-7D Flight Manual (Washington: US Air Force, no date, ca. 1984), TO-1A-7D-1

A-10A Flight Manual (Washington: US Air Force, no date, ca. 1984), TO-1A-10A-1

All Weather Approach and Landing Monitor, TC-121 (Paris: Thomson-CSF, no date)

Alpha Jet Head-Up Display and Weapons Delivery System (San Jose, California: Kaiser Electronics, no date)

AV-8A Flight Manual (Washington: Naval Air Systems Command, no date, ca. 1984), NAVAIR-01-AV8A-1

AV-8B Flight Manual (Washington: Naval Air Systems Command, no date, ca. 1984), NAVAIR A1-AV8BB-NFM-000

Collimateur à Tube Cathodique TC-121 (Paris: Thomson-CSF, no date)

CV-91AB Visual Guidance System (VGS) (Paris: Thomson-CSF, no date)

F-14A Flight Manual (Washington: Naval Air Systems Command, [no date, ca. 1984]), NAVAIR-01-F14AAA-1

F-15 Head-Up Display (St. Louis, Missouri: McDonnell-Douglas, no date)

F-15A Flight Manual (Washington: US Air Force, no date, ca. 1984), TO-1A-15A-1

F-16 Type WFOV HUD (San Jose, California: Kaiser Electronics, no date), brochure 0374M

F-16A Flight Manual (Washington: US Air Force, no date, ca. 1984), TO-1A-16A-1

F-18 Flight Manual (Washington: Naval Air Systems Command, no date, ca. 1984), NAVAIR-A1-F18AC-NFM-000

Head-Up Guidance System (Portland, Oregon: Flight Dynamics, no date), Pilot Guide

The Head-Up Guidance System (HGS) and the Bottom Line (Portland, Oregon: Flight Dynamics, no date)

Heads Up All the Way (Sugar Grove, Illinois: Flight Visions, Inc., no date)

Instrument Flying (Washington: US Air Force, no date, ca. 1986), AFM-51-37

JET 1000 HUD Series Head-Up Display System (Grand Rapids, Michigan: Jet Electronics and Technology, no date), brochure 1087/1M/DL

JET Series 1000 HUD (Grand Rapids, Michigan: Jet Electronics and Technology Brochure, no date), DL585K2

Light Line Head-Up Display System (Redmond, Washington: Sundstrand Data Control, no date), Pilot Handbook

MB-339C Aircraft Pilot's Guide (Varese, Italy, Aermacchi, no date, ca. 1993), PIPG01-9CB

Technical and Operational Description of CV-91AB (Paris: Thomson-CSF, no date)

Visual Approach Monitor (Redmond, Washington: Sundstrand Data Control, no date)

Subject index to bibliography

Note: please refer to main bibliography for full details of the references listed below.

HUD evaluations

Evaluation methodology

1979	Heffley, R. K.	1991	Newman, R. L.
1980	Herron, E.	1992	Adam, C.
1980	Schifflet, S. G.	1992	Andre, A. D.
1981	Schifflet, S. G.	1993	Bailey, R. E. (both refs)
1981	Smith, R. E.	1993	Cox, W. J.
1987	Papa, R. M.	1993	Eksuzian, D. J.
1988	Konicke, M. L.	1993	Haworth, L. A.
1988	Middleton, D. B.	1993	Metalis, S. A.
1990	Newman, R. L.	1993	Turner, A. D.
1990	(anon.) *Human Interface Design Methodology for Integrated Display Symbology*	1993	Weinstein, L. F. (both refs)

Flight test

1963	Ramsey, W. E.	1968	DeBotton, I.
1964	Johnson, R. K.	1970	Naish, J. M.
1966	Fry, D. E.	1971	Driscoll, N.
1966	Roscoe, S. N.	1974	Gold, T.

318

Simulator studies

1973	Harris, R. L.	1985	Weintraub, D. J.
1974	Harris, R. L.	1986	Armando, A.
1974	Weener, E. F.	1986	Desmond, J. P.
1975	Cronn, F. W.	1986	Frieberg, U.
1975	Dwyer, J. H.	1986	Kinsley, S. A.
1976	Harris, R. L.	1986	Roscoe, S. N.
1977	Haines, R. F.	1987	Abbott, T. S.
1977	Long, M. G.	1987	Henson, J. M.
1977	Mazza, J. D.	1987	McCormack, L. B.
1977	J. C. Penwill	1987	Mann, T. L.
1978	Haines, R. F.	1987	Newman, R. L.
1979	Fischer, E.	1987	Penwill, J. C.
1979	Haines, R. F.	1987	Way, T. C.
1979	Haines, R. F. and	1987	Zenyuh, J. P.
	Guercio, J. G.	1988	Carr, L. A.
1979	Heffley, R. K.	1988	Hasenbein, K. P.
1979	Smith, R. H.	1988	Konicke, M. L.
1979	Smith, W. D.	1988	Newman, R. L.
1979	Terhune, G. J. *Report to*	1988	Wells, M. J.
	ALPA on PERSEPOLIS	1989	Brickner, M. S.
	Simulations	1989	Deaton, J. E.
1979	Terhune, G. J. *Report to*	1989	Gawron, V. J.
	ALPA on TC-125	1990	Collins, P.
	Simulations	1990	Deaton, J. E.
1980	Adamson, J. C.	1990	Dryden, J. B. (both refs)
1980	Gibson, C. P.	1990	Ercoline, W. R.
1980	Herron, E.	1990	Hughes, T. C.
1980	Naish, J. M. (both refs)	1990	Penwill, J. C.
1980	Terhune, G. J.	1991	Ercoline, W. R.
1980	Wewerinke, P. H.	1991	Larish, I. A. (both refs)
1981	Tkach, M. J.	1991	Reising, J. M.
1982	Jewell, W. F.	1991	Weinstein, L. F.
1982	Lauber, J. K.	1992	Bailey, R. E.
1982	Penwill, J. C.	1992	Deaton, J. E.
1983	Detro, S. D.	1992	Haworth, L. A.
1983	Payne, J. M.	1992	Weinstein, L. F. (all refs)
1983	Penwill, J. C.	1993	Bailey, R. E. (both refs)
1983	Sexton, G. A.	1993	Cox, W. J.
1983	(conference) *Proceedings*	1993	Eksuzian, D. J.
	of the HUD/Instruments	1993	Lay, L. W.
	Conference	1993	Weinstein, L. F.

Symbology issues

Contact analog

1964	Sviden, O.
1965	Carel, W. L.
1965	Nordstrom, L.
1966	Klopfstein, G.
1970	Sherr, S.
1973	DeCelles, J. L.
1973	Foxworth, T. G.
1974	Pursel, R. H.
1975	Hutchinson, J. E.
1975	Walchli, R. M.
1976	Klopfstein, G.
1976	Terhune, G. J.
1977	Carel, W. L.

1979	Terhune, G. J. *Report to ALPA on PERSEPOLIS Simulations*
1979	Terhune, G. J. *Report to ALPA on TC-125 Simulations*
1981	Roscoe, S. N.
1982	Quinn, T. J.
1987	Way, T. C.
1990	Lintern, G.
1990	Way, T. C.
1991	Geiselman, E. E.

EADIs

1965	Carel, W. L.
1968	Walters, D. J.
1970	Sherr, S.
1971	Semple, C. A.
1975	(anon.) *Military Standard: Electronically or Optically Generated Displays for Aircraft Control or Combat Cue Information*
1977	Carel, W. L.
1979	Fadden, D. N.
1981	Hobe, G. A.
1981	Norton, P. S.
1981	Person, L. H.
1982	Reising, J. M.
1983	Blomberg, R. D.
1983	Simon, B.
1983	Summers, L. G.
1984	(anon.) *Military Standard:*

	Human Factors Engineering Design Criteria for Helicopter Cockpit Electro-Optical Display Symbology
1985	Silverstein, L. D.
1985	(anon.) *Indicator Group, Head-Up Display OD-(*)/ AVQ, Design Control Specification for F-14D and A-6E Upgrade Weapon Systems*
1986	Edwards, R. E.
1986	Hutchinson, J. E.
1987	McCormack, L. B.
1987	Abbott, T. S.
1988	Konicke, M. L.
1989	(anon.) *Military Standard: Aircraft Display Symbology*
1990	Lintern, G.
1991	Geiselman, E. E.

Pitch scale issues

1968	Walters, D. J.	1988	Reising, J.
1968	(anon.) *A Comparison of Electronic World and Flight Director World Head-Up Displays*	1988	Stephens, C. M.
		1989	Hall, J. R. (both refs)
		1989	Penwill, J. C.
		1990	Collins, P.
1971	Frieberg, U.	1990	Newman, R. L.
1972	Lincoln, R.	1991	Hughes, R. E.
1973	Naish, J. M.	1991	Weinstein, L. F.
1981	Smith, R. E.	1992	Bailey, R. E.
1982	Penwill, J. C.	1992	Hall, J. R.
1987	Henson, J. M.	1993	Eksuzian, D. J.
1987	Newman, R. L.	1993	Martin-Emerson, R.
1988	Green, H. B.	1993	Weinstein, L. F.
1988	Newman, R. L.		
1988	Penwill, J. C.		

Symbolic displays

1961	Naish, J. M.	1979	Frank, L. H.
1962	Naish, J. M. (both refs)	1981	Roscoe, S. N.
1963	Naish, J. M.	1982	Quinn, T. J.
1964	Naish, J. M.	1985	Adams, K. A.
1967	(anon.) *Procurement Specifications for Display Set*	1985	Koonce, J. M.
		1986	Kinsley, S. A.
		1987	Henson, J. M.
1968	Naish, J. M.	1987	Kama, W. N.
1968	(anon.) *A Comparison of Electronic World and Flight Director World Head-Up Displays*	1987	Way, T. C.
		1987	Zenyuh, J. P.
		1989	Ercoline, W. R.
		1989	Hall, J. R. (both refs)
1969	Naish, J. M.	1990	Collins, P.
1970	Sherr, S.	1990	Dryden, J. B. (both refs)
1971	Naish, J. M.	1990	Lintern, G.
1972	Lincoln, R.	1990	Way, T. C.
1972	Naish, J. M. 'Head-up display for the visual approach'	1991	Ercoline, W. R.
		1991	Geiselman, E. E.
1972	Naish, J. M. 'Application of the head-up display'	1992	Dryden, J. B.
		1992	Hall, J. R.
		1992	Weinstein (all refs)
1975	Cronn, F. W.	1993	(anon.) *Literature Review of HUD Symbology*
1977	Newman, R. L.		

Control law issues

Control laws

1983 Scott, B. C.
1983 (conference) *Proceedings of the HUD/Instruments Conference*
1983 (anon.) *System Description for FDI Model 1000 Head-Up Display*
1984 Herlt, S. M.
1984 Lowe, J. R.
1984 Mitchell, D. G.
1984 Powers, B. G.
1985 Innocenti, M.
1985 Lowe, J. R.
1986 Bailey, R. E. (both refs)
1986 Kessler, G.
1986 McCormack, L. B.
1986 Roscoe, S. N.

1987 Bailey, R. E.
1987 McCormack, L. B.
1987 Mann, T. L.
1987 Newman, R. L.
1988 Boettcher, K.
1988 Garg, S.
1988 Hasenbein, K. P.
1988 Stephens, C. M.
1989 Bailey, R. E.
1989 Gawron, V. J.
1990 Collins, P.
1990 Lintern, G.
1992 Bailey, R. E.
1992 Hall, J. R.
1992 Nagati, M. G.
1992 Weintraub, D. J.
1993 Cardullo, F.

Flying qualities

1973 Wanner, J.-C.
1978 Borodin, V. T.
1979 Smith, R. H. (both refs)
1979 (anon.) *Military Specification: Flying Qualities of Piloted Airplanes*
1980 Berry, D. T.
1981 Newman, R. L.
1981 Schifflet, S. G.
1981 Smith, R. E.
1982 Bakker, J. T.
1982 Smith, R. E.
1983 Payne, J. M.

1983 (conference) *Proceedings of the HUD/Instruments Conference*
1984 Herlt, S. M.
1984 Knotts, L. H.
1984 Mitchell, D. G.
1985 Innocenti, M.
1985 Newman, R. L.
1986 Bailey, R. E. (both refs)
1986 Kessler, G.
1987 Newman, R. L.
1988 Garg, S.
1989 Gawron, V. J.
1993 Cardullo, F.

Visual issues

Accommodation

1972 Larry, C.
1977 Chisum, G. T.
1978 Gibson, C. P.

1978 Iavecchia, J. H.
1979 Chisum, G. T.
1979 Haines, R. F.

324

Accuracy/disparity studies

Brightness

Peripheral vision displays

1981	Enevoldson, E. K.	1984	Malcomb, R. E.
1983	Liebowitz, H. W.	1989	Hameluck, D.
1984	Gawron, V. J.		

Superimposed fields

1960	Naish, J. M.	1985	Weintraub, D. J.
1964	Naish, J. M. (both refs)	1985	Menu, J.-P.
1965	Burroughs, A. A.	1986	Vallance, C. H.
1976	Terhune, G. J.	1989	Kimchi, R.
1979	Fischer, E.	1991	Foyle, D. C. (both refs)
1980	Bray, R. S.	1991	Larish, I. A. (both refs)
1980	Naish, J. M.	1992	Sanford, B. D.
1982	Barnes, G. R.	1993	Foyle, D. C.
1983	Martin, W. L.	1993	McCann, R. S.
1983	Vallance, C. H.	1993	Roscoe, S. N.
1984	Menu, J.-P.	1993	Sanford, B. D.
1984	Weintraub, D. J.		

Synthetic vision

1989	Brickner, M. S.	1992	Kruk, R. V.
1989	(conference) *Synthetic Vision Technology Demonstration Program*	1992	Mages, J. G.
		1992	Todd, J. R.
		1992	Tucker, R. R.
1990	Yenni, K. R.	1992	(conference) *Proceedings 7th Plenary Session of the Synthetic Vision Certification Issues Study Team*
1992	Adam, C.		
1992	Batson, V.		
1992	Conner, S. A.		
1992	Demonsthanes, T. A.		
1992	Foyle, D. C. (both refs)	1993	Burgess, M.
1992	Harris, R. L.	1993	Higgens, K.

Visual guidance

1964	Gold, T. (both refs)	1972	Gold, T.
1964	Sviden, O.	1972	Naish, J. M.
1971	(anon.) *Engineering Report, Delta Gamma Visual Landing System*	1972	(anon.) *Theory of Operation, Visual Approach Monitor Utilizing a Vertical*

Operational issues

Accident reviews

HUD failure detection

ILS approaches (all weather landing)

1991 Hutchinson, J. E.
1991 Steenblik, J. W.
1992 Batson, V.
1992 Demonsthanes, T. A.
1992 Mages, J. G.
1992 Todd, J. R.
1992 (conference) *Proceedings 7th Plenary Session of the*

Synthetic Vision Certification Issues Study Team

1993 Cox, W. J.
1993 (anon.) *Display Characteristics of HUDs Used in Civil Transport Aircraft*

Pilot surveys

1959 Cumming, R. W.
1973 Opittek, E. W.
1976 Barnette, J. F.

1980 Newman, R. L.
1981 Newman, R. L.
1989 Roust, L. M.

Spatial disorientation

1965 Benson, A. J.
1971 Benson, A. J.
1971 Dobie, T. G.
1971 Tyler, P. E.
1976 Barnette, J. F.
1980 Newman, R. L.
1981 Enevoldson, E. K.
1981 Jarvi, D.
1981 Newman, R. L. (both refs)
1981 Norton, P. S.
1981 Tkach, M. J.
1982 Taylor, R. M.
1983 (conference) *Proceedings of the HUD/Instruments Conference*
1984 Malcomb, R. E.
1984 Taylor, R. M.
1985 McNaughton, G. B.
1985 (conference) *Aircraft Attitude Awareness Workshop*
1985 (conference) *Flight Instrumentation Conference*
1985 (anon.) 'Jaguar hit trees'
1986 Guttman, J.
1986 Kinsley, S. A.
1986 Newman, R. L. (both refs)

1986 Roscoe, S. N. 'Designed for disaster'
1986 Roscoe, S. N. 'Spatial misorientation exacerbated by collimated virtual flight display'
1987 Haber, R. N.
1987 Henson, J. M.
1987 Iavecchia, J. H.
1987 Newman, R. L. *Evaluation of the FDI Head-Up Display*
1987 Newman, R. L. *Improvement of Head-Up Display Standards I*
1987 Newman, R. L. *Improvement of Head-Up Display Standards II*
1987 Newman, R. L. *Improvement of Head-Up Display Standards III*
1987 Newman, R. L. 'The HUD and spatial disorientation'
1987 Roscoe, S. N.
1987 Taylor, R. M.

Tactical applications

331

1988	Hickl, H.		*Manual*
1989	Hall, J. R. (both refs)	—	(anon.) *AV-8B Flight*
1990	Collins, P.		*Manual*
1992	Dryden, J. W.	—	(anon.) *F-14A Flight*
1992	Hall, J. R.		*Manual*
1993	Adam, E. C.	—	(anon.) *F-15A Flight*
—	(anon.) *A-7D Flight*		*Manual*
	Manual	—	(anon.) *F-16A Flight*
—	(anon.) *A-10A Flight*		*Manual*
	Manual	—	(anon.) *F-18 Flight*
—	(anon.) *AV-8A Flight*		*Manual*

Target detection

1979	Fischer, E.	1986	Norman, J.
1979	Roscoe, S. N.	1986	Roscoe, S. N. 'Designed
1980	Fischer, E.		for disaster'
1980	Frazier, M. L.	1986	Roscoe, S. N. 'Spatial
1980	Haines, R. F.		misorientation
1981	Watler, J. F.		exacerbated by
1983	Genco, L. V. (both refs)		collimated virtual flight
1983	Ginsburg, A. P.		display'
1983	Martin, W. L.	1986	Vallance, C. H.
1985	Matthes, G. W.	1989	Kimchi, R.
1985	Monaco, W. A.	1989	Steenblik, J. W.
1985	Morris, A.	1993	Roscoe, S. N.
1985	Roscoe, S. N.		

Training issues

1965	Carel, W. L.	1981	Watler, J. F.
1976	(anon.) *Head-Up Display*	1983	Kraus, J. M.
	Evaluation	1983	(anon.) 'Alpha Jet –
1977	Long, M. G.		further version for the
1977	Newman, R. L.		international market'
1979	(anon.) *Programme*	1983	(conference) *Proceedings*
	Simulateur – Approche		*of the HUD/Instruments*
	Automatique Mode Land		*Conference*
1979	(anon.) *A word from the*	1984	Knots, L. H.
	Navy	1985	Doten, F. S.
1980	Newman, R. L.	1985	Golovcsenko, I. V.
1981	Newman, R. L. (both refs)	1987	Newman, R. L.
1981	Norton, P. S.	1987	Roscoe, S. N.

1988	Agneessens, D.	—	(anon.) *Instrument Flying*
1988	Newman, R. L.	—	(anon.) *JET 1000 HUD*
1992	Foyle, D C.		*Series Head-Up Display*
1993	Newman, R. L.		*System*

Visual cues used in landing

1955	Cumming, R. W.	1979	Roscoe, S. N.
1966	Roscoe, S. N.	1981	Lowe, J. R.
1974	Riordan, R. H.	1993	Roscoe, S. N.
1976	Eisele, J. E.		

Wind shear

1978	Haines, R. F.	1986	Oliver, J. G.
1980	Haines, R. F.	1986	Trousdale, D. M.
1981	Newman, R. L.		

HUD state-of-the-art

Bibliographies

| 1966 | Andrew, I. D. | 1993 | (anon.) *Literature Review* |
| 1984 | Newman, R. L. | | *of HUD symbology* |

Helmet-mounted displays

1973	Hughes, R. L.		*Electro-Optical Display*
1980	Roscoe, S. N.		*Symbology*
1982	Barnes, G. R.	1985	Doten, F. S.
1984	(anon.) *Military*	1988	Wells, M. J.
	Standard: Human Factors	1989	Stinnett, T. A.
	Engineering Design Criteria	1993	Adam, E. C.
	for Helicopter Cockpit		

Holographic HUDs

1979	Berg, A.		*Aircraft*
1979	Chorley, R. A.	1983	Boucek, G. P.
1981	Berry, R. L.	1983	Desmond, J. P.
1982	Gard, J. H.	1983	Hussey, D. W.
1982	(anon.) *Holographic Head-*	1983	Kraus, J. M.
	Up Display for Transport	1983	(anon.) *System Description*

	for FDI Model 1000 Head-Up Display	1989	Steenblik, J. W.
1984	Desmond, J. P.	1989	(anon.) *FDI Model 1000 Head-Up Display System Specification*
1984	Wurfel, H. G.		
1985	Matthes, G. W.	1990	Desmond, J. P.
1986	Desmond, J. P.	1990	Hansen, R. C.
1986	Vallance, C. H.	1990	Johnson, T.
1988	Wood, R. B.	1992	Wood, R. B.

Reviews of HUD state-of-the-art

1966	Andrew, I. D.	1982	Bick, F. J.
1968	Jenney, L. L.	1983	Himmelberg, M. R.
1970	Sherr, S.	1983	Martin, W. L.
1972	Augustine, W. L.	1984	Lovering, P. B. (both refs)
1972	Smith, J. H.		
1975	Orrick, W. P.	1984	Newman, R. L.
1976	Barnette, J. F.	1986	Vallance, C. H.
1977	Green, G. N.	1987	Newman, R. L.
1977	Kiltz, R. M.		*Improvement of Head-Up Display Standards I*
1978	Egan, D. E.		
1978	Foxworth, T. G.	1987	Newman, R. L.
1979	Frank, L. H.		*Improvement of Head-Up Display Standards III*
1979	Haines, R. F.		
1979	Kiltz, R. M.	1988	Hickl, H.
1979	Naish, J. M.	1988	Isao, I.
1980	Newman, R. L.	1989	Gard, J. H.
1980	Roscoe, S. N.	1990	Stokes, A.
1980	Stonehouse, D.	1992	Weintraub, D. J.
1981	Maureau, C.	1992	Wood, R. B.
1981	Newman, R. L. (both refs)	1993	Adam, E. C.
		—	(anon.) *Instrument Flying*

Aircraft installations

A-6

1984	(anon.) *A-6F Head-Up Display (HUD Format*		*(*)/AVQ, Design Control Specification*
1985	(anon.) *Indicator Group, Head-Up Display OD-*	1986	Kessler, G.
		1987	Iavecchia, J. H.

334

A-7

A-10

AV-8 (Harrier)

F-5/T-38/F-20

F-14

1975	Doucette, A. R.		*Head-Up Display OD-*
1976	Doucette, A. R.		*(*)/AVQ, Design Control*
1979	Frank, L. H.		*Specification*
1985	Monaco, W. A.	1987	Guttman, J.
1985	Morris, A.	1989	Deaton, J. E.
1985	(anon.) *F-14D Head-Up*	—	(anon.) *F-14A Flight*
	Display Format		*Manual*
1985	(anon.) *Indicator Group,*		

F-15

1972	(anon.) *McDonnell-*	1987	Hannan, M. D.
	Douglas F-15 Head-Up	—	(anon.) *F-15A Flight*
	Display		*Manual*
1974	Behm, D.	—	(anon.) *F-15 Head-Up*
1974	Plummer, C.		*Display*
1981	Jarvi, D.		

F-16

1978	(anon.) *Prime Item*	1983	Swortzel, F. R.
	Development Specification	1983	Wurfel, H.-G.
1980	Frazier, M. L. (both refs)	1984	Heimple, H. H.
1980	(anon.) *F-16 Avionics:*	1984	Wurfel, H. G.
	Block 10 Changes	1985	Matthes, G. W.
1981	Berry, R. L.	1986	Dana, W. H.
1981	(anon.) *F-16 Avionics*	1986	Vallance, C. H.
	System Manual, Block 15B	1986	(anon.) *F-16C/D Avionics*
1981	(anon.) *F-16 Avionics*		*System Manual (Block 30)*
	System Manual, Block 25B	1986	(anon.) *Prime Item*
1982	(anon.) *F-16 Avionics:*		*Development Specification*
	Block 15B Improvements	1987	Papa, R. M.
1983	Genco, L. V.	1990	Hughes, T. C.
1983	Himmelberg, M. R.	—	(anon.) *F-16A Flight*
1983	Martin, W. L.		*Manual*

F-18

1979	Juergens, R. A.	1983	(anon.) *F-18 Head-Up*
1981	Adam, E. C.		*Display/Multipurpose*
1981	Tkach, M. J.		*Display Group*

HUD descriptions

Boom operator HUD

LANTIRN

1981	Berry, R. L.	1983	Martin, W. L.
1982	(anon.) *Prime Item Development Specification*	1984	Wurfel, H. G.
1983	Genco, L. V.	1985	Matthes, G. W.
1983	Himmelberg, M. R.	1986	Vallance, C. H.
		1987	Papa, R. M.

MARS

1976	(anon.) *Head-Up Display Evaluation*		*Retrieval System*
1976	(anon.) *System Specification: Head-Up Display (HUD) Air*	1977	Newman, R. L.
		1978	Augustine, W. L.
		1979	Heft, E. L.

VAM

1970	(anon.) *Technical Description of the Visual Landing System*	1974	Sorum, D. R.
1970	(anon.) *Visual Landing Aid System*	1974	(anon.) *The Requirement for VAM*
1971	(anon.) *Engineering Report, Delta Gamma Visual Landing System*	1976	(anon.) *Head-Up Displays*
		1977	Ernst, H. L.
		1977	Short, D. C.
1972	(anon.) *Theory of Operation, Visual Approach Monitor*	1977	(anon.) *System Specification: Visual Approach Monitor*
1973	Mackie, R.	1978	Short, D. C.
		—	(anon.) *Visual Approach Monitor*

FDI-1000/HGS-1000

1982	(anon.) *Holographic Head-Up Display for Transport Aircraft*	1984	Newman, R. L.
		1984	Steenblik, J. W.
1983	Desmond, J. P.	1985	Kyle, W. D.
1983	Kraus, J. M.	1986	Desmond, J. P.
1983	Ruhl, L. F.	1986	Trousdale, D. M.
1983	(anon.) *System Description for FDI Model 1000*	1987	Desmond, J. P.
		1987	Newman, R. L.
1984	Desmond, J. P.	1988	Green, H. B.
1984	Kyle, W. D.	1988	Johnson, T.
		1989	Steenblik, J. W.

TC-121/TC-125

1972	Reising, J. M.		*ALPA on PERSEPOLIS*
1973	Foxworth, T. G.		*Simulations*
1973	McCloskey, St. J.	1979	Terhune, G. J. *Report to*
1975	Hutchinson, J. E.		*ALPA on TC-125*
1976	Ertzgaard, J. H.		*Simulations*
1976	Terhune, G. J.	—	(anon.) *Collimateur à*
1979	Oliver, J. G.		*Tube Cathodique TC-121*
1979	Terhune, G. J. *Report to*		

Other installations

1964	Collins, L.		*Automatique Mode Land*
1968	Deliac, P. J.	1980	Lambert, M.
1969	(anon.) *80 Series Head-Up*	1980	Terhune, G. J.
	Display Fitted to	1981	(anon.) *Technical*
	McDonnell-Douglas DC-9-		*Description: AN/AVQ-24B*
	20		*A-4M HUDWAC System*
1972	Augustine, W. L.	1982	Hamilton, F. W.
1974	Pursel, R. H.	1983	(anon.) 'Alpha Jet –
1975	Kirschner, R. K.		further version for the
1975	(anon.) *Approache*		international market'
	Automatique Mode Land,	1986	Armando, A.
	Period Transitore	1986	Edwards, R. E.
1975	(anon.) *The Peri-HUD*	1987	Campbell, C. M.
1976	Tapia, M. H.	1987	Mann, T. L.
1976	(anon.) *Head-Up Display*	1988	(anon.) *Manuel*
	Evaluation		*d'Exploitation A320 Partie*
1976	(anon.) *Bendix Micro*		*Utilisation*
	HUD	1990	(anon.) 'The A320 head-
1977	(anon.) *Les Approches de*		up display'
	Prevision de Categorie III à	1991	(anon.) *Head-Up Displays*
	la Compagnie Air Inter	1991	(anon.) *Head-Up Displays*
1979	Frank, L. H.	1991	(anon.) *Head-Up Displays*
1979	Peer, Y.	—	(anon.) *Alpha Jet head-Up*
1979	Suisse, H.		*Display and Weapons*
1979	Terhune, G. J.		*Delivery System*
1979	(anon.) *Programme*	—	(anon.) *Light Line Head-*
	Simulateur – Approche		*Up Display System*

HUD standards and specifications

Civil standards

1968 Jenney, L. L.
1979 DeCelles, J. L.
1981 Newman, R. L.
1982 (anon.) *Minimum Performance Standards for Airborne Multipurpose Electronic Displays*
1986 (anon.) *Flight Deck, Head-Up Displays*
1987 Newman, R. L.
1988 Green, H. B.
1989 (conference) *Synthetic Vision Technology Demonstration Program*
1992 (conference) *Proceedings 7th Plenary Session of the Synthetic Vision Certification Issues Study Team*
1993 (anon.) *Display Characteristics of HUDs Used in Civil Transport Aircraft*

Military HUD specifications

1967 (anon.) *Procurement Specifications for Display Set*
1968 Jenney, L. L.
1972 (anon.) *Military Specification; Display Head-Up*
1975 (anon.) *AV-8A Head Up Display Modification Specification*
1975 (anon.) *Military Standard: Electronically or Optically Generated Displays*
1979 Frank, L. H.
1981 Newman, R. L.
1981 (anon.) *Technical Description: AN/AVQ-24B A-4M HUDWAC System*
1982 (anon.) *Prime Item Development Specification*
1984 Lovering, P. B.
1984 (anon.) *Military Specification: Displays, Airborne Electronically–Optically Generated*
1984 (anon.) *Military Standard: Human Factors Engineering Design Criteria*
1985 (anon.) *Indicator Group, Head-Up Display OD-(*)/AVQ , Design Control Specification*
1986 (anon.) *Prime Item Development Specification*
1986 (anon.) *Specification for Head-Up Display Set*
1987 Henson, J. M.
1987 Newman, R. L.
1989 Hall, J. R. (both refs)
1989 (anon.) *Military Standard: Aircraft Display Symbology*
1990 Bitton, F.
1991 Weinstein, L. F.
1992 Bailey, R. E.
1991 Hall, J. R.
1992 Weinstein, L. F. (both refs)
1992 (anon.) *Mechanization of the Instrument Flight Standardization*
1993 Bailey, R. E.
1993 Turner, A. D.
1993 Weinstein, L. F.

Non-traditional HUD applications

Automobile applications

1988	Brown, S. E.	1990	Goesch, T. C.
1988	Iino, T.	1990	Sojourner, R. J.
1989	Sojourner, R. J.	1992	Groves, D. J.
1989	Weihrauch, M.	1993	Knoll, P. M.

General aviation applications

1972	Therrien, R. L.		*Heads Up Display System*
1973	Harris, R. L.		*User's Manual*
1974	Harris, R. L.	1991	Newman, R. L.
1976	Fuller, H. V.	1992	Nagati, M. G.
1976	Harris, R. L.	1993	Newman, R. L.
1978	Schiff, B.	1993	(anon.) *Beechcraft King*
1985	Kyle, W. D.		*Air A100 Landplane Flight*
1990	Newman, R. L.		*Manual Supplement*
1990	(anon.) 'Through the	—	(anon.) *Heads Up All the*
	looking glass'		*Way*
1990	(anon.) *SZD-55-1 HUDIS*		

Helicopter applications

1969	(anon.) *Head-Up Display*	1978	Lebacqz, J. V.
1973	Hoerner, F. C.	1979	Heft, E. L.
1974	Gold, T.	1979	Lebacqz, J. V.
1975	Dwyer, J. H.	1979	(anon.) *AH-1S Cobra*
1975	Walchli, R. M.		*Attack Helicopter*
1975	(anon.) *AV-8A Head Up*	1980	Adamson, J. C.
	Display Modification	1982	Bick, F. J.
	Specification	1984	(anon.) *Military*
1977	Ernst, H. L.		*Standard: Human Factors*
1977	Newman, R. L.		*Engineering Design Criteria*
1978	Augustine, W. L.	1985	Doten, F. S.
1978	Borodin, V. T.	1989	Hameluck, D.
1978	Clement, W. F.	1992	Foyle, D. C.

Index

102, 104, 130, 131, 161, 170, 182, 191, 209, 210
Update rate 64, 159, 208, 216, 240, 314

V/STOL aircraft 79, 211, 251, 275, 276, 277, 280, 308
VAM 59, 64, 238, 263, 264, 265
see also Sundstrand Visual Approach Monitor
Velocity vector 15, 17, 19, 20, 22, 77, 80, 82, 83, 84, 91, 92, 102, 121, 123, 130, 131, 134, 144, 159, 160, 161, 163, 190, 193, 197, 198, 202, 210, 211, 225, 233, 235, 237, 238, 240, 241, 245, 262, 265, 277, 308
ghost 80, 83, 167, 180, 183, 241
see also flight path marker
Vertical speed 44, 45, 51, 98, 99, 128, 168, 172, 174, 175, 179, 196, 241, 251
Virtual image 2, 33, 34, 36, 139, 230,

231, 232, 244, 279, 282, 300, 302, 303, 304, 310
VISTA 221
see also Lockheed F-16
Visual meteorological conditions 10, 245
Vought A-7 9, 10, 11, 14, 37, 59, 64, 74, 79, 106, 112, 200, 248, 249, 270, 274, 276, 282, 289, 316
VTOL aircraft 10, 109, 171, 213, 281

Warning 119, 161
Waterline 48, 49, 78, 79, 81, 83, 84, 86, 91, 102, 105, 108, 109, 163, 167, 169, 177, 178, 182, 212, 235, 241, 257, 258
Weapon boresight 78, 120, 128, 177, 178, 246
World coordinates 240, 241

Zenith symbol 45, 88, 89, 90, 168, 306